# BRIGHT LIGHTS,
# NO CITY

## ALSO BY MAX ALEXANDER

*Man Bites Log: The Unlikely Adventures
of a City Guy in the Woods*

# BRIGHT LIGHTS, NO CITY

## An African Adventure
on Bad Roads with a Brother
and a Very Weird Business Plan

# MAX
ALEXANDER

HYPERION

New York

Photos are courtesy of Max Alexander, unless otherwise noted. Page iv courtesy Jennia Parkin; pages 254 and 321 courtesy Andrew Stewart.

Maps on pp. xvi–xvii by Tim Seymour.

Library of Congress Cataloging-in-Publication Data

Alexander, Max
  Bright lights, no city/Max Alexander.—1st ed.
    p.  cm.
  ISBN 978-1-4013-2417-9
  1. Business enterprises, Foreign—Ghana.  2. Burro (Firm)  3. Alexander, Max, 1957—Travel—Ghana.  4. Alexander, Whit—Travel—Ghana.  5. Storage batteries—Economic aspects.  I. Title.
  HF3932.A55 2012
  381'.45621312424 0922667—dc22        2011015658

ISBN: 978-1-4013-2417-9

Hyperion books are available for special promotions and premiums. For details contact the HarperCollins Special Markets Department in the New York office at 212-207-7528, fax 212-207-7222, or email spsales@harpercollins.com.

*Design by Susan Walsh*

FIRST EDITION

10  9  8  7  6  5  4  3  2  1

www.maxalexander.info
www.burrobrand.biz

*For my brother, of course, who put up with me,
and allowed me to put up with him.*

# CONTENTS

# AUTHOR'S NOTE

**G**hana and I were born seventeen days apart. On March 6, 1957, the British outpost known as the Gold Coast became the first sub-Saharan African colony to gain independence. Like other African nations that followed its lead, modern Ghana was forged like wrought iron—crudely, with rough hammers, in a white-hot fire of hubris and human misery. Yet for Ghana at least, that half-century flame has given way to an even brighter dawn. Today Ghana is a robust multiparty democracy with a free (even freewheeling) press, a highly engaged electorate, and a tradition of due process. Nevertheless, wealth and status in Ghana have accrued almost exclusively to well-connected businesspeople who curry favor with the ruling class, with whom they constitute a de facto oligarchy. Some would argue that comes close to describing the United States. A chief difference is that Ghana is a small country with a finely woven net of social and political connections; for a Ghanaian striving to better his life, a seemingly trivial affront to someone in power will not land him in jail, but it could very well wreck his career. As a result I have found it prudent to change the names of some Ghanaians. In the book, pseudonyms are always identified as such on first reference. Other than names, no facts have been changed.

"And logic? My dear new friend, it's logic, all right, oh yes—it's just not your logic. It's African logic."

—Redmond O'Hanlon, *Congo Journey*

"We had succeeded because we had talked with the people and by so doing knew their feelings and grievances."

—Kwame Nkrumah, the first leader of Ghana

# BRIGHT LIGHTS, NO CITY

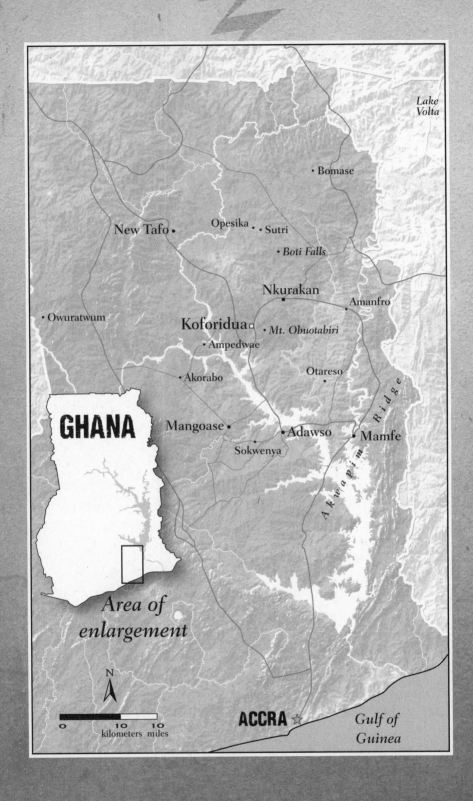

Lake
Volta

• Bomase

New Tafo •        Opesika
                            • Sutri
                         • *Boti Falls*

                    Nkurakan
                              •        Amanfro
• Owuratwum              Koforidua □   *Mt. Obuotabiri*

                    • Ampedwae

                 • Akorabo
                                      • Otareso

**GHANA**
                 Mangoase •                      *A*
                         • Adawso  *k*
                 Sokwenya     *w*   Mamfe
                            *a*
                          *p*
                        *i*
                      *m*

                        *R*
                        *i*
                        *d*
                        *g*
                        *e*

*Area of*
*enlargement*

N

0    10    10
kilometers miles

**ACCRA** ☆          *Gulf of*
                     *Guinea*

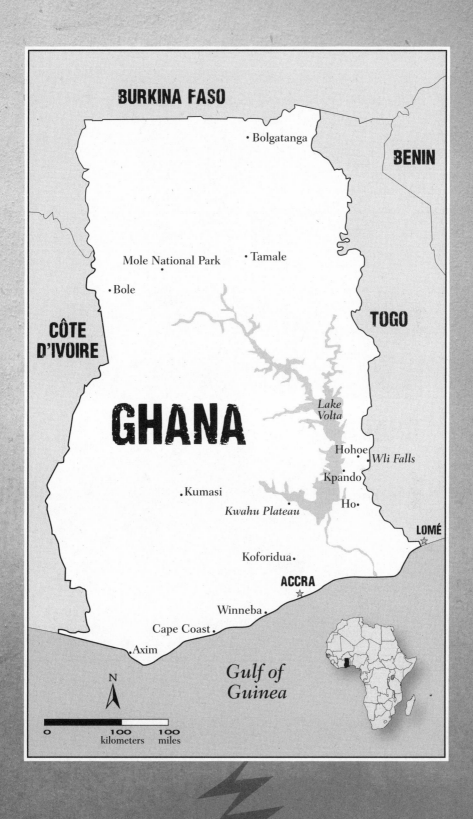

# PROLOGUE

**2008:** The setup

You had to be there: most of what my brother learned about starting a business in Africa he learned on the ground, from his customers.

**I** **never cared about Africa.** I never wanted to join the Peace Corps, raft the Zambezi, haggle in Fez or climb Kilimanjaro. My favorite Ernest Hemingway stories were set not in the blistering Serengeti but in familiar and temperate locations like Italy, France, and Michigan—places where insects are merely an annoyance and steaks are well marbled. I have no interest in a yam-based cuisine. It would never occur to me to attend a benefit concert for Africa. Except for a brief period as a boy after seeing the Howard Hawks film *Hatari!* I never even wanted to go on safari. Tanzania? I once interviewed Chuck Norris at his home in Tarzana, which sounded close enough.

But my brother Whit was starting this business in Ghana called Burro, renting batteries to people who earn a dollar a day, in a country with annual inflation exceeding 20 percent and a long history of military coups followed by firing squads. It sounded like an exceedingly bad business idea—in the pantheon of turkeys, I pictured it right up there next to the Edsel and New Coke—which intrigued me.

As a young man Whit had lived in Western Africa for several years, first as a student and then working on various aid projects, and he always believed that while many worthy charities are making huge differences for Africans, ultimately the marketplace—not government handouts or benefit concerts—would create lasting solutions to African poverty. Recently that's become a timely, even trendy, idea. From Davos to Seattle, in Zambia and New York, academics and business titans have been talking a lot about how to help poor people by giving them useful stuff to buy, and in the process creating enterprises that are sustainable, thus generating employment. But talking about bringing business to Africa is not much different than attending a benefit concert—it makes you feel good and requires no sacrifice. Saying good-bye to your family and touching down on an African tarmac with a business visa is quite another matter.

The touchdown is what intrigued me.

I was also fascinated by the risk—here I mean business risk, as opposed to the broader African risk of contracting a new strain of polio or having body parts removed by rebels—because I like few things more than tormenting my brother about his crazy start-up schemes. In 1997 he teamed up with Richard Tait, a former Microsoft colleague, to create a new board game. "A game where everyone shines" was the essence of Tait's original idea, and the two came up with Cranium. Whit hired me to write some of the questions for the first edition, a job I engaged with enthusiasm, but in my clearer moments I was lukewarm to the concept. With its mix of trivia questions, charades, word puzzles, whistling, and clay sculpting, it seemed too unfocused, too hard to get. I felt sorry for my brother because I was sure no one would buy the game.

Which goes to show how much I know about board games. Cranium, of course, became the hit game of the new millennium, embraced by celebrities like Julia Roberts and sold in Starbucks like brain food. Richard and Whit, "the Cranium guys," became minor celebrities in their own right, along the lines of Ben and Jerry. They were in *People* magazine. They made the cover of *Inc.* magazine. They were even featured in one of those Dewar's Scotch ads—my sloppy kid brother tricked up to look respectable in a Calvin Klein suit, Hugo Boss shirt, and even a necktie.

Over the years Cranium introduced many new games, and I was certain most of them sucked. I told Whit, "No one will buy that; it's got too many moving parts." Or "Kids will choke on those dice." Or "My cat could win this game." Many of them went on to be named Game of the Year at the annual New York Toy Fair. What did they know that I didn't?

It turns out that nobody knows anything. Innovators trust their gut much more than their brain, but most people aren't comfortable putting so much stock in stomach fluids, so we cling to the top-down, brainiac theory of innovation. We think of Bill Gates as a nerdy genius, which he probably is, but think about it: there had to be something in his gut to make him drop out of Harvard and start Microsoft. A truly brainy geek would have finished his studies.

In January 2008, Gates addressed the Davos World Economic Forum on the subject of what he called "creative capitalism." In his speech Gates called for businesses to develop innovative products that would serve consumers on the lowest rung of the economic ladder. He pointed out that charity wasn't enough to lift people in the developing world out of poverty.

They needed the power of the marketplace to invent solutions that would improve their lives. Come up with the right product at the right price, said Gates, and the poor will beat a path to your door. He described this model as a win-win situation: the poor improve their lives and become modern consumers, while companies make money and gain recognition. In some cases, he noted, corporations might even apply their third-world innovations to first-world markets. "This kind of creative capitalism matches business expertise with needs in the developing world to find markets that are already there, but are untapped," Gates said.

It sounded great. I pictured Indiana Jones riding shotgun with a spreadsheet across the savannah, Willy Loman shuffling through the casbah. But if they were out there, they weren't blogging, or hiring public relations agents. Maybe they only existed in speeches and polemical textbooks.

Whit knew a few people out there on the advance guard, both Westerners and indigenous pioneers, looking for new solutions in the developing world. But few were as passionate as he about applying conventional business approaches to financing and investors. Most were seeking some sort of start-up subsidy from the nonprofit realm, and very few were attracting profit-motivated investors. Nor did they seem as focused on brand development as Whit was. What's more, no one was documenting what it was really like on the ground, village to village.

The more I tried to learn, the more I saw my own brother as being pretty far out there on the edge—maybe one of the first few in a new movement. Maybe it would only last a moment. Maybe it would change the world. Either way, I wanted to be there, and not just because he was my brother. With the global economy imploding, jobs disappearing, banks tanking, and abandoned swimming pools across Southern California turning green with algae, I wondered if doing business in the developing world could do more than help the poor. I wondered if the poorest people could teach the rest of us how to live better.

In his 2007 best seller *Deep Economy: The Wealth of Communities and the Durable Future*, Bill McKibben argued that some bedrock tenets of modern capitalism—growth is good and more is better—are unsustainable in a world of finite resources and restless masses. He made a pitch for a new capitalist paradigm that separates more from better, and that nurtures small, local markets that might seem "inefficient" by conventional measures but may ultimately be more sustainable.

It's possible to imagine Ghana as a field test for some postmodern, localized, McKibben-style capitalism. More than half the population still lives off the electrical grid. Many citizens have never ventured farther than the nearest market town, perhaps half a day's walk from their own village. If you were looking to test a new paradigm for capitalism in a country of small, inefficient local markets, this could be paradise indeed. But my wife wondered if Africans need more "stuff," as opposed to, say, electricity and good government. Despite our good intentions, were we in fact just making the world safe for Walmarts in Rwanda?

"Your wife is a Waldorf kindergarten teacher," said Whit when I brought this up over the phone one day in late 2008. (He had arrived in Ghana that summer to start the business.) "She plays with sticks all day and doesn't let kids use video games. Of course she's worried about consumerism in Africa. I think she needs a hobby, something high-tech like laser-guided wood carving. I mean, she spends all her time around six-year-olds and you; imagine the warped perspective. Seriously, these people are so far away from the problems of materialism, at least out here in the bush. What I'm doing with Burro is nothing but a positive influence. Good God. There are shopping malls in Accra where flyers offering credit to anyone with any sort of job for any sort of purchase are being distributed en masse. Countless, pointless, consumer offerings are in play. They're plying all imaginable wares to the discretionary dollars of Ghanaian elites, and these people have no shopping chops; they're like lambs to slaughter. Burro is about supplying affordable, productivity-enhancing goods and services to low-income people, and doing it profitably so that we can continue to do so without infusions from governments or charities. How in God's name this might be a bad influence escapes me completely."

"I'd be careful how you invoke God over there," I said. "Those people are seriously religious, and they have voodoo."

He ignored me, which was becoming a theme in our conversations. Although I once managed a daily newspaper with an annual news budget of six million dollars, Whit generally assumed I had the business acumen of a cloistered nun. "Look, I'll grant you that Ghana is a relatively affluent nation by African standards," he went on. "It comes in tenth in per capita GDP in the sub-Saharan countries, if you don't count island playgrounds like the Seychelles. The World Bank considers it one of the most vibrant economies in Africa, which is one reason we're here. But it's all relative. All that basically means is that nobody's literally starving—for the moment. But malnutrition is rampant. Clean drinking water is a distant dream. The average adult has less than four years' formal education, and a fourth, maybe more, are illiterate. These people are a long way from your hamster wheel."

"I'm thinking I might be nuts to go over there," I said to Whit.

"Not my call," he said. "In the world of Burro we must each make our own risk assessments."

No, it wasn't Whit's call, but Africa was calling. I saw an opportunity to reconnect with my brother, a process that had begun a year earlier when our dad died suddenly and we were thrust into funeral planning. Besides, I had clearly misjudged his Cranium venture, and here was a chance to annoy him more intimately on his latest scheme. And as the oldest child, I was feeling the jitters of succession: with my father gone, there was no one left between myself and mortality, no buffer zone anymore. I was next. How many chances would I get to do something significant and crazy with my kid brother?

And while late 2008 may not have been the best time to start a new business in Africa (where local economies were crippled by the global recession), it seemed like a good time to be paying attention to that other half of the world. It's not like Whit was doing volunteer work, but his success depended almost entirely on his ability to understand what poor Africans needed and wanted; he would need to listen carefully, which is always a good place to start. As for me, all of my community-building efforts to date had been largely in my own backyard: helping at our kids' schools, the church soup kitchen, a grassroots conservation group in my town.

These were worthy efforts, but largely self-centered. Except for the soup kitchen, they all measurably improved my own family's quality of life.

We had moved to Maine ten years ago, after many years in New York and Los Angeles, hoping to raise our children in an environment relatively free of material clutter. The fact that Maine is one of only three states that outlaw billboards did not really play into our decision, but it did portend a place of kindred spirits. Over the last decade, however, the Internet has essentially turned every American home into a shopping mall; billboards or not, there is no escaping the consumer culture if you live anywhere within a five-digit zip code. So I saw Africa as another leap away from all the stuff we buy, and I wanted to know what that felt like. (Other than a few elite enclaves, Ghana has no door-to-door mail service, and post office boxes have long waiting lists, so ordering physical goods on the Web is simply not an option for most citizens.)

Little did I know that any given stretch of back road in Ghana boasts more liquor billboards than the Brooklyn-Queens Expressway. Or that in Africa, people make money by agreeing to have their entire home painted as an advertisement, which actually looks pretty cool. So it wasn't Bali Ha'i. But it was a broad new horizon.

I don't want to give the impression we lived like hippies. In fact, just pondering the plan, I could see my comfortable life fading like a Saharan mirage. I already saw Whit abandoning for months at a stretch his wife, Shelly Sundberg (a program officer at the Bill and Melinda Gates Foundation) and their two teenagers, Cameron and Rachel, back home in Seattle's Queen Anne neighborhood; paying two years' rent on an incredibly noisy seven-room office and living space in a provincial town with running water two days a week; investing hundreds of thousands of dollars of his own money; convincing Jan Watson, his former head of operations at Cranium, to quit her job at Microsoft and join him in Ghana; and hiring a full-time local employee with all the state-required benefits. I had a nice home in Maine, two amazing boys, and the world's greatest wife, plus a sailboat. What was I thinking?

There wasn't much research we could fall back on. My brother and I started a reading list, everything from the catalog for a 2007 exhibit on third-world product design at the Cooper-Hewitt Museum, to histories of Africa, its leaders, colonizers, and explorers. Yet the literature on grass-roots social entrepreneurship was thin, once you got below all the breath-less hype. There was no *Idiot's Guide*. Consider the reaction to Gates's Davos speech. Perhaps not since the Gettysburg Address has a short talk been so intensely analyzed and parsed. (At 2,765 words, Gates's speech was ten times as long as Lincoln's, but still brief by the gaseous standards of most executive presentations.) Yet at latest count, googling *bill gates creative capitalism* yielded about 141,000 entries. This is not surprising as Gates pretty much invited the world to come up with solutions to the problem of making capitalism work in the developing world. Furthermore it wasn't completely clear what he meant by creative capitalism, since plain-vanilla capitalism would seem to be creative by definition. So the floodgates opened.

A notable example was the book *Creative Capitalism,* a collection of online essays assembled by *Slate* editor Michael Kinsley in response to the Gates speech. There were some nuggets of wisdom, notably from econo-mist William Easterly, who has spent a lot of time working for the World Bank in poor countries. "You have to work very hard to figure out what the poor want and need," he wrote in the book, "and you have to work very hard to meet those needs *under local conditions* [my italics]."

Good point. But none of these writers offered any clue as to what it's really like to do so. How could they? Of the forty-two contributors to the book, only one—Loretta Michaels of HMS Wireless, which develops In-ternet technology for poor countries—was an actual businessperson doing deals on the ground in grubby foreign places. All the other contributors (besides Gates and Warren Buffett, both interviewed briefly) were profes-sors, journalists, consultants, and "fellows." I have nothing against these professionals. I am one myself. But anyone starting a business in the devel-oping world doesn't need navel-gazing economists and op-ed theorists. He needs a survival kit.

What kind of business models work in really poor and possibly danger-ous places, and who invests in them? Can you find competent employees? Don't these countries have absurdly bureaucratic regulations that hamper start-up business ventures? Are you even allowed to repatriate profits? Is there FedEx? What happens when the dictator dies? Aren't there crocodiles and snakes? On these and scores of other pressing real-world questions, the experts were silent, and the only sound coming from the developing world was the hum of the tsetse fly.

# one

# THE GONG-GONG MAN

**JANUARY 2009:** The pitch . . .

It's a showbiz thing: like many in his profession,
this gong-gong man appeared to enjoy an early cocktail.

## 1. Beyond the Horizon

**I**t was mid-morning and the gong-gong man was drunk. We sat, visitors in cheap folding camp chairs from the back of our Tata pickup truck and villagers in molded plastic patio chairs, under the canopy of a mango tree thick with weaver nests that hung like Christmas ornaments. The village of Ampedwae, near the regional capital of Koforidua, is like countless others in Ghana—countless because many are not on the government maps or even on an actual road and may go by several different names, depending on whom you ask and whether they speak Twi, Ewe, Ga, Hausa, or one of the more than seventy other languages and dialects of the country, not counting the official English.*

Villages in Ghana often have names that are devotional or inspirational in meaning. Ampedwae means "you should not boast" in Akwapim (the dialect of Twi spoken here)—advice the village seems to have taken to heart. Other than a stuccoed blue-and-beige schoolhouse, the built environment of Ampedwae is barely removed from the natural world: just a few dozen rectangular wattle-and-daub huts with bamboo or raffia roofs, their mud walls slowly melting from the rain back into the landscape, as if smeared together in wet oils by an artist. There would be no rain today; January is the dry season, which is one of the only ways to distinguish seasons in a country where every day of the year is hot and begins and ends around six o'clock. In January all of West Africa is dry, and the wind known as the Harmattan picks up the Sahara Desert—all 3.5 million square miles of it, as far as I could tell—and blows it south to the Gulf of Guinea—a thick, choking haze that stings your eyes and clogs your nose with the same brick-red dust that coats the broad leaves of the banana palms. Ampedwae—no electricity, no well—is bisected by a road of the same red dirt, and whenever a beaten Nissan bush taxi bounces by at high

---

* Of the roughly six thousand languages currently spoken in the world, some two thousand are African. Many local, unwritten African languages are disappearing, replaced by countrywide lingua francas like Twi in Ghana or Mende in Sierra Leone.

speed (which is the only speed driven in Ghana), it churns up a wall of dust that breaks like a tsunami over the squat village, scattering chickens and goats.

"Okay!" The gong-gong man rose shakily from his seat under the mango tree, stood at attention, and saluted us crisply with his right hand. In his left hand he held the village gong-gong, which is a hand-forged cowbell, and a foot-long stick. He wore brown polyester pants, sandals, and a filthy tan bowling shirt missing several buttons. In the back pocket of his slacks was jammed a liter-sized bottle of local gin, which must have made sitting as difficult as its contents had evidently made standing. He spoke rapidly in a slur as hard to grasp as mercury, while scribbling the air with his stick. I trained my digital camera on him and shifted the switch to video, which is why I know exactly what he said: "I know ya I say now listen up, so yo-yo come, ya make goo-gong. Okay." (Two raps of the gong-gong with the stick.) "Good-morning-good-morning-good-morning! How are you? Thank you! You are always will be here. You come and speak to us in under the good to Arno. Jesus la-la, Ampedwae, that's right. I going out now call every Jedi better come now and cure the sow."

At least that's what I got. It could have been a figure of speech. "Thank you," he concluded with a low bow. "God bless!" And he staggered down the road banging the gong-gong and announcing in Twi, *"Aggo! Aggo!"* Listen up!

Soon more villagers, alerted by the dull clang of the gong-gong, joined those already assembled under the tree. It was Thursday, which is rest day in Ampedwae—meaning the men were not tending their small cassava and cocoa plots and thus available for a town meeting. In theory the children would be at school, but although public school is free, many Ghanaian families cannot afford the required uniforms and books; children are also needed for labor—caring for smaller children, hauling water and wood, and tending animals. So throngs of barefoot kids in underwear waved from across the road, squealing *"Obruni! Obruni!"* which is Twi for "beyond the horizon" but in Ghana universally means "white man." (The Ewe slang for white man, *yevu*, seems to have originally meant "trickster dog," although this is debated.)

The children knew better than to cross the road. Important town meetings are for adults, and children in Ghana keep a prudent distance from their elders—not just out of respect. In Ghana if you beat someone else's child, his parents will thank you; the child must have deserved it. Other than Harper, my seventeen-year-old son, the only minor under the mango tree was an infant sucking at his mother's breast. She was one of just three women in the group of more than thirty. "Where are all the women?" I whispered to Jan Watson, who was sitting next to me in one of our camp chairs.

"Busy," she said. "Somebody has to pound the fufu," she added, referring to one of the national staples—boiled cassava and plantain pulverized in giant wooden mortars and formed into dumplinglike balls that are eaten by hand, dipped in peanut or palm nut soup. But soon enough the women straggled up, abandoning their long fufu pestles, and the meeting began. Ghanaians respect traditional gender boundaries—women cook and carry towering loads on their heads, men farm and carry machetes, sometimes on their heads—but some ethnic groups, like the Ashanti, are matrilineal: status is determined by your mother's family, a practical arrangement considering it is generally easier to be certain of your mother than your father. And in much of this predominantly Christian country, even Islamic women hold jobs, vote, frequent beauty salons (in roadside shacks on virtually every block), and allow the men to pretend they are in charge.*

Around strangers Ghanaians are formal, even courtly, so the first order of business was to shake hands with several of the important elders—ending with the village chief, a modest but mildly officious middle-aged man who seemed like the type who would refer to *Robert's Rules of Order* at an Elks Club meeting. His attire, an orange sport shirt and impeccably pressed sage green slacks, would not have looked out of place at the Seal Harbor Yacht Club. Every handshake ended with the elaborate Ghanaian mutual finger snap, along with the standard greeting "You are welcome!"—used in

---

* Women in Ghana also farm, sometimes small kitchen gardens but also substantial fields separate from their husbands' plots. Recent studies suggest that more women in Africa are farming as men leave their villages to seek work in cities.

Ghana as we would say "Welcome to my home" and not as a rejoinder to "Thank you." The local dignitaries moved down the receiving line, ending with my brother Whit.

Whit was born a few weeks before Barack Obama, who at age forty-seven had been sworn in as President the previous week. He is four years younger than I yet even grayer, his hair having progressed at a relatively young age to Steve Martin silver. He was wearing trendy gunmetal eye-glasses, a batik print shirt, high-tech travel pants, and khaki Crocs—the standard uniform of the hip West Coast entrepreneur. "Ties are for losers," Whit once told me.

Not that anyone in Ampedwae would have known that. In Ghana, a necktie means you are an important person, a college man, possibly even a Big Man, with a good job that doesn't require a machete. You might even work in an office that's air-conditioned and be able to sleep at your desk. Appearances matter: this is why Ghanaian men with office jobs tolerate ties and double-breasted woolen suits in blast-furnace climatic conditions. So Whit was bucking local custom, but he bowed formally as each village elder shook his hand. Then everyone sat down and waited for him to talk.

"Good morning," Whit began. "*Mente Twi.*" His admission that he did not speak Twi seemed to amuse the villagers, both for its contradiction (didn't he just say that in Twi?) and its self-evidence (white people rarely speak Twi). "We are starting a new company and we want to tell you about it," he continued. "It's a new way to use batteries that we think you will like. But first I'd like to tell you a little about myself. My name is Whit Alexander, and I am American."

After each sentence a man I'll call Kevin, Whit's first Ghanaian employee—short, stocky, goateed, and a former stage and TV actor in the capital of Accra—would translate into Twi, which required approximately five times as many words as the English version. ("Sometimes people would not understand the meaning so I have to embellish," Kevin told us later.) Most of the villagers spoke at least some English, so their reactions to Whit's original words and Kevin's translation reverberated like an echo chamber.

Whit continued: "I lived for many years all over West Africa. I did one year of university in Abidjan, Ivory Coast. After college I lived for a year in Niamey, Niger, working on a grain-marketing project. Then I spent two and a half years in Bamako, Mali, on a farming project. I have also traveled through Senegal, Gambia, Mauritania, and Burkina Faso. Now that my children are almost grown, I decided it was time to come back to Africa and start the business that I have always wanted to do."

"Farming projects" aside, as far as I was concerned Whit had been an Africa-based CIA agent. He's never admitted it, but then they don't tell their brothers, do they? After graduating from Georgetown's School of Foreign Service, Whit and Shelly (then his fiancée) did live in West Africa for several years. During that period I couldn't help but notice that for an African agricultural expert Whit knew almost nothing about farming. Yams, coconuts, carrots—all were the same to him. He called soil "dirt," none of which could be seen under his fingernails. And he seemed to spend a lot of time off the farm, in places like Washington, D.C., and the United Nations. Who was minding the melons? Letters to him had to be addressed via the State Department diplomatic pouch. Sometimes, on his U.N. visits, he would stay in my apartment in Brooklyn. Once after he went to bed I riffled through his wallet and found all sorts of official embassy clearances and passes. Confronted, Whit said he would now have to kill me. Then he pointed out that all the credentials were in his own name and granted him access to low-level areas like the American recreation center and the shopping co-op. I wasn't convinced. They practice saying that kind of stuff to throw you off track. In Bamako his private compound and swimming pool were guarded by a psychopathic monkey named Boo Boo who had fangs and was not afraid to use them. (He bit Shelly.) It was all right out of *Dr. No.*

At any rate, by 1990 Whit was back in the States and living in Seattle, Shelly's hometown. He dropped out of grad school in 1992 to take a job at Microsoft, where he produced the maps for the first Encarta Encyclopedia and then led the design and development of the more detailed Encarta World Atlas. (CIA agents would know a lot about exotic foreign maps, wouldn't they?) That was the stock-option heyday at Microsoft, when secretaries hired in the 1980s were retiring as multimillionaires. Whit came too late to win a game-ending jackpot, but after five years he too had "retired" at age thirty-five with enough options to sit back and plan his next move.

Within eight months he was off on a new venture, which became Cranium. After a ten-year ride to the top of the toy business, Whit, his partner, Richard, and their investors sold Cranium to Hasbro for more than seventy-five million dollars. With discretion reminiscent of his shrouded former "farming" work in Africa, Whit maintains that very little of that sum was available once investors and other debts had been paid off. All I know is, Whit then "retired" a second time.

The gong-gong man had returned. His bottle was empty.

"I respect how hard Africans work to provide for their families and build a better life," Whit went on, ignoring the fact that at least one community member was inebriated before noon. "I know that sometimes there are better ways to get things done. I have been searching for new ways to help people in Africa do more with their lives."

Growing up in a middle-class suburb of Grand Rapids, Michigan, Whit and I were not particularly close. He was the annoying kid brother who would tell your parents if he knew what was *really* happening after school. Whit was a techie nerd, before that term existed. He and some even nerdier buddies were programming a Wang microcomputer in high school, less than two years after Paul Allen had shown Bill Gates the first Altair microcomputer, which inspired them to launch Microsoft. By contrast I got through four years of college on an electric typewriter and a bottle of Wite-Out. Computers were forced on me by the workplace. "Here's a press release," said the editor on my first day as a salaried journalist. "Gimme a story by six." I peered at the blank screen on my new desk. "You need to turn it on first," he added.

Our parents divorced when I was seventeen. I got an apartment with a buddy, and Whit moved with our mother to Tucson, entering the slipstream of Sun Belt immigrants. That was the end of our life together, and for a while it seemed as though our paths would never again cross except at weddings and funerals. I was a rebellious loner, angry with my parents for their failed marriage and angry with myself for letting it happen. Anything my parents wanted me to do, such as college or even attending my high school graduation, I resolved to do the opposite. So I checked out. I drifted through jobs around the country. That might have continued forever had I not met Sarah, my future wife, an aspiring actress who was also trying to figure out who she was, albeit with considerably more poise and planning. Together we moved to New York, where I enrolled in college at age twenty-six.

Whit did everything in the proper order. He went to college right after high school. He never worked in a restaurant. He got good jobs, saved money, and tossed around phrases like "scalable business." He had financial planners and the right kind of insurance. Our dad, who fancied himself a keen judge of character, used to say, "Whit will get rich but Max will be famous"—not realizing in his Midwestern way that except in the case of presidential assassins, fame and fortune generally go hand in hand. Whit seemed on a path for both, and I wasn't strongly motivated for either.

And yet despite our differences, or maybe because of them, Whit and I grew closer over the years—or as close as two brothers could be who lived three thousand miles apart and saw each other once every few years. Our wives and children became friends. We shared a sense of humor, a love of wisecracks and mutual insults. Around me, Whit could loosen his (metaphorical) tie, shed the corporate jargon, and be a kid brother again. I wish I could say something lofty like we completed each other, but mostly what we did was make a safe place for fart jokes.

None of which could have indicated that someday we would be doing business under a mango tree in a village in Ghana.

"Don't fuck this up, asshole," I said, trying to be helpful. "You should have learned more Twi."

"Shut up," Whit whispered. I blew my nose and voided several ounces of red dust. Whit continued with his spiel:

"Our company is called Burro, and our goal is to help people do more. But I have to be honest with you. I am also trying to make money."

This brought polite laughter that, for a second, seemed in danger of breaking into a gale. It was unclear to me if the villagers were laughing with us or at us, but Ghanaians have a sharp sense of humor and are especially attuned to the absurd. When four *obrunis* show up in a brand-new pickup truck, they are either volunteers, Peace Corps workers, NGO reps, or governmental aid agents, all of whom are giving something away. But we were not building wells, digging latrines, or painting orphanages. In fact we were giving away nothing except a leftover stash of Obama campaign pins, and we were getting seriously low on those.

No, they understood that we had come to this village to convince thirty-three of the roughly one billion people on Earth who live on a dollar a day to give us some of their money.

As George Burns said, "If they laugh, it's funny."

"I believe Burro can only serve you continuously and sustainably if we make it a viable, profitable business," said Whit, bravely pressing on. "Then we can always be there for you." Although he didn't come out and say it, he was alluding to the problem of NGOs mobilizing an ambitious "project," then disappearing when the funding runs out—a problem all too familiar to rural Ghanaians. "We want to do many things, but our first idea is one that if you use a lot of batteries, you should be able to save money and do more. We want you to help us decide if the Burro offering is right for you."

A village man stood and said in Twi: "Tell us what these batteries do."

## 2. Fresh, Anytime You Want

It would be hard to overestimate the obsession with batteries in African villages with no electricity. For rural Ghanaians who live off the grid (in a country just north of the equator where darkness falls between five-thirty and six-thirty year-round), batteries power two essential appliances: flashlights and radios. Flashlights allow villagers to hunt at night for snails or bigger game like antelope and large rodents (all a significant source of income and protein), for children to do homework after dinner, and for villagers to feel safe after dark. (Perhaps because they have so little faith in law enforcement, Ghanaians are obsessed with security. Even remote village crop depots have more locks and bars than a Forty-seventh Street jewelry store.) Flashlights are also important in electrified cities, where street-lights are rare and the pavements present minefields of pedestrian obsta-cles, from sinkholes to open sewers to the mangled carcasses of wrecked autos that no one can afford to tow away. When you are walking around a dark African city at night, a flashlight can mean the difference between life and death.

Portable transistor radios offer many Ghanaians their only source of electronic news as well as entertainment. They listen to homegrown reggae stars like Blakk Rasta, who recorded a hit anthem to Barack Obama; the indigenous "highlife" beat that evolved after World War II from American jazz and R&B; its modern rap-inspired version, "hiplife"; and a particularly skin-crawling version of gospel music that is unfortunately not limited to Sunday mornings. Then there is the news. Ghana has a lively free press, and radio news is delivered at a constant yell in several languages. Life in Ghana happens out of doors (as near as I can tell, everything except sex takes place under trees), most of it to the soundtrack of a blaring boom box. This is not regarded solely as entertainment; farmers who bring their radios into the fields—those who do not superstitiously believe that music attracts snakes—claim to have more energy and be more productive.

A new use for batteries is evolving along with the adoption of cell phones, which are inexpensive in Ghana and have become the first and only tele-phone for most people. Of course, cell phones have proprietary batteries that need to be recharged, and when you don't have electricity this pre-sents a problem. Enterprising locals gather up phones in remote villages, then take them to the nearest on-grid charging location. But with fees approaching a dollar for a single charge if you factor in transportation costs, Africans are eager for a better solution. A handful of Chinese man-ufacturers have introduced cheap portable phone chargers that use a sin-gle AA battery to charge the internal phone battery. But their quality is uneven (some refuse to work right out of the box), the adapters included don't work on every phone, and the cheap non-alkaline AA battery available in Ghana isn't powerful enough to operate them at all. Whit was already looking into producing better battery-powered phone chargers, a product line that would not occur to anyone operating from an office in Europe or America.


**"How many of you use batteries?"** Whit smiled; he knew almost every hand under the mango tree would go up. One man stood and held up his radio. He opened the back, revealing three Tiger Head brand D batteries—cheap Chinese carbon zinc models, sold everywhere in Ghana, that perform poorly and are prone to leaking.* The man said he changed the batteries about once a week. Even these crappy batteries are a big expense for rural Ghanaians, who must work about half a day to buy a pair.

Whit pulled a battery out of his pocket—vibrant green with a black logo of a donkey on it. "This," he said, "is the Burro battery." It was, in fact, a rechargeable nickel metal hydride AA battery. "It looks small, but it has as much energy as the Tiger Head." From his other pocket he withdrew a matching green plastic tube the size of a D battery, then he inserted the AA battery into the adapter sleeve. "And it can be used like a Tiger Head." The audience gasped.

"The cost is 75 pesewa per month, per battery," said Whit. "Now, I know that is three times what you pay for a Tiger Head, but you are not really buying the Burro battery; you are buying *the power inside*. Burro batteries are fresh anytime you want. When the battery falls"—the charming Ghanaian term for a dead battery—"you take it back to your agent and get a fresh one—no pay. So if you use Tiger Heads and change them more than three times per month, you will save with Burro—and you can use ours all the time. So you can do more."

*Do More* was the Burro slogan, which Whit had craftily worked into his pitch.

A man held up a lantern-type flashlight that took four D batteries. He was already a Burro customer, he explained, having arrived from another

---

* Shortly after World War II, Union Carbide perfected the alkaline battery (sold under its Eveready name), which lasts five to eight times as a long as a carbon zinc battery.

village. "I used to turn my light off before sleeping," he said in Twi. "Now I leave it on all night for security." We could not have asked for a more ringing endorsement had we planted him in the crowd.

"There are other advantages," said Whit. "Has anyone ever had a Tiger Head leak and damage their device?" Many hands went up. "Burro batteries are better. If one ever leaks and spoils your device, bring us the battery and the device, and we will make it right. Finally, has anyone ever seen a child playing with a used battery they found on the ground?" Heads nodded. "It's not safe. With Burro, you don't throw them away."

A hand came up in the crowd. "What happens if my battery falls at the end of the month?" the man asked. "Do I have to pay to get it fresh?"

Jan joined in. "Yes," she said. "You are just *using* the batteries for a month; then you must pay for another month, whether the battery is fresh or fallen." Resorting to terminology now widely understood from the burgeoning cell phone market, Jan clarified, "You *prepay* one month. You get power from the battery that whole month. Then you *prepay* for the next month."

The man's question got at one of the biggest challenges in the Burro business model. Ghanaians don't really have a rental culture; despite the clearly compelling advantage of the offer, it takes time to explain to potential customers the basic idea of buying a service, as opposed to buying the physical battery. This is one reason why Burro was building its own network of trained agents who could explain the company's unconventional offering. A direct relationship between client and agent also ensured a level of trust that would enable the rental model to work. In a country with no reliable legal system for dispute resolution, and where most people have no identification, no bank account, and no street address, renting valuable merchandise to them for a fraction of its cost carried considerable risk. "You can't just set up shop on any street corner and hand out batteries to the first person who walks by," said Whit.

**So far the most promising** agent was Whit's man in Ampedwae—a local assemblyman named Gideon, with graying hair, a Fu Manchu mustache, and an entrepreneurial flair that impressed Whit and Jan. I found

Gideon's competence somewhat undercut by the fact that he worked out of a Spider-Man backpack, but after a while you get used to things like that in Africa, which is flooded with secondhand clothing and sports gear from America. I never saw a *Brady Bunch* lunch box, but it wouldn't have surprised me. After Whit finished his presentation, Gideon, who had organized our village sales meeting under the mango tree, opened up his backpack and promptly signed up several more customers. Later he explained that many Ghanaians distrust other Ghanaians and are reluctant to part with cash for a promise of "fresh" batteries that may or may not materialize. "They might not believe me," said Gideon, "but if the *obruni* shows up, they figure it must be real." At least until the brand was established, it was becoming clear that village "gong-gong" meetings would continue to be a valuable sales strategy.

The downside to the Ghanaian's good nature is that it can be hard to get at the truth; often, in the interest of politeness, deference, or perhaps some more calculated ruse that I have not yet gleaned, he will tell you what he thinks you want to hear. So Whit was working hard at training his associates to talk straight with him. "Tell me," Whit asked Gideon as we were loading up the truck, "what could I have said better?"

"You might have talked about the environment," he said thoughtfully. "You know, you mentioned how the old batteries are dangerous for children, and that was good, but I would also talk about how our batteries do not litter their village." It was a good point, albeit one riddled with contradiction. Ghanaian cities are filthy, and people litter with abandon. For all its Eden-like rain forests, vertiginous waterfalls, and flocks of exotic birds and butterflies, modern, urbanized Ghana is no paradise. But these small ancestral villages are conspicuously tidy. The trees along the main roads are often pruned into aesthetic submission, and purple bougainvillea vines are artfully trained over entranceways. The floors of the village huts may be of dirt, but they get swept several times a day. Even the outdoor spaces are swept daily, leaving the unintentional broom tracks of a Zen garden. I wondered if it was part of the Ghanaian ownership culture: big cities don't really "belong" to anyone, but these villages represent home and family, even for Ghanaians who have left the farm. I wasn't sure yet how Burro would fit into that proud, poor culture, but I was beginning to see that the only way to do business here was to respect the simple logic of village life. When we sat under the mango tree and followed the rhythm of the gong-gong, we did well.

"Now, before you go, I have a present for you," said Gideon. From the bed of the truck he hauled out a four-liter plastic jug with a loose-fitting cap and sticky white foam oozing from the lip. "Fresh palm wine, very sweet!" Gideon poured the unfiltered milky brew into a plastic cup; specks of dirt and a small bug or two floated like coffee grounds on the surface. "Don't worry about the dirt, we always pour the first sip on the ground for our ancestors," he said. "They don't mind." He tipped the cup in front of him and poured off the dirt, took a slug, and passed the cup to Whit. "Today we rented many batteries," he said. "To Burro."

## 3. Planners and Searchers

As Bill Gates freely acknowledged, he did not originate the idea of doing good by doing well. As far back as 1959, the Pakistani activist and social scientist Akhter Hameed Khan realized that charity on its own was unsustainable as a model for third-world development. He pointed out that infrastructure such as schools, wells, and sewers needed ongoing maintenance; simply building them wasn't enough. Who would pay for their upkeep after the volunteers left town? Working with the Pakistan (now Bangladesh) Academy for Rural Development, Khan initiated the Comilla Cooperative Pilot Project, a system of local cooperatives that integrated public and private enterprise to improve roads and irrigation systems, train administrators and accountants, and develop village economic plans that would carry improvements forward. Other programs followed.

Khan's initiatives had varying degrees of success but were ultimately hampered by a lack of central control. In the 1970s, building on the work of Khan, the Bangladeshi economist Muhammed Yunus began developing a model for a centralized bank that would finance small rural businesses at more favorable rates than those offered by local moneylenders. Traditional banks ignored this market because it was difficult to enforce repayment contracts. But Yunus realized (this was his breakthrough) that when loans were made to groups of villagers (mostly women), repayment was essentially self-enforced by peer pressure. If someone did not pay back her loan, no one else in her group could take out a new loan. Thus was born the concept of microfinancing. In his book *Banker to the Poor: Microlending and the Battle Against World Poverty,* Yunus wrote: "We were convinced that the bank should be built on human trust." Yunus's Grameen Bank (which means "village bank") has now loaned more than ten billion dollars to poor families while experiencing very low default rates; his success has inspired similar banks all over the world.*

In 1980 the American management consultant Bill Drayton founded Ashoka: Innovators for the Public, a sort of nonprofit venture capital firm dedicated to encouraging innovations that serve the world's poor. Drayton popularized the catchphrase "social entrepreneurship." In this context, *entrepreneur* did not necessarily mean someone looking for financial profit, but rather someone who sought opportunistic solutions to seemingly intractable social problems like hunger, infant mortality, illiteracy, and environmental degradation. Drayton and his associates traveled the globe seeking pioneers, then looked for ways to support them through grants, professional services, and joint ventures. He recalled his simple but audacious goal to David Bornstein, author of the recent *How to Change the World: Social Entrepreneurs and the Power of New Ideas*: "Was it possible to create a system that would, with high reliability, spot major pattern-changing ideas and first-class entrepreneurs before either were proven?" The answer was yes. With a current annual budget of thirty million dollars, Ashoka has supported more than two thousand fellows in over sixty countries.

If social entrepreneurship was a religion in search of a bible, the scripture came in 2004 when the Indian-born University of Michigan business

---

\* The rapid growth of for-profit microfinance banks has sparked controversy, with critics citing the potential for exploitation of the poor. In 2011, Yunus himself was forced to resign as managing director of Grameen Bank, in what may have been a politically motivated sacking.

professor C. K. Prahalad published a seminal book called *The Fortune at the Bottom of the Pyramid: Eradicating Poverty Through Profits*. Prahalad, who died in 2010, was brave enough to argue that Westerners needed to stop pitying the poor as victims and start respecting them as value-conscious consumers and even small-scale entrepreneurs. He defined the bottom of the economic pyramid as those earning less than two dollars a day—some four billion people worldwide. Obviously these poorest of the poor do not consume at the level of Westerners—their buying is overwhelmingly focused on needs, not wants, and impulse purchases are mostly on the level of snacks and trinkets like key chains—but their total spending power amounts to trillions of dollars. "This is not a market to be ignored," wrote Prahalad. Indeed, even a casual visitor to all but the most destitute and autocratic third-world countries cannot help but be amazed by the vibrant local food and clothing markets—to say nothing of the roving snack and trinket sellers who ply traffic jams—where buying and selling takes place in environments of such unfettered chaos as to seem physically unsafe. And of course some Western corporations, like Coca-Cola, have done very well by selling to the world's poor.

All of these observations suggest that the idea of *poverty* is highly relative and impossible to separate from context. In Ghana (as I was to learn), small-plot cocoa farmers and other cash-crop growers are in fact diligent savers. They often barter for daily needs, breaking into their cash hoard only when something they regard as extraordinarily desirable comes along. Put in business terms, their balance sheet is sterling. Such people certainly do not think of themselves as poor, especially when their own measurement of happiness is less contingent on material possessions and more heavily weighted toward the security and support of family and friends. These are the billions of Africans and Asians and Latin Americans who appear "poor" to us but in reality bear no resemblance to the belly-swollen refugees with outstretched hands that epitomize the Western image of the developing world's population.

But from one village to the next can be night and day. Plenty of rural Ghanaians really *are* poor, even by their own standards, often desperately so, and in debt to boot. The point is, you can't tell who is truly poor and who is not just by looking at them. And you certainly can't tell by giving stuff away to them; who wouldn't accept a free well or clinic? The only way you can tell who has money and who doesn't is by offering to sell them something they want and need at an honest price.

By the time Gates gave his speech at Davos, backlash against conventional foreign aid was growing. In 2006, the year microlender Yunus won the Nobel Peace Prize, economist William Easterly published *The White Man's Burden: Why the West's Efforts to Aid the Rest Have Done So Much Ill and So Little Good*. As the title suggests, the book is a scathing polemic on the failure of governments and nonprofits (including Easterly's former employer, the World Bank) to make any significant dent in the problems of the developing world. "The West spent $2.3 trillion on foreign aid over the past five decades and still has not managed to get twelve-cent medicines to children to prevent half of all malaria deaths," he wrote, comparing this tragedy to the marketing push in the summer of 2005 that sold nine million copies of the sixth Harry Potter book in a single day. "It is heartbreaking that global society has evolved a highly efficient way to get entertainment to rich adults and children, while it can't get twelve-cent medicine to dying poor children."

According to Easterly, one problem is that well-meaning but clueless bureaucratic "Planners" have created a culture of freebies in the third world that makes it difficult for market forces to find a viable niche. When a charity gives away mosquito nets, what happens to the local entrepreneur who is trying to make and sell mosquito nets at a reasonable profit, running a business that employs villagers and sustains itself? Easterly compared the Planners to those whom he called "Searchers." The Searchers are experimenters who don't claim to have all the answers but are willing to hit the ground and find out—especially if it leads to some personal reward. "Searchers have better incentives and better results," he wrote. "When a high willingness to pay for a thing coincides with low costs for that thing, Searchers will find a way to get it to the customer."

It's a compelling argument—but searching takes time. Gates himself recognized the challenge: "Sometimes market forces fail to make an impact in developing countries not because there's no demand, or because money is lacking, but because we don't spend enough *time* studying the needs and limits of that market."

Which helps explain why so many market-based innovations for the developing world are large-scale corporate mobilizations. Gates mentioned the efforts of GlaxoSmithKline to develop affordable drugs; Prahalad wrote about Unilever's success inventing a more effective way to iodize salt using molecular encapsulation, preventing mental retardation in Indian children while making money. These are multinational behemoths that can easily drop a few million into research and development with relatively little overall risk. Their developing-world missions are the corporate equivalent of the World Bank, or the Peace Corps—admirable business ventures, but hardly *adventures*. I was looking for the place where venture and adventure intersect. As I was about to learn, it was a dangerous crossroads with no traffic light.

# two

# AFRICA IS STILL ON FIRE

**JANUARY 2009:** The start-up

Boys swimming at the village of Nzulezo, which is built entirely on stilts over a lake. The water appeared quite foul.

## 1. Dead Heat

**O**ut of the plane and onto the molten tarmac of Kotoka Airport, you smell it right away. Africa has a smell as distinct as the subway of Manhattan or the eucalyptus of Laurel Canyon—pungent and exotic yet vaguely familiar, like burley pipe tobacco or pontifical incense.

"Welcome to Ghana," said Whit as we walked through immigration, past a large sign warning that pedophiles were decidedly unwelcome here, and into the January glare of my first morning on the oldest continent. The previous afternoon we had met at JFK—he from Seattle, me from Maine, along with Harper—to connect to Accra. Whit had been in Ghana, laying the groundwork for Burro, from August to November of 2008, and Jan had been in charge since he left. So far the company consisted of Whit, Jan, Kevin, the Tata pickup, and a few thousand batteries. My plan was to spend the first month of 2009 there with my son (who had been given an independent study project on recording Ghanaian field music for his high school), during which time I would annoy Whit as much as possible, explore the country, and, if things worked out, prepare for a much longer stay later in the year.

Outside the terminal, a gang of aggressively friendly touts immediately surrounded our luggage cart, fighting for the opportunity to guide us to a taxi. "No, no, no thank you, we're okay," said Whit, but nobody listened or cared. The rule seemed to be that anyone with his hand touching any bag on the cart was entitled to a tip, so a dozen dreadlocked men with outstretched arms frantically huddled around us, tripping over one another, grasping at luggage and arguing as we pushed through the crowd, looking like a giant moving tarantula. "We're waiting for someone," said Whit. "We have a ride. No taxi. No thank you." Harper, dazed with jet lag, wandered off to the snack stand and came back with two Red Bulls. One was already empty and he was working on the second. "He's gonna come down hard," said Whit. "Charlie!"

Across the parking lot, waving from the door of an older Mercedes-Benz, was a big, tall, athletic man with a wide smile. He was wearing gym

clothes and shaking his head at the gang surrounding our overflowing luggage cart. "Hey, Whit! Sorry, I can't get any closer." Whit's Ghanaian business partner waited for us outside the security cordon. We piloted the
luggage cart and the attached porters in his direction. Charlie (not his real
name) yelled at them in Twi and tossed some brightly colored bills. He
hugged Whit. "Welcome back!"

"You still driving this old wreck?" said Whit.

"Who can afford a new car?" said Charlie. "We have not rented enough
batteries yet. Besides, it holds a lot of baggage."

It did, amazingly, and we were off to Koforidua on a Sunday afternoon.

I liked Charlie right away. Like many Ghanaians I would come to know,
he was generous, sincere, and completely unflappable, relying on an endless
taproot of humor to cope with the daily indignities of African life. Stopped
at a red light in front of Ghana's new presidential palace, a curvilinear
metallic ziggurat that is meant to suggest a traditional Ghanaian chief's
throne (called a stool) but looks more like a rocket launch pad from the
1939 World's Fair, Charlie stuck his arm out the window and gestured to
a tall young woman selling bags of fried plantain chips from a bowl on top
of her head. He quizzed her in Twi in what was obviously some form of
mock indignation, and the two exchanged pleasant banter until the light
changed and we sped off.

"What was that about?" asked Whit.

"I asked her why she is not in church today," Charlie replied, laughing.
The son of a Unilever executive who was a part-time minister, Charlie,
fifty-six, inherited the preacher's ardent voice if not his precise spiritual
calling. Although like most Ghanaians he is among the faithful (and married to a devout Catholic, a minority religion in this former British colony),
mostly Charlie proselytizes for business. His upbringing was middle class
by American standards but relatively privileged for Africa. After attending
Accra's Achimota School, a boarding institution from the colonial era and
one of the most prestigious secondary schools in Africa, he majored in
biochemistry at Kwame Nkrumah University of Science and Technology,
anticipating a medical career. But the physician's life was not for him, and

he went on to study timber management. Most of his business ventures have been in the building trades—manufacturing high-quality construction materials—and he owns several properties around Accra and farther to the east, in the Volta Region of his ancestry. Charlie is a member of the Ewe tribe; besides English he speaks Ewe, Twi, and Ga, which is Accra's indigenous language.

"Look at this," said Charlie, this time in English, gesturing over the hood as we idled at another red light.

In front of us, a truck carrying maybe thirty young men in its open cargo hold lumbered past, hiplife music blaring from speakers, the men dancing and waving red, white, and blue flags picturing an elephant and the letters NPP—the National Patriotic Party. "Let's hope they are going home," said Charlie as the music slowly faded and the truck disappeared into the heat, shimmering like a mirage. "Enough of this already."

One month earlier, Ghana's presidential election had been too close to call. The sitting president, John Kufuor of the NPP party, had served his two-term limit, and his potential successor, Nana Akufo-Addo, was running against John Atta Mills of the opposition National Democratic Congress (NDC). The dead heat had forced a runoff just a few days before our arrival, and Mills, a fifty-six-year-old lawyer and university lecturer with a gap-toothed smile that made him look like a black David Letterman, won. But in Africa, elections are never over when they're over. While most Ghanaians were expressing pride that the country could now count two consecutive democratic transitions to opposition parties (a record for postcolonial Africa), plenty of NPP loyalists were still agitating, claiming the election was rigged, a challenge for any party not in power, to be sure. (Observers from the Carter Center said it was largely free and fair.)

Swirling under the surface was an undercurrent of ethnic animosity. Ghana has taken measures to ensure that its political parties are not tied closely to ethnic groups. National parties must have viable offices in every region, and parties may not include ethnic names or symbols in their regalia. Nevertheless, the NPP stronghold is the central Ashanti tribal region, while the NDC was founded by a member of the Ewe tribe—the former

military head of state, Flight Lieutenant Jerry John Rawlings.* Although
Mills is not Ewe, he was Rawlings's vice president. And Rawlings—who
sent three former dictators and five generals to a firing squad in June of
1979—was still very much on the scene, speechifying and prognosticat-
ing. Further stirring the pot was the country's partisan tabloid press,
which regularly ran block-type headlines proclaiming NDC THUGS RAID
NPP RUMPUS or NPP PLOTS NDC MAYHEM.

Compared to many African countries, tribal tension in Ghana burns at
a very low flame; it rarely rises above the level of ethnic humor. Any serious tribal conflict seemed unthinkable, but the election did seem to be
bringing out the worst in people, and some of the roving bands of political
supporters acted more like street gangs cruising for a fight. These were not
gangs you would want to engage in political debate.

"So what happens next, Charlie?" Whit asked. He had been home in
Seattle for six weeks over the holidays, following the Ghanaian election on
the Internet, and he was anxious to catch up on the ground.

"I think things will be okay," Charlie said. "People are starting to calm
down. But right now the problem is that Nana has not conceded. He
needs to get up and say that."

We were heading out of town on the main road north toward Koforidua,
two and a half hours away. Whit had chosen the town for his test branch
because it was within a day's round-trip drive to the air and shopping hub
of Accra yet far enough away to be out of the limelight. As our car switched
back and forth up the Akwapim Ridge, Charlie pushed the accelerator to
the floor and passed a banana truck on a blind curve. This was not a lightly
traveled road; I estimated the chance of an oncoming vehicle to be high,
perhaps once every few seconds. I closed my eyes, and when I opened them
I noticed other cars doing the same thing, going both ways, as if it were
completely normal to risk an explosive, dismembering head-on collision to
gain a relatively small time advantage on a Sunday afternoon. Harper, who

---

* Rawlings is half-white, the son of an immigrant Scottish pharmacist and his Ghanaian mistress.

had just finished driver's ed back in Maine, gave me a wide-eyed look. "Don't try this at home," I said.

We climbed higher, dodging trucks and taxis. Soon Accra and the Gulf of Guinea spread out below us, felted in dust and smoke. Along the highway, fields had been set ablaze by farmers clearing underbrush before planting. Adding to the haze were street vendors, who fanned flaming charcoal fires below rice pots and shards of sizzling cocoyam and plantain.

"Dad, they're selling dope all along this road," Harper said to me in a whisper, apparently not wanting Charlie and Whit, in the front seat, to know that he was onto an incredible scam.

"What?"

"*Dope.* Pot. Mar-i-juana. I can smell it. These guys are dope dealers, and they're burning samples."

"They're not selling dope," I said dismissively, ignoring for the moment how he knew what dope smelled like. "And even if they were, why would they be burning samples? This is not Jamaica."

"Rita Marley lives up on this ridge," said Whit on cue, playing tour guide, ignorant of our conversation in the backseat.

"That's right," said Charlie.

Okay, maybe they *were* selling dope. Maybe the free samples were some native Ghanaian version of creative capitalism. But no, it didn't smell quite like dope. Then I placed it. The smell of Ghana was the smell of burning leaves from my childhood, a time before anybody cared about mulching or recycling or even air pollution, when leaf piles were set ablaze at the curb every fall. The burning fields and the charcoal fires smelled the same. In my youth the cities and suburbs of America were regularly on fire, and autumn was delirious and orange and black with smoke. I was ten in the summer of 1967 when Detroit was in flames during the race riots, and it seemed perfectly normal to me, just a little early. Africa is still on fire.

"How did you guys meet?" I asked.

"Serendipity," said Whit. "We met last May in Accra. I was still just kind of noodling the whole Burro idea back in Seattle, and I found out there was a World Bank conference called 'Lighting Africa' in Accra. I thought that was a perfect excuse to come over, do some initial market research, and scope out possible partners."

"Why did you want a partner?"

"Well, it certainly makes things easier. You can be one hundred percent foreign-owned in Ghana, but it's a bit tricky. I really wanted someone on the ground who knows the terrain. Anyway, I had arranged a meeting with this guy who heads up the Ghanaian branch of a U.S. NGO that helps jump-start small- and medium-scale business enterprises in developing countries. They do the largest annual business-plan competition in Ghana, so I wanted to meet with them to get the lay of the land. In the back of my mind I thought maybe they would be a sponsor, and maybe they would know whom I should talk to as a potential partner.

"So on the day of our meeting, the guy got called away on an emergency and he arranged for me to meet with another person from his group, a very smart woman named Afi. We met, and I could tell she was pretty excited about my idea. They hear all kinds of bullshit stories over here, and they've been through the wringer with snake-oil Western no-ops coming over. Charlie's been screwed by these types in the past. So Afi was definitely sizing me up. I could tell we were connecting, and she was figuring this guy seems real and has integrity.

"She told me she knew a lot of potential partners. 'Let me think about it and get back to you,' she said. The next day she called and said she had a guy she wanted me to meet. So we all met at the Golden Tulip Hotel—me, Charlie, and Afi. Charlie and I hit it off right away. I was very impressed with his entrepreneurial background; he had tried a lot of things. I could tell he was passionate about creating things that make a difference while making money at it. And because of his forestry and construction background, he loves managing work in the field; he doesn't want to sit in an office like a lot of Ghanaian businessmen."

Charlie laughed. "Offices are so *boring*."

"Well, about fifteen minutes into that meeting, Afi dropped the bombshell that Charlie was her husband."

Charlie laughed harder. "She didn't want that to influence anything."

"Afi did say she knew a couple of other people as well, but my time was short and I felt great about Charlie, I felt this could work. So it wasn't the most rigorous executive search in the world, but I think it turned out really well."

"You could do a lot worse," said Charlie.

"No shit. I could have gotten a total operator who's just a crook, some flashy guy tooling around in a Mercedes—"

"What are you saying? I drive a Mercedes."

"I meant a *late-model* Mercedes, the kind with air bags and a CD player."

"Oh you are bad!"

Just when I thought that our luck in overtaking large vehicles up steep hills must surely run out, the gods took pity on us and we pulled into the traffic of downtown Koforidua, where passing became impossible even by the relaxed standards of Africa.

## 2. Living Hell

Ghana is a country of striking beauty, roughly the size of the United Kingdom yet considerably more diverse in climate and landscape. The lower third of the country is dominated by verdant rain forests teeming with neon-colored birds and orchestrated by the treetop chatter of the white-tailed colobus monkey. Along riptide-laced Atlantic beaches, hundred-foot-tall coconut palms (in their prime natural habitat) hover like extraterrestrials over raffia huts where fishermen tend their nets in brightly painted dugout canoes. Colonial-era rubber and palm plantations march along the coast road, which winds through beachfront villages huddled below the white-washed parapets of slave castles—the oldest European buildings in sub-Saharan Africa, illogically bright and romantic, the kind of places that in the West would be converted into boutique hotels with horizon pools and mojito bars, but in Africa crumble inexorably, like decaying teeth. In the north, the rain forest gives way to drier savannah, and villages far off the missionary track are clustered around medieval mud-and-stick mosques—pincushion palaces with the uninhibited creative charm of a child's sand castle. Herds of migratory elephants, hippos, and waterbucks roam vast reserves that are barely accessible and (unlike the travel-magazine game parks of Tanzania or Botswana) virtually un-touristed. Way up near the Burkina Faso border are communal lodges painted in striking geometric patterns, sacred colonies of giant hammer bats, and strange tribes where women still wear "lip plugs"—six-inch wooden discs inserted (one can only imagine painfully) in distended, pierced lips to create the effect of grotesque cartoon duck bills. The east of the country is defined by claw-shaped Lake Volta, the largest man-made lake in the world (created in the 1960s by the Akosombo Dam, which powered my brother's battery chargers), where moldering steamers straight out of *The African Queen* chug hesitantly between forgotten outposts with pulp-novel names like Kpando and Yeji, and waterfalls sluice down jungle escarpments.

Koforidua is not one of these places. Koforidua—population roughly one hundred thousand, the same as Gary, Indiana, which could well be its sister city—is the kind of place that guidebooks euphemistically refer to as "a good jumping-off point" or "a decent enough base for exploring the wider region." In other words, "the bus turns around at this backwater, so we are obliged to tell you something about it." Perhaps it is unfair to say that Koforidua is to Accra what Gary is to Chicago. It is, in fact, the capital of the misnamed Eastern Region (the Volta Region lies farther east). In Europe, Koforidua would be the kind of busy small city, like Tours or Sheffield, that offered a range of hotels and restaurants to suit any budget, plenty of public transportation, and convenient access to nearby tourist attractions. But Koff-town (as it is called), while undeniably busy, is not in Europe. It offers no nearby tourist attractions save a couple of admittedly decent waterfalls and a weekly bead market of regional and, arguably, even international importance so far as handmade beads go; it boasts only three substantial restaurants, serving related pathologies of the same brown food; and it lays claim to just a few overpriced hotels inconveniently located several miles outside of town.

Hotels, at least, were not our issue. We had a home. Of sorts.

My brother's rented quarters, which tripled as residence, Burro corporate office, and its first pilot field branch, occupied the entire second floor of a two-story colonial-era municipal building on a busy downtown street called Hospital Road. (The local hospital, may God have mercy on your soul, was indeed a short walk east.) The first floor accommodated a grocery store the size of a bus shelter and—taking up the remaining fifty feet or so of street frontage—a cluttered electronics concern, open until well after midnight, that mostly trafficked in gargantuan secondhand sound systems powerful enough to shake paint off the walls.

With the entire street façade devoted to commerce, entrance to Whit's flat was through a paved rear courtyard shared by another block of buildings behind us. This communal outdoor living space served as a playground, laundry room, kitchen, and bathroom for perhaps a dozen large families. Along one side of the courtyard ran an open concrete sewer, perhaps eighteen inches deep and as wide, through which coursed a slow-moving stream of soapy gray effluvia and floating trash. While genuine sewage of the toilet-flushing variety did not appear to drain into this fetid trough, my brother's kitchen and bathroom sinks could be plainly traced as tributaries, from drainpipes running down the side of the building. At any rate, the sewer's status as a conduit of relatively innocuous sink water was undermined by the fact that most of the courtyard's residents—men and women alike— freely peed into it. At least one uninhibited child regularly emptied his bowels into the babbling slipstream. The courtyard itself was sloped so rainwater would roll into the trench—along with every child's ball and other toys, which then got picked out, occasionally washed, and put into play again. In short it was a pathologist's nightmare, and a perfect example of why diarrhea is endemic to children in Africa.

At the rear of the courtyard, a double flight of red-painted concrete steps led up to my brother's flat. The door opened to a long perpendicular hallway off which two main rooms faced a colonnaded veranda, accessed through French doors, above the street. In the first room, makeshift wooden tables were covered with batteries, chargers, and extension cords, over which an industrial-sized metal fan throbbed loudly in a vain effort to keep the electronics cool. The other main room, larger, had a dining room table and chairs, and walls plastered with regional maps and whiteboards listing agent names and rental volumes. At either end of the hallway was a pair of smaller rooms, one front and one back. The back room on the west side was Whit's bedroom; the street-facing room adjoining it was the Burro office, with two desks, bookshelves, and a massive built-in safe with a keyed lock that no one could open and contents, if any, that remained a tantalizing mystery. The office could be accessed from Whit's room or the veranda. Over on the opposite side, the rear bedroom was occupied by Jan, and the front room, also accessible from either Jan's room or the veranda, was to be Harper's and mine. Behind Jan's bedroom, forming a sort of ell, was the small kitchen (sink, narrow fridge, Lilliputian four-burner gas stove) and a shower room, toilet cabin (with a commercial jet–siphon flushing action that I came to appreciate after a few meals at the local dives), and separate bathroom sink.

These cooking and ablution facilities, while Spartan by North American standards, were in fact pharaonic according to the dim expectations of Africa—particularly the keg-sized hot water heater above the shower, which apparently had no temperature setting cooler than scald. (Months later, Whit found the thermostat.) By contrast the kitchen sink provided only cold water, so dishwashing was accomplished by transferring a bucket of hot shower spray into the kitchen sink. Having running water at all was a minor engineering miracle: the murky public supply ran only twice a week, so at great expense Whit had installed a pair of 1,800-liter plastic tanks on the roof, creating a 950-gallon reservoir. In theory these backup tanks would fill when the utility gods deigned to open the communal spigots; after the town water went dry, we would subsist on this bacterial oasis cleverly cached on our roof. (Less fortunate residents of the block got by on dry days by hauling water from a large communal cistern located in another courtyard behind ours. When *that* ran dry, they had to buy water, per bucket, from a vendor across the street.) In practice, however, with a full house including one American teenager who showered twice a day, we ran out of water often, so the normally routine act of turning on a faucet was freighted with suspense; you never knew if you would get water (or what color it would be), a blast of pressurized air, or a pathetic burp followed by nothing.

I had to commend my brother for putting up with these inconveniences; I can't picture a lot of multimillionaire middle-aged American businessmen voluntarily living this way, particularly those happily married with a family eight thousand miles away. I regarded it as testament to his entrepreneurial commitment. In fact, he admitted, he would have gladly put up with even more straitened arrangements had he not been worried that Jan, who made no demands but also lived comfortably in the North-west, might run out of enthusiasm for cold bucket showers. At any rate, the place was actually rather charming and comfortable in a rakish, retro way. It was clearly built at a time when the Brits were doing things right, with high ceilings, lots of cross ventilation, and hand-carved mahogany doors and transom windows. The building had originally been the regional office of the British American Tobacco Company; later it was the office of the state labor department, and it was still known to locals as "Old Labor."

When Whit came into town looking for digs, the real estate agent drove him around to look at villas on the outskirts, down dark rutted roads and behind high walls. But that would never work for a business that was going to need a visible presence in the city. "I was like, 'Dude, you don't get it,'" Whit told me. "'We want to be in town—*right* in town.' The agent said, 'Oh, there is no place suitable for *obrunis* in town.' I said, 'Try me.'"

The place was cheap—two hundred cedis a month, payable in advance for two years (typical for Ghana), which came to about three thousand dollars. But it wasn't exactly in move-in condition. "Oh man, this place was three inches thick in dust when we first saw it," said Whit. "The kitchen had no appliances, no counters or cabinets—just a sink hanging in midair from pipes. The toilet was there, I just had to replace the seat."

"What was wrong with the existing seat?"

"It was there."

Some problems ran deeper. Above the coffered plywood ceiling was a corrugated metal roof dulled by rust and thus incapable of reflecting the relentless tropical sun. With no insulation of any kind, the roof was a heat sink. So, despite ceiling fans in every room and huge louvered-glass jalousie windows, the flat was transformed into a living hell roughly fifteen minutes after sunrise every day. Closing windows was unthinkable; in that stifling cloister, the slightest breeze was greeted like an apparition of Our Lady of Guadalupe. As a result, the flat was so noisy—horns, roosters, music, screaming children, and motorcycles—that you had to stick a finger in your ear to talk on a cell phone. This was indoors. Out on the veranda, otherwise a lovely vantage point above the street commerce—young men splitting coconuts with machetes, women selling sliced papaya snacks in front of plywood stalls hawking used brassieres (something about the coconuts and the brassieres suggested a small-time burlesque routine)—conversation transpired at a yell. Although we could and often did cook our own dinners from provisions gathered at the town's huge outdoor market, at the end of many days all we wanted was to go somewhere that had not been baking under a tin roof since six in the morning. Usually, that was the Linda Dor restaurant.

## 3. The Gold Coast

As Whit had predicted, Harper was down for the count by sunset; while he slept off his Red Bull bender, Whit and I ambled out for dinner at the Linda Dor, a few blocks down Hospital Road. "Watch every step you take, and don't ever stop watching," he said as we shuffled down the dark road, jumping over open sewers and dodging the jagged metal stumps of former signposts. "There is no concept of liability in Africa, and no one to blame if you fall into something. Also, I can pretty much guarantee that your medevac coverage won't airlift you to Germany for a twenty-inch gash in your leg; you'll be stuck with the local clinic, followed by a very unpleasant ride home on that shitty Delta plane. Or you could fork over four grand for a first-class seat."

Like our living quarters, the Linda Dor possessed a faded colonial charm. It had certainly seen better days, and its dingy décor and dark recesses suggested that there was much concerning this establishment that you really didn't want to know about, at least not before dinner.

We sat near the door and I opened the menu warily. Much to my surprise, laid out across its greasy pages was the promise of an intercontinental repast without equal. Steak frites, pasta Bolognese, boeuf Bourguignon, and Chinese stir-fry, not to mention African delights like peanut stew and the ubiquitous fufu, were all possible. Years of living in New York had trained me to be suspicious of restaurants that "specialize" in more than one ethnic approach; purveyors boasting simultaneous expertise in Korean and Mexican were not likely to create edible versions of either. But the menu at Linda Dor took multicultural cuisine into bold new territory. Clearly, behind the stove of this unassuming chow house reigned a polyglot chef of global ambition, a Baedeker of the broiler.

"What do you recommend?" I asked Whit.

"Nothing. But don't worry, they won't actually have any of this stuff— well, maybe one Chinese dish, but it won't be anything like Chinese food you've ever seen. I'd stick with the Jolof rice."

Rube that I was, I had not yet learned that in Ghana, restaurant menus are merely aspirational. Any given establishment, no matter how remote, may boast on its menu anything from Castilian tapas, Lebanese mezze, Auvergnian biftek, and Venetian fritto misto, none of which has ever been prepared within two thousand miles of the place, even if the ingredients were available. A request for any of these exotic belt-stretchers is invariably met with the response "It's finished."

Looking over the pages devoted to reliably available local fare, I saw something even more curious. "What's grasscutter?" I asked Whit.

"Rat. Well, a ratlike rodent. They eat regular rats here too, but grasscutter is big—bigger than a rabbit but with a ratlike tail. Maybe like a muskrat. Lives in the tall grass. It's a delicacy. Men hunt them with shotguns and sell them by the side of the road for extra cash."

It turns out that the grasscutter market is the subject of ecological controversy because hunters typically flush out the animals by setting grasslands on fire, contributing to the alarming deforestation of West Africa. Reckoning that one sample of the tender viand (in the interest of journalism) was unlikely to raze the African savannah, I pressed ahead bravely: "I'll have the grasscutter stew with fufu, please."

"Fufu is finished," the waitress replied meekly. "We have banku."

Whit explained that banku is a fermented version of fufu. I consented. He ordered the Jolof rice.

"Is the food better in the former French colonies?" I asked Whit.

"Considerably."

"So why are we here?"

He shot me a weary look. "Well as much as I like good food, there were some other considerations, some of them obvious, others not. Before last summer I had never been to Ghana, although I came close on New Year's Eve of 1981. I was in a bush taxi at the border in Burkina Faso, which was still called Upper Volta. That was the night of the second, and successful, J. J. Rawlings coup, when they sealed the borders."

"Whit, you were in the CIA. You let a closed border stop you?"

"Only that one time, and only because I left my decoder pen and shoe phone at the hotel. So I always felt kinda ripped off, like my Ghana trip had been taken away from me somehow. For years I toted around my unused Ghana visa as a shameful badge of travel curtailed. But since then, Ghana has gone through a pretty phenomenal evolution. There's a very free press; in fact the press is rated freer than in some of the Eastern European countries. There are very strong democratic institutions, albeit still fragile at times, as we are learning in the election just finished. But the country has now had five presidential elections, at least the latter three of which were widely acclaimed as substantially free, fair, and transparent. The first one, when Rawlings won in '92, was rigged, but the second one, in '96, was much more fair, and they have been since then."

My stew arrived, bony chunks of skin-on grasscutter in a thick brown slurry. On the side were two softball-sized gray dumplings—the banku. Whit explained that traditionally one eats the banku (or fufu) by hand, small pieces dipped in the soup like a doughnut in coffee. It is also considered rude to actually chew it, which, upon tasting the gelatinous paste, did not seem much of a sacrifice. "Go ahead and eat," said Whit a bit too forcefully, as if addressing a reluctant child staring at his vegetables. "There's no telling when mine will come. Ghana has no traditional restaurant culture;

they just bring food out whenever it's ready." I nodded and tucked in to my rat, which, as I had hoped, tasted much like rabbit.

"So you've got strong democratic institutions, and a strong civil society as well," Whit continued. "There are a lot of professional organizations and associations and church groups that really push for a better society and are working in various ways to improve things. And it's a relatively well-educated society. Ghana used to have the best education system in Africa; it's probably suffered in the last twenty years. It's also got a history of a monetized rural economy, so that was very important. You go to some countries, like Ethiopia, and the rural economy is very much at the subsistence level, maybe with some barter. Here there's a long history of cash-cropping and monetization, so people are used to earning money in a wide variety of ways and living in a cash economy."

This commercial bent seems ingrained in the Ghanaian culture, a legacy of the country's rich gold mines—the region's most valuable natural resource before the transatlantic slave trade, and still the second most important export after cocoa. The Brits of course called Ghana the Gold Coast; under their rule, Ashanti tribal leaders were groomed as business partners, a transformation that accelerated in the early twentieth century. In 1930 one of them, Kofi Sraha, described the situation in terms that would sound familiar to the most acquisitive baby boomer: "We turned ourselves from Warriors into Merchants, Traders, Christians and men of properties, [kept] moneys in the Banks under British Protection and began to build huge houses." It was easy to see Whit's Ghanaian partner Charlie as the modern descendant of this legacy.

A loud *crack* ricocheted inside my skull, and pain I had never felt outside of the dentist's chair bored through a maxillary molar. I reached inside my mouth and extracted a mangled shotgun pellet. "*Fuck*, look at that."

"Holy shit," said Whit. "I knew there was a reason I never eat the grass-cutter. Chew carefully." Indeed; by the end of the meal I had extracted five pellets. (I later learned from Charlie that you *want* your grasscutter to have pellets. "That proves they were properly shot, and not killed with rat poison," he said.) Whit's rice arrived just as I was finishing up.

"Ghana is a beautiful country too," Whit continued. "That's also important because I'm trying to attract and retain American and other partners as we grow. And obviously the English language here helps with that as well. The business climate is also very friendly to foreign investment. There's guaranteed repatriation of profits, albeit with an eight percent dividend tax. So you've got a very positive and improving business climate for outside investors. Put all those factors together and it just makes sense."

It was late, still quite hot. Jet lag was winning. I paid the check, gathered up my shotgun pellets, and we left for home. "Let's take the scenic route," said Whit. "I'll show you a bit of the town."

We tramped down gloomy side streets, where African men leaned against sheds, sharpening machetes along smooth stones and eyeing us with curiosity. I briefly weighed the relative benefits of getting hacked up by a sharp versus a dull machete, deciding the difference would be largely esoteric in the moment. White people are a rare sight in Koforidua, and it felt strange to be such a visible minority. For the first time in my life I felt some visceral awareness of what it must be like to be black in a largely white society, to be stared at like a freak. I wasn't sure if our route was prudent; these were not streets I would walk down at night in, say, Detroit. But we weren't in Detroit, and it was fine. Whit said "Good evening!" to everyone we passed, and the sullen faces would suddenly beam. My dopey kid brother was at home here, and I was glad to be with him.

three

# THE HORN OF AFRICA

**EARLY 2009:** The business plan

I know I'm confused: a typical road scene in Ghana.

## 1. The Last Unlucky Place

"It's Italian for butter."

"Huh?" Whit, behind the wheel of the Tata, glared at me, then swerved to avoid a woman balancing a two-foot-high pyramid of loose eggs, stacked like cannonballs at a Civil War monument, on a tray over her head.

"Burro," I said. "It means 'butter' in Italian. That could be confusing in Italy."

"We're not doing business in Italy, asshole. It's not a developing country."

"But what happens when you expand into francophone West Africa? Do we call it Buerre?"

"Shut up."

"Seriously, don't you think it's a little weird that you're starting a business with a Spanish name on a continent where virtually no one speaks Spanish? I mean, the Spaniards were smart; they stayed away from this miasmic hell-pit except to pick up slaves. They had experience. They knew what relentless heat can do to the human soul. There's like one country the size of Rhode Island that speaks Spanish here."

"Are you finished?"

"Just watch the road. You can get the death penalty for hitting a pedestrian here, especially if you knock eggs off her head."

We were headed down the coast from Accra to Axim, a 150-mile stretch of surf to the lagoon border with Ivory Coast. It was a working holiday with Harper. We had planned a rolling tour of the slave forts, while scouting expansion locations for Burro, plotting back roads on our GPS and following the power lines—mostly to see where they end and where the battery-powered villages begin. It didn't take long to figure out that the existence of power lines did not mean a village was electrified. Often the main three-phase lines would run right over a large settlement—with no step-down.

"There's no money to bring power down to these villages," said Whit.

"And they have to stare at those power lines every day. Must be like dying of thirst on the ocean."

"Of course that's assuming the power is actually running. You never know."

We pulled into the seaside town of Beyin and parked next to Fort Apollonia, a decrepit British outpost from 1770. By far the largest and most successful capitalist venture in the history of Africa was slavery. No other natural resource—not diamonds or gold, not copper or bauxite or oil—has shaped modern Africa, and the mind-set of Africans, like slavery. The slave trade literally wiped out generations of Africans; the latest scholarly assessments, using sophisticated computer models, suggest that more than eleven million sub-Saharan Africans simply disappeared (think Nazi Holocaust times two), mostly young men. But as Americans know from our own history, a centuries-long conflagration like slavery doesn't simply end when it ends. In Africa the long-term effects of slavery, still being felt, include the rise of militaristic native governments (armies were needed both to protect against rival slave raids and to gather slaves for trade); tribal and ethnic distrust; an obsession among leaders with opulent trappings of power at the expense of normal citizens (the slave trade enriched African rulers and desensitized them to the plight of the poor); primitivism (consider that the height of the slave trade was during the Age of Enlightenment); and pervasive poverty that breeds desperate acts of violence. Anyone doing business in modern Africa must contend with the legacy of the continent's dark capitalist history, which did not begin with the Europeans.

Today we tend to think of Africa as a place of teeming masses—and in fact, modern African cities are hives of sweating, coughing, chaotic humanity. But the larger story of Africa is the story of underpopulation. Poor soils, extreme climates, and a host of natural diseases and predators kept the African people in check for millennia. Simply put, there were not enough bodies to do all the work. As a result, the medieval kingdoms of Africa were constantly at war for the express purpose of collecting slaves. In West Africa, along the humid Atlantic tropical belt, slaves made it possible to clear the rain forest and establish agricultural settlements. These communities grew to become the cities and capitals of modern nations, including Ghana. In fact, when the Portuguese slavers first arrived at what is now Ghana, the local tribes were not sellers but buyers: between 1500 and 1535, the Akan tribes, from whom most modern Ghanaians descend, bought between ten thousand and twelve thousand slaves with local gold. (The slaves came from what are now Benin and Nigeria to the east.)

Taken as a whole and looking back over thousands of years, the scale of pre-colonial slavery on the African continent cannot be explained away as opportunistic capture on the battlefield. Clearly, indigenous African slavery was a stand-alone business, and a large one.

And yet—what the Africans themselves started and the Portuguese refined, the British took up with organizational zeal. They turned the Gold Coast into the center of the West African slave trade, and Cape Coast Castle was their corporate headquarters. At the height of the trade, in the eighteenth century, it is estimated that about six million West Africans were shipped into slavery, mostly to plantations in Brazil and the Caribbean. Scholars now believe that between 1720 and 1780, 5 to 10 percent of the Gold Coast's entire population was enslaved. As William St. Clair points out in *The Grand Slave Emporium*, while the slave trade did not exactly drive the Industrial Revolution, the agricultural commodities (like cotton) that slaves produced in the New World contributed hugely to the success of British manufacturing in the nineteenth century—well after 1807, when England abolished slave trafficking. This is not a fine point. It means that England and other European countries continued to profit indirectly from slavery long after they had formally washed their hands of it.

And perversely, abolition encouraged a second wave of indigenous slavery in nineteenth-century Africa, since the vast business infrastructure of the slave trade didn't just disappear overnight. As Europeans shifted to legitimate trade in African agriculture and other resources, slaves were needed to tend the fields and extract the minerals. In some parts of Africa, such as Mauritania, slavery still exists openly.

Today eleven of Ghana's coastal slave fortifications are UNESCO World Heritage Sites and international tourist attractions. African Americans come to find their roots, and they stay in hotels and eat in restaurants and take pictures under the Door of No Return and buy handicrafts from the locals. For the diaspora tourists it is a bittersweet journey. It is not uncommon for African American visitors, upon seeing firsthand the reality of modern Africa, to express perverse gratitude that their ancestors were among the enslaved. (The descendants of Haitian slaves are presumably less buoyant about their fate.) There is no doubt: chained and beaten, raped and ruined, wherever they landed the slaves were surely the unluckiest of all humanity. But Africa, it turns out, is the last unlucky place.

## 2. What Has Upset the Gods?

Through the terminally gridlocked traffic in Accra, narrowly escaping from Nkrumah Circle and its armies of prostitutes and panhandling children of Tuareg nomads from the southern Sahara (sent out by their parents to beg in traffic all day and making the universal hand-to-mouth sign of hunger), we passed a large hand-painted billboard for a skin ointment with the query: SUFFERING FROM BUMPS AND KELOID? followed by detailed illustrations of various worms and festering skin ailments.

"They don't leave much to the imagination, do they?" I said.

"Oh that's nothing," said Whit. "Wait till you see the signs for diarrhea meds."

To the catalog of African miseries, add a modern plague: driving. It is possible to imagine a more dangerous contact sport than driving in Africa, but if so, it has managed to fly under the radar of even the most ratings-desperate television networks. Numbers are sketchy since even serious accidents often go unreported in the developing world, but Africa easily boasts the highest traffic mortality rate on the planet. A 2004 study by the World Health Organization found that of every hundred thousand Africans, 28.3 will die in car accidents, compared to just eleven in Europe. Children are particularly at risk, as pedestrians: in Ghana, about 20 percent of the nearly two thousand annual traffic deaths are children walking to and from school or playing in roads; most are boys, under age ten.

Along the road between Cape Coast and Accra were several billboards that said OVERSPEEDING KILLS! This is presumably opposed to regular speeding, which is generally accepted. Beneath that loud warning was a grim tally of traffic deaths at that particular intersection. The first sign said: OVER 12 PERSONS DIED HERE. And the next one, a few miles down the road: OVER 70 PERSONS DIED HERE. You see these signs all over Ghana, always with an inexact body count that suggests the authorities simply got tired of tallying up the limbs and settled for a guesstimate.

Reasons for the carnage include the previously mentioned penchant for mindless passing; spectacularly overloaded and unsafe vehicles (trucks piled two stories high with cargo, devoid of tire treads and listing like drunken sailors); scarce medical facilities with limited training in trauma care; low to zero enforcement of speed limits (the Ghana national police, uniformed in blue camouflage and shouldering Kalashnikov rifles, seem to exist all too frequently to shake down drivers for bribes at roadblocks); roads cratered with chassis-twisting potholes; deep, open concrete roadside sewers that leave no shoulder and no room for error ("pulling over" to avoid an accident could be more disastrous than the collision itself); for the same reason, no place for pedestrians except in the roadway; an obstacle course of countless rusting hulks of previous accidents that never get towed away, causing new accidents (the African traffic nightmare has been called "the hidden epidemic," but in fact you can see the pathology along any ten-kilometer stretch of road); and, at night, a lack of streetlights or reflective roadway markings combined with the inescapable logic that the less often headlights are used, the longer they will last.

These are just the material causes. Whit speculates that the real, underlying problem is the African's innate fatalism: "When it's my turn to go, it's my turn to go" is a common sentiment. It's in the hands of God, so why not pass a double tractor-trailer over a hill in a rainstorm? This is not a private spiritual matter. Trucks, cars, buses, and taxis throughout Ghana are adorned with Christian aphorisms surrendering their drivers to a celestial traffic code. I don't mean discreet bumper stickers; I'm talking about large-scale decals that cover the entire rear window (which, come to think of it, could be another cause of accidents). "It Is God's Will" might be the motto plastered across a seventeen-foot-high banana truck with six bald tires. "In Thy Name Alone" christens many a speeding taxi. "God Is In Control" is another favorite—no need to steer those cars. One day, we got stuck behind a massive cargo truck that featured a professionally hand-painted message laid out in twelve-inch-high circus font across the back: RELIGIOUS CONFUSION. Below, the left mud flap said MASTER and the right said JESUS. Often the message is in Twi, the most common phrase being *Gye Nyame,* which means "Except for God" and is meant to suggest His omnipotence. On the road in Ghana you put the pedal to the metal, but the real power hovers somewhere above the hood, so it's okay. Not to worry. *Gye Nyame.*

On its website for travel advisories, the U.S. State Department summarizes driving conditions in every country in the world. Here are some insights they provide for travelers to Ghana:

> The road from Accra to the central region tourist area of
> Cape Coast continues to be the site of many accidents.
> Travel in darkness, particularly outside the major cities,
> is extremely hazardous, due to poor street lighting and
> the unpredictable behavior of pedestrians, bicyclists and
> farm animals, particularly goats and sheep. Aggressive
> drivers, poorly maintained vehicles and overloaded vehicles
> pose serious threats to road safety. The safety standards
> of the small private buses that transit roads and highways
> are uncertain.

Very few Africans own cars—in Ghana about one in two hundred people. As a result, "nobody knows how to drive here," says Whit, "especially the people who drive." But that doesn't mean a lack of cars. With very little infrastructure of public transportation—the few trains stopped running reliably years ago, intercity buses don't cover the deep countryside where so many Ghanaians live, and even Accra (population two million) has no mass transit of any kind—getting around Ghana has devolved into a free-wheeling circus of enterprising shared taxis and their downscale stepcousins, the battered private passenger minivans alluded to in the State Department brief, known as *tro-tros*. (The name derives from the Twi slang for the small coins once used to pay for passage.) The nomadic and wild-eyed drivers of these vehicles will take you from one end of the nation to another, and anywhere in between; you see them bouncing along dirt tracks dozens of kilometers from anywhere, groaning under rooftop baggage loads, their unbelted passengers practically spilling out the windows and the open sliding doors. Neither taxis nor *tro-tros* have meters; the fares are highly competitive and based on destination, which means profit is a factor of three inputs: extreme speed, maximum passenger load, and as little money wasted on maintenance as possible. Maybe you could add speed again.

The result is chaos. Car accidents pose a far greater threat to visitors than any of the country's myriad tropical diseases, flesh-eating parasites, and venom-spitting reptiles. Guidebooks and websites warn visitors not to even consider getting behind the wheel, even in broad daylight; driving at night is considered evidence of criminal insanity. Hertz of Ghana will not rent its vehicles without a hired driver, and local agencies are nearly as insistent. Of course this adds considerably to the expense of tourism—at least for those unwilling to ride cheek-to-shoulder with the perspiring masses in *tro-tros*—as the driver must not only be paid but also fed and housed along the road. It's oddly colonial, and disjointing in a modern tourist context. There is something Kipling-esque about the well-heeled German sightseeing couple nosing around the slave dungeons of Cape Coast Castle as their African driver waits in the blinding sun of the whitewashed courtyard, jangling keys and speaking Twi into his cell phone.

But we are not tourists, and our business in Ghana requires driving—lots of driving. So we drive. Everywhere. Sometimes even at night. Driving here is not fun, even if, like me, you love to drive. It is exhausting because African driving requires constant vigilance; take your eyes off the road for one second and you miss the darting child, the stubborn goat, the open sewer an inch from your tire, the oncoming *tro-tro* in your lane. Death waits around every curve and over every hill, and there is simply too much life happening in too little space. On the road in Ghana, mistakes are unforgiven, and physics can provide a harsh and messy lesson.

Here is what happens, all too often: In February 2009, a bus carrying thirty-three passengers along the road between the northern towns of Tamale and Bolgatanga was passing two larger buses at high speed when it collided head-on with an onion truck. Everyone on the bus and the truck was killed, and dozens more in other vehicles were injured. In the gritty, repulsive-attractive style of African journalism, the *Ghanaian Chronicle* reported: "Most of the victims had their skulls broken, while others had disfigured faces and mutilated bodies. The accident was so horrendous that one could easily describe those with broken legs and arms as having minor injuries."

One month later, a gasoline truck circling a busy roundabout in Winneba, along the main Accra–Cape Coast highway, blew a tire. The driver lost control and careened into an Opel sedan. The tanker exploded into the proverbial ball of fire, incinerating more than a dozen people on the spot, including an entire family, and sending three dozen more to the hospital with severe burns. Most of them would die later. "Almost all of them came in with their whole body burnt, both the frontal part and posterior part, including the head," a doctor at the local hospital, which quickly ran out of bandages, told a reporter. "For most of the kids it also involved their private parts. . . . We are beginning to lose them one by one. It is quite hard."

The same day, in Eastern Region near Whit's home in Koforidua, at least four people died when a bus collided with a truck carrying acid. Responding to all these accidents, a Ghanaian editorialist wrote:

> We are dying on our roads like flies. It is as if some
> wicked gods have decided to exact retribution for some
> national sin we have committed and decided that our
> roads are the best place to exact the sacrifice. If this was
> happening in the old days in a village with responsible
> leaders, they would go on "abusa" [asking a deity for an
> explanation] to find out what has upset the gods.

As always in Ghana, it's in the hands of the gods. But spend enough time behind the wheel and you start to see rational patterns in the chaos, clues to the seemingly random behavior. You get better at it, although with practice comes the danger of complacency. The Maine woodsman who taught me how to cut down trees warned me that most chainsaw accidents happen to people who've been using them for years; they stop fearing the blade, and they get careless. The same could apply to driving in Africa.

"It's all about the horn," said Whit as we threaded through afternoon traffic in Cape Coast. "You gotta get the horn thing down," demonstrating with a short blast while swinging wide around a man on a wobbly bicycle balancing a large piece of lumber on his head.

"You know, to a bicyclist there's nothing worse than jerks who honk when they pass," I said. "You think a guy on a bike doesn't know a car is coming?"

"Not the point. It's a conversation," he said, flipping his thumbs across the horn buttons in a staccato rhythm.

The conversation. It has been observed that in Africa the car horn takes the place of the brake, but I think it is more than that. The horn is more like the muse of the African driver. Honking, which Ghanaians call *hooting*, in the British manner, constitutes a tribal language of its own, with grammatical rules. In a Ghanaian traffic dispute, "But I hooted!" is a perfectly legitimate defense. Likewise, "Why didn't you hoot?" is not a rhetorical question but a serious level of inquiry. It is not considered rude to hoot; in fact hooting is often an expression of gratitude. When someone has courteously allowed your car into the traffic lane, you give them a civilized hoot. When a Ghanaian driver wants to pass another car, he hoots to signal his intent. The driver of the forward car will then hoot back in acknowledgment, hopefully communicating some important traffic information from his vantage point. A quick, light hoot (more of a toot) means "all clear to pass." A long, forceful hoot (here the word *honk* makes more sense) means "not a good time to be in the oncoming traffic lane." As the rear car swings around to pass, both cars will re-hoot in recognition of a job well done. This orchestra is accompanied by a dance of arm waving and hand signaling out the windows of both cars. Meanwhile, one potential source of confusion for Westerners is the practice, also common in Latin America, of using turn indicators to communicate to other drivers what they should be doing, rather than what the driver who signaled intends to do next.

All of it—the hoots, the waves, the high fives, the brush-offs, and the finger snaps that keep cars moving in Ghana—would be impossible in air-conditioned vehicles hermetically sealed from the outside world. Driving here is an intimate ritual, as hands-on as haggling over slabs of goat meat in the public market.

Hooting reaches its apex in Ghana's ubiquitous and traffic-clogged roundabouts, which are considerably more freewheeling than their Western counterparts. In theory, the Ghanaian rotary follows the usual international rules: traffic already in the circle has the right-of-way. In practice, however, it's more like a bumper-car ride at the state fair: no matter where you are or which way you turn, someone else is bearing down on you illogically, and the worst possible thing you can do is nothing. In this situation the call-and-response of the hooting breaks down into gibberish, but it could be my lack of fluency.

It would not be far-fetched to make a connection between African hooting and traditional African drumming, which was also a form of communication in motion. In the slave-trade era, British soldiers at Cape Coast were amazed at how quickly news traveled between the Fante villages. The arrival of a Portuguese ship at a fort several days' march away would be known to the natives within hours, long before the Brits had a clue.

It was the drums. Talking drums, some more than eight feet tall, with the tonal register of an earthquake, used animal hides tensioned with a series of wooden pegs that could be adjusted to vary the pitch. In this way, drummers wielding carved sticks could actually mimic the local tongues, which were more tonally complex than the written languages of Europe and thus lent themselves to percussive interpretation.* Of course this required a

---

* Ghana's tribal languages, perhaps eight thousand years old, are members of the Niger-Congo linguistic family, which predominates from Senegal to Tanzania and includes virtually all of the African equatorial belt.

great deal of skill; communications were relayed by drummers positioned every few miles, and the musicians needed to be able to comprehend the message as it was received, then pass it along faithfully. It required virtually perfect pitch and an unerring rhythmic sense. Talking drums have been compared to Morse code, but that's inaccurate. Drummers did not use a semaphore, or an algorithm of the language. They were actually *drumming the language*. It was more like amplification. Like a horn.

African languages really do sound like they evolved to be spoken in motion—they literally roll off the tongue—a trait with practical advantages in modern Ghana, where road conditions make it difficult to converse while driving, at least in the precise diction of Western tongues. People who have never been to Africa cannot fully appreciate the exquisite torture of the road surfaces. Dirt roads are universally creased with washboard ruts that make you feel like your eyeballs are vibrating out of your head. These roads go on for hundreds of miles and connect major settlements; it's not like you can avoid them. Now, any country boy knows that washboards can be planed over by driving at a "sweet spot" speed, typically around forty miles an hour; only city slickers lunk along at jogging speed. Unfortunately, in Ghana, the dirt roads are also sluiced with washouts, craters, and deep sand pits, making speed impossible. All you can do is creep forward as your tires feel their way through every rut like a blind man looking for the curb. You might think the paved roads provide some relief, but they don't. For one thing, in Ghana even major paved highways sooner or later become dirt roads, often without warning. Second, the pavement is generally mined with bathtub-sized potholes that could possibly be negotiated by some form of military transport but not vehicles designed to carry unarmored passengers on welded steel frames suspended over bald tires. That doesn't slow down Ghanaian taxi and *tro-tro* drivers, who simply swerve like pinballs around the holes. As a result, the highways have the feel of test tracks; there are not so much "lanes" as paths through the obstacle course, and cars are constantly weaving and dodging at high speed within inches of each other.

Sometimes, of course, cars and trucks moving at 150 kilometers per hour will misjudge a pothole's depth or location. When the front tire hits one of these black holes at high speed, all is lost. In Africa you need to throw out every preconception that you have about road construction and maintenance. You need to understand that even a very bad road in America would qualify as above average in Africa.

Conversing over these road conditions is like speaking into a vibrato synthesizer. One day on our coast trip, winding along a rutted track past fishing villages along the beach near Axim, I tried engaging Whit in a discussion about seasonal income and how it applies, if at all, to Ghanaian fishermen. It might have been a fascinating exploration of emerging-market microeconomics—the kind of conversation I pictured myself having with Bono and Bill Gates at a Davos cocktail party—but instead it sounded like a couple of fifth-graders making burp-talk on the playground. I was getting heartburn.

By contrast, the two Ghanaian peasant women in the backseat—one of them pregnant, both wearing wraparound shifts printed in bright patterns of banana leaves and flowers—were chattering away like weaver birds. At least to my ear, their native dialect spilled effortlessly off their tongues, completely uninhibited by the lurch and sway of our truck.

The back of our truck was rarely empty, because we stopped constantly to pick up pedestrians—usually women on their way to the local market, their heads balancing giant enamelware bowls and plastic laundry baskets of cassava root, rice, bananas, oranges, peanuts, yams, smoked fish, and rolls of colorful fabric. It is not unusual for women to walk ten miles every day under such loads. In the evening, many also haul water in twenty-liter jugs, which weigh forty-four pounds full. You want to admire their grace and stamina, but health experts say that over a lifetime these loads cause crippling spinal deformations in women across the developing world. And while physical violence is not a major concern in Ghana, women in many poor countries are vulnerable to sexual attacks while on the road.

So we picked up women, and men, everywhere we went, and they beamed over their good fortune to be on the right road at the right time when the white men in the truck came by. They would set their loads in the bed of the pickup and climb into the cab thanking us, sometimes in English, and when the cab was full of passengers, they climbed into the bed, which always seemed to have room for one more dusty traveler. I often wondered what these poor Ghanaians, who are extremely respectful to family members, made of the two bickering *obruni* brothers in the front seat.

## 3. Where Electricity Comes From

"Listen to this," said Whit, spinning the dial on his MP3 player, which was plugged into the truck's stereo.

"Whit, Daddio here." It was our father's cracking voice, desiccated by old age as if speaking through a Lintophone wireless, captured on Whit's voice mail. He had died a year earlier after a long bout with Alzheimer's that left him unable to manage his finances. After he lost thousands of dollars entering bogus junk-mail sweepstakes, we took away his checkbook and put him on an allowance. But he lived in Michigan and we didn't, and even though he had plenty of cash and the comfort of caregivers, his mind was unable to do the math, as they say. So he would call constantly, imagining himself broke and launching paranoid voice-mail rants against the nursing agency, his bank, and finally us. It was sad.

But to be perfectly honest, it was also funny. One time he called Whit and said he was tired of getting all these small bills that don't buy anything: "I need some sixties and some eighties, man," he insisted.

Our dad was capable of great kindness and generosity. But he could also be emotionally cruel, especially when he drank. He was what Lenny Bruce called the white-collar drunk—buffed nails, bespoke suit, bombed out of his mind. Unlike working-class drinkers (such as our maternal grandfather, a Slovak immigrant who painted Chryslers for forty years), Jim Alexander, the successful advertising man, never raised a hand against his children. That could get messy, and Alex, as his friends called him, was a meticulously tidy man. Today he would probably be diagnosed with obsessive-compulsive disorder, but in his era he was simply a clean freak. One inviolable hygienic rule in our family was that the limes he squeezed into his gin-and-tonics had to be scrubbed with a brush under hot soapy water. Limes were the only things green and fresh he was ever known to eat, and he went through crates of them. In hindsight his frenzied scrubbing was perhaps sensible, given the current hysteria over food-borne illnesses. But his concern was not strictly biological, as he had full faith in the power of corporate America and chemicals to deliver safe food to the local grocery store. Rather, his agricultural anxiety was ethnically motivated. Approximately once a week he would remind us that "some Mexican picked his nose and then picked that lime." It was one of his favorite lines, especially once he became aware of how much we hated it.

Averse to the persuasive power of the belt, Dad's brand of retribution was discourse and humiliation. After a flight of gin-and-tonics he would bait us into arguments about his favorite bêtes noires, namely bedwetting liberals, ecology, and creeping socialism. One night he got me to take the bait on energy conservation, which as far as he was concerned was invented by Karl Marx as part of his unified proletarian enslavement theory. Our dad tried to leave every light in his house turned on all night, just to thumb his nose at the bedwetters, the hippies, and Karl Marx.

"Dad, do you know where your electricity comes from?" I asked.

"Of course I do. It comes from Consumers Power Company."

"Okay, but do you know where they get it?"

"They own it."

"Fair enough, but how do they generate it? Kite strings?"

"I haven't the slightest idea, and I don't care."

"Well then you might be surprised to know that they make it by burning coal. Every time you turn on a light you burn a piece of coal."

"That's the stupidest fucking thing I've ever heard."

After the Alzheimer's kicked in, Dad forgot to drink and became a sort of benign version of his old aggressive, ranting self.

The phone message continued. "I think you were out yesterday," Dad said into the machine, "as many people were. I said something about six bucks a month from the crazy people with the money? Forget it, uh, what

I need—what I'm gonna need, is like a hundred dollars a month, every month. And you sure got that kind of money. That's money I made way way way back when I was makin' big-big-big-big money. So give me a call when you can, I may be out on a brief errand or something like that, but give me a ring because I'm in touch with Palmore [his broker] and we got some things to talk about here, so I'd like to hear from you, okay? Bye."

I looked in the rearview mirror at the two Ghanaian women, who had stopped chatting. I wondered if they understood enough English to comprehend my dad, and if so what they could possibly be thinking.

Dad again, next message: "Yeah, Whit. I don't know what the hell is goin' on down there, but I'm getting very very upset. This goddamned buncha nitwits that sent these girls [his caregivers]. The girls are terrific, but then the company steals this, they steal that, they steal everything within sight, it looks—it appears that way. Anyway I find out, I find out—*heh heh*—when I call the company—what the hell? What's all this business? *Blah blah blah.* It's Whit and Max. And it's *pay! pay! pay! pay! PAY! PAY! PAY!* Jesus Christ! I spent a lifetime, *a fucking lifetime of my life* puttin' bing-bing-bing-bing together for you and your brother!"

I checked the women in the back. No reaction. Ghanaians are familiar with all the major English curse words, but they are considered shockingly rude and almost never uttered, even by men.

"And what the hell?" Dad carried on. "And then whaddya doin' with the money? You're sendin' it to Palmore! Boy, he needs money like—*heh heh*—like a cop needs a cigarette. Jesus Christ! I've gotta go out for another hour here in a minute. Gimme a call, and I wanna know what's gonna happen here. If you guys wanna be in my will you better make a change in your lifes [sic] right now, you and Max, okay? Good-bye."

"Like a cop needs a cigarette," I repeated, musing on the analogy. One fortunate aspect of life in Ghana is that almost no one smokes, perhaps because they inhale enough smoke preparing their food. Outside, along the side of the road, a man was holding up a rat for sale—a real rat, not grasscutter. It had been dried and smoked and stretched over a rack of twigs, ready to eat.

"I wonder what Dad would think of us now," I said.

"He would love it over here," said Whit, unconvincingly. Our dad lived in the same Michigan town his entire life, had no patience for strange foreign countries like Canada, and never ate rodents. An exotic meal for him was Boston baked scrod. He was a businessman of the first world (American version), and he was not much a part of our own world as kids—checked out on booze or on the 5:39 to Chicago. He was absent, and come to think of it, now so were we.

The Ghanaian ladies indicated we had arrived at their corner, and we pulled over. "Thank you and God bless you," the pregnant one said from the road. "Safe journey!" Apparently their English was pretty good, but who knows? "Safe journey" is a common farewell pleasantry in Ghana. But like "slave tourism," "safe journey" has a disconnected ring to it. There are no safe journeys in Africa, and never have been.

**"Why are we here, Whit?"** Back on the main road toward the industrial port town of Takoradi, through a pinball course of roundabouts, the pavement had improved enough to make conversation possible.

"You mean, why are we on a road with post-colonial asphalt? Or here on Earth? Is your question navigational or existential?"

"I guess I mean, why batteries? How did this idea get started?"

"It all goes back to my childhood."

"I was there. In fact, I remember when you came home from the hospital. It was a tragic mistake; we were supposed to get another perfect child, but Mom had been taking some new pain reliever and we got you."

"Shut up. Batteries. It all goes back to my Major Matt Mason Space Station. From an early age I realized that the moon crawler never had enough battery power. I loved that moon crawler, and yet every time I would get near the base, the batteries would die. So I vowed from that day forward that someday I would have a battery that is fresh anytime you want. That was the origin of Burro batteries. And I named it after the Italian word for butter because I love butter and I love Italy."

"So the Major Matt Mason Space Station was sort of like your Rosebud."

"That's it."

"Wow, I remember that stupid toy, but I never knew it meant so much to you. I think Bob Zaroff and I set it on fire once. We wanted to watch the plastic melt."

"Don't go there."

"I think you need to work on your backstory."

"Okay, here goes. I didn't start with batteries. I started with a broader idea. I actually started with the idea of the brand, of really focusing on a range of goods and services that would be affordable to low-income people and would improve their personal productivity. This all goes back to my first days as a student in Ivory Coast. I just felt there was so much economic opportunity. When I was working on aid projects I felt like, why don't people come over here and start businesses? That always seemed to me the best way to make a sustainable difference—create a for-profit business that employs people. Of course I was very naïve—there are all sorts of barriers and difficulties—but the idea stuck with me. So when we sold Cranium to Hasbro, you know, I was forty-seven years old and I just thought to myself, if I don't do this now, when am I ever gonna do it?

"My first idea was that we actually would be based in a capital city and we would target products to urban elites, who often go back to their family villages. And there's an expectation that you bring something back to the village when you come. Often that can just be a farm animal or alcohol, bread or money, and I thought, wouldn't it be great if we could have like an African version of Home Depot that would be sort of like a Nike store—a retail destination that would really be kind of like a showroom, a proving ground almost, for all these different product ideas, and people would take these things back to the villages and generate demand for them.

"So I employed this recent University of Washington graduate, a really smart young guy named Ben Golden, to come over here. He spent about six or eight weeks in Ghana for me, traveling all through the country, and he interviewed all sorts of people about all these different wares."

"What kind of wares?"

"Solar battery chargers, improved mosquito netting, battery-operated fans for your hut, water filters, improved pumps and irrigation systems, better cookstoves—all kinds of stuff that people typically mention when they talk about better products for people in the developing world. He came back and he said, 'Yeah, everybody loves this stuff, but nobody's got any money. There's just so little discretionary income.' And I said, 'Well Ben, that's what we've gotta figure out.'

"Eventually it dawned on me that we were kidding ourselves to think that we could come in with this broad line of products and all of a sudden create demand when there's so little budget available. I mean, anything that would be perceived as a luxury or secondary would be hugely problematic if we're trying to reach a mass audience. There are all kinds of things you could do with the elites—frankly I see tons of business opportunities in Ghana to better service the elites. But that's not what I was interested in.

"So that's what got me to think deeply about what it was really gonna take. And what I eventually came up with is that, first, what if our products directly enhanced income-earning capability? What if we stepped back one level and said that our business was really selling a business? What if we were actually trying to create these little—and I actually was naïve enough to think I had coined the phrase—micro-franchises? Then I thought, well great, how do we do that? I started to look at some of the models—you know, Amway, Avon.

"So that was the first thing—the realization that you've got a much greater chance of success if you're setting people up in a business, and that your business is really creating success for them.

"And the second thing was, since you're not gonna generate new spending, you need to find a product that would displace existing expenditure—the better mousetrap. So I needed to find out where poor people are already spending money and come up with a better alternative that either saves them money or gives them better value for the same money.

"So those became my two critical criteria. And I started combing through

Ben's reports and looking more at the literature, and I really just asked myself, what are people in Ghana spending money on? And batteries kept coming up. The data aren't great, but there are a few ways to back into it, and pretty much every estimate starts to converge around the typical African family spending somewhere between two and five dollars a month on throwaway batteries.

"Now I had recently converted our family over to rechargeable batteries, and we were saving a ton with them. I did a little research online and discovered that rechargeables deliver ten to thirty times more energy than throwaways, per dollar spent. And I thought, wow, here's something: a better battery.

"But then you gotta ask yourself, if they're so great, how come no one in Africa is adopting them? Why don't you see them? Well it makes sense when you realize that the primary thing people are after here is minimizing current out-of-pocket expenditure. There's so little cash flow that people are watching every penny. And even though rechargeables save you money in the long haul, they are tremendously more expensive initially. The batteries themselves cost more, and you have to invest in a charger. And then, most significantly for rural Africans off the grid, you've gotta have a way to power the charger.

"So that's when I started to ask myself, well how do you get over these hurdles? What are other businesses where you've got a very high initial capital cost that you want to spread out over the lifetime of the goods, so it's affordable? There are all kinds of models for this in the first world, from tool rentals to video stores. So it became clear that renting was a way to spread out the capital costs and allow a consumer with less upfront money to still take advantage of the long-term savings of rechargeables. But it was also clear that to make a rental model work over here, you had to have a first-person direct-selling system, like the Avon lady or the Tupperware party. The salesperson has to actually know the renter, and be able to get the batteries back if the person decides to stop renting. And I knew we'd need that direct, personal relationship to be able to adequately explain new offerings like Burro's batteries to prospective clients.

"That's when everything started to fit together: the rental model opened up the economy of rechargeable batteries to a much wider audience, and improved the productivity of poor people because of these greater economies. It required a model where our business would be setting up these little businesses—these independent agents—who would be carrying Burro wares into their own villages. So it was right on brand for us. A great place to start."

Traffic slowed in front of a roadblock. On the left, a trooper from the Ghana National Police, in stiff blue camo and matching visored cap, glanced at the insurance and registration stickers in the windows of slowly passing cars, occasionally motioning one over to the side of the road, where two other police holding Kalashnikovs performed their shakedown on the unlucky driver. As we approached the head of the line, I thought I saw the cop signal Whit to pull over. "Aren't you gonna stop?"

"It's not me, he's going after the taxi behind me," said Whit, eyeing the rearview mirror. "Don't ever stop unless it's completely clear they mean you. Don't look them in the eye, don't say hello. Just give them a little nod and keep moving."

"How much do you have to pay if they pull you over?"

"*Whatever is in your heart.* That's what they say."

"And what's typically in your heart?"

"A couple of cedis, but never offer it. Wait for them to demand it."

"Okay, so then what?"

"Then you don't get 'arrested' on some trumped-up charge."

"No, then what happened with your battery idea?"

"Oh. Well, this was probably back in December of '07. I was still in Seattle, just noodling on it more, thinking about names, starting to protect IP, researching batteries and chargers. But bear in mind this was all taking place against the backdrop of the Cranium sale to Hasbro, and then Dad died, so I didn't have a lot of brain cycles to spend on Burro until maybe the end of January '08. So then, once I had locked in to Ghana as the best place to launch, I started to realize I better get over there. That's when I heard about the World Bank conference in Accra. I spent about three quarters of a week at the conference, met Charlie, then a good week and a half on the road conducting on-the-ground market studies."

"How did you find people?"

"It was not as rigorous as you might want. We would just storm into a town or a village and find people who looked like they had time and might be potential clients. I had a driver, Asare, and we had Martin Aponsah, a translator; he's the brother of Rachel and Cameron's high school guidance counselor in Seattle who is actually a traditional Ghanaian chief. We went as far west as Takoradi and up to Koforidua, and then all along the coast road here. We interviewed people up and down the Akwapim Ridge. We stopped at places on the grid, off the grid, villages, cities, towns. We brought a bunch of batteries so we could show people what we were talking about. And then we interviewed people as potential agents as well as clients. We talked to probably seventy or ninety people around the country, and these were detailed, sit-down focus groups, albeit very informal."

"And?"

"What we found was incredible receptivity to the idea. I was cautioned by someone at the conference, 'Oh yeah, people will tell you they're interested until you ask for money.' But I know a little bit about market studies, and I could tell we were getting pretty straight answers from people. I mean, I think I came away feeling like there would be stronger demand than we've seen in urban areas, but I really underestimated the demand in off-grid rural areas. We've had trouble cultivating the urban demand, at least in Koforidua, but we've also had trouble getting good agents there. So I think the verdict is still out on the potential in urban areas. Obviously what we've learned is our sweet spot is the rural areas in general, and particularly off-grid areas.

"But the May trip confirmed that people were in fact spending between two and five bucks a month on throwaway batteries. Moreover, it suggested that many people were going through their batteries three or four times a month *in any given device*. That's what we were most after, because that's where they start to see the economies. Unless somebody is burning through batteries three or four times a month in a particular gizmo, they're not gonna be a good customer for us. There's no point in putting rechargeable batteries in a wall clock—at least not when you're asking for a fixed fee per battery every month.

"And the other thing that became clear was people were having to carefully ration their device usage. For me, that was the tip-off that people are gonna respond to the all-you-can-eat promise we were making. Assuming we could make the economics work on our end, we would be able to keep people at about the same battery budget they were at now, but with comparatively unlimited energy potential.

"So on that first trip it all became pretty clear to me. Originally my objective was to find a Ghanaian partner and do a more detailed market study, maybe spend ten thousand dollars or something. But I came away from that trip feeling like a study was gonna be a waste of time and money, because I was just blown away by the response. It was so strong. I was like, okay, we're just gonna roll the dice and roll this out. Can you drive for a while?"

We pulled over and switched seats, and I pushed the pedal down hard. The road was pretty good, only a few potholes, and we wanted to get back to Kof-town by dark. Tomorrow morning was the battery route, and we needed to drive it ourselves. Kevin was still learning how to drive (Whit was paying for his driver's ed classes) and had not yet received his learner's permit. I was amazed that Ghana even had such a formal process for driver training, but apparently attempts are being made to rein in the highway slaughter, and education (along with "overspeeding" signs) is one of them.

It was a big step up for Kevin, who was thirty-seven. He lived alone, in a studio apartment on the south side of Koforidua with a sink, shower, and cold running water twice a week—comfortable by local standards. When he saw I was interested in Ghanaian cuisine and willing to eat anything, he adopted me as a lunch partner. We would head into the market and his favorite lunch stands (Kevin had no stove in his apartment), where he introduced me to various offal-based delicacies like stewed pig intestines and goat kidneys. When he cooked at Whit's place, he used lots of garlic and hot pepper. Originally from Kumasi, he was college educated and read the newspaper every day. He was worldly by Ghanaian standards, having once been to Nigeria, and he wanted to visit London, where his brother lived. He was engaged to an Ashanti woman who lived in Kumasi. Kevin was not a bachelor. He was a widower. In 2006, his wife and seven-year-old son were killed in a *tro-tro* accident. It happened on his thirty-fifth birthday. They had been visiting her family, and they were coming home to celebrate.

## four

# DOWNSIDE

**EARLY 2009:** The risk

*"I confess that in 1901 I said to my brother Orville that man would not fly for fifty years."*

—Wilbur Wright

Half an aphorism: the shutters on this remote village hut probably featured a quote from the Bible.

## 1. A Dangerous Place

In a 2007 op-ed piece in the *Los Angeles Times* titled "What Bono Doesn't Say About Africa," William Easterly chided rock stars and their corporate sponsors for perpetuating an image of Africans as downtrodden victims. "Africans are and will be escaping poverty the same way everybody else did," he wrote, "through the efforts of resourceful entrepreneurs, democratic reformers and ordinary citizens at home, not through PR extravaganzas of ill-informed outsiders."*

When it comes to Africa, charity bashing appears to be catching on. In 2009 the young, Harvard-educated Zambian economist Dambisa Moyo wrote a best-selling book with the eye-poking title *Dead Aid: Why Aid Is Not Working and How There Is a Better Way for Africa.* Asked by the *New York Times Magazine* what she believes has held back Africans, she replied: "I believe it's largely aid. You get the corruption—historically, leaders have stolen the money without penalty—and you get the dependency, which kills entrepreneurship."

It sounds ridiculous to say that entrepreneurship is risky. Of course it is, even when carefully conceived. Investing time and money in any venture that doesn't generate a paycheck within a month is risky. But as time went by, what struck me was the prolonged nature of Whit's risk; it was like betting on a horse the day it was born, then waiting three years for the Kentucky Derby. Even so, it became clear that Whit and Jan needed to figure out a faster way to deal with agent reconciliation, or get better agents, or both.

---

* In fairness, Bono himself has said as much. In an April 2010 op-ed piece in the *New York Times,* he reported on a recent pan-African visit to observe entrepreneurship in action. "Smart aid can be a reforming tool," he wrote, "demanding accountability and transparency, rewarding measurable results, reinforcing the rule of law, but never imagining for a second that it's a substitute for trade, investment or self-determination." He recounted a meeting in Ghana with the Sudanese-born cell phone mogul Mo Ibrahim, who told him, "Ghana needs support in the coming years, but in the not-too-distant future it can be giving aid, not receiving it; and you, Mr. Bono, can just go there on your holidays."

"Seasonal income is a big issue," said Whit one January night, back from our coastal trip, as we sprawled across the rattan sofa on his second-floor veranda. "When we started in the fall, people were harvesting their maize and they had lots of money, disposable income," he went on. "But because they can barely meet their needs, they spend it when they have it, without a whole lot of thought to what happens next. So now it's the dry season—no crops, no money. I had assumed people would still buy batteries in hard times, but we're finding that many people really do live without them in the lean months."

Whit had only been in business for a few months, but already he was seeing kinks in the plan. He had assumed customers would recognize the obvious advantage of the Burro offering and keep renting every month, exchanging their old batteries for new—establishing the sort of recurring annuity stream that gets venture capitalists salivating. But a number of factors led to renewal rates lower than the high client satisfaction reports had predicted, not least of which was the issue of income volatility.

"What if you got people to pay an annual fee when they have the money?" I asked.

"That's a lot of money for these people, even in the good season. Maybe with microfinancing. Maybe we get into a model where agents get microfinancing so they can stock up on batteries from us."

Whit poured a sweaty bottle of local Star lager into a pint glass and took a long swallow. "Initially we were focusing on signing up new customers," he continued, "and I think that also hurt our renewals. We hadn't prepared the first class of agents for the challenges of renewals. Some agents feared that collecting batteries from people slow to pay would terminate the relationship for all time, and even jeopardize their standing with friends and neighbors. Some even went so far as to continue providing fresh batteries to clients who kept promising to pay 'tomorrow.' We had to put a stop to that, but saving face is very important here. So Jan and I came up with revised terminology. Instead of *canceled*, nonrenewing clients were said to be *on break*, and we trained agents to remove any stigma from the collection of batteries. You know—'It's fine to go on break, many clients go on break, and Burro will welcome you back when you are able to pay.'

"The third problem is that a lot of customers seemed to be testing our resolve. So many charities and NGOs have provided so many services at little or no cost to these villages that expecting something for free from white people has become perfectly rational behavior. Once we made it clear that Burro was not only refusing to offer credit but was also being hard core about collecting batteries on unpaid accounts, renewals began to improve."

Down on the street, a minivan for Fred's Medicated Soap crawled past, its roof-mounted speakers blaring ad slogans in Twi. On the side of the truck, next to a crude painting of a topless woman with one breast cartoonishly larger than the other, was inscribed in English:

> *Indication: Treatment of Breast Cancer, Boils, Conjuncti-*
> *vitis of Eyes, Treatment for Broken Bones, Waist Pains,*
> *Rheumatism, Menstrual Pains, Severe Headaches, Stom-*
> *ach Aches, Rickets Fibroid, Whitlow Piles, Stroke & Ba-*
> *bies Facing Hard in Walking.*

"Jesus," I said. "We're doing business in a country where people buy soap to cure breast cancer."

"Ghanaians are obsessed with cleanliness," said Whit. "Which is amazing considering they have no running water and live on packed dirt. They take bucket showers twice a day, and you've no doubt noticed the beauty salons on every block. Frankly, they find white people rather slovenly."

"Well they're used to Brits," I noted. "Which reminds me, what's up with all the ironing? These people are constantly ironing clothes, and with no electricity. Have you seen those irons that hold a chunk of red-hot charcoal? Amazing. I've never seen such a crisply creased bunch of people. I feel like such a slob by comparison."

"Well, you are a slob, but the ironing is a health issue," said Whit, draining his beer. "Mango flies, also known as putsi. They lay their eggs in drying laundry, hanging on the line. When you put the clothes on they hatch and the maggots burrow under your skin, leaving nasty boils. The only cure is to squeeze them out by hand. You put Vaseline on the boil, and the little fucker sticks his nose out to breathe. Then you pop him out like a zit—but the trick is, they have barbed spines and they hold on, and if you break them off they get infected. Before you know it you're a walking pus-bomb. Sepsis is a big issue here. It's so hot and humid that even minor insect bites get infected; you can imagine what a rotting half maggot under your skin looks like after a week. Anyway, ironing kills the mango fly eggs."

"Holy shit. As if these people didn't have enough to worry about. No wonder they buy medicated soap."

"It's a dangerous place. Americans have no idea. By the way, did you know your son bought a bottle of Scotch yesterday?"

"What?"

"Scotch."

"Where'd he do that?"

"At the liquor store, duh."

"Were you with him?"

"Yeah."

"And you let him?"

"I'm not his dad. But I figured you'd want to know."

"I figure his mother will not want to know. Hey, Harper!" No answer from inside the apartment.

"He went down to the market," said Whit.

"Great. What's the drinking age here?"

"Eighteen."

"He's seventeen."

Whit laughed. "This is Africa. Like they check IDs."

I took away the Scotch.

## 2. It's My Brother's Fault

Seasonal income was one challenge facing Whit. Another, more vexing problem for Burro was the complexity of agent reconciliation. Twice a week, Whit, Jan, Kevin, Harper, and I spent the day driving to villages around Koforidua, meeting with Burro's dozen or so field agents to exchange dead batteries for fresh ones and collect the rent money. It was an absurdly complicated process with reams of paperwork to keep track of who had paid, who hadn't, who was going on break and who was renewing, to say nothing of how many batteries each customer was using and the frequency of their replacement. We all knew there had to be a better way, and Jan and Whit were developing more efficient accounting systems, but Burro hadn't gotten there yet. One idea was to give more autonomy to agents; Burro would rent batteries to them and not worry about the end users—sort of like Avon ladies. But for the pilot program, Whit felt it was important to understand how villagers were using the batteries, and how often they needed to "refresh." So the tedious reconciliation days continued. We'd sit for hours in our camp chairs, eating peanuts and grilled plantains under the midday sun as Kevin and the agents pored over numbers, flicking biting red ants off their paperwork.

One day we sat under a tree in the village of Adawso, a pleasant junction town with a busy market, near a group of teenage boys playing a menacingly physical game of Ping-Pong at an outdoor table. It reminded me of the cutthroat Ping-Pong Whit and I used to play in the basement rec room of our split-level suburban house. One of the boys was wearing a T-shirt that said IT'S MY BROTHER'S FAULT. Whit and I went over and posed with him for a goofy picture. Agnes, an agent for the nearby village of Gbolokofi, arrived and spread out her paperwork. Her wide, soft face was framed by a knitted headband around her smartly coiffed and straightened hair. She ran down the list of her clients: Kwaku Afo, Kwei Norley John, Ogbey Samuel, Kwame Oparre, Regina Awuku . . . twenty-eight in all. This week she added a new client, but some of her existing clients who owed money appeared to be missing in action. "What about Neil Armstrong?" Kevin asked her.

"He went away," replied Agnes. I think we all said "To the moon?" in unison, and Agnes laughed. (When signing on for his Burro batteries, Neil told Agnes his first name was spelled "like the moon astronaut," which is what she wrote down.)

Another man "has a program with the radio and he has traveled," she reported. "I can't find him. But he's not done yet"—meaning he has not formally canceled.

"Did anyone go on break this week?" Kevin asked.

"*Dabi dabi!*" No, no.

The boys at Ping-Pong reached an impasse over a play and were now arguing loudly, slamming fists on the table and threatening each other with the paddles. High in a papaya tree in the courtyard of a pale colonial government building, African pied crows—black with distinctive white breasts and shoulders—cawed aggressively as if mocking the Ping-Pong brawl below. Agnes finished her paperwork. She unknotted the waist wrap of her skirt and carefully pulled out her money, paying Kevin one cedi and fifty pesewa—about $1.20.

It would all make more sense if the agents were moving more product, but after four months it appeared that very few were able (or willing) to rent more than a hundred or so batteries per month. Agents made a fifteen-pesewa commission on each battery rental, and in theory it could be a relatively lucrative full-time job for an aggressive salesperson. But virtually all of the agents worked at other jobs. Some were schoolteachers; others were farmers, bar owners, tailors, even local politicians. Moreover, there did not seem to be a lot of aspiration to wealth in rural Ghana; people tended to work until they earned what they needed, then stop. They were not trying to "get ahead," a Western notion of individualism that seems alien to the Ghanaian mind-set, at least outside of the capital. Africans are adept at making from scratch things that Westerners simply buy—homemade rat traps from inch-and-a-half-thick chunks of mahogany, bamboo flashlights, sandals from old tires that are sewn together at lightning speed by cottage tailors on almost every city block, to say nothing of the huts in which they live and the charcoal fires by which they cook. But for all their sense of invention, they seem to have no thought of reinventing themselves. This medieval acceptance of the status quo is the antithesis of the modern West. We need experts to build our homes, fix our cars, and grow our food, but we try on careers, religions, and identities as if they were new clothes. The Ghanaian sense of contentment is admirable, but also maddening in a modern business context.

## 3. Politicking

Harper and I went home at the end of January. Whit and I stayed in touch over the phone, by email, and on Twitter; Jan's blog posts also kept me informed.

Movement came soon. Whit called to say that on February 23 he added seven new agents in one day. Best of all, their work would be coordinated by two new "team leaders"—which meant more sales and less reconciliation for Burro. The Avon model seemed to be panning out. "These guys are great," said Whit, referring to the team leaders. "One is a man named Jonas who won Farmer of the Year for his district. The other, George, is a shopkeeper in a pretty big junction town."

"How did you find them?"

"Both were recommended by a district assemblyman. We met the assemblyman at a meeting we had in the village of Korkorom; he was in the audience. He signed up for batteries and told us he could help us find agents in the other villages. The guy was amazing—he took a workday off and introduced us to chiefs and elders."

"What's in it for him?"

"He gets perceived as bringing services to the villages he represents. It's a way for him to get visibility. So it's politicking, plain and simple. The question is, can it be modeled? Gideon is also an assemblyman, but he's taking a different approach; he wants to be an agent himself. Either way, we're now seeing evidence that we can build some sort of dynamic relationship with civic-minded local assemblymen."

"What's the district assembly?"

"We don't know exactly yet. It seems to be vaguely Napoleonic—an outreach of the executive branch, not legislative. Each region has fifteen to twenty districts, and each district has an assembly. Each assembly has fifteen or twenty-five smaller assembly areas, and an assemblyman represents that area, which is like eight to fifteen major villages or towns. They get paid a small stipend, basically expenses for when they go to meetings. We don't have an electoral map, at least not one that's up to date, but we're trying to get one."

"How long do they serve?"

"They stand for election every four years, and they are apparently nonpartisan. The district is managed by the district chief executive or DCE, who is appointed by the president. So individual assemblymen are nonpartisan and elected, but the DCE is appointed, although he must be approved by majority vote of the elected assembly. Meanwhile, each DCE reports to the regional minister—again, very Napoleonic."

"If it's not legislative, what can they do? Can they raise taxes?"

"Not really. Impose fees, perhaps, but apart from that one-shot chance to vote up or down the president's choice of DCE, they seem to have virtually no substantive power. It seems mainly to be a bottom-up steam valve to vent local disputes and resolve grievances. For example, each village has a unit committee, which meets with the assemblyman. I went to one of these meetings with Hayford Tetteh, who translated."

"I thought English was the language of government."

"Not at this level. It's in Twi. Anyway, the assemblyman was reading from this very official-looking document that obviously came from higher up the chain. These were his top-down notes for points he was supposed to be making. In this case there was a dispute between two youth sports leagues, two groups in two different villages including this one. Every time these kids got together they ended up in a brawl, so the DCE decided that sporting events were 'rescinded' between the two villages until the dispute was resolved. This is what the assemblyman was reading. One of the opinion leaders got up to speak. 'The elders of both villages have met, and the issue has been resolved,' he said. 'There will be no more trouble.' The assemblyman said, 'Good, but I need the elders to draft a letter to show the DCE so that he will lift the ban.' Case closed."

"Man, I'd be careful getting involved in local politics."

"We are definitely staying out of the politics, but this looks like a good way into the villages. And it gives us a fallback if an agent screws up; we can call the assemblyman. Anyway, business is growing by about a hundred and fifty batteries a day. There are plenty of scary details still, including the fact that we've got six thousand new batteries held up in customs in Durban, South Africa, which is bullshit because the batteries aren't even landing in Durban; they're en route from fucking China."

On February 23, I emailed Whit: "What are the chances that this all goes belly-up?"

The next day, he called: "Best case? Our new model works. We solicit the support and cooperation of locally elected assemblymen. They go around with us in a single day to every one of their major off-grid villages and introduce us to the most trustworthy, hardworking agent candidates, with blessings and endorsements from elders, opinion leaders, and chiefs. We work out the kinks in our 'group leader' model so that we can aggregate all of these folks into one or two 'super agents' to reduce our reconciliation burden. This enables us to add the former equivalent of four to six agents a week to the model, with a management burden little more than one of our former agents. Each of these has the potential to grow within one month to a five-hundred- to thousand-battery business. This puts us on track to getting to full branch capacity in something like nine months. We build out a serious local corporate capability that allows us to staff, train, and manage branches autonomously. Koforidua turns profitable by August or September or October. We launch a second branch in July or August or September. We are able to raise prices while sustaining subscriptions. We add wildly well-received items for sale including improved lighting devices, better, cheaper phone chargers, low-power battery-operated televisions, etcetera. We evaluate self-funding versus seeking outside capital. We opt for ever more rapid growth and so create a compelling financing story and receive five million dollars in VC money. We accelerate local branch roll-outs and by March 2010 have begun to establish two branches per month in Ghana with five already well established. We kick off operations in a neighboring francophone country, probably Burkina or Togo. I'm invited to speak at Davos.

"But there is potential downside here. We may be unable to resolve operational challenges related to efficient branch operation."

"Speak English."

"Management issues. It could be hard to recruit enough motivated agents to drive the business forward autonomously. There are technical concerns. Our batteries may all of a sudden collapse in month nine versus month thirty-six. Politics: sustained civil strife may break out across the country. I may chicken out before plowing in the three hundred to four hundred K to make the best-case happen. Lots of unknowns. It's risky. It's Africa. The reality will probably fall somewhere between best and worst case— much closer to best case because I am paying attention to things."

On March 11, Jan left for Seattle. She had not been home in six months, and she was more than ready for a break. Whit called after taking her to the airport: "I am utterly terrified of leaving this business alone when I go home in May."

"When's Jan coming back?"

"Mid-June. I'm putting all my energy into recruiting some more bench depth here before I leave. There's a great candidate I met at a job fair in Accra, a young woman who just graduated from Ashesi University College, a private college run by this Ghanaian former Microsoft manager named Patrick Awuah. She totally gets it and seems to want to work on a start-up, but it's hard to know. Maybe she's just looking for an air-conditioned office job in Accra like everybody else and we're like her third or fourth choice. We'll see.

"I'm also trying to design a computerized field management system that we can use with cheap netbooks. That should let us build a client-level database, and then we can create an output for agents—you know, 'Kwame is overdue, he's your number-one effort, dude. He doesn't own a cell phone? Have you asked him lately? Maybe you should ask him right now.'

"Ultimately this will give us a direct-marketing database with half a million cell phone numbers. But in the near-term it's all about helping agents do their job. They can't track it all on paper."

On April 16, Whit called with good news: "I hired Rose Dodd, the Ashesi grad." She drove a hard bargain, demanding six hundred cedis a month—about four hundred dollars—a handsome salary for an entry-level worker in Ghana.

"My new accounting guy started last week," Whit added, "and Kevin passed his written exam today and takes the driving test tomorrow. He's still a little scary behind the wheel; he's not a natural driver, and he's pretty rough on the clutch. But man, I think I pulled it off; this place is actually going to be running itself when I'm gone."

Other personnel issues appeared less sanguine. "Gideon is turning into a major flake," Whit said. "It's partly our fault; we let him get overextended. It doesn't work for one guy to cover fifteen square kilometers. He had a bunch of personal issues. He crashed on his bicycle and injured himself. He had malaria or something for a while, and then things got really busy in the district assembly—like they had to do actual work. So he got completely distracted by all that. He just basically went missing on us. He lost his phone, he had to travel to Tema to visit his family, on and on. His business is a fraction of the size it was. I lent him a cell phone, but he never turned it on, so I still couldn't reach him. Finally I said, 'Dude, bring back my phone.' He's definitely not the superstar we thought at first. But he is very good at selling when he's in front of somebody."

"Too bad," I said. "I like that guy."

"We'll see; maybe he can unwind it all. Our new superstar is Jonas, the Farmer of the Year. Get this: His wife is almost full-term and had a complicated labor last night. They lost the baby. So the guy's up all night with his wife near death, loses his full-term baby, and he's still fucking showing up at ten A.M. today to swap batteries with Burro. Can you imagine in America? He'd be out of pocket for a month."

"And rightly so. That's awful."

"And that's not all. Remember Agnes from Adawso?"

"Of course, the biting red ants and the Ping-Pong table."

"Yeah, well, she gave her business to Hayford. It just wasn't working for any of us, and we sort of agreed she would be better off doing something else. It was sad because she was our first agent. Anyway, her husband died last night."

"Are you serious?"

"Yeah. So we had two weird deaths in the Burro family last night. Oh, and here's another charming development. A little while ago they put a new billboard up that you can see from our balcony: BREAK THE CYCLE OF DOMESTIC VIOLENCE, REPORT PERPETRATORS TO POLICE. So a woman in the courtyard got beat up by her husband pretty bad two days ago. I mentioned the new sign and she just laughed. 'The police won't do anything,' she said. I checked with Charlie and he agreed. 'Some white people came in and gave the locals some money for a program,' he said. 'The sign makes them feel like they've done something useful.'"

"Your tax dollars at work," I said, assuming the sign was paid for by some Western aid program.

"Actually just yours," said Whit. "To pay taxes you need to make money, which I'm not doing yet. Which reminds me—the batteries got loaded on a ship in Durban today; they sail Friday or Saturday. Not sure how long it takes, but pretty soon we'll have six thousand more batteries. Did I mention inflation here is running at twenty-two percent right now? We just raised prices on the rentals yesterday, and so far we're not hearing any massive revolts."

"Speaking of revolts, what's going on in the government? Is Rawlings gonna stage another coup?"

"Charlie feels it's a bunch of bluster and hot air. Some say Rawlings has no substantive support or effective power within the military at this point. And he is aware enough of his legacy that he won't do anything to endanger that. I mean, he did run for election and relinquish power voluntarily. There's a good chance history will treat him favorably as the George Washington of Ghana, albeit a George Washington tainted by the murder of four Supreme Court justices. When are you coming back?"

"June 13. I got on the same flight as Jan. When are you headed home?"

"May 15. Can't wait to get a haircut."

"You haven't cut your hair since January?"

"There is no one in Koforidua who has ever cut a white person's hair. Do I want to be the first?"

"Man, you can't let your hair get long over there; you'll get lice. Why don't you just shave your head?"

"Shelly will leave me."

"It will grow back."

"She's not that patient."

"Hey, leave a light on for us, in honor of Dad."

"I need your baggage allowance. I've got five hundred cell-phone chargers to bring over."

I was becoming the Burro mule.

## 4. Noise Awareness

*Today is National Noise Awareness day. Someone forgot to tell the roosters. And the dick with the 5:30 AM radio blaring.*

**—Whit on Twitter, 5:54 A.M., April 16**

On May 12 I called Whit. "Didn't sleep too well last night," he said. "You haven't met this guy Dave, a former two-term Peace Corps worker who's been living here four years, about two miles down the road. He runs the bike shop around the corner. A couple of nights ago he was the victim of a home invasion and an armed robbery. They beat him twenty times with a board; his eyeball socket is all but broken. He woke up to the sound of these guys busting his front door down, and next thing he knew he was getting hit over the head with a board. They were screaming in pidgin English, 'Where be the laptop? Where be the money? Where be the phone?' He thinks they were Nigerian from their accents. He's all bandaged and bruised. Told me in four years he's never had any trouble here. The worst of it was that the neighbors didn't do anything to help."

"Holy shit," I said. "And I was sleeping behind nothing but a screen door off that balcony."

"Yeah, I know. I mean, I feel a little better that we're on the second floor, and I don't think they would come in through the front balcony. The street merchants are out there most of the night, and the bank across the street has night guards. If they came in here it would be through the back, up the stairs. But we definitely need to be more careful. I want to get a bar for the door. It's going to be an exciting summer."

five

# TIGER BY THE TAIL

## SUMMER 2009: The relaunch

The Burro truck drew a crowd everywhere we went.

## 1. Beginner's Luck

In June, Jan and I returned to a Ghana cleansed by monsoon rains. Outside the airport, steaming puddles filled every hole in the pavement, forcing us to negotiate our sagging baggage cart around small lakes of unknown depth. The sky was sea blue, the landscape green and polished like waxed limes, and the dust and haze of January had been wiped away like a smudge on a lens. This time, our drive up the Akwapim Ridge was rewarded with breathtaking views over Accra and the ocean we had just crossed. If only things were as clear with Burro.

Even before he left for home in mid-May, Whit realized that Burro was not growing fast enough to create what he called "a compelling business case"—meaning a business that could be duplicated and scaled across a whole country or, optimistically, a continent. His worries drove my own sense of doubt.

"Whit, I hope I haven't hitched my wagon to a loser."

"Huh?" he replied over the phone, distracted as usual.

"You. Your business."

"Max, I feel your pain, but right now I'm packing for China."

On some level, it was certainly possible to position Burro as successful: in just nine months, business had grown from nothing to an efficient network of more than thirty agents spread around a fifteen-mile radius from Koforidua. Whit, always the computer geek, had created a field management program for Burro using Microsoft Access, which he impishly named Fodder. It vastly simplified agent reconciliation. Under his new system, agents completed their paperwork on their own, which was then left in a zippered and locked bag, along with used batteries and revenue, at prearranged drop points in villages along the route—just the sort of thing an ex–CIA agent might design. Kevin would then circulate to the drop points on scheduled days and exchange fresh for fallen batteries, collecting cash and paperwork. A young accountant I'll call Adam was hired to manage the Fodder system in the office, entering in the day's receipts.

Fodder mostly eliminated the tedious practice of waiting under trees, sometimes for hours, for agents to show up on bicycle or on foot from far-flung villages. (Punctuality is not a character trait to which even many enterprising Ghanaians aspire.) The drop points made it possible to expand the agent roster dramatically without hiring legions of drivers; one employee could service the entire route.

So far, so good. But many problems shadowed growth potential. First, it was becoming clear that local disposable income was tied heavily to the seasonality of small-farm economics. When the corn and cassava were harvested and farmers had money, they could afford to pay the monthly battery fee—currently 1.70 cedis for a pair. But in lean or dry times, that much cash was simply out of reach. Unfortunately, Burro's renewal plan was tied to inflexible calendar dates—clients could renew only on the first and fifteenth of the month. Such a plan was essential from a business standpoint—trying to manage thousands of rental policies coming due on any random day would be a logistical nightmare—but was completely at odds with customers' financial reality.

And even when customers had cash, the monthly fee was a major stretch, especially when they could get *some* battery use for just half a cedi—the price of a pair of Tiger Head throwaways. It was easy enough to say that over the course of a month, the Burro offering of unlimited battery use for 1.70 cedis per pair was a far better deal than .50 cedis for a pair of throwaways. Heavy users exchanged their batteries twelve times per month, which made each renewal effectively cost .14 cedis per pair—a cost advantage of more than 350 percent over Tiger Head, assuming equivalent battery performance. Over the course of a year, a customer who used a four-battery radio would save over 100 cedis, given equivalent usage. Considering that most rural Burro customers lived on 1 or 2 cedis per day, the customer would be *saving* as much as a third of his total annual income.

But that's like telling an American he could save tens of thousands of dollars over the next thirty years by paying cash for his house. The only difference is the scale of the investment. Few Americans can afford to pay cash for their homes, but many go to Sam's Club and buy bulk packs of batteries, which represent a small fraction of disposable income even for relatively poor people. To many Ghanaians in the dry season, the bulk battery deal wasn't like buying batteries at Sam's Club. It was like paying cash for a house.

Furthermore, Burro's value proposition was not immediately obvious to typical prospects because they had never experienced the advantage of "bottomless" battery use. Even heavy users of Tiger Heads probably changed them only five or six times per month; it was simply too expensive to buy more. Instead, they grew accustomed to rationing batteries and couldn't readily picture what it would be like to leave flashlights on all night or play the radio all day long. There was a huge learning curve inherent in the business plan.

Meanwhile, intermittent battery users—those who got by just fine on changing their batteries under three or four times a month—gained no advantage from the Burro offering. That effectively eliminated the urban electrified market (where battery-powered devices were more of a convenience than a necessity), as well as users of long-life devices such as wall clocks. Explaining to prospects that they would be wasting their money by paying a monthly fee to power a wall clock was a potential source of confusion. Whit wanted to help customers, not rip them off.

None of these issues was a total surprise, of course. Back in January we had seen drop-offs in renewal rates associated with the dry season (no crops, no money), and Whit had led many discussions about alternative ways to structure the offering. But it took months in the field to really discern patterns and averages—and by May, the numbers were not looking great. For one thing, Burro's market share was not nearly as high as Whit had expected. Data was sketchy and basically involved polling local village shops on their Tiger Head sales, but it appeared that in villages where Burro was operating, its market share ranged from as low as 5 percent to perhaps a high of 60 percent. In short, Tiger Head D batteries (and the primary AA brand, a low-power Chinese entry called Sun Watt) were still dominating the market, despite Burro's long-term cost advantage and (in the case of Sun Watt) much better performance.

Clearly, battery customers were focused on minimizing daily out-of-pocket expenditure, not on saving over the long term.

The upshot was a constant churn in the customer base, as clients went on break when they could no longer afford the monthly fee, and agents scrambled to line up new customers. The Fodder program showed that only 45 percent of clients were renewing on any given renewal date; the majority simply went on break.

Burro agents, almost all of them working part-time and juggling other jobs, in theory had a relatively straightforward duty: keep their clients happy by exchanging old for new batteries, thus fulfilling the company's promise of "Fresh, anytime you want." Instead, agents were forced to spend most of their time chasing renewal payments from clients, or retrieving batteries from clients on break. This was not a model for large-scale success. Nor was it a great way to build the Burro brand.

It is at this point in any new business venture when genuine entrepreneurs can be separated from mere poseurs. Faced with such obstacles, lesser mortals throw in the towel and retreat to the comfort of the familiar, or panic and overreact—barking orders to underlings, grasping at quick fixes, or, as is so often the case with developing-world initiatives, finding a deep-pocketed charity to come to the rescue. (Selling your product to an NGO is a time-honored loser's game in the developing world; since the charity is giving the product away, nobody has to worry if it fulfills a genuine need.) Another reaction is to simply ignore the evidence and hope things will get better.

Whit, on the other hand, stayed calm and logical. Without minimizing the very real challenges, he remained confident in the business and intent on finding a more compelling sales model. So in late May he convened a brainstorming session at his home in Seattle. Sitting around the living room were Jan; three members of Burro's advisory board (Michael Connell, Cranium's former creative director and art director for Burro's brand identity; Jim Moore, a seasoned executive with extensive developing-world and venture-capital experience; Chris Legler, Cranium's former finance director); Adam Tratt, another former Craniac and a guerrilla marketing professional who had studied one summer in Niger; Derek Streat, a serial entrepreneur who was then with UNITUS, a Seattle-based NGO working to accelerate the growth of microfinance organizations; and Charlie Wood, another former Microsoftee now at the Grameen Foundation, where he literally wrote the book on how to replicate Grameen's successful village-based phone business in new countries.

Implicit in the discussion was the need for two basic changes to the business model: first, customers needed to be able to rent batteries whenever they wanted, not according to a set schedule; and second, Burro had to be the lowest-cost option for battery power *today* and every day. The best way to do that was to charge per use rather than per month. Find a way to make that usage fee less than the price of a Tiger Head, and you'd have a tiger by the tail.

There was just one problem. You still needed to get the dead batteries back so they could be recharged.

The obvious solution was a deposit, which is a concept that Ghanaians understand from their soda and beer bottles. But bottles are cheap, and their deposits correspondingly insignificant, whereas a rechargeable battery is inherently valuable. A deposit that covered Burro's actual battery cost—to say nothing of its potential retail value—would be far out of reach of an average Ghanaian.

Then again, a deposit doesn't necessarily need to cover the replacement cost of a product. You leave a credit card number at a rental car agency, but unless you have a very high credit limit, Avis won't be charging a new car if you drive away and keep going. What makes you come back (other than honesty) is the knowledge that Avis has enough information about you (from both your credit card and driver's license) to track you down. So long as a deposit ensures *return* in most cases, it doesn't need to ensure *replacement*. Likewise, in states with beverage container deposit laws, some people can't be bothered to return their cans, but the deposit is enough to ensure that someone will find it worthwhile to do so.

What if the battery deposit were one cedi? That would be less than the cost of the battery, but equal to a day's pay to some customers, and real money to virtually every Ghanaian. Furthermore, the dead battery only had value to someone with the ability to recharge it. Since most of Burro's customers had no electricity, much less access to a charger, why wouldn't they return it for a cedi?

But what if they didn't? And what about urban, electrified customers, who could presumably obtain a charger? A well-organized scam artist could clean out the business quickly by stealing expensive rechargeable batteries for less than half their wholesale cost.

These issues bothered Whit. He considered the possibility of adding a chip to the batteries that would only allow them to work in a dedicated charger. That would be expensive, and perhaps impossible: charging simply completes the same circuitry as usage, but with current flowing in reverse; a diode could simultaneously prevent charging and still pass current through to a load, but some energy would be lost, and even more daunting, how could the relatively low voltage of a single cell enable control of the diode in a handshake with Burro-authorized chargers? Tech solutions were looking pricey at best, and the seemingly intractable issue of theft and loss, and how to prevent it, went around and around during the Seattle meeting. Finally Derek said, "Whit, don't hose your business worrying about a problem that might not happen."

## 2. That's the Way We Are

"Charlie, are you following this? You look confused." Back in Koforidua on the third day of our return, Jan was leading a meeting of the team to discuss the new pay-per-use offering with a deposit. Charlie had driven up from Accra; also sitting around the dining room table were Kevin, Adam, and myself. (Whit was in China, meeting with manufacturers.)

"I just think the client will be suspicious," said Charlie, shaking his head. "You know, 'Now these batteries are cheap; why did you let me pay so much before [under the monthly plan]?' They will be suspicious. That's the way we are."

By *we*, he meant all Ghanaians, for whom Charlie had appointed himself national apologist. Mention any Ghanaian custom that might be ascribed to some character flaw, from police corruption to gasoline meter "inaccuracies" to wife beating, and Charlie's generic response was "That's the way we are." Not that he approved of this endless screed of African transgressions; on the contrary, Charlie brazenly lectured cops demanding bribes at roadside checkpoints, and his business dealings were unfailingly ethical. He was just being realistic, I suppose. But it was strange all the same, like an American explaining Charles Manson by saying, "That's the way we are."

"But we don't need to convert existing clients," countered Jan. "We can test this in a new area."

Jan was at the whiteboard, laying out the plan. "We were thinking of three price points. You can buy an individual battery charge for 20 pesewa. A purchase of ten charges would cost GH¢ 1.50, or 15 pesewa each, and buying twenty charges would cost 2 cedis, or 10 pesewa each. Agents would get a 20 percent commission on each rental. So even the most expensive plan—pay as you go, one charge at a time—is still cheaper than Tiger Head. In fact, the first charge is free; when you pay your one-cedi deposit, you get the battery charged and ready to use. And the more charges you can afford to buy, the cheaper it gets. For the multicharge plans, the idea is to print up booklets of tickets or coupons—Adam, what's the best word to use?"

"Coupons."

"Coupons—which keeps us true to our promise of 'Fresh, anytime you want.' This should also open up the urban market. And it totally simplifies reconciliation, because once customers pay their one-cedi deposit, we don't really need to know who they are. Charlie, you're sitting there with your arms crossed. Your body language says 'I'm not buying this.'"

Charlie shook his head again. "The deposit—that pokes a hole in the concept." He paused. "That's not to say we shouldn't try it."

"It's like cell phones," said Jan. "You can buy phone minutes on every street corner here for next to nothing, but you still need to invest in a phone initially."

"Yes, and that's why people steal the phones," said Charlie, triumphant at the opportunity to catalog another Ghanaian character flaw. "It's the way we are."

"Are you saying we're going to create a whole new subculture of battery thieves?" asked Jan.

"Don't rule that out," said Charlie gravely. "People here are desperate, they have nothing to lose."

Kevin turned to Charlie: "At first I was thinking like you. People are gradually warming to our current plan, the agents are getting used to it, and now we are entering the harvest season. I thought, maybe we should get through the harvest and see what happens. But now I'm thinking we should try it. Nothing ventured, nothing gained."

"Okay," said Charlie. "But what village? Where haven't we been? Tell me."

## 3. The Bead Makers

The road from Koforidua northeast toward Lake Volta bisects a striking landscape of verdant mountains fronted by rolling hills planted in rows of corn and cassava. I had not been on this road before, and it reminded me of parts of Appalachia or central France. Nor had Burro developed an agent network up this way, so it was a perfect area to test the new offering. Unfortunately for Burro, most of the villages along the main road appeared to have power; maybe not every hut was electrified (it's expensive to get wired), but clearly "light," as the Ghanaians call power, was available somewhere in most towns. We took a left at a small junction town called Akatawia and decided to try our chances up a road that had once been paved but was now potholed into a post-nuclear landscape.

"Pick up this woman," said Charlie from the front passenger seat as we bounced along at little more than walking speed. "Maybe she can tell us what we will find up here." Jan pulled over, and Kevin and I made room in the back for the young woman, who explained in Twi that she was headed to the Wednesday market in Sekesua, a village some eight kilometers up the road, to buy fish. She and Charlie spoke for several minutes. "She says most of the towns around here have light, even down this road, but Bomase does not."

Four kilometers and twenty minutes later we hit Bomase, which looked more like a hamlet than a village, situated at a T junction where a wide dirt track led down to a bridge over a stream. Several young men and older boys were sitting under a blooming acacia tree, playing cards, oblivious to the explosion of yellow flowers in the branches above them.

Charlie greeted them in Twi, but the response stopped him short. "What language do you speak?" he asked in English.

The citizens of Bomase were Krobo, which is also the name of their native tongue—one that even Charlie didn't understand, although they were able to converse with us in a mixture of broken Twi and English. "Why aren't you in school?" Charlie asked one boy.

"We are on break," the boy said defensively.

"Then why aren't you helping your father farm? Are you lazy?" Charlie was capable of maintaining a straight face through this kind of wise-guy routine for a long time. It seemed an odd way to engage potential customers in an important new test market, but who was I to question Ghanaian business manners? Often, late at night sitting on our veranda, I would hear Ghanaian men down on the street, quarreling strenuously. As they invariably discoursed in Twi, I could not understand the specifics of their briefs, but the tone always suggested violence was imminent. Yet every time—just as I braced for the dull clang of machetes, followed by the police siren, the wails of the wounded, and the collection of stray body parts in the street—the tone changed to laughter.

"We do not farm here," said the boy in a tone that mixed pride and apprehension over speaking so forthrightly to an adult. "We make gari and beads," and he pointed across the road to an open-sided bamboo shelter that housed a diesel-powered cassava mill. Gari (not to be confused with the pickled Japanese sushi ginger of the same name) is a popular Ghanaian instant porridge made by toasting ground cassava root in metal bowls over fires. The bowls are set in a round form made of dried mud, under which a wood fire is lit. As the cassava heats, the worker uses a piece of hard, dried gourd skin like a scoop to turn and mix the meal, preventing it from burning. Gari is the Ghanaian version of convenience food because it only requires adding hot water. "Students eat it," said Kevin. "It's not what you would expect to be served at home, but it's actually quite good for breakfast with sugar."

The other local Krobo industry was making the colorful glass beads sold every Thursday at the bead market on the soccer field in Koforidua. Ghanaian beads are justifiably famous and a signature craft, with collectors around the world, and the Krobo are skilled practitioners. The process begins with ground glass—old bottles and jars, laboriously hand-crushed with mallets—which is sifted into ceramic molds and then fired in mud kilns. The hole in the center of the bead is formed with a tiny cassava stalk, which burns away during firing. Some beads are made with layers of tinted glass for multicolored effects; others are hand-painted after being fired.

So we had unwittingly stumbled upon an unusual place: a busy craft village with no electricity in an electrified farming region, and a populace who spoke a language that even our polyglot Ghanaian colleagues could not speak. (We soon learned that the place had no cell phone reception, also unusual in Ghana.) Part of me wondered if it made more sense to find a more "average" location for our first market test, but Charlie had already established his street cred with the local youth group (whom he was now loudly beating at cards), and Kevin was already taking out the batteries. Bomase, here we come.

As curious villagers wandered up to the corner, Jan started explaining the offer as Charlie translated into Twi (which was then retranslated into Krobo by other villagers for the people who couldn't speak Twi). This all took a long time; Jan was careful to explain that with any payment plan the customer chose, the Burro batteries would cost less than Tiger Heads, and she wanted them to understand exactly how much cheaper they were. I held my breath when she got to the part about the deposit (which in Ghana is pronounced with the accent on the first syllable: *DEH-posit*), expecting a litany of complaints.

Except there were none. Nobody seemed to have an issue with the *DEH-posit*.

At that point the chief walked up, a handsome man in his forties named Victor. He was a bead maker and, it turns out, one of four chiefs in the village. Apparently Bomase had some sort of governance dispute at one time, and the village broke into four separate chiefdoms. The bad feelings had been long since resolved, but the village retained its four-part structure. As the entire village appeared to consist of three huts and a cassava grinder, I asked Charlie if there were any braves, so to speak, for all these chiefs to rule.

"Victor says the village is very spread out, all along these paths," Charlie replied, pointing off into the jungle. "It is much bigger than it looks—five hundred voters, according to the census, he says."

Several residents had wandered off to get their radios and flashlights, anxious to verify that the Burro batteries would in fact work in their devices. This was common whenever we first went into a new village, and it seemed like a strange compulsion—but we were dealing with people who had never seen anything but a Tiger Head D battery in their lives and rarely had the opportunity to make any kind of consumer choice; the concept that another product might be able to do the same job for less money had perhaps never occurred to them, and naturally required prudent investigation.

More people arrived, and soon we had a mob of potential customers, all of them trying to explain the deal to one another loudly while exhibiting Burro and Tiger Head batteries like actors in a TV commercial. A man walked up holding his baby daughter, who took one look at me and burst into tears. "She has never seen a white man," explained the father apologetically. Charlie decided it would be hilarious to sneak up behind the little girl and make a monster face, which caused her to wail like a shrew. "You see, the black man is even scarier than the white man!" he said, guaranteeing years of therapy for the girl.

Finally the crowd ebbed, and the chief stood up and addressed Charlie.

"What did he say?" asked Jan.

"He says, 'How soon can we get these batteries?'"

## six

# WHERE THE BIG MEN LIVE

### SUMMER 2009: The agent

*If I could do it all again I'd be a farmer.*

—Mobutu Sese Seko, self-appointed president
of Zaire from 1960 to 1997

David and Goliath: Jonas attempting to keep birds from
nesting in his plantain trees. Good luck with that.

## 1. Everything God Does Is Good

**W**hen I told my African friends that I wanted to spend time living and farming in the remote, off-grid villages where Burro was doing business, they responded with polite laughter. When I convinced them I was serious, they reacted as if I were proposing missionary work in a leper colony.

"That is a very hard place to live," cautioned Kevin. "No toilet facilities, no water, the food is very different from what you see in town; you will surely get sick. And the work is very hard. I am not sure you will like it."

"It isn't really about *liking* it," I replied, sensing a bit of projection on his part. Kevin is in a small minority of Ghanaian men who might be called husky—not grossly obese, but a long way from six-pack abs; it would be hard to picture him scampering up a coconut tree with a machete. "It's more of a learning process," I added.

It was the summer of 2009; Whit was still in China talking to manufacturers. The new pay-as-you-go deposit system was proving a big hit in the new Krobo territories. Jan, Kevin, Rose, and Adam could barely keep up with growth. More batteries were on order. With Whit returning in a month, it seemed like a good time for me to get out of the stifling city and learn more about village life than you could glean in a one-hour gong-gong.

"In the rainy season?" said Charlie. "What you will learn is the meaning of a nightmare!" He went on to stress that—in the right season, of course—he too would love to get back to his "roots" with a village stay. It would be difficult to imagine Charlie thriving without the restaurants and international shops of Accra, or the fresh-baked bread delivered daily to his home. But put him in a small African village of mud huts and cook fires and he waxed as pastoral as a Hudson River School painter. "Ah, you can really *breathe* out here!" he would say whenever we traveled to a Burro village. "And the people are so real, so friendly. This is surely the life for me."

With his worldly wisecracks and flirtatious humor, Charlie was an exotic urban sophisticate to these simple villagers. But at least he was Ghanaian. I, on the other hand, was a space alien. "We can receive you," was the stiff reply from an agent for the village of Adenya named Ebenezer Yirenkyi Kissiedu—a former civil-servant turned farmer. "But we are human."

I think he meant human in the Paleolithic sense—*Homo sapiens* at his most essential. "We have no light," he continued grimly, "and in the night there are small ants which will bite you and leave black spots all over your body. Then the mosquitoes will come, and you will get malaria." His use of the nonconditional tense suggested this was an inarguable certainty, like a biblical plague on the pharaoh.

To all of these concerns I was tempted to reply, "No worries, I've been camping lots of times." But equating their given lot of grinding survival to an enchanting frolic in a national park seemed to trivialize their very existence, and I couldn't find the words. What would you say? "Yes, when I grow exhausted from a week of staring at my computer screen, and the Red Sox are playing some shitty National League team and there are no good movies and the restaurants are crawling with tourists, I love to get away from it all and recharge with a weekend in the mountains. This should be cracking good fun! Lawn darts, anyone?"

Instead I fell back on a more estimable chapter of my biography: "I used to have a farm in America."

Ebenezer looked at me like I was a pair of Siamese twins. "It must have been a *mechanized* farm, no?"—spitting out *mechanized* like an epithet.

"No. I worked it by hand," I replied, forgetting for the moment that once a year I did hire a local guy to come over with his tractor and till my larger plots. But mostly it was backbreaking hand labor. Still, I didn't add that it was a "hobby farm" and my survival never depended on it.

"You have boots and a cutlass?" he asked, using the local term for a machete.

"I do."

He seemed a bit more convinced that I might survive a brief sojourn in the bush, but you couldn't say he was anxious to secure the arrangements.

Jonas Avademe, on the other hand, was practically falling over himself to arrange my visit to his village. So it was that I found myself one afternoon behind the wheel of the Tata, dodging craters on a washed-out dirt track to the distant village of Otareso, population 144 according to the recent census. (In Ghana, census data only counts adults of voting age; Jonas said that children probably brought the total number up to about 200.)

The sole written historical record for Otareso is penned in Jonas's hand on a sheet of ruled school notebook paper, which he keeps in his mud-walled hut. It reads:

> Otareso is a village located in the Akuapim-North District. It is said to have been established in the 1930s. The name of this village was named after a stream called "Otare."
>
> The origin of the people in this village are said to have come from Abiriw-Akuapem, led by Mr. Kwabena Botswe. Later, Mr. Christian Mensa Tugbenyo from Agorvee in the Volta Region, led a group of Ewes who also settled in the village.
>
> Their main purpose of settlement was to tap palm wine and to distilled [sic] into alcohol as well as farming activities.

And not much has changed since then. "I am very proud in my village," said Jonas in his pidgin English after I had transcribed the history into my notes. Whether he meant he was proud *of* his village or that his village is proud of him I cannot say, but both are plainly true. At forty-one (broad-faced, fair-skinned, medium build, with thin mustache and goatee) Jonas is hardly an elder—there are many older men and women in the village, including his own parents—but he is a respected leader and a diligent promoter of his community. He is also a lay leader in his local church, a parish of the Apostles' Revelation Society—a seventy-year-old Ghanaian institution with its roots in the Ewe tribal region of Lake Volta. This is the same faith in which Charlie's father preached.

Jonas's local stature was enhanced in 2008 when he won the title Farmer of the Year for his district, competing against hundreds of other men in dozens of villages. The award is prestigious but also remunerative. This is what he won:

- five cutlasses
- two bars of soap
- one pair of rubber boots
- a polytank for storing water
- a knapsack
- a backpack pump sprayer
- some cloth
- a six-battery tape player and radio
- a bicycle
- a certificate

The award was based on productivity per acre, and after spending a few days with Jonas it was easy to see why he was a good farmer. The man was almost artisanally obsessed with detail, attentive to the point of fussiness. As he sat around his family compound before a meal, his eyes never stopped moving. While speaking to me in English he would stop mid-sentence and issue a stern observation in Ewe that caused family members to scramble in response—rearranging a wooden table, moving a lantern, fetching a pan of water, sweeping the dirt floor—in short, keeping the jungle feng shui of Jonas in order. This is an unusual trait in Ghanaians, who generally take a relaxed approach to life even when they are working very hard.

For his farm, Jonas maintained detailed rainfall records ("I have all the patterns," he said). He worked with an adviser from the government agricultural station, who helped him learn green-manure techniques such as alternating soil-depleting crops like corn with nitrogen-fixing legumes like cowpeas. (Although green-manure practice is a cornerstone of organic farming, Jonas, like virtually all Ghanaian farmers, also used chemical fertilizers, pesticides, and herbicides.) He laid out string lines and planted his corn in perfect three-foot rows for maximum production, as opposed to simply scattering the seeds. (Other Ghanaians plant in rows too, but

Jonas was the first in his village.) And he shared his knowledge with the whole community in a small demonstration garden he planted to teach other farmers.

On my arrival, Jonas led me on a tour of his land. We walked down a footpath through a plantain orchard, broad leaves bending in the breeze above thick green clusters of the large fruit, until the landscape opened to long, dramatic views across the corn to the distant heights of the Akwapim Ridge, ten miles away. There, high above the cultivated plots of the villages, sprawled the gated villas owned by the Big Men—the important government and business elites of Accra who kept weekend homes in the cool elevations. In the dry season of winter, the dust and haze obscured the ridge completely, but in summer the rains cleared the air and lifted the veil, and the poor farmers and the rich city men looked out on each other every day. Fast-moving thunderheads tacked like sailboats above the ridge, slicing shadows across the whitewashed mansions.

Jonas, who had only an elementary school education, did not envy the ridge dwellers. "I am very happy," he said. "If I had gone on to second cycle," the term for post-elementary school, "I would not be in this village; I would be working in an office somewhere." He paused, then added, "Everything God does is good."

Jonas's father, a wiry little man with a crinkled brow, a silver Hitler mustache, and several missing fingers, emigrated from Benin; his mother is an Ewe from Ghana's Volta Region. Jonas speaks Ewe first but also Twi, Ga, French, and English. "I can hear several more African languages," he adds, meaning he can understand them but not speak in return. It turns out that many of the citizens of Otareso are from Benin and Togo—the pair of geographically narrow and politically fragile francophone countries east of Ghana—which explains why several residents (but not Jonas) smoked cigarettes, a distinctly foreign custom in Ghana.

Jonas farmed eleven acres outside of town, land on which his grandparents once lived. Their family compound—two tiny one-room houses, a cooking hut, a storage hut, and a bamboo corn crib—now belonged to Jonas; he called this place his cottage, distinct from his home in the village center, a five-minute walk away. His grandparents were tenant farmers, paying forty cedis a year in rent to a landowner; after they died, the owner offered the land for sale, and Jonas bought it in the year 2000, for sixty cedis per acre. It was a smart move: today, said Jonas, farmland like this along a road—as opposed to far back in the bush, where transport is difficult—sells for five hundred cedis an acre, when you can even find it. "Many more people are farming today than when I started twenty years ago," he said, in part because people like his neighbors have emigrated from Togo and Benin, lured by Ghana's stronger economy and greater freedom.

As we walked, Jonas identified trees and plants along the trail. There was odum, a hard red wood for making furniture, and ktsensen, a more common tree with white wood used for planks and scaffolding. Achampo is a medicinal herb that looks something like basil and is sold in bunches in the Koforidua market. "If you wound yourself with the cutlass," said Jonas, "you rub the leaves in your hand with some water to make a paste, then you put it on the cut and tie it. It will heal more quickly." We passed under a moringa, the wide, drought-resistant tree whose dime-sized leaves contain complete proteins and have saved Africans and their livestock from starvation when crops fail. "Also very good medicine," said Jonas. "It cures ninety-nine diseases."

We stopped to pick and eat large red berries from the asoa tree— "sweeter than sugar," said Jonas, and he was right. He pointed out the four varieties of plantain trees on his land: *apim*, meaning "thousands," yields a lot of plantains; *sawmynsa* produces three bunches; *sawunu* yields two very big bunches; and lowly *pentu* translates into "doesn't give much."

Sometimes his meaning got lost in pronunciation. "This tree is called *ofram*," he said. "We use the wood to make the stew."

"You make stew from wood?"

"Yes, is very nice for that."

"It must be very soft wood."

"Soft? No! Is quite hard!"

"You must have to cook it for a long time."

"Pardon?"

"In the stew."

"*Stools*."

"Stools! You have hard stools from eating the wood. You should eat more mangoes."

"No, no! We don't make the feces. We make the *stool*—how do you say?—*throne* for the village chief out of this wood."

And so it went, until we had returned to his cottage and he introduced his wife, Gifty, a shy and quiet younger woman who spoke neither English nor French, bent over sweeping the dirt courtyard with a whisk despite having lost her baby—and nearly her own life—a month earlier. Jan had told me that Jonas's wife ran the village shop, so I inquired, through Jonas, how things were going at the store. "Oh no," said Jonas, "my other wife runs the store." My surprise must have been evident; polygamy is uncommon in the Christian parts of Ghana, although keeping a mistress is considered perfectly normal—what Ghanaians call tending the farm and the garden. "I will explain it all later," said Jonas. "But now is time to help with building our neighbor's house."

It was Monday, which is rest day in Otareso—meaning it is taboo to farm. Friday is also a rest day, and Sunday is reserved for church, so actual farming only happens on four days. The taboo against farming on rest day is taken seriously. "If you are caught farming against the taboo," said Jonas grimly, "you must pay seven rams to the elders." (Otareso has no chief.) Upon closer questioning he acknowledged that the ram tax is more tradition than modern reality, but he insisted that no one farms on Monday or Friday.

That is not to say that rest day means no work. People have to eat, which means the women still have to cook. And men devote their rest day to communal activities. Today's job was building a new house for a recently arrived Beninois family. The house had been framed with lengths of dried bamboo, split in half with machetes and nailed crosswise in a grid pattern between thick timber corners and door posts. The walls were being raised in mud—plain, red mud from a pit dug behind the house and filled with water from buckets and rain. I pulled on my Italian-made rubber farm boots (twelve cedis in the Koforidua market)* and took my place inside

* Whit later laughed at my naiveté; Africa is the Wild West of counterfeit products. "I don't care what they say on the soles," he said. "I guarantee you those boots are made in China. They are, however, probably better than the ones made in Italy."

one of the rooms, where workers had piled a small Kilimanjaro of mud and were scooping handfuls into the spaces between the bamboo cross members. "You take it and push down, like this, between the wood," said the Beninois man next to me in French, ramming a slab of mud into the wall. "If you see an air space, take like this and throw it in, *comme ça*"—and he demonstrated by hurling a mud pie into a cavity at close range. This was work that any kindergartner would love, and the men—it was only men— were having a grand time, laughing and shouting while getting covered with muck and sliding around the floor like hockey players.

Most of the men worked shirtless, and they all had biceps like steam-engine pistons, and chests that could have been carved out of onyx. Fourteen-year-old boys looked like young Cassius Clay. Here was an entire village of big musclemen who had never done any "exercise" in their lives.

The last step of the day's work was texturing the walls by running our fingertips all over the wet mud to make deep grooves. After the mud dried, the grooves would hold the plaster, which was the final step before painting. (Homes are generally plastered smooth, inside and out, then painted; lesser shelters like storage rooms and outdoor kitchens are left as mud.)

We rinsed our hands and arms in a bucket of water and walked back to Jonas's main family compound, where his other wife, Rebecca, was preparing dinner. She was an older woman of spherical build who, over the course of my three-day visit, appeared in a permanent state of bending over a fire. Until I came back to the village for a Sunday church service, during which she danced like Aretha Franklin, I don't recall ever seeing her fully upright. Despite what must have been a life of backbreaking toil, Rebecca was cheerful to the point of disbelief. "You are welcome!" she said with a wide smile that revealed several missing teeth.

Then there was Jonas's younger sister, Charity, perhaps in her thirties, tall and beautiful with the sultry pout of a 1930s blues singer. It was unclear to me if she had a husband, and I could not tell how many of the children in the compound were her own, but her primary job in life appeared to be serving as Jonas's scullery maid, fetching him water for washing, and serving the meals that Rebecca had cooked.

Several men of the village had gathered around the Burro truck and were looking curiously at the GPS receiver on the dashboard. "Is it a compass?" asked one.

"Well, it can work like a compass," I said, "but it does much more. There are twenty-four satellites in space, and they talk to this machine. They can tell you exactly where you are, anywhere in the world."

"Satellites!" said another man knowingly, and they all nodded. I zoomed out the screen to show all of Africa, then zoomed back in to their village (which I had already labeled with a waypoint) and they gasped and pointed. "Africa! Otareso!"

Another man, older and animated, said something in Ewe. Jonas translated: "He says that's why we call white men trickster dogs."

It was now five-thirty on the day after the summer solstice. Back home in Maine it would be light until well after nine o'clock tonight, but here it was already getting dark, and quickly. I told Jonas I needed to pitch my tent while I could still see. "Okay, you have a choice," he said. "You can set up here or at my cottage. Here you may find it noisy at night because I sell alcohol from the store, and the men come around."

"I'll take the cottage," I said. We walked back down the path to his cottage compound, and I spotted a nice location under a mango tree on the perimeter of the courtyard. But Jonas insisted, "No no, you set up here, next to my house, under the roof." There was indeed a small protective eave, and I had been worried how my twenty-dollar Walmart tent would hold up in a monsoon downpour. So against my first instinct to put some space between us, I relented and pitched under his eave.

## 2. My Favorite Food

Although I was looking forward to a big family meal, Jonas had decided that he and I would eat separately from the rest of the group, which was clearly meant to convey that we were two important men, discussing the affairs of the world, and not to be bothered by mere women and children. He issued an order in Ewe, and Charity sashayed over with a small wooden table. Children arranged our plastic chairs on either side; we sat down and awaited the repast.

Then he told me the story of his two wives. "Rebecca is first wife," he said. "After many years she could bear me no children, so with her permission I also married Gifty. So I have old wife and I have young wife, who has given me four children." I later learned from Charlie that Jonas's church, while nominally Christian, is devoted to the Old Testament. "They are very tolerant of polygamy," said Charlie, "because you have the biblical story of Abraham and his wives."

Jonas's kids range in age from thirteen to three. "My children live here with old wife," he said (I didn't need to ask which wife he slept with), which seemed strange since their real mother, "young wife," lived a five-minute stroll down the path in an identical hut. But it didn't take long to realize that the main purpose of these children, at least for now, was taking care of Jonas and helping prepare the family meals. Perhaps to demonstrate how it worked, Jonas removed his farm boots and yelled in Ewe. Within seconds, a boy of about six who had been sweeping the dirt compound (on Rebecca's orders) dropped his broom and rushed to his father's side. He took away the farm boots, went into the hut, and returned with sandals, carefully placing them, left and right, at his father's bare feet.

Charity then served dinner, arranging two small covered casserole pans on the table. Before we started, she placed a pan of rainwater and a container of liquid hand soap on the table. (The village has a drilled well with drinkable water about a quarter mile down the road, but carrying water is hard work, so in the rainy season everyone collects rainwater in round clay cisterns fed by elaborate split-bamboo gutter systems around their roofs.) I held my right hand over the pan and she squirted a dollop of soap into my palm. Ghanaians generally eat with their hand, and always the right hand—the left being reserved for what one local guidebook calls "the filthy activities." So after some one-hand scrubbing, I rinsed in the pan as Charity poured water over my hand from a cup. I felt like a Roman emperor; it was mildly embarrassing. I wondered if she realized that I was just being a polite guest and would never, in my own world, ask a woman to wash my hands—even one of them—before a meal.

Jonas removed the two lids from our dinner service. One pan held the usual brown peanut-based soup (which we would share), laced with spicy peppers and a few bits of bony chicken; the other contained two familiar starchy beige blobs. *"Akple!"* said Jonas, salivating almost audibly.

"Akple?"

"An Ewe specialty. My favorite food."

It looked conspicuously like fufu, my least favorite African food, but Jonas explained that unlike fufu it was made with the addition of corn, and it did seem somewhat more palatable than the all-cassava goo I had come to know around Koforidua. "It's all stomach filler," said Jan later when I described it to her, which is true—a cheap gluten blast for people who do extreme physical labor, can rarely obtain meat, and have no oven in which to bake their carbs into crusty loaves. Fufu, akple, whatever, is in fact cooked; the cassava, plantains, corn, and other ingredients are boiled before being pulverized into mush. But to my palate it still managed to taste like raw bread dough.

In modern Africa, fufu and its relatives are both a required and an acquired taste. What I mean is, fufu is survival food in these subsistence villages, but even elite Ghanaians with access to pizza love their fufu—although, like Charlie's family, they buy the just-add-water version from the grocery store. "We don't pound," Charlie told me dismissively. "All the neighbors will hear you," suggesting a stigma attached to the labor-intensive pounding process.

All of this is not to say I dislike African cuisine. Charlie's wife Afi is one of the finest home cooks I have ever met, in any culture; her versions of the classic Ghanaian dishes—peanut soups, tilapia stew, fried plantains (*kiliwili*), spicy rice and beans—are bright-tasting, deceptively simple, and stunning on the plate, like the best Mediterranean food. "Okay, now I get it" is about all you say after an all-day feast from her small home kitchen. Like all good African cooks, Afi knows how to extract deep flavor from one-pot meals that do not involve browning, traditionally a prerequisite of

Western stews and braises. As with Indian cuisine, which also does not generally start with browning, Africans get flavor from spices and aromatics (dried chilies, onions, garlic) and from long, slow cooking, not from the carbonization that enhances Western meals. This stems from necessity: when you cook over an open wood fire, you are limited in the sauté arts. Also making up for the lack of browning is the earthy flavor of peanuts and the raw taste of bright-red palm oil, the primary cooking fat of Ghana. Palm oil production is a primitive and ancient village industry; all along back roads in southern Ghana, women tend giant boiling vats over charcoal fires, rendering the oil from the fresh crimson palm nuts, a fruit similar to olives that grows in tight clusters the size of beach balls. (What Americans think of as palm oil is what Ghanaians call *palm-kernel oil,* a clear and more refined product mechanically pressed from the pit, or kernel.)

Jonas said a brief grace in Ewe (concluded by "Amen" in English) and we dug in, tearing off small sticky pieces of akple, which we rolled in our fingers and then dipped in the communal dish of soup. We took turns fishing out pieces of chicken and gnawing off the meat and skin. As we feasted, Jonas explained the economics of farming in Ghana. He recited the annual expenses for his eleven-acre plot:

- Fertilizer, seventy-seven cedis
- Pesticide spray, eighty-eight cedis
- Water delivery in drums for pesticide spraying, ten and a half cedis
- Herbicide (which he calls "weedicide"), ninety cedis

Other expenses include market transportation: the bush taxis charge twenty pesewa for driving his sister to market—plus twenty more pesewa for each bag of cassava that she stuffs into the trunk. (Virtually no farmers in Ghana own cars. Jonas has a Chinese motorcycle that he rides only on back roads around his village because he cannot afford the twenty-cedi registration fee and can't risk the fifty-cedi fine if he's caught by police on main roads.)

He pays two cedis per month in dues to his regional agricultural group (the organization that named him Farmer of the Year), called the Akua-pem Award Winners Association.

A huge nonfarm expense is education; his three school-age children each cost about one hundred twenty cedis per year to attend private school, one in Accra (where she lives with another sister of Jonas's) and two in Adawso, the market town ten miles away. Public school would cost slightly less, but the difference is not great because most private schools are church-subsidized, and even public education requires uniforms, books, and fees that parents must provide. The two boys who go to school at the Miracle Child Academy in Adawso ride their bikes to a junction and then take a bush taxi, which is yet another expense.

"The only good thing," said Jonas, licking his fingers, "is I'm not buying foodstuffs," which is not entirely true. To supplement his own corn and cassava, he buys a bit of dried fish in the market once a week for add-ing protein to soups, as well as tomatoes, which he does not have time to grow. (His own chickens, goats, and sheep provide occasional meat, although they are thin because all they get to eat is what they can forage; and he is fattening two wild grasscutters—with grass, of course—in a hutch.) Of course, he can't grow his laundry soap, matches and other ne-cessities.

In all, his family and farm expenses come to about seven hundred ce-dis per year, or five hundred dollars. In a good year, he said, he can make eight hundred cedis selling his produce in the market. In theory that leaves him with one hundred cedis in savings, which could be applied to expanding or improving his farm. But in practice, he said, "the rain can fail you at any time." Last year it was dry, and he ended up losing money.

Jonas would like to improve his already productive farm. With a power tiller (three hundred fifty cedis) he could work more land. A palm-kernel press (one hundred eighty cedis) would let his family extract more oil, and thus profit, from their small palm plantation. But such investments were out of reach. He applied for a loan at the Akwapim Bank, where he saves a little of his profits, and the manager turned him down. In 2007, his agri-cultural association petitioned the government to provide low-cost loans for farm improvement projects. The 531 members were granted a total of five thousand cedis, or less than ten cedis each. "It wasn't even worth doing the paperwork," Jonas said.

While the government claims it does not have money for farm loans, or road improvement, or bringing electricity to these villages, in January 2009 it did find the cash to give outgoing President John Kufuor two fully furnished residences; six new vehicles, fully insured, fueled, and maintained, to be replaced every four years for the rest of his life; forty-five days' all-expense-paid travel outside Ghana for him and his wife plus a staff of three, every year for the rest of his life; and the equivalent of twelve years' presidential pay. Kufuor was president for eight years, the term limit, which means his pension will total more than he made on the job (at least officially). He left office voluntarily, which has been rare in post-colonial Africa. But after the payout was announced, critics wondered why anyone but a fool or an utter despot (and Kufuor was neither) would not go quietly given such a lucrative exit package. It could be argued that African leaders like Kufuor are, in effect, paid off to leave peacefully.

Jonas and Rebecca also made money from their store, a rickety wooden stall stocked with sundries and dry goods they bought in the Adawso or Koforidua markets and resold for a tiny profit. More remunerative was the nighttime business, when the store functioned as the village bar, selling only one libation: ten- or twenty-pesewa shots of Jonas's home-brewed *apio*, a powerful moonshine distilled from palm wine, with a taste that resembled cheap tequila.

Then there is Burro, from which Jonas earned perhaps ten cedis per month in commission. He said he spent three or four hours a day servicing clients, but much of that time was multitasking—stopping by the huts of clients on his way to and from farming or while running other errands. Being the Burro agent for his village also clearly enhanced Jonas's already high status. Now, besides being Farmer of the Year and local shopkeeper, he was the go-to guy for rechargeable batteries.

We had finished eating, or so I thought. As I rinsed my hand in the water bowl, signaling I was "satisfied," as Ghanaians say, Jonas reached over and picked up one of my chicken bones, which I had stripped clean out of respect for the fact that meat is a special treat. He popped the joint into his mouth and crunched noisily. "The marrow is good, many calcium," he explained. After extracting every digestible molecule from the bone, he spat the masticated shards onto the ground. His flinching dog, so thin you could almost see through him, stopped snapping at flies and rushed over to devour the bone fragments.

Dinner was over.

## 3. I Think It's Going to Rain

Jonas explained that Charity would now tend to my evening bath, at which point I confess my mind wandered. "Do you prefer hot or cold water?" she asked—twice, I believe, but possibly more. Appreciating that hot water would expend precious firewood, I finally vouched for cold, which also seemed wise in the event Charity's responsibilities proved arduous. As things stood, it was a stuffy, humid evening—and after a big meal of steaming hot akple and soup, a cool bath sounded refreshing.

Although the idea of being sponged clean by a nubile Otaresan had its cultural appeal and could have been justified journalistically, it transpired that Charity's sole task was delivering a bucket of water to my bathing stall. As in most Ghanaian villages, bathing took place in a simple enclosure of woven bamboo and grass walls while standing on a few flat stones. You dip a small bucket into the larger bucket of water and douse yourself. Then you soap up and rinse. As it was already well past dark, I did all this by the glow of a flashlight balanced on one of the walls.

Bathing accomplished and immensely refreshed in clean clothes, I returned to the compound and pulled a plastic chair up under the grass-roofed gazebo that defines the communal space of many African villages. Or rather, I allowed one of Jonas's sons to fetch me the chair, which I then tried to move surreptitiously into position before he could see me and pounce to help. I have no idea if the Queen of England ever thinks about this, but sometimes I get a feeling that I'd just like to do a few things myself—a challenge when you are an honored *obruni* guest in an African village.

While Jonas bathed, villagers arrived from their own dinners, the dancing beams of their flashlights drawing closer. A table was pulled up under the gazebo, three kerosene lanterns came alive, and five children gathered to do homework from an arithmetic exercise book. The lantern light was dim and the music from Jonas's Burro-powered radio (resting on two nails driven into the plaster wall of his house, left of the door) was loud, but life in Africa is naturally distracting and noisy, and I did not sense the children were at all disturbed. It was an average night.

A few men, some of them smoking cigarettes, sauntered up to the storefront and dug into their pockets. Rebecca went behind the counter and carefully poured each man a measured shot of *apio*, then took their small coins. They drank quickly, in one gulp, then shuffled over to the dirt courtyard and began to dance in the dark among themselves as the radio blasted a Congolese soukous rhythm. Oddly, in a country where homosexuality is a criminal offense, Ghanaian men interact physically without inhibition. Grown men often hold hands in public—indeed, Jonas held my hand as we walked through his village—and dance together, much as women do in the West. They have a completely different code of male bonding that does not rate the insult as the highest expression of affection. This can lead to confusion when traveling with my brother.

Jonas returned from his bucket shower and took his place in the shop stall, portioning out liquor shots to the dancers. "I don't take alcohol," he said, "just a soft drink," and he pointed to a bottle of Malta, the molasses-like carbonated beverage popular in Africa and the Caribbean.

We sat together under the gazebo and watched the dancers. The music changed to reggae, and Jonas sang along. At ten-thirty I signaled I was ready for bed, and we switched on our flashlights and walked down the path to his cottage. The sound of the radio slowly faded; crickets rose in chorus from the black jungle outside the narrow beam of our lights.

I said good night and crawled into my tent. The crickets were loud, but I didn't mind because it was not the street noise of Koforidua. Alas, rapt appreciation of nature is not the Ghanaian way. In hindsight I might have guessed that Jonas had another Burro-powered radio in his cottage hut, and that the musical soundtrack that accompanies all life in Ghana (and for that matter death, when you consider the country's raucous funerals) was not over just because it was bedtime. A night satellite image of Africa shows a dark and isolated continent. But if that photo could record sound waves—like the psychedelic blinking "light show speakers" I had in high school—Ghana would glow like a halo.

It was after midnight when Jonas clicked off the reggae music. Two hours later, the rooster started crowing right outside my tent, which I soon realized had been pitched in the middle of the chicken yard. Still, there were no downshifting trucks, no horns, no shouting *tro-tro* drivers or whining scooters, and I finally dozed off.

At five-thirty I woke to the rumble of distant thunder. A moaning wind beat against my tent, and I heard the sound of footsteps around the dirt yard. I stuck my head outside, under a charcoal gray sky, and saw palm trees arcing in a gale. Chickens scurried for cover and Gifty was quickly taking laundry off the line, which whipped in the wind. "Mister Maxwell!" said Jonas, emerging barefoot from his hut. "I think it's going to rain—now!"

"I believe you could be right," I said, leaping from my tent.

"Quick, come inside!" I ducked into his hut just as the monsoon hit. It was the hardest rain I had ever seen in my life, an epochal torrent so loud that we had to shout to be heard.

Jonas's one-room hut was about ten by fifteen feet in size, with a concrete floor, plastered walls, and a corrugated metal roof supported by tree limbs. On the long side facing the courtyard was a simple plank door with a padlock. The door swung in; on the outside, a handmade paneled half screen door allowed mosquito-free ventilation and a view of the compound. The only other light inside came from a small window, eighteen inches square, on the opposite long side of the hut. This window also had a screen, which hinged inward; on the outside, a wooden shutter could be closed for privacy. Next to the door, a simple worktable, about three feet long, held Gifty's manual sewing machine and a pile of fabrics. Under the window, a smaller, low table stored an assortment of nested aluminum cookware and plastic buckets. On one end of the hut, farthest from the door, a double-sized foam mattress was laid out on the floor. Above the mattress ran several rope lines, which sagged under clothes. On the floor, a few plastic laundry baskets held more clothes. There were three molded plastic lawn chairs, two adult-sized and one miniature child's version. The only wall decoration was a calendar from the Apostles Revelation Society. If Jonas were to have cataloged his household goods for an insurance company, that would have been the long and short of it.

We sat in the chairs for half an hour, looking at the rain through the screen door and watching rivers of red mud branch and course like lava through the compound. Gifty had disappeared earlier, perhaps to the kitchen hut. Jonas said that while the rain in general was good, he worried that these gale-force soakers would knock down his corn stalks. "But I mostly worry about hail," he said. "Hail is very bad." And then the rain stopped and the sun came out. "Now we must pay our respects to the elders," said Jonas.

"To thank them for the rain?"

"No no. Because you are an honored guest in our village."

"Oh, that."

We walked up the path, now slippery with mud, to the hut of Francis Ahorli, a tall gray-haired man with fine features and the distinguished countenance of an economics professor. From a shady calabash tree in his courtyard hung round gourds the size of basketballs, the type used to make bowls and scoops. "Life here is quiet, but isolated," Francis said. "Now farming is good; we have the rain," and he looked up at the sky. "But I have been around long enough to remember the times of no food. The politicians care about the people in the cities; they can organize and make trouble. Out here, we do not get heard. We need good leaders in our country who will keep us from hunger."

Francis joined us for the short stroll to the home of the village's most important elder, Kofi Adri. We sat on a wooden bench on his porch and were joined by Joshua Asinyo, the village linguist. (In a formal meeting, it is considered disrespectful to speak directly to a chief or elder; instead, you speak to the linguist, who then speaks to the chief. As the chief is sitting right there and can obviously hear you, it feels a bit forced, but that's the tradition.) Joshua was a middle-aged man severely afflicted with late-stage yaws, the disfiguring African disease related to syphilis but not transmitted sexually (it generally attacks children). Of all the developing-world ailments, yaws is especially tragic because in its early, highly contagious stage it can be cured with a single dose of penicillin. Without that simple treatment, however, it advances to an incurable scourge. The result could be seen on Joshua, whose entire body, including his face, had been transformed into an unrecognizable mass of giant wartlike welts. It was frankly hideous—if he were a monster in a horror movie you would jump out of your seat—but the bigger surprise was how utterly cheerful and content he was, despite his unsightly plague. Like most Ghanaians he was deeply religious (also a member of Jonas's church), and he had obviously found some transcendent inner peace that was enviable.

Jonas spoke to Joshua in Ewe, and Joshua then repeated to the elder. I had brought along the traditional offering of a bottle of schnapps, and it was ceremoniously presented to him. He thanked me for my interest in his village and, through Joshua, ordered a gong-gong meeting for the next morning to discuss the use of Burro batteries. After receiving his permission to leave, we shook hands and walked back to Jonas's main compound for breakfast. Jonas's children served us steaming cups of tea sweetened with Milo (the Nestlé malted chocolate drink) followed by delicious omelet sandwiches in sweet tea bread. At the window of Jonas's shop stall, several men were getting fortified for their morning farming with a shot of *apio*. I thought of rural France, where I had often seen men knocking back "eye openers" of pastis before heading to the vineyards.

Soon Joshua returned to announce tomorrow's gong-gong. He was also the village gong-gong man, a job he had redefined with modern technology. Instead of the typical cowbell, Joshua's "gong-gong" was a battery-powered megaphone—the sort that might be used by the fire marshal in a small-town Fourth of July parade. While Jonas sharpened my machete on a flat rock next to his shop, Joshua turned on his megaphone and marched up and down the dirt track, announcing tomorrow's meeting through the tinny, crackling loudspeaker.

Moments later Jonas's children, who had evidently bathed after preparing our breakfast, emerged from their huts in crisply pressed school uniforms. They grabbed their knapsacks and headed off, on foot and bicycle, to secondary schools in the outlying market towns and larger villages. Otareso has its own informal elementary school (there is no building), but its status is in limbo. Jonas introduced me to Georgina, the young woman who is the teacher for the village. "When does school start?" I asked her.

"We don't start," she said. "I expelled the students last week because the parents don't pay me." She said this without anger or malice, simply as a fact. "And when we have a PTA meeting, they don't come. It's very painful, but I have to feed and clothe myself. Until the parents come up with something reasonable . . ." She shrugged.

## 4. White Man Swings a Blade

It was time for work. Jonas and I slipped on our boots, grabbed our machetes, and walked to the fields. The morning job was planting cassava cuttings—inch-thick stalks that take root in the rainy season. To use his land most efficiently, Jonas interplanted cassava between the corn stalks, which were perhaps a month away from harvest. By the time the slow-growing cassava was ready to harvest early next year, the corn would be long gone. So by timing his interplanting, Jonas was able to grow two crops on the same plot at once.

Along the path, Jonas marshaled two women to join us, speaking in Ewe. We arrived at a field that had grown cassava last year and was now fallow. A few days earlier, Jonas had gathered two large bundles of five-foot-long stalks and tied them with strips of palm frond. "The women will carry these to our field," he said.

"What do we carry?" I asked.

"Our machetes."

I shook my head. "What if we made four bundles and we helped? Then the women would not have to carry so much."

"In our African culture," he replied in a tone that brooked no argument, "women carry." Chivalrous African men like Jonas, however, do make it a point to arrange the loads properly on the ladies' heads. We hefted the giant bundles aloft and followed the women as they walked—erect, straight, and perfectly balanced—to the cornfield ten minutes away.

Jonas had a distracting habit of gesticulating wildly with his machete as he talked, and I was careful to keep some space between us on the trail. Finally we reached the corn, about knee-high, and he ordered the women to drop the bundles. They left, and our work began. Jonas showed me how to bore a shallow hole in the soil with the tip of the machete, push the cassava stalk in at a slight angle, and deftly whack off the stalk about a foot from the ground. Then he moved to the next space between the corn, dug another hole, pushed in the stalk, and whacked it off as well. It took practice to make a neat slice of the stalk in one cut; even though my machete was razor-sharp thanks to Jonas (I jokingly tried shaving with it, and it worked), I was too timid in my attack. The result was a mangled stalk. I also had to practice not making the hole too deep, which Jonas said would cause the cassava root (which is the edible part) to grow too far under the surface. On my own, I recognized the additional importance of avoiding my feet on the downstroke; my rubber boots were not steel-toed. But after about an hour I was almost keeping up with Jonas's steady rhythm of *dig, poke, whack . . . dig, poke, whack.*

I was also foaming with sweat like a draft horse. My clothes, the latest in high-tech "wicking" fabrics from REI, were as soaked as if I had stood out in the morning monsoon, the memory of which had now long faded. The sun attacked without mercy; I felt we were on some other planet, several million miles closer to the fiery ball in the sky. As I bent over my machete, perspiration dripped like steam from my brow, stinging my eyes and fogging my glasses. I had a small digital camera in my shirt pocket, which was now soaked through; I tried to find a dry pocket, but there was none anywhere on my body. There was no shade within sight. It was still early morning.

"Are you hot?" asked Jonas.

"Just a bit," I allowed, between panting breaths. "How about you?"

"No." Jonas was wearing corduroy pants and a pilled polyester golf shirt under a heavy wool gabardine top, buttoned at the cuffs. His brow was completely dry. "The rain has cooled the day nicely."

Although I cannot back this up scientifically, I am certain that after three hours planting cassava, my machete had gained approximately ninety pounds, and I had lost perhaps half that in water weight. I did not protest when Jonas decided it was time for lunch. We had planted perhaps half an acre; only about ten more to go.

Lunch back at the compound (cooked by Rebecca and served as always by Charity) was banku and fish soup, deliciously spicy.

For our afternoon work, Jonas apparently took mercy on me and decided we would work in the shade of the nearby plantain grove. As we walked down the path, he unsheathed a slingshot from his back pocket and fired rocks into a mango tree, causing hundreds of weavers to scatter in a cloud so large it momentarily blotted out the sun. "Those birds, they spoil the plantains," he said spitefully. I wasn't sure if his slingshot attacks would do much to prevent them from nesting in his plantain trees, but they seemed to make him feel better. A few yards farther down the path, a goat was busy uprooting cassava stalks Jonas had planted last week. He loaded his slingshot and fired a rock into the goat's hindquarters, which sent it braying across the field. You don't mess with the man's crops.

The plantain grove was spread out along the main road to the village. Here too, Jonas was attempting to use his land as efficiently as possible. "These are orange trees I have planted between the plantains," he explained, pointing out the two-foot-high saplings with their shiny leaves. "We need to clear the brush around them"—a foot-high shag carpet of grass and woody clumps that grow like mildew in the relentless heat and sun of Ghana. He demonstrated how to use the machete like a scythe, swinging wide arcs parallel to the ground—ideally without lopping off the orange seedlings.

We got to work and I was soon dripping again, despite being in the shade. This time, however, our labors were highly public, as villagers passed in a steady flow of foot traffic along the road, carrying water jugs on their heads. As far as I can tell, few entertainments are as capable of sending Ghanaians into knee-slapping hysterics as the pantomime of a white man performing manual labor, and I endured several hours of exuberant laughter and catcalls. Sometimes people would simply stop and watch for several minutes, as though taking in a sporting event. This is understandable when you consider that the African's relationship with the white man has long been one of servant and master, and I'm not even talking about slavery. During the colonial era, it was considered perfectly normal for Africans to carry the British around on throne-like hammocks. In his 1883 book *To the Gold Coast for Gold*, the British explorer Sir Richard Francis Burton decried the incompetence of his Ghanaian porters, whom he felt were overpaid:

> As bearers they are the worst I know, and the Gold Coast hammock is intended only for beach-travelling. The men are never sized, and they scorn to keep step, whilst the cross-pieces at either end of the pole rest upon the head and are ever slipping off it. Hence the jolting, stumbling movement and sensation of feeling every play of the porters' muscles, which make the march one long displeasure. Yet the alternative, walking, means fever for a newcomer.

An arduous journey, indeed. When you consider that Burton was in fact a seasoned adventurer and keen student of indigenous culture—he spoke many African and Asian languages and once visited Mecca in disguise as an Arab—you can imagine how a less dogged Western traveler would expect to be coddled by the Africans. No wonder the locals marvel when a white man swings a blade.

By the end of the day, I had earned my farm credentials. "You know," said Jonas at one point in the afternoon, "I believe Americans are stronger than Europeans."

"Yeah, those Europeans," I said, looking up from my labors. "What a bunch of pussies!"

"Pussies! Ha!" said Jonas.

"To be honest," I said, "my grandparents were European."

"Really?" he said, as if I had suggested they were Uighur herdsmen.

"Yes, from Eastern Europe, like many immigrants to America. And it's pretty unlikely the gene pool has evolved much over two generations to make me noticeably stronger. Besides, there are many strong Europeans. Look at Andre the Giant. He was French."

"I don't mean giants," he said, "just regular people."

The conversation segued into a discussion of the American melting pot. Jonas pointed out that Otareso is also a melting pot, being a haven for migrants from Benin and Togo. "That explains why we are so friendly," he said. "We like foreigners because we are foreigners."

Back at the compound, we peeled off our farm clothes and bathed before dinner. "You should not leave your boots in the bed of your truck like that," Jonas told me as I combed my hair by the side-view mirror. "Someone could come by and take them."

It struck me as an odd concern in a village of two hundred people who know one another like family. "Is there a bad man in this village?" I asked.

"Oh no, there is no bad man," said Jonas. "But you never know." (A few months later, someone broke into Jonas and Rebecca's store in the middle of the night, on a looting rampage.)

Dinner was more starchy mounds, more brown soup. Again the women served us. A soccer game played on the radio, announced in Twi. I tried to strike up a conversation with a young village boy who had been eyeing me with curiosity. "He speaks no English," said an older boy. "He doesn't go to school." The boy kept staring at me. I asked the older boy if he liked football, and he said he listened to the Phobia games; Phobia is the nickname for the Accra premier-league team. I asked if he liked to play football himself. "I would," he said, "but the village has no ball."

Five degrees above the equator, the sun does not linger at the horizon, and darkness descended quickly on Otareso. My energy faded with the light; I was exhausted. As Jonas and I headed down the path, twirling our flashlights, I remarked on how the whole village seemed to just disappear into the sudden blackness of night. "We will get light soon," he said. "It is coming to our village."

Actually it isn't, no matter what the politicians promise. Electricity will not come soon to these villages. But wherever I went in Ghana, that's what people said: *It is coming soon. We are next. Very soon.*

Instead of light, they get stars. There was no moon and the night was clear, and the Milky Way split the sky in two. The stars faded along the southern horizon, where the glow from electrified Accra washed out the black sky. And along the western horizon, high up on the Akwapim Ridge, the lights were coming on in the houses where the Big Men live.

# seven

# A MILLION TINY MOSQUITO BITES

## SUMMER 2009: The cash crop

Cocoa connoisseur: Hayford inspects cocoa beans in a split pod.

## 1. Cocoa Man

**A** **week later I arranged** a village stay in Sokwenya with Hayford Atteh Tetteh, one of Burro's first agents and, at age sixty-four, the oldest. Hayford, a farmer, was a member of the Shai tribe, a subset of the Adangbe nationality, which is itself part of the larger Ga-Adangbe ethnic group. Although lumped together as descendants of ancient Nubian fishing people who settled in and around Accra, the Ga and the Adangbe now speak distinct languages—Ga and Dangbe—that are mutually unintelligible. However, as in Jonas's village, Sokwenya was vibrantly multicultural; despite the presence of many Shai, the chief was Akwapim.

Sokwenya lies off a formerly paved, primary route that was now a virtually impassable dirt road several kilometers west of the market town of Adawso. The morning of my visit I met Hayford in Adawso, where he had been delivering batteries on his bicycle from a cheap zippered red shoulder bag emblazoned with the word FLORIDA; we loaded the bike into the back of the truck, shifted into four-wheel drive, and headed out of town.

A wiry, gray-haired man with a long face and a seemingly permanent smile, Hayford was possibly the most pleasant individual I had ever met—and that's saying a lot in Ghana, where people seem to be genetically good-natured. He had a mannerism that involved laughing and extending a handshake whenever conversation reached a point of agreement or empathy—as if to say, "I'm with you, let's shake to that!" For example, told that I once lived in New York, Hayford replied, "I have a cousin in New York!" followed by a laugh and a conspiratorial handshake. To spend an hour with Hayford is to shake hands elaborately more than several dozen times, to the point where I started to wonder if it made more sense for us to simply hold hands and be done with it.

Unlike his cousin, Hayford had never been to New York. He had never been to neighboring Togo, or even to most places in Ghana. But he was proud of his ten years' formal education (at the Old Mangoase Presbyterian School from 1956 to 1966) and he spoke English better than most younger Ghanaians—well enough to converse freely. As we drove, he expressed pointed curiosity about race relations in America. As an elected subchief of his village—his title was *amankrado* or "opinion maker"—Hayford was an important elder. He was also a leader in his Presbyterian church.

"Do whites and blacks mix?" he asked.

"That's a hard question to answer," I said. "It's a big country. In some places they do, in others not so much."

"Do they marry each other?"

"Sometimes. My brother is married to a black woman."

"Whit's wife is black?"

"Another brother. And many if not most African Americans have some white ancestors. They're not as dark as you."

Hayford laughed at that, and we shook hands. We drove on, slowly. The recent rains had turned an already bad road into a theme park ride of mudslides and yawning sluices. We passed several bush taxis and *tro-tros* fender-deep in muck, their passengers engaged in strenuous efforts to push and pull the vehicles free as the tires spun out ribbons of red clay. Occasionally we stopped to pick up a pedestrian or a waylaid taxi passenger—Hayford knew practically everyone along the road—and load their plantains and sacks of cassava into the truck. When the cab filled, more people jumped into the bed along with the produce; soon we were bouncing along under a mountainous load of human and vegetable cargo, plus several bicycles.

The passengers in the backseat did not seem to speak much English, so Hayford and I continued our own discussion. "Where are your Negroes *from?*" he asked, meaning where in Africa.

"All over. Some know, but most don't," I said.

"Really?" That seemed inconceivable to him.

"It was a long time ago, and slaves were not exactly encouraged to re-member their past. At this point they just consider themselves African American. You know, I can't think of a single black American I know who identifies with a particular African country or ethnic group."

"Obama does; he is from Kenya."

"Well, he's different," I said. "He's not from slaves, like his wife. I doubt if she knows where her ancestors are from. *Whoa!*"

I stepped on the brakes. Just ahead, around a bend, the muddy track ended at the shore of what looked like a small lake. The road simply disappeared into the murky, brick red tarn. In the distance I could vaguely make out the track as it reappeared from the far shore. I looked at Hayford. "Now what do we do?"

"It's okay. Let's go."

"Through that water?" I glanced in the rearview mirror at the bed of the truck, overflowing with produce and people. I wondered if the Tata could float, and if not how I would explain a sunken truck to Whit. "You're sure?" There were waves breaking across the surface of the water.

"Let's go."

I shifted from four-wheel high into four-wheel low and inched forward. In we went, deeper and deeper. The water swirled around the doors. I sensed a current pulling us sideways, then realized that what I thought was a lake appeared now to be a fast-moving river. At this point the mass of humanity in the bed of the truck struck me as an advantage; I hoped the weight would act like a sea anchor to keep us tracking through the gulf.

We made it, finally, and crossed a couple more streams before Hayford indicated I should pull over on the right, in a jungle clearing. "We shall walk from here," he said. I parked, and our passengers began unloading their goods. Across the clearing, several men were laboring over steaming cauldrons that indicated a backwoods distillery. "This is where we make the alcoholic," announced Hayford.

The nerve center of the operation was a sealed fifty-five-gallon steel drum perched on rocks over a searing wood fire. Inside the drum, palm wine boiled and evaporated into a length of copper tubing fitted into the lid. The tube then coiled around and circulated through two more drums filled with cold rainwater, which condensed the vapor into alcohol. At the bottom of the last drum, the tubing emerged over a filter funnel placed in a large plastic jug, which rested in a hole in the ground. The clear condensed alcohol dripped slowly from the tube, into the funnel, and down to the jug. The filter seemed to be a good idea because the surface of the liquid, which was backed up in the funnel, was covered with a silvery skin that looked like mercury. I wondered if metallic scum was a normal by-product of the distillation process, or if it had something to do with the use of old oil drums.

"Very strong alcohol," said Hayford.

"What's that stuff in the filter?" I asked.

"We take it away," he replied dismissively, waving his hand in the direction of the jungle, like a public relations officer for a chemical plant. Fortunately, a tasting was not in the morning schedule. Like Jonas, Hayford was happy to make and sell moonshine but never touched the stuff himself.

"Let's go," he said, and we gathered our stuff and headed down a jungle path so narrow that I could barely put one foot in front of the other. Soon we came to the bank of the Osoponu River, a brown, fast-moving stream. There was no bridge, just a few rough-cut timbers balanced precariously on rocks and logs across the deeper parts of the ford. "Follow me," said Hayford. "Step where I step," and we proceeded slowly over the rickety boards. Hayford carried his bicycle, and I carefully held my sleeping gear above my head. Halfway across, the boards ended and we stepped into the stream, which began swirling around the cuffs of my calf-high rubber farm boots; I sincerely wanted to avoid having my boots fill with water, but for Hayford the problem was immaterial as his own farm boots had gaping holes in the toes and heels. We made it without incident, and on the far bank the overgrown trail continued half a mile to the village itself.

My earlier stay in Otareso with Jonas had left me feeling well prepared for the rigors of Ghanaïan bush life, but I now realized that Jonas's village was Shangri-La compared to Hayford's grim outpost. Where Otareso was situated on a high, grassy plain with big views of the sky and cooling breezes, Sokwenya was claustrophobic, damp, and dark—a haphazard collection of compounds strung along the densely wooded canyon of the riverbed. The town had no well; water was carried in jugs from the muddy river or collected in rain barrels. The air, or what passed for it, was stiflingly humid, like breathing through a wet sponge. It was, ecologically speaking, a perfect malaria microclimate, and clouds of tiny mosquitoes vibrated like auras around our heads.

And yet this seemingly cruel human environment was perfect for growing cocoa, which thrives in warm, humid zones, generally within fifteen degrees of the equator. Cocoa was Hayford's primary cash crop, and indeed the most important source of income for many of Burro's customers; it made sense to see where their money came from. He also planted half an acre of maize and cassava, and he grew some plantains, okra, tomatoes, and peppers. But by his own admission he was getting too old to wield his machete across large fields of annual crops. Mostly he tended his valuable cocoa trees.

"You will stay here tonight," he said as we rounded a bend in the trail and emerged in a clearing where a long tin-roofed hut, its beige stucco walls crumbling, slumped behind a cracked concrete patio on which cocoa beans dried in the sun. We entered the hut, which had two rooms. Hayford pointed to a spot on the floor where I could sleep. I set up my mosquito netting and unrolled my bedding. "I was born in this room," he said, with his twin brother, which explains his name. In Ghana, the older of male twins takes the second name Atteh, while the younger is known as Larweh.

Now the compound belonged to Hayford's sister Agnes, who was queen mother of the village. Contrary to how it sounds, a queen mother is generally not the mother of the chief. Her role is more that of wise counsel and keeper of all genealogical knowledge. As such, she plays a key role in choosing the chief. She is also treated with great deference—a custom not lost on Agnes, a physically substantial woman who apparently did not share Hayford's easygoing nature. When I reached out to shake her hand, she pointed at my feet. "Give me those boots!" she said. "Mine are worn. I need new ones."

"Umm, no thank you," I said, not really knowing what else to say when the queen mother asks for your only shoes.

The silence was awkward, and I was glad when Hayford yet again said, "Let's go." We walked another hundred yards down a trail to his own compound, where his wife, Rose (small and quiet, gray hair under a green head scarf) was tending the cook fire and his grown daughter, Dora (tall, with straightened hair pulled into a bun) was washing clothes in a bucket. They smiled and waved. Hayford went inside to change into his farm clothes, apparently a different ensemble of tattered polyester slacks and golf shirt than those he was wearing. My phone rang and I engaged in a brief transatlantic chat with Sarah.

"I like your phone," said Dora when I hung up.

"Oh, thank you," I replied, finding the compliment strange, as even by African standards my cell phone was a no-frills el cheapo. Except for an obviously fake iPhone I once saw (spelled *IPHOUE* and bearing no resemblance to the real thing apart from its counterfeit Apple icon), my phone was about as crappy as they get in the developing world.

"Will you buy me one?" she said. Now I understood. In Ghana, praise is often a hint for a gift. Whit later told me he'd first noticed this years ago when learning that a single word in one of the neighboring lingua francas means both "to like" and "to want." Clearly the gimme culture was alive and well in Sokwenya.

Whit and I made it a policy never to give in to begging in Ghana, except for cases of the obviously homeless and handicapped—conditions sadly on the increase, according to our African colleagues, as modernity erodes traditional family values and the weakest members of society lose their support system. But often healthy and secure Africans (in a relative sense, granted) will ask for money, or gifts, simply because they know some Westerners will "pity" them and take the easy path of tossing a few bills. Thus encouraged, they naturally beg all the more, which leads to cynicism and the opposite of the enterprising spirit that Whit was trying to develop. "If you give me forty cedis," I said, "I will buy you a phone just like this one and have it brought to you." She frowned and went back to her laundry.

Hayford's dogs were even skinnier than Jonas's, so slight and thin that at first I mistook them for purebred Chihuahuas. During my medical checkup before coming to Ghana I declined to buy the eight-hundred-dollar rabies vaccine (why is it forty dollars for dogs?), vowing to my doctor that I would steer clear of vicious village pets. But these starving and no doubt worm-infested mongrels appeared too fragile to bite anything; I worried that a strong wind would turn them to dust, like Egyptian dog mummies.

Hayford emerged with his machetes—three styles, each for a different task. He examined my own blade carefully. Even though Jonas had recently honed it to a razor's edge, Hayford pronounced it hopelessly dull.

He stooped over his sharpening stone and worked the blade back and forth for a good twenty minutes. "That's better," he said. "Let's go." He untied a goat that had been leashed to a tree and pulled and dragged the loudly complaining animal down a steep trail as I followed closely behind.

In a few minutes we arrived at a field of elephant grass under the power lines, which traversed his property but of course did not provide any electricity to Hayford's village and probably never would. He tied the goat to a bush and left him to graze while we continued on. Soon we came to his cocoa plot, spread out along the bank of the narrow river.

Cocoa trees are small and gnarly, almost like overgrown bushes, with long, oval leaves. The cocoa beans grow inside strange football-shaped pods that emerge from flowers on the trunk. The pods grow to around ten inches long and start out green but turn lemon yellow or bright red (depending on the variety) as they ripen. In the right environment, a cocoa tree can produce beans for seventy-five years, but they are finicky. Besides heat, they need around eighty inches of annual rainfall and filtered shade, which is why they do well along sheltered riverbanks and under larger trees with broad shade-producing leaves, like plantains and bananas.

Hayford whacked a pod off a tree with his machete, then deftly wielded the blade to split it open. He held out the dissected pod in his long, creased fingers. Inside, rows of thumb-sized purple cocoa beans—the tree's seeds—were embedded in a fibrous white pulp. To yield the cocoa, Hayford explained, he would ferment the bitter-tasting beans between wet banana leaves for six days, which removes the pulp and develops flavor. Then he would dry them in the sun for five days before selling them to processors, who roast the beans, then remove and discard the outer shell. The remaining portion, called the nib, goes through further elaborate processes (including the addition of milk solids and sugar) to become chocolate. To someone like myself who could eat chocolate at every meal, Hayford's cocoa plot was the Garden of Eden. "Let's go," I said.

"First we shall pray," said Hayford, bowing his head. "Oh Lord, we have come here to work, so you shall abide us so that we don't have any troubles."

As it happened, Hayford's cocoa trees were having some troubles of their own—an outbreak of powdery mildew after the rains. "I need to buy copper spray," he said.

"Fungicide," I said. "We use the same stuff on fruit trees in Maine. But, Hayford, look at this." I pointed to the base of the trees, ringed with thick mats of brush and weeds. The river had obviously overflowed its banks recently, and all the floating debris had been trapped around the trunks of the cocoa trees. "Look, I don't know beans about cocoa, but that can't be good for the trees," I said. "It's probably choking them, and I think it's encouraging the mildew."

"Yes yes, I see," said Hayford. "We should remove it."

So we did, pulling away the brush with the curved points of our machetes, then chopping down the surrounding vegetation. Next Hayford walked through the grove pulling up tiny cocoa shoots that had sprouted under mature trees. "We will plant these in better places," he said, explaining that the new shoots need more sun. We carefully cleaned and trimmed the roots, stripped off the leaves to encourage new stem growth, then poked holes in the ground with a sharpened stick and replanted the shoots.

"So next week you'll have new trees here?" I said.

"Hah!"

"Seriously, how long before these yield beans?"

"About two, three years," he said.

"That's all?"

"They grow very fast," he confirmed. "Some hybrids, even faster."

We moved downstream, clearing more brush with our machetes. It was pleasant work in the shade of the trees, even with the mosquitoes. "Are you tired yet?" Hayford asked.

"No," I said. "I'm fine." Which I probably would have said even had I been close to sunstroke, but this time I actually meant it.

A few minutes later he asked again. "Do you need to rest?"

"I'm fine."

The third time he asked, it dawned on me that maybe Hayford himself was tired and was trying to save face, so I agreed to head back.

At Hayford's compound, we drank tea and listened to a soccer game on the radio; Accra's Phobia was playing the All-Stars of Wa, a provincial capital in the north. Hayford had become his own best Burro customer: he told me that he used to ration his radio use carefully, but since signing on as an agent he played it all the time—mostly gospel music. .

After an hour or so, Dora's sons—four of them, all under ten or eleven—returned from school. Hayford has seven offspring and an indeterminate number of grandchildren because, he says, "some of my kids live in the forest, so I don't know how many children they have." While Hayford resharpened my machete, I sat down on a bench with Maxwell, Adjei, Amos, and Samuel as they worked on their math books. Adjei, the youngest, had bare pink spots the size of nickels all over his head— ringworm. All the boys had scabby insect bites all over their bodies.

"Do you have mosquito nets for your beds?" I asked.

"No," said Maxwell, the oldest. "We get sick."

Dora snapped an order at the children, and they scurried to round up fallen coconuts from the surrounding trees. They took turns hacking away at the shells with a machete, preparing them for tomorrow's market day. It looked incredibly dangerous; I figured no amount of practice could give ten-year-olds the physical coordination to use a machete safely. After a few minutes I turned away, unable to watch. An older boy in a school uniform, whose name I didn't get, came home, pushing a bike with a flat tire. He went into the hut, came out changed, and proceeded to repair the flat tire on his bike. His mobile phone went off; the ring tone was the Shaker hymn "Simple Gifts." He set down the tire and spoke on the phone in Twi for several minutes.

It was dinnertime. Hayford and I ate first, sharing fufu and a bowl of bright red palm nut soup with a few chicken livers and gizzards. Hayford made sure to offer me the livers first. After we ate, he carved a couple of toothpicks from twigs and handed me one. He went to bed at eight, and so did I.

A goat in my room woke me early the next morning. I shooed him out, then followed through the door to brush my teeth. I was greeted by a boy of about nine named Sammy, who handed me a plastic cup of rainwater. The index finger of his left hand, or the half that was left of it, was wrapped thickly in gauze. "What happened?" I asked. He spoke no

English. I pointed to the wound and he made a chopping motion with his other hand.

Breakfast with Hayford was a shared bowl of sweetened porridge and tea bread. "When did the boy lose his finger?" I asked.

"Last Tuesday. He was in a cocoa tree with the cutlass, holding a branch with his left hand. He's a lefty so he was trying to cut with his right, which is not good."

I wanted to add that perhaps it wasn't good for ten-year-olds to be pruning trees with machetes, but I held off. A billboard seen along roads all over Ghana said AGRICULTURE WITHOUT CHILD LABOUR IS POSSIBLE! Maybe so, but for most Ghanaians it certainly wasn't practical. A September 2010 report by Tulane University's Payson Center for International Development said hundreds of thousands of children work on cocoa farms in Ghana and next-door Ivory Coast; many are trafficked and forced into labor.

"Did he get medical care?" I asked.

"There is a clinic in Adawso." Remembering the road we had taken, I imagined a long, agonizing trip.

I had to get back on the road to Koforidua, but first Hayford wanted me to meet one of his brothers who was a preacher—not his twin, another brother, named Kwesi, which means "born on a Sunday." We walked up a hill to Kwesi's house and sat in chairs under a raffia awning. It looked like rain; Hayford was wearing a long trench coat and complaining about the cold, even though it was in the eighties.

"Are you Christian?" Reverend Kwesi asked me.

"I grew up Catholic."

"Do you believe in the Holy Spirit?"

"It's an important part of Catholicism," I replied, trying to stick to the facts as I remembered them from Sister Madonna's second-grade classroom.

That seemed to satisfy him, and he abruptly changed the subject. "Do you grow cocoa in America?"

"Oh no," I said, somewhat relieved that we had moved on from the Holy Spirit to agriculture, a subject on which I felt firmer terra. "Too cold. Not even in the far south. Not even Hawaii."

"Does it snow where you live?"

"Very much. And the lakes freeze so thick you can walk on them."

"No!"

"I swear it. Like Jesus on the water."

"Hah! Like Jesus!"

"You can even drive cars on the ice when it gets really cold." This was a bridge too far, beyond Ghanaian comprehension, and I gathered they thought I was joking.

"Of course, every year, someone's car goes through the ice," I added. Kwesi thought that was hilarious, which it sort of is, if not to the driver.

Hayford's brother had a Chinese bike that needed fixing—not a Walmart Chinese bike with sparkle paint and a pseudo-English name, but a real made-for-Shanghai bike, plain black with Chinese writing. Could I take it into the shop in town? I agreed, and accepted a ten-cedi note for the repairs. The bike was a mess—flat tires, bent rims, missing brake cables, no doubt much more. In America and probably even China it would go to the dump, but not here. I was looking forward to meeting Dave Branigan, the American who ran the bike shop around the corner from us—the former Peace Corps worker who had been beaten in his own home by Nigerian gangsters.

## 2. Guilty

Back in Kof-town I coaxed the bike across the street—the rims were so bent they thumped like a djembe on the pavement—and down the alley to the shop for Ability Bikes, the nonprofit venture that Dave ran. Three Africans—one woman, two men, all of them polio victims on aluminum crutches, were hard at work on various disabled bike frames. At the front of the shop, working on another bike, was a blond white guy in his mid-thirties with a nasty fresh scar under one eye.

"Excuse me," I said. "I need to get this thing ready for the Tour de France."

He looked up and extended a hand. "You must be Whit's brother."

"I'm Max. You must be Dave."

"Pleasure. Where's Whit?"

"He's in China on mission impossible—trying to get factories to make twenty-dollar flashlights for fifty cents. Speaking of China, I've got one of their finest for you."

Dave looked at the bike and exhaled deeply. "Bad timing. I'm on my way to Tema. Container of bikes just came in. I'm swamped. But let's take a look."

The way Dave's business worked was he got charity bikes sent over from the States—wrecks that somehow escaped the dump—which he reconditioned on the cheap for local consumers. In the process he trained disabled Africans to repair bikes, building skills for people who might otherwise end up as beggars. His venture was affiliated with a Boston organization called Bikes Not Bombs that promotes bike empowerment in poor countries around the world, as well as in American cities.

"Thanks, Dave," I said. "By the way, our agent gave me ten cedis to fix this thing."

"That'll be tough," he said, stooping to examine the twisted carcass. "Let's see . . . definitely needs tubes and tires. I've got some used tires I can throw on, and if I buy the cheap Chinese tubes he'll save a couple cedis. We can probably straighten the rims rather than replace them; they'll be good enough to ride, anyway. Brake cables, I've got some used over there. Looks like the whole front brake assembly needs replacing." He started writing down figures.

I wanted to ask Dave about getting cracked over the head with a mahogany plank in his own bed ("What's that like?"), but it didn't seem like the right time. "We'll need some grease, maybe an hour of labor . . . ," he went on. "I'm guessing this all comes to about nineteen cedis."

"Let's do it," I said.

Dave looked up at his workers. "Anybody have time to do this job over the weekend?"

"I will do it," said a tall man on crutches with toothpick legs and a bodybuilder's chest popping out of a bright red Arsenal soccer jersey.

I thanked Dave, made a mental note to ask him later about Nigerian thugs, and walked back across the street to home and a hot shower. On the way I ran into Kevin, who had just come back from his route.

"Hayford says you worked very hard on his farm," Kevin said.

"Well, I wanted to work even more, but I think he was tired."

"Oh, he told me about that," said Kevin. "He said he was afraid you were going to cut your leg off with the cutlass."

Back in our flat, I stood under the shower and watched the mud of Sokwenya swirl around the drain, and I felt deliriously comfortable and guilty. A white person in Africa can feel guilty about almost anything. I felt guilty that I could be enjoying a hot shower when people like Jonas and Hayford had to bathe in a bucket; guilty that I used conditioner in my hair; guilty that after dark I could turn on lights and cook over a shitty but serviceable gas stove, or (if I wanted) drive to get a shitty but edible steak in a hotel restaurant; guilty that I didn't chew my chicken bones; guilty that I accepted ten cedis from Hayford for the bike repair when I could easily afford to foot the whole bill myself; guilty that I did not give my farm boots to the queen mother and go barefoot like so many Africans I saw every day; guilty that we were trying to make money off people who were so poor they needed to let their children work with machetes; guilty that I could go home.

Yes, it's easy to feel guilty in Africa, but it was also easy to forget that Whit was giving people jobs and teaching them skills; that I was paying for half the bike repair; that I gave Hayford and Jonas nice gifts (heavy-duty Coleman flashlights unavailable in Ghana) and that I helped them on their farms without cutting off any body parts; that I was a long ways from home in a dangerous place. All these conflicting feelings rose and fell like a blush, and soon they disappeared like the red dirt down the shower drain, and all that remained was a million tiny mosquito bites.

# eight

# POWER POWER

**SEPTEMBER 2009:** Quality control

*In many ways, a rechargeable battery exhibits human-like characteristics: it needs good nutrition, it prefers moderate room temperature and, in the case of the nickel-based system, requires regular exercise to prevent the phenomenon called "memory." Each battery seems to develop a unique personality of its own.*

—Isidor Buchmann, *Batteries in a Portable World*

The voodoo priest who, at my instigation, single-handedly transformed Burro's business through black magic, although that analysis is debated by my brother.

## 1. Personality Crisis

could handle the concept that batteries need good nutrition and regular exercise. It was the last sentence that got me: *Each battery seems to develop a unique personality of its own.* I was out on the veranda reading Isidor Buchmann's battery bible, hoping to learn more about the product at the center of the Burro business. Buchmann is a Swiss-born Canadian inventor who, according to Whit, made a small fortune in the early days of the cell-phone business by helping phone manufacturers get a handle on runaway battery returns. He helped them figure out why seemingly good batteries went bad—that is, failed to take a charge—and how to analyze and recondition them. Being a techie nerd, Whit loved this kind of stuff; he went so far as to telephone Buchmann, twice, exchange several emails and, on one trip home to Seattle, have lunch with him over the Canadian border. I, on the other hand, expected his book to be eye-glazingly technical and dry as a camel bone. In fact it was surprisingly readable. To be honest, I soon found myself transported far from the dusty streets of Koftown to a science-fiction netherworld where batteries were like HAL, the malicious computer with a mind of its own in *2001: A Space Odyssey.*

If Buchmann can be taken literally (and the man is nothing if not a precise writer), batteries are not merely good or bad, strong or weak. He says *each battery* develops its own personality. Think about it: that's a lot of personalities. Taking Buchmann's analogy to its nightmarish conclusion, batteries have the potential to be temperamental, stubborn, melancholic, curious. And that's just a four-pack. It gets worse. Much like a misunderstood lad who adopts a life of crime after meeting more hardened youths in reform school, it seems that a perfectly good battery can be spoiled by other, more delinquent cells in proximity. Bad personalities rub off. Imagine if all the batteries in the world banded together under one type-A personality battery (a triple-A making up for size?) bent on global domination. Chances are good it could happen here in Africa, which has bred despotic dictators since the colonial masters showed the Africans how it's done. Then what? Look out is what. I could scarcely imagine the outcome, mainly because like most people I don't think much about batteries until they die, at which point I curse them and move on.

By the fall of 2009 this whole battery personality business had become a big issue for Burro. Jan and Whit first started getting indications about battery problems in the summer—customers, the agents said, were complaining about noticeably shorter battery life. "I am worried," said Kevin one day after his route. "The agents say they don't want to go out and sell because they don't want to hear the complaints."

This was puzzling because in tests back at the office, the batteries seemed to be doing fine. Granted these early tests were not the most scientific; without sophisticated electronic analysis equipment, testing basically involved running batteries through a discharge cycle (a feature on the chargers that simply reverses the current flow) and timing how long it took. The batteries were rated to deliver 2.3 amp-hours of current, which in battery-speak is expressed in one thousandths of an amp-hour (one milli-amp-hour), written like this: 2300 mAh. In practice, said Whit, it was more reasonable to expect around 1800 mAh per battery at this stage in their life cycle. (You could compare this to the difference between a car's official gas mileage rating and its actual mileage in traffic after a little wear and tear.) Since the chargers had a metered discharge rate of 300 milli-amps per hour, it ought to take around six hours to completely discharge a healthy battery.

Which it did.

So the batteries seemed fine—but to be sure, Jan also tried running down fresh batteries in a variety of flashlights and radios, and timing the results. All these tests had begun as soon as we arrived in June, and the batteries seemed to be holding up well, certainly as well as Tiger Heads. Still, the complaints continued. What was going on? What kind of weird personalities were we dealing with?

## 2. Animal Electricity

The battery was invented in 1800 by Alessandro Volta, a physics professor in Como, Italy. Volta had studied the experiments of Luigi Galvani, a

Bolognese physician who observed that a frog's leg twitched when connected to two dissimilar metals. Galvani thought the phenomenon was due to what he called "animal electricity," but Volta realized that the moisture in the frog's leg was actually facilitating a chemical reaction between the two metals that caused a transfer of electrons—an electrical charge. Put another way, chemical energy was being converted into electrical energy. Volta refined the process, using brine-soaked blotter paper instead of a frog's leg to create a steady electrical current between plates of copper and zinc stacked up within a glass tube. His battery, known as the Voltaic pile, was itself of little practical value. It was large, fragile, and prone to internal leakage of the brine (known as the electrolyte), which caused short circuits. It also had a tendency to generate bubbles of hydrogen gas which, besides being explosive, increased the battery's internal resistance and limited its useful life to about an hour.

But the principle was revolutionary. When you consider that the electrical generator was not invented until 1831, by the British physicist Michael Faraday, Volta's battery represented the first form of continuous electricity (as opposed to static charges) known to man. Today—at least in the modern West—we think of batteries as a convenient supplement to generated electrical power, yet in fact they came first. By the time Faraday was demonstrating his first electromagnetic generator, incremental improvements on Volta's design had already led to batteries with steady currents capable of lighting rooms, albeit not for very long.

And then something special happened. In 1859 the French physicist Gaston Planté replaced the copper and zinc electrodes of the Voltaic pile with alternating plates of lead and lead oxide. Then he used an acid solution as the electrolyte. The acid interacted with the two forms of lead to generate a sustained current unlike any previous battery. Planté's lead-acid battery had genuinely useful applications; his 150-year-old design was essentially the same as the battery in your car. But his findings went beyond inventing the first practical battery. Planté also realized that after the lead-acid battery ran down (converting the two types of lead into lead sulfate), it could be brought back to life by reversing the process and feeding a current back into it. Thus in one swoop, Planté had also invented the rechargeable battery.

The 1880s saw the development of dry cells (made of carbon and zinc), which made it possible to produce small, portable batteries. Dry cells are not totally dry—it's a relative term compared to the watery liquid in lead-acid batteries. They do, however, leak a gooey, corrosive electrolyte when run down very low. In 1898 the National Carbon Company introduced the first D-cell, a carbon-zinc battery whose direct descendant is the Tiger Head sold in Ghana today.

A Swedish inventor named Waldemar Jungner created the first rechargeable nickel-cadmium battery in 1899, but it was expensive and impractical as it required venting of internal gases. It wasn't until the late 1940s that sealed NiCd batteries (which recombined the internal gases) were developed, opening up the consumer market for rechargeables.

NiCd batteries proved to be workhorses that dominated the rechargeable market for decades. They are relatively inexpensive, tolerant of deep discharge, can handle high loads (such as those required for power tools), recharge quickly, store well, and last for more than a thousand charge cycles. On the downside, NiCds have low energy density, meaning power comes at a cost of weight and size. The batteries also develop crystals on the cell plates that reduce charge capacity over time—that familiar phenomenon called "memory" that can be especially problematic if NiCds are repeatedly charged without having been fully discharged. Finally, cadmium is extremely toxic in the environment, complicating transportation and disposal of NiCd batteries.

The next major battery improvement was the development in the 1980s of the nickel-metal hydride (NiMH) battery. NiMHs have several advantages over NiCds, namely far less memory effect, as much as 40 percent higher energy density (meaning smaller size for equivalent power), and only mildly toxic ingredients, greatly simplifying disposal and transportation. But there are trade-offs: NiMHs don't last nearly as long as NiCds (you get roughly three hundred charge cycles); they can't take high loads as well (making them less suitable for power tools); they are less tolerant of deep discharge; they take longer to charge and generate more heat while charging; and they have a greater propensity to "self-discharge"—that is, they lose their charge relatively quickly during storage. Oh, and they also cost about 20 percent more than NiCds, although the price difference seems to be narrowing as NiMH technology has improved and come to dominate the consumer market.

Given all the disadvantages associated with NiMHs, you might think the old standby NiCds would be the way to go in Ghana. But Whit ruled them out for one simple reason: because of the NiCd's low energy density, it was impossible to get the power of a D battery in an AA-sized cell. This was a deal-breaker because a big part of Burro's business model was the two-for-one offer: an AA battery that slips into an adapter for D-powered devices. Then there was the environmental issue: "Do I want to be the guy bringing tons of cadmium into Africa? I don't think so," said Whit.

NiMHs, on the other hand, were environmentally friendly and dense enough to deliver the big power in a small package that Whit needed. From the beginning, they were the only real choice.*

## 3. Nights in the Battery Room

Whit arrived from China in July with an array of geeky testing gear—a battery analyzer with a serial port interface to his laptop, and a regulated DC power supply that could be adjusted to deliver a constant source of either amps or volts.† Using these machines, he could run calibrated loads on batteries to mimic the load of any device, such as a flashlight or a radio. Then he could monitor how long it took for the battery to run down—the point where the voltage dropped so low as to be effectively useless. The analyzer plotted the results as a graph on his laptop.

Whit connected a cheap Chinese LED flashlight—the kind many Burro customers use, bought at the market in Koforidua—to the DC power supply

---

* Lithium ion batteries like those used in laptops and cell phones are lightweight, powerful, and have no memory issues. But they are expensive and fragile, requiring complex circuitry. Moreover, they are not compatible with the huge installed base of devices owned by Burro customers.

† An electricity primer: Amps are a measure of *current*, often compared to the amount of water that flows through a hose; the larger the hose, the more water flows. Volts are a measure of *force*, equivalent to the pressure of water in a hose. Amps times volts equals watts, which is the measure of *power*.

unit, using alligator clips. The flashlight was meant to be powered by two 1.5-volt D batteries, so he set the power at three volts. The beam was clear and bright. Then he dialed the voltage lower and lower, watching the light grow increasingly dim. At one volt (half a volt per battery), the flashlight gave off only a faint glow. We turned out the room light (it was nighttime) and could barely see ourselves in the orange cast. It was dimmer than a candle. "I would argue that's the bottom end of useful light," said Whit. "I mean, it's beyond any functional task lighting; you couldn't read by it. But I suppose you could argue it still works as a night-light. Basically it's dead."

"Agreed," I said.

Knowing that the flashlight became useless at one volt, Whit could now measure how long various batteries could reasonably power the light—that is, deliver more than half a volt (considering there are two batteries) at the constant current being drawn by the bulb. He began by connecting a new Tiger Head to the battery analyzer, then entered the following parameters on the laptop interface: start at 1.5 volts and draw down steadily at the flashlight's current load until .5 volts. "So we'll time that and see how it does," he said, "then we'll do the same with a Burro battery starting at 1.2 volts, which is its top-rated voltage."

By the next afternoon, we had the results. Both batteries had comparable duration: the Tiger Head dropped to half a volt in six hours and thirty-eight minutes; Burro hit the same target in six hours and fifty-seven minutes—about twenty minutes longer. But the big difference was in overall performance, as plotted on two graph charts. The Tiger Head was obviously brighter at first, since it starts out delivering 1.5 volts compared to Burro's 1.2. But after just forty-eight minutes, the Tiger Head had dropped below 1.2 volts. By contrast, the Burro kept running at 1.2 volts for more than six hours—virtually its entire life. In other words, Tiger Head was brighter for forty-eight minutes, and then Burro outshined it for five more hours. The graphs made the difference clear: Tiger Head's power drain charted a steady decline from the get-go, but Burro's graph was essentially flat for six hours—dropping off rapidly at the end. Burro truly delivered on its promise of more power.

(Whit later learned that the popular LED-powered flashlights were not drawing a constant current but were in fact drawing less and less current as the voltage decreased. Recalibrating the test with that information showed that the Tiger Head–powered device was brighter for about six hours, then Burro was brighter for about thirty hours, at which point Tiger Head hobbled along at one tenth its original brightness for another couple of days.)

That was good news, but it didn't explain the complaints about bad batteries. Obviously not every battery was performing up to snuff. Whit started running batteries through the analyzer and found that on average, the batteries had lost about 20 percent of their original capacity. This was not too surprising—it's what happens to rechargeable batteries over time, and some of these were nearly a year old. Still, the drop-off was more than Whit had expected. "The business model is based on batteries lasting three years—two years at least," he said ominously.

"What do you think's frying 'em?" I asked.

"Could be a lot of things. Some of the original chargers we had might have damaged them; they were putting out way too much power. It didn't help that the second load sat in a can for five months." What he meant was that the shipment from China had been held up at port in Durban, South Africa, due to an incompetent shipping agent; the batteries spent months in an airless metal container. Heat can cause permanent damage to NiMHs.

"And they could just be low-quality to begin with," said Whit, who was up at five every morning to email China, looking for a better battery manufacturer, among other product sources. "And frankly, I think usage patterns could be hurting them. People are using this fairly sophisticated battery in all these dumb devices, and they're just running them until they quit working—which is how they use throwaways. Some are coming back at zero capacity, and NiMHs don't like to be run down all the way to nothing. It's best if you leave some capacity in them. In some cases I think these things are getting run down until they reverse polarity, which is really bad."

Whit began a reconditioning program for batteries that had been returned as faulty from the field. He stayed up for hours after dinner, sitting at a small desk in the battery room, discharging bad batteries, then applying small currents to jump-start capacity before charging them again. Mostly it worked—the reconditioned batteries performed as well as average and went back into service. But some were beyond repair, or even understanding.

"Max, check this out."

I looked over Whit's shoulder at the laptop. "So I just reconditioned this one, and it's showing good capacity. But when I put any kind of load on it, it drops right off a cliff, down to nothing." He pointed to what indeed looked like the profile of a cliff on the chart. "Then, when I put a charge on it, instead of gradually climbing, it spikes like a rocket, then it drops as soon as I take the charge off. I can't get any accurate capacity reading, and the power curve is just nuts. And the really scary thing is, when I test it in the little hand tester, it reads fine. But the customer sticks this thing in a tape deck and it runs right down. They seem to have capacity, but they don't produce current flow. What the hell does it mean?" said Whit.

"You're asking me?"

"Only rhetorically, because you're an idiot. Frankly, so am I. I only know enough about batteries to be dangerous, and I have no clue what this means."

"How many are doing that?"

"I don't know yet."

"You're so fucked."

"Only if I can't identify them. Right now I'm just trying to stem the damage to the brand and pull them out of circulation. I'm working on a quick, production-oriented approach to culling bad batteries."

"English, please."

"I'm starting with Jan's idea of using the discharge function on the chargers—setting a timer and pulling any that discharge fully in under five hours and putting them in a bin for reconditioning later. The ones that last over five hours, I'll put on the analyzer and run a medium-high rapid-load test to make sure they can pull a good amp out and still put out at least 1.1 volts. If it passes that test, I'll put a blue mark on it and send it into the field. Any that don't pass get shitcanned. When the batteries come back from the field, any that don't have a mark I'll run through the test. Eventually we'll get every battery in the field through this level of certification. What stinks like a dead animal?"

"A dead animal. I bought an antelope hide in the market today. A bushbuck. I don't think it's fully cured."

"That's disgusting. Where is it?"

"I put it on your bed to air out."

"You asshole!"

"Speaking of bed, I'm turning in. Good luck with those batteries."

In fact, if it were my company, I would have locked up the office, thrown away the key, rolled up my antelope hide, and bought a plane ticket home. But not Whit. His nights in the battery room grew later and later. Surrounded by buckets of green Burro batteries and racks of blinking chargers, he worked, bent over his testers and coils of wire, like a mad scientist. Sometimes I could hear him talking to himself—grunting and sighing over his Sisyphean toils.

"How's it going?" I asked him one night around ten, after my evening shower—the only time of day you could get clean and hope to stay dry for more than ten minutes in the oppressive humidity.

"Pretty good. I'm getting a handle on this. It looks like about ten or eleven percent of our stock is failing."

"Wow. That's not good."

"Well, it's certainly not sustainable. I mean, overall we're hearing customers are very satisfied, but long-term, if you've got ten percent of your product not performing, that's insanely high. It's not gonna lead to ninety-eight percent customer satisfaction, let's put it that way. And the problem is, the people it impacts the most are our best customers—the guys with these massive high-powered radios and tape decks that use lots of batteries. You know, these culls can run flashlights no problem—put a little fifty- or hundred-and-fifty-milli-amp load on them and they're fine. But those boom boxes pull much higher loads; they take six or eight batteries, and it only takes one bad one to shut it down. So let's say there's a one in ten chance he's got a stinker; if he changes batteries twice in an eight-battery device, he's almost certain to get one stinker. The radio shuts down, and he thinks they're all stinkers."

"Ouch. So you get rid of the stinkers, but what's the long-term fix?"

"Well, chipped batteries would solve the problem."

"Chipped?"

"Add some circuitry to the battery that cuts it off at nine hundred milli-volts, so people don't run them down so low. And if you did that, you could have circuitry that prevented charging in unauthorized chargers, which would eliminate theft issues once we expand to big cities. For that matter, a chip could track cycle counts, capacity, total power in and power out—basically get a running health report. We'd probably have to order like a hundred thousand of them, so it's big money. And I don't even know if any of this is possible in a double-A; there might not be any room for the circuitry. I'm pretty sure you'd need another contact point too, for data. To my knowledge nobody else is using rechargeable double-A's in a rental business model, so I doubt if anybody has even tried to make a smarter double-A battery. But I don't know."

"Hold on, Einstein. Let's say you can chip these batteries. And let's say some woman is out hunting snails in the bush at midnight, and suddenly her flashlight battery clicks out when it hits your little voltage cutoff. She's stranded in the jungle, with the pythons. Oops! Bad idea."

"I hear you. But the thing is, by the time that battery's only pushing nine hundred milli-volts, it's practically dead anyway. It's just not giving her much light at all, certainly not for walking around the bush at night. I don't think she goes out to the bush with a flashlight that weak to begin with. And the time for an LED flashlight to go from nine hundred to four hundred milli-volts is less than ten minutes, so it's not like the client is getting a lot less use. The client utility at that point is effectively nil."

Batteries weren't Whit's only worry. During a company meeting the next day, Jan and Whit brought up another looming concern: the potential for counterfeit exchange coupons. The first coupons were simple black-and-white A4 printouts from Burro's HP Officejet, which were then cut into individual coupons and stapled together. We knew that was asking for trouble, but it seemed like an acceptable risk for the first test market in Bomase, which everyone was anxious to get going. By mid-July, as the pay-go (short for "pay-as-you-go") offering expanded across the test region, we had added a multicolored hand stamp with the Burro logo.

"Fortunately the value of a coupon is fairly low," said Jan, "so the cost of photocopying and cutting may be prohibitive to a thief, but we need to take steps to make it more prohibitive."

"I can see all kinds of solutions long-term," said Whit, "printing in China with the Burro color, adding a watermark, finding a local printer who specializes in security printing. But we need something in three days." ·

For now, Jan and Whit decided to engage the services of a local printer, using colored ink. That came with its own dangers, namely the potential for a dishonest employee at the print shop to take advantage of the relationship. "If we serialized the coupons, that would be a higher bar," said Whit. "Adam, find out what the incremental cost is for that. And I'm thinking if we put a wavy pattern in the background it would be harder to pull out the stamp image and re-scan it. And maybe the stamp could be in a blue ink that doesn't photocopy. Let's see what all this does to our costs."

## 4. Voodoo Economics

On the road between Nkurakan and Amonfro, about a twenty-minute drive from our office, lived an Ewe fetish priest named Torgbe Ahluame. Fetishism is an ancient belief system that West Africans call Vodun, an Ewe word from which the word *voodoo* derives. It revolves around one god but with many "helper" deities or spirits—frequently the spirits of ancestors, who exist alongside the living. These spirits are manifested in talismans like animal parts and sculptures—the fetishes around which worship takes place. Voodoo and other fetish religions are still practiced in much of Africa, thriving alongside Christianity and Islam.

Torgbe's site was impossible to miss, marked by a six-foot-square painted concrete sign that said POWER POWER on each side, along with his name and two mobile phone numbers. One side of the sign featured a pair of African mermaids with long, straight black hair that tumbled and curved around their exposed breasts. One of the mermaids was holding a white dove in her left hand and a long, straight knife in her right; the other was admiring her visage in a hand mirror. On the other side of the sign were painted two men. One wore a traditional grass skirt and seemed to be dancing, or writhing in ecstasy; the other had a kente robe around his waist and was standing erect. Both were brandishing knives. Between the two men was a bizarre composition whose iconography I can only guess at: a figure in the shape of an African drum, but with a human face and cowry shells for eyes, was balancing on its head two large metal bowls—the type African women carry on their heads to market. The top bowl was inverted over the lower bowl, as if to cover something inside. And here was the strangest thing: the rims of the bowls were clamped tightly shut with a pair of massive padlocks.

I took a picture of the sign and showed it to several Africans I knew well. None could say exactly what it meant—it didn't appear to be any conventional symbolism—but the general speculation was that it conveyed great power inside the bowls that had to remain under lock and key.

I wondered what kind of power this priest could unlock from the spirits. "Hey, Whit," I said casually one afternoon, "what say we take some of these bad batteries and go see the fetish priest."

"The fetish priest?"

"You know, the Power Power guy—up on the Amonfro road."

"You're joking, right?"

"Not at all. Maybe he can put more power into these batteries. Look, you said yourself you don't understand what the hell is happening to the bad ones. They go up, they go down, it makes no sense. So maybe we need some voodoo. That guy who wrote the battery book says every battery has a personality all its own. Maybe this priest can tap into that."

"Have you been drinking?"

"Of course not. Let's go check it out."

"I will do no such thing."

"Oh, come on! What can it hurt?"

"Human sacrifice is what can hurt. I hear it hurts a lot."

"They don't do human sacrifice. Not very often." I had heard lurid stories of fetish priests demanding blood sacrifices (called *mogya sika duro* in Twi) from customers who came in search of riches. In most cases, blood was obtained relatively harmlessly—from the menses of a woman, or a small cut—but in some parts of Africa, albinos have been murdered at the behest of fetish priests. Such crimes are rare; fetishism is broadly accepted in Ghana, and you don't read about humans being sacrificed left and right. Still, in 2008 Ghanaian police arrested two men for selling a sixteen-year-old boy, who was being offered for body parts to fetish priests. At last report the police were having a hard time locating the boy's family—raising suspicions that relatives had been complicit in the sale.

"I have no idea what they do, and I don't feel like finding out," said Whit. "Those guys are scary."

The next day, I asked Kevin what he thought. "Oh, don't get involved in that," he said gravely, shaking his head.

"Why not? What could happen?"

He thought for a few seconds. "You will maybe get into something you had not expected. It will cost you."

"You mean money?"

"That, and possibly more. Once you visit the fetish priest, it is hard to remove yourself. That is all I can say."

This was starting to sound like heroin. I told Whit that if he didn't come I would go by myself. I was bluffing: I had no intention of going alone. One blazing hot Sunday afternoon he finally relented. "Okay, I'll go, but only to make sure you don't do anything incredibly stupid that jeopardizes our business," he said. "I'm not saying anything, and I'm sitting close to the door."

An hour later we pulled into Power Power, partially hidden behind a bamboo fence. At first it looked like a typical rural family compound: metal-roofed square clay huts to the left and right were bunted with the usual assortment of drying laundry; children played under the shade of wide eaves. But straight ahead was something out of the ordinary: two more connected huts, their entrances veiled in curtains and shaded under eaves, were painted with more colorful scenes of knife-wielding mermaids and priests; these were obviously the temple rooms. The children shouted "*yevu!*"—Ewe for white man. A young woman approached. I asked for the priest and she led us into one of the family huts off to the side, where we sat in a bare room and waited for our consultation. On a small table rested three intravenous vials of ampicillin, a strong antibiotic. "There's your 'magic,'" said Whit with a sneer.

"Shhh, he's coming."

"Good afternoon. I am Torgbe Ahluame." I was expecting a wizened old sage in a robe, but the figure who stepped through the doorway was an athletic man in his early thirties wearing gym shorts and a Nike T-shirt. Behind him followed a slightly younger man whom I took to be the sorcerer's apprentice. Both shook hands with us, sat down, and smiled.

"So?" Torgbe asked.

I told him about Burro and the problems we were having with some of the batteries, extracting two bad ones out of my shirt pocket. "We need more power in these batteries," I concluded, handing them over.

"Not just these, but all of them," Whit whispered in my direction.

"I thought you weren't talking." He glared at me.

"These and many more," I added. "These are just two examples."

Torgbe held the batteries and pondered the problem for about two and a half seconds. "It can be done," he ruled. "The spirit can help you."

"Oh, thank you, sir," I said respectfully, bowing my head. "What must we do?"

"It will require alcohol," he replied.

"Ah, so we should go buy alcohol and return?" I asked, mentally kicking myself for not having thought of that. Of course it would require alcohol.

"No," said the apprentice. "We will take care of it. Give us two cedis and we will bring the alcohol for the spirit." I unfolded two cedi notes from my pocket and handed them over, relieved that the price of entry was so reasonable. "Please follow me," said the apprentice as Torgbe disappeared into another room.

We stepped back into the sun and crossed the dirt yard to the first of the two temple rooms. "Remove your shirts and shoes," he said at the entrance. Whit and I glanced at each other. The apprentice was now holding a knife very similar to those in the paintings. We disrobed and entered the temple.

The windowless room was dark and stuffy. The only light came from a candle burning in a large metal bowl on the tile floor, which was mostly covered by animal hides. From the glow of the candle we could see more wall paintings. One showed a bearded Old Testament priest with his hand on the forehead of a prone man who was obviously sick. Next to that was another buxom mermaid, this one I think modeled after Charo. On the next wall was a bearded man sitting under a tree with a snake in the branches. Over to one side, the room opened into a small alcove, which was hidden from view by a gauzy curtain. Next to this alcove was a carved wooden bust of a woman almost completely covered in hardened drips of candle wax—the fetish.

We sat in plastic chairs next to the man with the knife, sweat pouring down our exposed chests. Soon Torgbe entered. He was now shirtless himself, with a muslin wrap around his waist. He sat in front of the gauze curtain. He had a bottle of schnapps. "The spirit has requested three hundred to be summoned," he said.

"Three hundred cedis?" I asked, fairly choking.

"I think he means three hundred *thousand* old cedis," said Whit.* This confusion, combined with the fact that English-language numbers could be difficult for uneducated Ghanaians to master, often complicated financial negotiations. "Is that right?"

"Yes," said Torgbe.

"So you mean *thirty* new Ghana cedis?" I said.

He thought for a minute, doing the mental math. "Yes."

"Wow," I said, peeling off three ten-cedi notes, about twenty dollars, from my bankroll. I handed them to the assistant, who passed them along to Torgbe, who stuffed them into a small woven basket. Then he draped the curtain over his head, rattled a shekere (a percussion instrument made from a gourd covered with cowry shells), and began chanting what sounded

---

* Although the national currency had been revalued to account for inflation more than a year ago (the new cedi was equivalent to ten thousand old cedis), many Ghanaians still expressed monetary amounts in the old system. The old currency had the advantage of not requiring knowledge of decimal points, since a cedi was the smallest denomination. Under the new system, a cedi was divided into one hundred pesewa.

like gibberish in a strange tongue. He poured a shot of the schnapps into a small plastic cup, recited some invocation, and poured the liquor over the wax-covered fetish. This was presumably the offering to the spirit. He poured another shot and downed it himself. His apprentice took the bottle, poured a generous shot on his own account, and then poured one for Whit and finally me. The liquid was strong and coarse, and I had to choke it down. I felt bad for Whit, who had been suffering an all-too-common bout of intestinal dysfunction; the last thing I'm sure he needed was a long slake of moonshine. But it seemed clear that to refuse the alcohol would anger the spirit. Plus we had paid for it.

The libation completed, Torgbe was ready to engage the spirit. His face was still concealed behind the curtain. There was more shekere rattling, lots of strange yelling, and suddenly a cloud of "smoke" that smelled remarkably like talcum powder filled the air around the curtain. I was beginning to feel like Dorothy meeting the Wizard of Oz. And then the spirit spoke.

Or I should say, squeaked. The all-powerful spirit, it turns out, had a voice closely related to one of those plastic dog chew toys that squeaks when you squeeze it. And the spirit apparently had a lot on his mind, because the squeaking went on for some time. I looked at Whit. His eyebrows were approximately on the ceiling, and his jaw was stretched tighter than a drumhead. He was trying his best not to roll over laughing.

"The spirit says you are welcome," said Torgbe, emerging briefly from behind the curtain.

"Please tell him thank you for us," I replied.

Torgbe drew the curtain closed again and chanted some more, which was followed by more spiritual squeaking.

"The spirit says he can give the batteries much power," confirmed Torgbe, again pulling aside the curtain. "But there must be a sacrifice."

"Of course," I replied.

"We must kill a cow," he said, and at that moment his apprentice demonstrated by drawing the knife close to his own throat. "From the blood will come the power. Also three bottles of alcohol and fifty million cedis."

"*Fifty million cedis?*" I asked. "So that's, let me see . . . five thousand new Ghana cedis?"

"Yes."

"Five *hundred*, right?" suggested Whit hopefully. "You mean five *hundred* new cedis."

Torgbe, whose English was rudimentary, seemed confused. (We learned later that he was in fact Togolese, although his French was also weak.) He reached behind the altar and withdrew a ruled student notepad and a ballpoint pen. On the pad he wrote the numeral five, followed by four zeros—no commas or decimal points. "That is how much," he said. So did he mean fifty *thousand*? In old or new currency? Now it was our turn to be confused.

"Can I see the pad?" asked Whit. He took the pen and started writing. "So ten thousand old cedis equal one new cedi, right?" He wrote down the equation. "And one hundred thousand old cedis equals ten new cedis, okay?" He wrote the numbers below the first set.

"Right," said Torgbe, looking on closely.

"Okay. So one million old cedis equals one hundred new cedis, yes?"

"Yes." Whit wrote down the numbers.

"Now. That means five *million* old cedis is the same as five *hundred* new." He wrote it down.

I was getting slightly embarrassed for the spirit, who was waiting patiently behind the curtain while this currency conversion played out. "So the spirit is asking for five *hundred* new Ghana cedis, right?"

"No," said Torgbe firmly. "Fifty million old, five thousand new."

"Really?" said Whit.

"And a cow."

"Oh, the cow is not included in the price? How much is a cow?"

"Maybe three hundred cedis," said Torgbe.

"Old cedis?"

"New cedis."

"Wow," I said. "I don't have that much, and I'm not sure I can get it."

"When can you come back?"

"Well, I can come back any day, but I don't think I can get that kind of money."

"You will check and come back tomorrow," Torgbe commanded. I was starting to see what Kevin had meant when he said it's hard to extricate yourself from these guys. "Now, we will pray for you. Come."

Torgbe and his man Friday led us out of the hut, back into the glinting sun, next door into the other windowless temple room. We stepped into the dim light and almost fell over from the stench of rotting flesh. After our eyes adjusted to the dark, we saw, in the center of the floor, a large pile of cow horns and jawbones, still slippery with dark, coagulating blood. In a far corner I made out nine African peg drums of different sizes, stacked up. On the other side was a high altar topped by several wood sculptures of African priestesses and other traditional figures. In the center of the altar, piled almost to the ceiling, was another gruesome tableau of rotting animal bones—at least I hoped they were animal bones.

"You must kneel," said Torgbe, pointing to a goat hide in front of the altar. I got down on my knees over the blood-matted fur, trying to breathe through my mouth so as not to vomit from the vile odor of the room. "The spirit needs twenty cedis."

"I have only ten," I said.

"Okay." Clearly the spirit, as channeled through Torgbe, was negotiable.

I fished out the note. Torgbe set the crumpled bill on top of the cow bones. He chanted for several minutes. "You may go now," he said.

"Can we have our batteries back?"

We took our batteries and left, but not before Torgbe's apprentice got my cell phone number. We drove out, past the bamboo fence, past the sign with the mermaids and the knives, and we did not stop until we got home to Koforidua.

"You *ass*hole!" said Whit, speeding into town.

"What?"

"*What?*" he repeated in a mocking falsetto. "This guy's on our route, and if we blow him off he'll be pissed, and he'll totally fuck my business— not with his lame Donald Duck spirit but in real ways, like telling people not to buy the batteries. You asshole! This is all your fault. You need to talk to him and figure out how to get out of this gracefully. Maybe the spirit will need five hundred cedis, I don't know, but you need to figure it out before you slink out of here, asshole."

"I'll talk to the man tomorrow."

That night, the power went out. Torgbe called me twice over the next few days. I told him both times that I didn't have the money. I never went back.

# nine

# WILLY LOMAN IN THE CASBAH

**FALL 2009:** The bottom line

Pyramid scheme? Whit finally found a shopkeeper who
let him set up a display, albeit behind boxes of Tiger Heads.

## 1. Burn Rate

In September Burro had its first birthday and was still not breaking even; far from it. In fact, the trailing thirty-day revenue of about two hundred cedis was roughly one tenth of what Whit called his "burn rate" of two thousand cedis a month—another way of saying negative cash flow.* On the bright side, growth was phenomenal: revenue was doubling every two weeks. The new offering was catching on, so it appeared to be a question of conscripting enough agents, getting them trained, and getting the word out. Whit and Jan crunched the numbers and figured break-even (and possibly modest profit) would happen when the branch had roughly one hundred agents renting one hundred batteries each, so "100/100" became the rallying cry. Almost all of Burro's "corporate" energy in late summer was focused on signing new agents. Every morning the staff split into teams and fanned out across the region. One day it might be Jan and Rose in the truck, heading up north toward Bomase, while Adam and Whit took the Kia Pride (another used car Whit had bought, known in the United States as a Ford Festiva) south, through towns along the road to Mamfe, a busy junction town on the Akwapim Ridge just before the road descends into the dust and chaos of Accra. Kevin, meanwhile, spent a lot of time managing the twenty-six agents still working under the old, monthly rental system, a job that included preparing them (and their clients) for conversion to the pay-go plan in early September. On some days Adam would stay in the office and work on the books while Kevin and Whit, or Whit and Rose, or Jan and Kevin went off on the routes. It was a rotating chain of teams, everyone vying for time in the two vehicles because the alternative was taking *tro-tros*. Sometimes we would get stranded in a remote village with no *tro-tros* or taxis, and then we would walk, down dusty roads that traversed cocoa farms, thick bamboo stands, and high, grassy plateaus.

---

* The burn rate included salaries for the three Ghanaian employees plus operating expenses. It did not include Whit and Jan's travel expenses, or Jan's salary, all of which were paid from the U.S. holding company.

Sometimes we saw snakes, mostly small neon green varieties—almost Burro green—that probably weren't poisonous, but we didn't know, so we kept our distance. Once a python—a small one but a python just the same—slithered lazily across the trail in front of us. Had a local farmer been with us, he would have surely hacked it apart with his machete. Visitors often find this brutal, but snakes in Ghana kill people in very ugly ways. The Armed Forces Pest Management Board of the U.S. Department of Defense lists twenty-four venomous snakes in Ghana, including, besides pythons, many varieties of cobra, viper, adder, and mamba. Some carry venom that is hemotoxic—causing internal bleeding and death—but most are neurotoxic, shutting down brain functions like breathing and heartbeat. Death in either case is agonizing, and not fast enough. Some venomous snakes won't actually kill you; they just cause "tissue necrosis" (in the words of the Defense Department), requiring amputations. These are not anomalies. I couldn't find numbers for Ghana, but it's estimated that perhaps a thousand people every year die of snakebites across Africa, and many more thousands are wounded and maimed. Potentially deadly encounters with snakes are quite common in Ghana, and there is no 911, no ambulance to rush you to the ER for some antivenom. If you are in the bush in Ghana and you are bitten by an Egyptian cobra, you will die of respiratory failure within five hours.

Watching carefully for snakes, I tagged along with one or another of these groups (including the *tro-tro* excursions) on most days. We would pull up in a new town, survey the market and the shops, unload our plastic tubs full of batteries and flashlights, draw a crowd (not hard for a white person in these outposts) and start walking and talking—looking for the important people, the opinion leaders, maybe even the chief or at least a shopkeeper with a good reputation. Kevin and Adam and Rose would talk in Twi or Ewe or Ga; Whit and Jan and I would embellish in English (and sometimes French if the people were from Togo or Benin). Whit and I would make funny faces at the children who crept up to stare at us; they would run away squealing in laughter as we bared our teeth and shook our arms and pretended to be monsters. Then we would open our plastic bins and pull out our wares and demonstrate our batteries. Villagers would leave and return with radios and flashlights, and we would take them apart and pull out leaky Tiger Heads, sanding down rusty terminals (with scraps of sandpaper kept in our road kits) and inserting new Burro batteries. *"Ahaahh!"* they would say in appreciation as we turned on the radio and blasted them with their favorite station—hiplife or reggae or news or talk or soccer, whatever. *"Ahaahh!"* they would say again. And we would smile and say to the growing crowd, "Who would like to start saving money on batteries today?"

The towns had strange, exotic names like Huhunya, Agogo (as in "whiskey-*a-go-go*"), Tinkong, Nkurakan, Beware (*Beh-WAH-ray*), and Bo-somtwi (*Bo-SUM-chwee*). But after a few weeks they could as well have been Moline, Youngstown, Danbury, or Duluth. After a couple of months they all started to blur together—an endless brown palette of mud huts, fire pits, flinching dogs, fly-covered goats, peanut stews, tattered and stained laundry draped limply over frayed nylon lines, and half-naked children with their ceaseless cries of *"Obruni! Obruni!"*

"That's my name," I'd say, "don't wear it out."

*"Obruni!"*

*"Wo te brofo, anaa?"* I would ask. Do you speak English?

"Yes," they would say.

"My name is Max. What's yours?"

*"Obruni!"*

The daily word games with children devolved into a certain sameness, but at least it was fun to make them laugh. Far more tedious was the sales pitch. There were days when I felt if I had to listen to the battery spiel one more time I would crawl out of my skin, slither under a rock, and renounce my citizenship in the human race. But if you're going to be a good salesman, you have to get excited about your product every day, with every customer. It's new to them, no matter how familiar it seems to you. Before coming to Africa, I joked about finding Willy Loman in the Casbah. Now I was becoming him.

Almost every week brought a gong-gong, crucial for building brand awareness and acceptability in villages where new products, or better ways of buying existing products, were virtually unknown. The format had not changed since the first gong-gong in January—a formal introduction to the chief and elders, sometimes followed by a Christian prayer in the local language, then our pitch.

Not that any two gong-gongs were quite alike. In Mangoase, a cocoa-growing center of three thousand voters, the gong-gong man insisted that everyone speak through his new, out-of-the-box megaphone. This seemed of dubious necessity given that only nineteen citizens showed up for the gong-gong at the town well, and we could hear one another just fine without amplification. Maybe he felt a jolt of technology would help revive his town, which was long past its prime. Mangoase was once an important railway depot on the line between Accra and Kumasi, and its hilly streets were lined with stately colonial buildings. But the trains stopped running years ago—the tracks reverting to bush—and the only roads into town were washed-out dirt tracks. The colonial buildings were now faded and crumbling; despite an impressive public market basilica, Mangoase had the claustrophobic melancholy of a dying New England mill town.

Unfazed by his community's wounded pride, the gong-gong man jumped energetically from speaker to speaker with his megaphone, as if working the audience of a TV game show. Most of us were largely unfamiliar with the operation of a megaphone, and its employment by untrained hands presented no small amount of danger. If the person next to you was speaking, you had to duck when he turned his head, to avoid getting whacked by the device or, worse, suffering permanent hearing damage from a point-blank acoustic blast of the speaker—powered, I might add, by Burro batteries.

The pitch for those batteries had evolved under the new pay-go system. No longer were batteries "fresh, anytime you want," which reflected the monthly rental system of unlimited free recharges. Now our mantra was "better battery, half the price"—since a two-cedi Burro coupon book yielded sixteen individual refreshes, versus buying eight Tiger Heads for the same price. (To simplify the offer, the 1.50-cedi coupon booklet was changed to one cedi, which bought seven refreshes.) Whit and Jan perfected the pitch over several weeks, trying to boil it down to simple phrases, easily understood. They identified six reasons why Burro was a better battery:

1. Half the cost
2. More power
3. No-leak guarantee
4. Two in one (AA and D, using the adapter sleeve)
5. Cleaner and safer
6. First charge is free (you pay only deposit first time)

It seemed clear enough, but when Kevin, Rose, and Adam gave the pitch in one of the country's native languages, we couldn't understand what they were saying. And it often seemed like their spiel was taking a long time, even factoring in the consonant-laced African vocabularies. But over time we got better at recognizing their phrases, in part because many modern words have no local linguistic equivalent and are simply repeated in English—like *battery*, although in Twi the phrase we most heard was *battery-nie*, which means "these batteries." And apparently there is no way in Twi to say "better for the environment," because Kevin always said that in English.

After the pitch came questions and demonstrations. Then Whit would say, "So who wants to be the first person to start getting batteries for half the money?" Someone would step forward with a few wadded up cedi notes in his hand, and we would lead the crowd in applause.

Or not. Sometimes no one came forward. Sometimes no one showed up at all. One Friday in late August we arrived at two different gong-gongs in far-flung villages that somehow never got organized. This happened a lot, sometimes after driving for an hour down a road that was little more than a footpath. Sometimes the road itself ruined the gong-gong. One day, Jan and Rose were driving on a back road in the Kia when an exposed tree root punctured the sidewall of a tire. They jacked up the car and put on the spare—which was flat. They walked over a mile in the punishing sun to a village, where a man with a bicycle pump accompanied them on foot back to the car. They got home late, well after dark, hungry and tired. This sort of thing happened on an almost weekly basis.

Occasionally the gong-gong no-shows were understandable: someone had died in the village, and funeral arrangements had to be made quickly, out of respect and, in places with no refrigeration, sanitation. But sometimes the excuses boggled us: "It is cloudy, so the people lost track of the time." Never mind that virtually every adult in the realm had a cell phone with a clock. Time is simply not tracked precisely by people who live by the sun and the planting seasons. When rural Ghanaians do think about specific times, it is usually in the past tense—as in the time of the ancestors. Time as a future concept is rarely considered. Meetings will happen when they happen; what is the point of worrying about it? Likewise it is nearly impossible to get a Ghanaian to give you a realistic distance between villages. The next village is as far away as it always has been, and you will get there when you get there.

This Zen-like concept of time and distance, while charming and possibly even wise, made it difficult to do business in the conventional sense. Often the closest we could get to pinning down a gong-gong was for "Friday" or "Tuesday." We considered ourselves lucky if we could at least specify morning or afternoon.

You might think that the Ghanaians' laid-back approach to time would make them readily available to start a meeting as soon as we arrived, but no. Often we sat around an hour or more, watching goats have sex, waiting for things to get going. We occupied ourselves playing our usual games with the children. We started responding to their calls of "*Obruni!*" by pointing at them and saying "*O bebeni!*" (Oh, black man!), which made them laugh. I learned how to say "I am not a white man; I am a black man" in Twi ("*Menye obruni; meye bebeni*"), which got them thinking. Whit and I decided to teach them some American rap lingo, so we invented a greeting, recited with the appropriate hip-hop arm gestures:

"Yobruni!"

"'Sup, bebeni?" And so on.

In one village, out of boredom, Whit caught a striking red-speckled grasshopper. Knowing the African child's pastime of putting insects on "leashes" made of strings, Whit gave the bug to a small boy. He dropped it and stomped on it.

Often there would be something culturally edifying to watch, like the Krobo bead makers in Bomase. In the village of Twum, a man named Foster Appia made sturdy rattan market baskets while listening to his Burro-powered radio. One time I saw two men by the side of the road flip a live sheep onto its back, tie its legs together, load it into the trunk of a taxi-cab, and drive off. I thought that was pretty impressive, but the next day I saw a taxi with two sheep in the trunk. At one gong-gong, the chief, who had been drinking *apio*, was having trouble getting a sound out of the shell horn he used to start the meeting. Jan offered to try, and the villagers laughed. But Jan had played saxophone in school and was the bugler at her summer camp. They cheered when she belted out a perfect note.

One day Kevin asked if I could go with him to a gong-gong. "I prom-ised this village an *obruni*," he said, which always seemed to help drive interest in the batteries. "If you can't, no problem; I can tell them my white man has traveled."

"It's fine, I can be your white man," I said. But we got there and every-one was too busy: a government-sponsored malaria control program had villagers clearing brush from around their huts.

At a gong-gong in a school in Behanase, a man in an Obama T-shirt who had lost his right leg at the knee in a car accident was complaining to his neighbors that someone was stealing from his farm. "If I catch them I will cut off an arm," he said. "If a cripple like me can farm, then able-bodied people should be able to do their own farming."

Another time, Rose and I had a meeting with a chief in a small village called Meawm'ani. A gray-haired man in his sixties who wore a traditional African tunic, the chief seemed like a wise and thoughtful leader. But after examining a battery and listening to Rose's introduction, he demanded twenty cedis for organizing a gong-gong, a request that bordered on extor-tion. If he thought Rose would be a pushover, he was very mistaken.

"Twenty cedis!" said Rose. "I have never paid more than five cedis for a gong-gong."

"Okay, five," he said, "but you must pay me now."

"No," she replied. "I will give you two now, and three later if you make it happen."

"I want five now," he insisted, "and I will give you back three if it doesn't work out."

Rose shook her head. "You know, where we live there is electricity. We can go home tonight and turn on lights. So we are just trying to help you and your people in this village. Yes, we want to make some money, but we are not making that much." None at all so far, she might have added. The chief finally agreed.

The process of training agents was arguably even more important than the gong-gongs, because the agents would be on the front line of battery sign-ups every day. The gong-gongs were a key driver of initial interest in the program, but if the agents didn't get it—and feel inspired to promote it—the whole thing would collapse.

One day we trained three new agents in Amonfro, a village on a main road out of Koforidua, toward the Akwapim Ridge. One of the agents, Enoch, owned a small chemist shop in town; the other two, George and Monica, were shopkeepers in nearby, smaller villages. Whit began the training session by outlining the company's values:

"The first is *respect*—for you the agents, and the clients. We follow the Golden Rule of do unto others as you would want them to do unto you. We will always respect you and be honest with you, and we need you agents to show respect for the clients. And we hope you will have respect for us and the company and what we are trying to do.

"Number two is *innovate*. We are still learning. We are always looking for better ways to do things. We are a team, and we can go farther if we share ideas. So please do not hesitate to tell us when you have an idea for a way we can serve our customers better and help them do more.

"The final value is *empower*. Burro is about helping people do more. So talk to your customers about doing more. Our offering is very simple: better battery for the half the price. You need to spread the word that people can do more with our batteries.

"We will come to visit you two times a week to change batteries and collect names of new clients and money. Your commission is twenty percent on batteries, ten percent on merchandise like the phone charger. You can take your commission then, or if you like, we can hold it for safekeeping until you want it.* Are there any questions so far?"

"How do we sell the batteries?" asked George, a handsome, thoughtful man whose nearly identical (but not twin) brother was also an agent.

"That's a very good question," said Whit. "Let's talk about selling. When someone comes the first time to get batteries, you need to take a deposit of one cedi for each battery. This is very important because the battery is very expensive. You need to tell the client two very important things. The first thing is that the battery is not for sale. They are borrowing it. The second thing is that they can get back their deposit any time they want if they bring the battery back and do not take fresh.

"Now, the client has to join the program the first time. That's how you sell batteries. So the first time only, they must fill out the form."

Whit pulled out a printed form the size of a filing card. "You have on this card client one, client two, and client three. First you get their surname—the name they gave at school. Then you write down any other names, their phone number—"

"Not all have phones," said Monica, a quiet young woman.

"That's okay," said Whit, "but please ask. It will help us to market to them, which will mean more sales for you." (Cell phone penetration in Ghana reached 75 percent by the end of 2010.)

He went on: "Then you get their birth date or age—if they don't know how old they are, just make a guess. Check whether they are male or female, on grid or off grid; that means if they have light. You mark the date they started, how many batteries, and if they took them alone or with an adapter. That's it. You only need to do this the first time they sign up. Any questions?"

---

* Roughly 90 percent of agents were asking Burro to hold their commission for a month or more. In that sense the company was functioning as a rudimentary bank for agents with no other savings account. Stashing money with Burro prevented theft and eliminated the cultural pressure to share earnings with extended family—everyone from siblings to cousins. Burro did not pay interest but did not charge any fees—unlike the informal local savings banks known as *susus*, which charged customers for the service of saving their money. In the developing world, this is called earning negative interest.

George again: "What about the coupons?"

"Another very good question. When they use the batteries and come back for fresh, they have three choices. If they want to pay half the price of Tiger Head, they must buy a coupon book for two cedis." He held up the book. "With this they get sixteen batteries, or eight pair. And now, for a short-time promotion, they get four extra. So twenty batteries for two cedis.

"They can also buy one battery at a time, for twenty pesewa each. We call this *pay as you go*. It's still less than Tiger Head, but not as great a savings.

"Finally, if they can't afford two cedis but want a better deal than pay as you go, they can buy a one-cedi book, which gives you seven batteries.

"One more thing on the commission: with the coupons, you get ten percent when you sell it and ten percent when the coupon is redeemed. So you should always redeem coupons, even from clients who did not buy them from you. If anyone has a coupon and a fallen battery, they are entitled to get a fresh battery—even if you don't know them—and you will get ten percent commission on their coupon.

"Now, we would like to set you up with fifty batteries and twenty adapters. You put the fallen batteries in the red tub; we will pick those up and give you fresh. Keep the fresh in the green tub. Please do not mix them up! Are there any more questions?"

None.

"Okay, thank you," said Whit. "If in four weeks you are still selling any Tiger Heads from your shops, you are doing something wrong."

He was kidding, because he knew Tiger Heads had one clear advantage. One day we watched a man listen carefully to the Burro pitch in front of a shop, then plunk down one cedi for four Tiger Heads. Whit shrugged. "We are definitely not the cheapest battery today. You can get Tiger Heads cheaper the first time."

Kevin said, "That man stood there for a long time listening. He wished he could get the Burros, but he needed four and did not have the money for the deposit."

## 2. Smoking Wheels

Batteries were not the only unpredictable technology in the business. Burro's "Avon lady" model depended on vehicles to deliver fresh batteries to villages along routes that Whit, Jan, and the employees had designed. When the business was new and concentrated along just a few main roads leading out of town, route management was relatively simple. But as business expanded in several directions and Burro started racking up dozens of agents in an ever-widening circle around Koforidua, scheduling the cars became a math puzzle. In particular the route teams competed briskly for use of the Tata, which had four-wheel drive and high clearance and could go where the tiny Kia could not. There was little room for error in the schedule; if someone came back late from a gong-gong or a meeting with a new agent, events for the rest of the day tumbled off the calendar, like a blizzard at O'Hare rippling into flight delays across the country. Complicating matters were Ghana's punishing roads, which sent both cars into the shop constantly. Flat tires were relatively easy to fix; a major breakdown was inevitable.

One Tuesday morning in August, Whit, Adam, and I were driving the Kia to Mamfe to train two new shopkeepers as Burro agents. It was a key expansion, the closest we had come yet to Accra: one shop was in the busy *tro-tro* station and another on the town's main roundabout. Both had the potential to move tons of batteries, but we had almost no experience in urban, electrified markets, where customers would almost certainly be more transient and anonymous. Would they return the batteries?

Suddenly, rounding a tight curve at about fifty miles an hour, the Kia shuddered violently and swerved right. "Hold on, kids," said Whit as he gripped the wheel and pulled hard left, trying to stay on the road.

"Whoa, that doesn't feel like a flat," I said.

"I think it's a wheel bearing," said Whit. He drifted to the side of the road and limped another hundred feet to get past the blind curve. Fortunately there was no open gutter along this stretch, but the shoulder was still nonexistent. Overloaded trucks, hauling tomatoes and bananas to

Accra, were bearing down on us at high speed, horns blaring and stones flying. We pressed open the doors a crack and escaped into the tall elephant grass along the side of the road. The right front wheel was smoking from the hub. It was starting to rain.

"This business is hard," said Whit in a mock whine. The metaphor nobody mentioned was obvious: were the wheels also falling off the business? "It was so much easier to sell board games," he added.

"And as I recall you took the bus to work."

"I did."

Whit got Kevin on the phone. "We're past Adenya junction, near Kwamoso. I'm wondering if we should call a mechanic in Kof-town or get Samuel up from Accra." (There is virtually no concept of tow trucks in Ghana; most mechanics, few of whom have their own cars, travel with their tools by taxi or *tro-tro* and make repairs at breakdown sites, working in traffic. Often they have to travel twice—once to assess the nature of the repair, then back to get parts. If you can be sure of the problem in advance, your mechanic can arrive with the right parts the first time.)

Kevin advised calling Samuel, Charlie's mechanic in Accra, who had in fact checked out this car and recommended it for Burro—not least for the very good reason that it is a common car in Ghana with readily available parts. Whit reached Samuel, explained the situation, and hung up. "He can't leave Accra until noon, so he'd get up here on the *tro-tro* around two." It was now nine-fifteen.

Whit called Kevin again and asked him to contact the Koforidua mechanic we'd used in the past. "Maybe he can get here sooner than this afternoon," said Whit. We sent Adam back to the office in a *tro-tro*; no sense in three of us eating dust all morning when Adam could be working on the books. Whit and I walked ahead another hundred yards to a small turnoff—nothing more than a path to a small settlement in the forest—where a woman and her two young children were selling bags of gari under a bamboo shelter. "If we can get the car here, we can pull it off the road and jack it up," said Whit.

"Well, the bearing's obviously fried so I don't think we can hurt it any more," I said, conveniently ignoring the unpleasant possibility of toasting the entire hub with more driving. "Just take it slow." We nursed the Kia up to the clearing, backed into a spot next to the gari stand, and hauled out the jack as the gari lady and her children looked on curiously. Kevin called back with news that he could come down in the Tata with the mechanic in an hour or so. "We got the tire off," said Whit, "and it's definitely the bearing, maybe also the hub. But I doubt he can pull the bearing without a press, so he should probably bring a whole hub. I'll leave it up to him, but don't let him come down here without parts."

Whit and I hailed a taxi and sped up the ridge to Mamfe for our training session with the two shopkeepers. Obviously, we were late. Fortunately, shopkeepers are usually around their shops. We sat in the usual plastic patio chairs, but this time we weren't under a mango tree in a village with a gong-gong man. This time we gathered under the awning of the Redeemer shop at the noisy *tro-tro* station. In case anyone might miss it, the store said REDEEMER REDEEMER REDEEMER across the cornice. Redeemer sold the usual mix of everything, Africa's version of a New England general store—from aluminum bowls to spaghetti to matches to cans of Malta and penny candy in jars. And batteries—both Tiger Head Ds and Sun Watt AAs.

The owner, Emmanuel, was a gray-haired man in a bright red traditional African robe with fancy black piping that is typically worn for funerals. He greeted us with the usual Ghanaian smile and warmth—"You are welcome," he said—and went off to get his wife, Janet Twumasi.

It soon transpired that Janet was the real boss, for as soon as we sat down she announced she was no longer interested in selling our batteries. "It's too complicated," she said. This was not a total surprise, as she had relayed as much to Kevin a few days earlier. He had talked her back into the program, and as far as we knew she was on board. But now she was waffling again. Whit whipped out his phone and dialed Kevin, then put her on. Several minutes of Twi later, she was back in the program, but I didn't sense much enthusiasm. It seemed clear that the conventional Burro training process—starting with the inspiring rundown of the company's values and commitments to empowering Africans—would fall flat here.

"You better cut to the chase," I murmured to Whit.

"No kidding."

We were joined by Christy, the daughter of the shopkeeper a hundred yards away in the roundabout. Christy seemed more plugged in to the concept. "If someone comes in to buy Tiger Head, I will tell them that Burro is a better deal," she said.

No such insight from Janet, who seemed mystified by the whole coupon-book thing. She was, however, laser-focused on the twenty-pesewa individual purchase offer—even though that cost customers more money and earned her less commission. Undoubtedly she was planning to push individual recharges, and not even tell customers about the "complicated" money-saving coupons.

We walked over to Christy's father's shop, where she worked behind a five-foot-long glass display case that contained nothing but packaged cookies—I counted a dozen varieties of chocolate chips, ginger snaps, and others. I'm no expert in merchandising, but it seemed an odd use of prime retail frontage considering the cornucopia of wares on offer in the shop—especially as each cookie brand was piled several packages across. Assuming it was essential that her customers see every brand of cookie available, wouldn't it suffice to display one example of each? I caught Whit's eye and nodded toward the display case. He politely suggested to Christy that she might consolidate the cookies and make a little room for a stack of Burro batteries. She nodded in agreement. Whit and I looked at each other as if to say, "No time like the present!" But that's not how time works in Ghana. Several days later, there were still no batteries on display—only cookies—and this was a merchant who seemed excited about Burro.

Whit and I clambered into a packed, sweaty *tro-tro* for the forty-minute ride back to Kof-town. "So you're back on the bus after all, Whit," I said. He ignored me and turned to the *New York Times* on his smart phone, looking up only to glance at our sad, broken-down Kia as we flew past it, still jacked up in the clearing by the gari stand.

A few days later, Kevin reported that both Mamfe shopkeepers were still pushing back on the process of taking down clients' cell phone numbers and other information. "Christy says many people do not want to fill it out," he said. "Also the people at Redeemer say it is too much trouble."

"Okay, then let's close them down," replied Whit.

"So we lose that money?" asked Kevin.

"Yes, if they won't do it our way. Look, I hear you—maybe long-term we do it some other way, but I'm just not ready to give that up yet, for several reasons. Fraud is one, also marketing and brand building. The sign-up makes it clearer that the customer is entering a program, not just buying a Tiger Head. That's really important. I mean, I think we have a really compelling offer here, and frankly I don't want to do what Cranium did with Walmart, which is when they say 'Bend over,' we say 'How far?' So you should tell agents that gathering this information will help us to market to their clients, which will earn them more money. And another way to put it is that people are giving us one cedi for a battery that's worth like six or eight cedis. So we are essentially loaning the client several cedis. Ask them, would they give away five cedis to a complete stranger without getting some information from them?"

"But if someone wanted to steal," said Kevin, "he could just give a false name and phone number." Kevin was beginning to sound like Charlie.

"Right, but most people won't," said Whit. "There may well be some theft, but we don't want to make it easy for them. And I think some people will just forget, or lose batteries, and this gives us a way to track them. Again, Kevin, I hear you on this. But we need to test it. If we never test it in a big urban market, we'll never know if it works or not. We need leadership from you guys in the field on this. You can't seem to be waffling and say, 'I'll go to the obrunis and see what they say.' You need to be in charge and explain it."

"Oh no no no," said Kevin. "I will explain it to them."

"Okay, good," said Whit. "Keep in mind that when we get smart cards, which is the holy grail, it's not gonna be any easier, because agents are still gonna have to fill out the card when they sign a new client so we track their usage and make offerings. So this information is a huge advantage to us and the agents, and you have to make that clear to them."

Most of Burro's business was still in small villages around Koforidua, where personal relationships with agents and clients made a huge difference. So even while expanding to the big city, we were talking about seeding goodwill in villages—the process of greeting chiefs, queen mothers, and youth leaders and giving them free battery coupons (they still needed to sign up and pay their battery deposit) in order to spread the word. "That's a very good thing to do," said Adam, whose late father was an Ewe sub-chief in the Volta community of Adaklu, actually a collection of thirty-nine villages around a sacred mountain of the same name. "The chiefs can be very helpful to us."

Or not. One day we trained a shopkeeper in the largely Ewe village of Mintakrom, where the chief had seemed cool to us. After sitting through a one-hour training session, the man stood up and spoke to Adam in Ewe. "He says the commission is not enough for him."

"Okay, I respect that," said Whit. "We'll find another shop owner."

"He says they will all say the same thing."

"Do you interpret that to mean they've been told to say that?"

"Yes."

We drove on. "Adam, what about the whole schnapps thing?" Whit asked. The traditional gift to a chief is a bottle of Dutch schnapps, which costs anywhere from five to ten cedis, depending on quality—and the chiefs know the difference. "We've been burning through cases of schnapps, and I'm not sure it's really necessary."

"If you are just stopping by to meet a chief, then I would say no," said Adam. "That's more for a formal meeting with the chiefs and the elders."

"They won't be offended if we don't always bring schnapps?"

"Oh no."

"That's good, because I see huge value in this approach Jan has been using of just pulling off the road, finding a group of people, and building enthusiasm. That creates a very different dynamic than showing up and immediately going to the chief. All of a sudden it's very proscribed—you know, the chief says, 'This guy will work with you, he will show you around.' We don't get to tell our story and pick who we would pick to be the agent. We get stuck with the chief's son or something. So we need to balance the formal approach and the gong-gongs with the guerrilla tactic. And yeah, I can see where we should then go greet the chief and say hello—you know, 'If you have time next week we'd love to sit down with you and the elders and explain the program.'"

When the routes started overlapping, banter between the teams grew more pointed. Jan and Rose came back one evening with the news that they'd secured a potential agent in the key junction town of Nkurakan. "You know, the guy in the polio shirt," Jan said.

"*Polo* shirt?" said Whit.

"No, *polio* shirt, like Hayford wears—the polio eradication Rotary Club shirt. Well, actually it *is* a polo shirt, so a polo polio shirt. Anyway, he was great, showed us all around town, actually made us late for a meeting."

"Wait a minute," said Whit. "This is gonna cause problems because Nkurakan is a nexus for both our routes, and Kevin and I already had our sights on Yoko Ono in that town. She has the best shop."

"There's a woman named Yoko Ono in Nkurakan?" I asked.

"Yes. We drive through Nkurakan twice a week," said Jan.

"So do we," said Whit.

"Well, Kevin already said it was okay."

"Look, Jan, keep your mitts off our turf in Nkurakan."

I never settled the issue of the woman named Yoko Ono. The guy with the polo polio shirt turned out to be a dud.

## 3. Secret Farms

Out in the rural villages, we started ramping up the guerrilla forays— touching down in a new location and identifying our agents and shops first, while still being careful to pay respects to the leaders and schedule gong-gongs, which usually led to lots of new sign-ups.

One day Jan, Rose, and I headed north from Huhunya, following a dirt road that runs past Boti Falls, a one-hundred-foot cascade and one of the country's major scenic attractions. Joining me in the backseat of the Kia was our newest agent, a smart young man I'll call Nkansah, who plied these roads weekly (on foot and by bush taxi) as a "medicine man," delivering drugs to villagers.

"What kind of drugs do you deliver?" I asked Nkansah as we bounced along.

"Mostly painkillers," he said. "Farmers hurt their backs a lot. Also Chinese herbal medicines for hypertension. You drink it in tea. I bring a machine to measure blood pressure."

"That's really a problem here?" I asked, wondering how people who did so much hard physical labor could be hypertense.

"It's a very big problem in Ghana," he said. "Too much palm oil in the diet. There is also a lot of diabetes."

Nkansah's genuine concern for the health of these villagers belied his long-term goal in life, which was apparently to become the Sammy Glick of Ghana. He was diligently saving his money, he said, so that he could afford tuition for business school in Accra. He wanted to study marketing. Already he was combining his health-care expertise with business acumen: "My uncle and I have brought some moringa cuttings from Tamale, and we are raising our own crop to sell for diabetes patients." (Studies have shown that the leaves of the moringa, the so-called miracle tree, which Jonas had told me cured ninety-nine ailments, can help control glucose levels.)

We turned left at the Don't Mind Your Wife Drinking and Chop Bar,* then headed deep into the bush on a bad road to the twin villages of Opesika and Sutri (the first was an Akwapim tribal stronghold, the second Krobo). Jan was getting concerned that these villages were too far off the route track, too difficult to service, but Nkansah insisted: "I will come every Thursday and the people will be ready then. There is a lot of opportunity here." Jan relented, and we drove on to the villages, which turned out to be unusually pristine. Almost every house looked freshly plastered and painted, as was the shared school. A small health clinic seemed well stocked and was staffed by two workers. The children spoke excellent English—sign of a good (meaning well-paid) teacher. Opesika and Sutri felt like Hollywood movie versions of African villages.

We got out of the car, and Nkansah immediately started moving from door to door and shop to shop, showing batteries and launching into his spiel. Just about every person got it immediately and promptly whipped out cash for several batteries—lots of cash. Typically, when poor villagers

* *Chop* is the Ghanaian slang for food.

make the important lifestyle decision to sign up for Burro, they carefully unwrap their savings from a handkerchief or skirt tie—a few filthy cedi notes and pocket change. But these people were flashing the Ghanaian version of a Philadelphia bankroll. Just about every customer paid with a crisp, new ten-cedi note, quickly draining our cash box of change. When one guy pulled out a twenty (the first I had ever seen in Ghana outside of a bank), I shot Jan a look; she raised her eyebrows. On the drive back, Jan asked Nkansah where these villagers got all their money.

"Oh, they have secret farms," he replied.

"Secret farms?"

"Indian hemp. Marijuana. They grow marijuana." Nkansah said this as if the crop in question were rutabagas, or pomegranates—a curious specialty item in the grocery store perhaps, but nothing out of the normal agricultural sphere. This was surprising because Ghana is not some stoner's paradise; Bob Marley may be the most popular musician in the country, but his drug of choice is strictly illegal here—possession can bring a sentence of ten years' hard labor—and not at all common outside a few Rastafarian enclaves in beach communities frequented by student travelers. "A farmer can sell a sack of Indian hemp for one hundred fifty Ghana cedis," Nkansah the entrepreneur added. "Very good business."

"Indeed," said Jan, no doubt mentally comparing hemp profits to Burro's languid balance sheet. "Do they hide it in between their regular crops?"

"Oh no, they just plant the whole field with it," he said. "When the police come, the farmers pay them."

Coincidentally, the very next day Whit saw an article in one of the papers headlined POLICE WILL "NOT RUSH" IN YILO KROBO NARCOTIC CASE. Yilo Krobo was the district we had been driving through the day before. "The Police Administration says it would 'not rush' to prosecute police officers alleged to have been taking bribes from Indian hemp farmers at Yilo Krobo," the article began. Officials said they would instead follow due process and conduct an orderly investigation, after some politicians complained that police bribery had encouraged more farmers in the region to take up hemp farming. Given that the crop has brought obvious prosperity to Krobo communities and (to my observation) no local drug problem whatsoever, it seemed likely that any political pressure to "clean up" the district was window dressing.

If only every new village were as flush as the secret farmers. After a one-hour gong-gong in Twum, a village on the other side of the route, with no secret farms, the large crowd fell silent. "I guess what I want to know," said Whit, "is why would anyone still use Tiger Head?"

A few people finally straggled up, mostly out of curiosity. Others admitted they simply had no money at the time. And for others, the issue of timing loomed large: someone who has just bought a new set of Tiger Heads needs to wait until those run down before buying Burro replacements. As we drove off in the dusk, lunking down a warped dirt road, Whit reflected: "It's increasingly apparent that this business is brain-dead stupid simple and really hard at the same time." It was getting dark fast, we'd never had lunch, and we were looking at nearly an hour's drive home. It was a road we knew as well as one another, but you can never get to know the potholes because they change daily, so we stayed vigilant, trying to avoid fatal complacency. "But we're gonna change this country," said Whit, banging the steering wheel. "We're gonna change this country one battery at a time." That was when I began to see Whit as the gong-gong man.

## 4. Heads or Tails

Lunch on the road was usually the most basic street food: salty boiled peanuts (just like the kind you get in the American South), grilled plantains, an ear of grilled corn, sometimes a hard-boiled egg with homemade hot sauce (tomatoes, rock salt, onions, and searing Scotch bonnet chilies, pulverized with a mortar and pestle), all of it washed down with purified water in five-hundred-milliliter plastic "sachets." But this simple repast was rarely enough for Kevin, whose knowledge of Ghanaian cuisine was encyclopedic and in constant need of fact-checking. He ate perpetually and with abandon. Entire dried mackerel, heads and all, disappeared into his mouth like a sea lion. I too enjoyed the ubiquitous dried fish of Ghana (in a country with very little refrigeration, every size and species of marine life, from

minnows to tuna to shrimp and clams, is preserved by smoking or salting),
but eventually swore off it on sanitary grounds; it was simply impossible to
know how it had been handled. Whit simply hated everything about it. For
him, the very smell of dried fish—and it was pungent—filled him with in-
choate revulsion, although we both liked the fresh tilapia from Lake Volta.

Not everything Kevin ate agreed with me. He exhibited a passion for
deep-fried chunks of cocoyam that to my palate tasted (and to my eyes
looked) like Ivory soap. And he reserved his greatest ardor for fufu, the
gooey Ghanaian staple that Whit and I both agreed was not so much awful as forgettable. Kevin could go only so many days without tucking into
a massive sticky ball of fufu, and I'm not counting his dinner, which for all
I knew included fufu every evening. One day, scouting new territory up on
the ridge with Whit, the fufu jones got ahold of him.

"Kevin browbeat me into fufu for lunch today," said Whit that night
over dinner at the Capital View Hotel. "I told him, 'Dude, I'll be honest
with you. I've got a real problem eating with my hands.'"

"You're eating with your hands right now," I pointed out.

Whit dropped a French fry on his plate and glared at me.

"I told Kevin I'd eat fufu if I could use a knife and fork, but if that was
gonna cause an international incident, we better forget it. He said fine. So
we get to this place and there's like two choices: fufu with brown goat
soup and fufu with brown fish soup. The goat looked like pieces of gristle.
The fish soup at least had recognizable cross-sections of fish, but there
were also lots of heads and fins floating around in there. You had a choice
of one or two pieces of meat. I ordered the fish with two pieces, figuring
the chances were fifty-fifty that I'd get some meat and not just heads."

"Maybe you could flip a coin and get heads or tails."

"I think the tails are for garnish. Anyway, Kevin got the goat. I couldn't
tell what the hell those pieces were. It was like goat kneecaps or fetuses or
something. Of course he wolfed it down. I think he ate the bones."

Yet even Kevin had his limits, his culinary no-go zones. One day, in
the village of Nyame Bekyere (which means "God will provide" in Twi, and
is the name of possibly six dozen villages in Ghana), Whit was meeting
our agent, Nana Bekoe, while Kevin and I waited in the car. Nana, an Ewe,

ran a local drinking spot whose walls were plastered in posters of Flight Lieutenant Jerry Rawlings, the former military coup leader. Like his political hero, Nana was a man of status, albeit in a very small village—a distinction that in his mind excused him from a life of drudgery and toil. He spent most of his time engaged in heated games of checkers under a palm-frond canopy next to his drinking spot, surrounded by his acolytes and multiple litters of mangy, featherweight cats. When it became apparent that being a Burro agent meant distracting interruptions of actual work, Nana recruited a gang of older boys and young men to be his battery runners. The details of this business arrangement remained obscure to Whit, but he assumed Nana collected a hefty percentage as the godfather of this makeshift syndicate.

After a few minutes, Whit returned to the car and said, "That was weird. I was petting one of Nana's kittens and he said, 'When they get bigger I will give you one.' I said 'Yeah, just what I need is a cat.' And he said 'Don't you eat cat?'"

Whit turned to Kevin, who was driving. "He was kidding, right?"

"Oh no," said Kevin. "The Ewe, they eat cats."

"Oh come on," said Whit. "You're not serious!"

"Yes, they do. They call it Joseph."

"*Joseph?* You mean, like pig is pork, cow is beef, cat is Joseph?"

"Yes."

"I don't believe you. I'm calling Charlie."

"He will confirm it."

Whit picked up his phone. "Good afternoon, Charlie. I'm calling you with a quick question. Kevin says that the Ewe eat cats, and they call it Joseph. Is it true?"

There was a brief pause.

"Really! Do you eat it yourself? Okay, thanks, Charlie."

He hung up. "Charlie says it's true. He said, 'Don't ever leave your cat with an Ewe.'"

"I told you it was so," says Kevin.

Back in the office, I decided to confirm this revelation with a second Ewe source. "Adam, do you eat cat?"

The young accountant looked up from his laptop. "Yes."

"Joseph, right?"

"Yes. It's very nice."

"Nice? Yes, most people would agree that cats are nice. Why is it called Joseph?"

"I don't know why," he replied, pondering the question as if for the first time.

"How do you prepare it?"

"Oh, in a stew," he said with a tone of surprise at the inanity of the query. Everything in Ghana is prepared in a stew.

"What does it taste like?"

He thought for a minute. "I don't know how to describe it."

"Like chicken?"

"No, it doesn't taste like chicken. More like rabbit. Do you eat rabbit?"

"Indeed," I replied, which made me wonder why we find it so repulsive to eat certain pets (assuming one eats any kind of meat at all). The Ewe also keep cats as pets, but they are somehow able to compartmentalize Tabby while dining on Joseph. But they regard the consumption of dog as absolutely barbaric. I posted the whole Ewe cat food thing on Facebook and got a lot of responses. My friend Steve Vickery suggested serving cat topped with dried cat food, "for extra crunch." Don Rainville wondered why we abhor eating pets since we have no problem eating vegetables, even though we keep house plants. It's a good question, but I decided I would politely turn down offerings of Joseph, unless doing so would cause grave offense to a village chief.

## 5. Do More

The first counterfeit coupons showed up on 9/11. To a casual observer they were not obviously fake, but Jan was no casual observer. It was Friday, the end of a hectic week and her last day in the office before a three-month trip home. Over the summer, while Jan worked in Ghana, she and her partner Leslie had bought a house in Medford, Oregon—four hundred miles from her previous home in Seattle—where Leslie had taken a job as pharmacy manager for a local hospital. Between packing for her trip and looking forward to seeing her new home, Jan could easily have been distracted enough to miss the eight fake coupons in the cash box from that day's route. But she thought they looked funny, so she looked again. They were the right size—one and a half by two and three quarter inches—with the right words ("ONE BURRO EXCHANGE, FRESH BATTER-IES ANYTIME"), but the font looked just a little too small. And the image of the Burro battery with the donkey logo was grainy. What's more, the fakes had a dotted-line border around the edge, like a cutting guide, which the real coupons did not. Also there was no staple mark; these coupons had never been part of a booklet. Obviously someone had made a copy of an original coupon, then copied it several times more, compromising the resolution just enough to be noticeable if you took the time to compare. "Hey, Whit, look at this," Jan said.

"Holy shit," he replied, staring at the bogus slips, holding them up to the light. "Wow. That didn't take long."

"Definitely from Bomase," said Jan. "It's the only place we collected at least eight tickets today. And they came from either Seth or Dorothy," two Burro agents there who had redeemed a bunch of coupons. Seth was a smooth-talking farmer with a cool straw hat whom we had met on that very first day in Bomase; Dorothy was the wife of a former assemblyman and the town's youth leader. Both were high-performing agents and among the first under the new system.

"Do you think Seth or Dorothy know?" I asked.

"I don't know, but I doubt it," said Whit. "Most likely one of their clients, without their knowledge."

"Just one?" I said. "Don't kid yourself. Those Krobos have been copying Venetian glass beads since the fifteenth century. Even the Arab traders couldn't tell them apart. Have you ever looked at some of the patterns on those things? Faking up some Burro coupons would be child's play to them. You're in deep shit. And did I mention they also grow dope?"

"This is nuts," Whit said. "As if this business weren't hard enough." He slumped in a chair and opened a beer. "Today I drove for ten hours, covered a hundred and eighty kilometers, and came home with forty cedis and some counterfeit coupons. Totally nuts. We need a lot more volume."

We were all feeling a bit violated by this breach of faith. Charlie always said, "You try to help poor people in this country, they just take advantage of you." Whit and I had always hoped he was just being overly fatalistic, but maybe he was right. Maybe you couldn't help poor people. Obviously bad guys were out there watching us, looking for ways to game us. Fix this leak and they'll spring another one, somewhere else in the system. *Do More*, indeed. They were mocking us!

"What are you gonna do?" I asked Whit.

"Nothing yet. Wait and see. Let's monitor the situation, see who's turning them in. I don't even want to tell the agents yet. When we find out who it is, maybe we pay them a visit with the assemblyman and the police. We may need to do a currency call-in—you know, exchange your old coupons for new ones, and after thirty days we won't honor any coupons without the new stamp. Shit, I don't know. This business is hard."

ten

# A CULTURAL DESIGN

**FALL 2009:** The per diem

Night school: Jan leading the kids in an educational card game.

## 1. Feeding Time

The rain dampened the dust and cleared the view from our second-floor terrace of the twin fifteen-hundred-foot hills that rose, like the humps of a Bactrian camel, a mile southeast of downtown Koforidua. They are known as the Obuotabiri Mountains, and tradition says they are the home of the local gods as well as mysterious dwarves. That legend is somewhat trivialized by the mountains' current status as a broadcasting relay station—eight blinking antennae sprout from the highest peak. But just as modern African village chiefs enjoy listening to soccer on the radio, so perhaps do the gods of this noisy merchant town find it expedient to keep abreast of the mortals through the evening news.

Thanks to the broadcast towers, a rutted dirt track to the summit is sporadically maintained and negotiable by truck seasonally and by foot always, affording a fine view of town and a refreshing breeze. Yet despite this relatively reliable access to a pleasant vantage and clime, human habitation ends about a third of the way up; from there, houses give way to slopes dense with tall grass and banana palms, above which tower eighty-foot-tall silk cotton trees with wide, smooth gray trunks and umbrella tops. Below this verdant crown the dirt brown city, much of which we could take in from our terrace, sprawls chaotically, and watching the passage of humanity through this maze was an endless source of entertainment. On any given day there were parades of youth groups running through the streets carrying school banners and led by frantic drummers; groaning livery trucks unloading dozens of market-bound farmers from the outlands, who hefted coffin-sized sacks of cassava root; rattletrap *tro-tros* bound for the town of Suhum and heralded by the throaty *"Su-Su-Su!"* call of the driver's mate; and men and women carrying loads on their heads that defied physics. I distinctly recall one man, who in America could find good work in the rings of Barnum & Bailey, balancing a full sheet of plywood on his head while riding a bicycle.

Yet as far as some of the locals were concerned, the real show was up on the veranda where the *obrunis* lived. We were out there all the time—it functioned as our living room—and since no other white people lived in the city center, our highly public existence was, for them, a spectacle worthy of footlights. From morning until late at night we endured the interminable cries of "white man!" and *"obruni!"* from strangers who mostly just wanted us to wave. Nothing wrong with that, of course—except that by the tenth or eleventh wave it got a little old, and it was still morning. By the end of the day, it could actually be anxiety-inducing. I realized with discomfort what it must be like to be a celebrity, and I suddenly felt sympathy as I never had before with the plight of the famous, who so defensively guard their privacy.

We weren't famous, of course, just very different from most humans in their orbit, which I suppose made us rather nonhuman in their eyes. I don't recall exactly when I began to feel like an animal on display, but I do recall a torpid night, just before dinner, when I turned to the assembled onlookers, some of them particularly strident in their catcalls, and yelled, "The zoo is closed, it's feeding time," before disappearing through the screen door.

**One day out on the veranda,** I was reading Ryszard Kapuscinski's 2001 book *The Shadow of the Sun,* and I think I found my muse. Not the author—the late Polish journalist and *New Yorker* contributor who filed thoughtful, funny, and harrowing dispatches from Africa starting in 1958 (his first stop was newly independent Ghana)—but rather one of his subjects in the book, another journalist, named Felix Naggar.

In the early 1960s, Naggar was the Hemingway-esque East African bureau chief for Agence France Presse. He lived in a sumptuous villa in Nairobi's exclusive Ridgeways neighborhood, which he apparently rarely left—gathering news over the phone and dictating stories to his staff of Indian copyboys, who sat at teleprinters and transmitted his reports to Paris. To hear Kapuscinski tell it, Naggar was a Mozart of the news dispatch: perfectly composed stories flowed effortlessly from his mouth, ready for the printed page. With no need to labor over his copy, he had plenty of time on his hands for a trifecta of more edifying pursuits, namely cigars, cuisine, and crime novels. "He was either supervising his cooks—he had the best kitchen in all of Africa," writes Kapuscinski, "or sitting in front of the fireplace reading crime novels. In his mouth he held a cigar. He never removed it—unless it was just for a moment, in order to swallow a bite of baked lobster or taste a spoonful of pistachio sorbet." The phone would ring, a source would reveal a tidbit of breaking news, and Naggar would dictate the breathless dispatch to his aides. At that point, says Kapuscinski, Naggar would "then return either to the kitchen, where he would stir something in the pots, or before the fireplace, to continue reading."

This was a job I was cut out for. I was already the de facto chef at Burro world headquarters, where among my duties I had taken on the task of daily market shopping and dinner prep. (The alternative was eating in one of the town's handful of vile restaurants, as Jan rarely had time to cook and Whit seemed incapable of making steam from boiling water.) I have enjoyed cooking since childhood, as much for the process as the food itself. I began, like so many cooks, at my mother's side but soon moved on to cookbooks. As an adult, and after years cooking in restaurants, I graduated beyond the need for cookbooks except as they provided broad outlines for unfamiliar dishes or critical measurements for more technical creations. Over the years, in Europe, New York, and Los Angeles, I found myself drawn to the public green markets and food stalls, and I gained confidence in heading out to shop with no particular menu or ingredient list in mind but rather determined, like a Neanderthal to the hunt, to see what I could find and cook whatever followed.

I didn't think about any of this before coming to Ghana, but soon after I arrived it became clear that my hunter-gatherer abilities were about to take on new significance. With nothing even remotely resembling a Western grocery store in Koforidua, food shopping was a daily scavenger hunt, and improvisation a survival skill. Most of our shopping was done in the town's sprawling and odiferous public market, a maze of wooden stalls wedged

into narrow walkways bisected by open drain channels clogged with vegetable trimmings in various states of compost. Here, every day of the
week, anyone with a few cedi notes in his pocket could choose from hundreds of neatly constructed pyramids of tomatoes, peppers, onions, garlic, ginger, cabbage, cucumbers, avocados (charmingly known as "butter
pears"), limes, lettuce ("salad leaves"), mangoes, papayas, pineapples,
plantains, bananas, coconuts, rice, peanuts, eggs with anemic pale yellow
yolks (precisely why I don't know), green beans, dried beans, yams, egg-
plants ("garden eggs"), dried and smoked fish and shellfish of every size,
and (in the rainy season) wild mushrooms and live snails as large as a
baseball. In other sections of the market you could find bolts of fabric, handmade leather shoes, hair weaves, charcoal, cookware, and stiff switches
with which to beat your child.

Considering that many African countries regularly contend with drought
and famine (as did Ghana in 1982), the availability of so much cheap food
was an unqualified blessing. And yet (to qualify anyway) this relative cornucopia was aggravated by two factors. The first was a numbing lack of
diversity within each category (except when it came to dried fish); every
stall with tomatoes, for example, proffered the exact same type of tomato,
at the same price. While arguably fresh, sun-ripened, and juicy, they were all
the same, everywhere and every day. It was as if every farmer in the country had sworn allegiance to the One Tomato; likewise every other species
of vegetable and fruit. At first this lack of innovation puzzled me; why
wouldn't an enterprising farmer grow something different—an exotic
tomato, a striped eggplant, a wax bean—and corner the market? Instead,
with no distinguishing product, sellers resorted to a curious form of competitive begging:

"*White man!* Please buy from me!"

"*White man!* I have what you need!"

"*White man!* Come and see!"

I tried to spread the wealth and buy from different sellers every day, a
strategy, I began to learn, that makes friends of no one. Bargaining was
fruitless, as it were, although I never ceased enjoying the effort. Whit and

I had developed a sort of vaudeville routine that shamelessly milked humor from the recent currency devaluation, in which one new cedi replaced ten thousand old cedis. I would give a mock shudder at the stated price, then say, "*Old* cedis, right?"

Usually that drew a laugh. "Oh no! *New* Ghana cedis!"

"Wow! Is that *obruni* price?"

"Not *obruni* price! *Everybody* price!" I rated the whole routine mildly amusing, but Ghanaians regularly doubled over in laughter at the exchange.

"Okay, but I want a gift." A "gift" was the traditional extra tomato or two thrown in, as gratitude for your business. Most sellers kept a special pile of less-than-perfect or overly ripe produce just for these gifts. Otherwise, it was exactly the same as the regular produce.

Everywhere I went in Ghana, I kept an eye out for that unusual tomato or strange eggplant, but it didn't exist. Over time and through our own business dealings, I began to understand how poverty depresses innovation and entrepreneurship, even on the level of the produce market. Although times are relatively good right now, Ghanaian farmers live constantly on the edge of disaster. A crop destroyed by pests, or one that simply doesn't sell, can ruin lives. There is no margin for error. Risk is simply too risky.

So the proven tomato, the one that does well in the local soil and sells well in the local market, is the one whose seeds get saved and replanted. In the long term, of course, that practice promotes a dangerous lack of biodiversity; sooner or later a new pest will come along that positively adores the Ghanaian tomato, and then there will be none. This is what happened in Ireland during the potato famine of the nineteenth century. But then as now, a farmer living on a pittance will always focus on his family's needs today, not a theoretical caterpillar of tomorrow.

(This hand-to-mouth lifestyle had clear implications for Burro. In the first battery offering, the monthly subscription price was too much money for most customers, even though it saved money in the long run. And for a lot of customers under the new, pay-as-you-go system, the one-cedi deposit was a big hurdle, again despite the savings.)

The second problem with food shopping in Koforidua was the long list of staples that were completely unavailable—like coffee, except for instant Nescafé, which is synonymous with "coffee" in Ghana. Or dairy. The country simply has no dairy culture, and gold bullion could not buy you a drop of fresh milk or cream in Koforidua, although a couple of stores sold boxed milk. Butter could be found at great expense (imported from France and quite good; how it found its way to our Anglophone *banlieue* I have no clue), but cheese might as well have been moon rocks. Nor was there yogurt, except in presweetened and artificially flavored children's drinks. Olive oil was considered medicine, like castor oil, and had to be bought from the pharmacist. All of these exotic alimentations could be bought, expensively, at the Western-style supermarket in Accra, but that was a full day or overnight trip.

The daily scavenger hunt for groceries really became an adventure when it came to buying meat. Poultry was relatively simple: both chickens and turkeys could be bought live in the market (you could always find someone to butcher them) or dressed and frozen rock hard from one of several "cold stores"—modest but busy shops with a few chest freezers and a scale. Cold stores also sold frozen fresh fish, as opposed to the dried fish in the market, and, oddly enough, factory-made hot dogs, rather optimistically labeled "sausages." Red meat beyond processed frankfurters, however, necessitated a visit to the abattoir, a windowless octagonal house of horrors within the public market. Under this squalid dome lay a tableau that might have been shot by Brady at Antietam. Counters lined in bloodstained vinyl sagged under the hacked carcasses of large mammals, hooves akimbo, skulls cleaved and bellies ripped open. Shirtless butchers in stained aprons wielded machetes over these dishonored corpses, sending bits of bone and flesh flying.

"*White man!* You want filet?"

Of course the white man wants filet. White men always want filet.

The abattoir had no refrigeration, and the ninety-degree slabs of meat dripped grease slicks across the floor, so you didn't so much walk as skate along the aisles.

"*White man!* I have fresh cow!"

Beef was called cow, mutton was simply sheep (lamb was nonexistent), and then there was goat. In deference to the large Muslim population, there was no pork.

"*White man!* Goat is very good today!"

The flies certainly thought so. I removed my glasses and used my T-shirt to smear the grease around the lenses, then examined the animal more closely. As far as I could tell there were never any tender cuts like steaks, which I assumed went to buyers from the hotel restaurants before the abattoir opened. What was left for the *lumpenprol* were the heavily muscled and gristly undercarriages—cuts that are delicious enough but require grinding or long stewing to become palatable. Also on display, and wildly popular with the locals, were the so-called variety meats—kilometers of coiled intestines, bushels of spleens and livers, bowls brimming with dark hearts and kidneys, plus brains on the half shell, so to speak.

Adapting to the ingredients at hand, I bought a manual meat grinder to make hamburgers on our little charcoal brazier. Unfortunately, buns were impossible to find and it was far too hot in the flat to bake our own, so we used the spongy "tea bread"—a Ghanaian staple, sort of a baguette-shaped Wonder bread laced with sugar—sold in the market. With all the avocados, guacamole became a daily treat—but with no corn chips, we had to substitute the fried plantain chips sold by ladies (from huge bowls balanced on their heads) in the traffic circles. We bought a blender and made mango smoothies every day until the blender motor burned out, filling our tiny kitchen with acrid electrical smoke. (Jan later had it fixed for a few cedis; nothing ever gets thrown away in Africa, and there is always someone who can fix something.) On my second trip to Ghana I actually brought over several pounds of Parmesan cheese, along with a few small plants to start an herb garden on our terrace. (Rosemary, basil, parsley, oregano, and sage were nonexistent in the markets.) Whit thought I was nuts, but I noticed he ate everything.

Cooking for my brother every day made me feel a little bit like his wife, especially as he was the guy running the business. I grew weary of hearing "Hi, honey, I'm home! What's for dinner?" But I was good at it, and it made me feel like I was doing my part. "What would you eat if I weren't here?" I asked him once.

"Cereal."

"No, I mean for dinner."

"Cereal. With bananas."

"Who would slice your bananas?"

"Very funny. I would hire someone."

Our clan does not excel at self-reflection; we are generally much better at reflecting on the deficiencies of others. Yet one night over dinner, I recalled a time when we were kids and Whit gave me a spiral-bound Betty Crocker cookbook for my birthday. I must have been fourteen or fifteen, making Whit just ten or eleven. It was an enormously thoughtful gift for a small boy, reflecting his understanding of his older brother's love of the kitchen. But when I unwrapped the gift, in front of all my friends at the party, I was embarrassed; at that time my cooking was a closet affair. In a misguided effort to save face with my peers, I sniffed at the gift and replied cruelly, "A cookbook? What would I ever want with this?" Little Whit's face collapsed at that moment, and I immediately hated myself.

When I retold the story that night in Ghana, Whit said he had no memory of it. I found it amazing that an incident that had haunted me for decades was unremarkable in his own eyes, but such are the vagaries of human memory.

"Well, I'm glad it didn't ruin you for life," I said. "But I always regretted it, and it was really the first time I ever learned not to be ashamed of who I am. So I can thank you for that."

After dinner we called our mother, slowly fading in a nursing home in Chicago. It was her eighty-first birthday. "Hey, Mom," I said. "Guess where we are?"

"Where?"

"Africa."

There was a long pause while she processed the information. "That's nice."

## 2. Anything to Call Their Own

Jan was in many ways my opposite—one of those keenly scientific people for whom every problem in life was simple once you knew the equation— and we complemented each other. Logic was in essence her profession. She had majored in math, naturally, at Washington State University. "I loved math, but I didn't know what I wanted to do," she told me one night. "I didn't want to be an actuary. Then I took a three-hundred-level course in operations research, and I loved it."

"Operations research?"

"Yeah. It's like, okay, you have to visit twelve cities in one week to do business; what's the most efficient way to do it? I loved it because it was applied math. After the three-hundred-level course, I had one more se- mester in my senior year. I purposely left myself one credit short of gradu- ating so I could take the four-hundred- and five-hundred-level course classes in my second senior year, during which time I decided on graduate school."

Which ended up being the University of Illinois, Urbana-Champaign, where she earned a master's in industrial engineering. Before joining Whit at Cranium, Jan had spent twelve years at a management consulting firm, earning a partnership. After Cranium she worked at Microsoft but longed for something more entrepreneurial, even adventurous. Rejoining Whit, she gave up a "safe" career in return for an equity stake in Burro and the chance to do something very different.

Jan loved the Ghanaians, but one significant aspect of Ghanaian cul- ture failed to soften her: the country's hyperventilating version of Christi- anity. Several evangelical churches operated within a few blocks of Burro, and they all had raucous services lasting late into the night on various staggered evenings. The meetings were characterized by mindlessly out- of-tune gospel singing accompanied by drums and brass amplified to distortion levels, alternating with hysterical sermons in Twi, delivered at jet-turbine decibels. These Nuremberg rallies often went on until long after midnight and were impervious to earplugs, prayer, or agnosticism. Suffice it to say the Christian soldiers weren't winning many converts on our side of the road.

"An agent asked me to go to church today," Jan said one night, raising her voice enough to be heard over the din of a particularly discordant hymn from across the street.

"And you agreed?" I asked.

"As if! When I said no, he said, 'Don't you believe in Christ?' I said, 'It doesn't really matter to me.' He said, 'Then you will go to hell.' I said, 'I don't believe in hell.'"

"Wow," I said. "Now you're definitely going to hell."

"I told him, 'You learned about hell from some white missionaries who came here two hundred years ago, and now you're trying to tell it to me! Do you think all those thousands of generations of Africans before the missionaries are burning in hell?'"

"Score one for you," I said, "but I do think religion has in many ways been a force for good here. It certainly gives people a sense of community, and the churches have encouraged democracy and social progress."

"Well, they had all that before, in their own communities and with their native religions," Jan replied. "It just got translated into Christianity."

She had a point, adding on further thought that religion had also encouraged a culture of passivity; when everything will happen "by God's will," why bother trying to be on time for a meeting, or even trying hard to sell more batteries?

This blithe acceptance of fate was not, however, a universal Ghanaian belief. In fact, Whit noted that in recent years even the collective benefits of organized religion in Ghana had been sacrificed at the altar of "personal empowerment." The late Reverend Ike, who drove Rolls-Royces around Harlem, used to preach, "If it's that difficult for a rich man to get into heaven, think how terrible it must be for a poor man to get in. He doesn't even have a bribe for the gatekeeper." Even without a punch line that would resonate in a graft-ridden African society, that sentiment pretty well describes the spiritual imperative in modern Ghana. Like their telegenic cousins in the West, the most popular Ghanaian preachers today promise an answer to the question "What can God do for me?"

Of course not all churches in Ghana have taken the *us* out of Jesus. One Sunday morning I ventured out to Jonas Avademe's village for the service at his Apostles' Revelation Society. "It is the special Children's Day program," said Jonas over his cell phone when he called to invite me a few days earlier. "You will like it." I had a new soccer ball I wanted to deliver to the kids in the village, so it seemed like good timing.

The church was actually in a nearby village that was closer to the main road and thus had electricity. I pulled up a few minutes early in front of a long, neat rectangular building. A set of wide double doors had been thrown open, as were the shutters of several large windows, and the congregation was taking seats in rows of wooden benches. Jonas met me at the door and instructed me to remove my shoes, as in a mosque. Inside, above a concrete floor, rough-hewn wooden trusses supported a raked and corrugated metal roof, which, in its own modest way, lent the feeling of a vaulted basilica. Behind a lectern, Jonas was adjusting the dials on a public address system. Fluorescent shop lights buzzed overhead.

The rudimentary accommodations were belied by the women of the church, who arrived turned out in the most arrestingly beautiful dresses (and matching head scarves) I have ever seen. Each was handmade from printed, woven, or embroidered fabrics in a constellation of African patterns—floral, spiral, checked, geometric, brocade, vine—and in colors from vermilion to indigo that vibrated with energy. Some of the men wore impressive traditional robes, but most arrived in Western dress shirts and ties. I was ushered, undeservedly, to an honored seat with the elders to the right of the altar. The service began with the beating of a gong-gong, hanging from a mango tree outside. As the gong-gong man sounded his call, the choir—five men and six women (including Jonas's sister Charity, stunning in a white linen dress embroidered with lavender and silver threads) circled the outside of the church, ringing bells and shaking a tambourine. They entered and took seats, the men behind large peg drums. On cue from the pastor, a dour-looking man in a dark robe, the choir began to sing a buoyant Ewe hymn, accompanied by the drums and tambourine, as a procession of several dozen children entered and took seats in front. The children, roughly age five to sixteen, were as vibrantly attired as their parents, with one more amazing addition: every child's face, neck, and bare arms were "tattooed" with circles transferred by dipping the rim of a drinking glass in cream-colored makeup. Jonas later told me that this striking decoration had been traced to Nigeria, where the Ewe originated in ancient times (they are related to the Nigerian Yoruba ethnic group) before migrating west to Benin, Togo, and Ghana. He could not say what it meant other than to describe it as "a cultural design for the body." Nor could anyone one else in his village elaborate.

The service itself was in Ewe, but in deference to my presence the gong-gong man translated. Speaking to the children, the pastor stressed the importance of fealty to elders: "If you always obey your parents, you will grow old and you will grow wise," he said. "You will not die prematurely."

There was more singing, followed by an unusual offertory. Instead of passing the basket, church members formed a conga line and, without a trace of the stilted self-consciousness that would mark a Caucasian dance on Sunday morning, shimmied their way to the front, dropping coins in a box, as the choir sang and the drummers pounded.

What followed was even less conventional. Small groups of children performed a series of skits and songs whose words I could not understand (the translator thankfully did not interrupt the drama) but which seemed to be demonstrations of correct child behavior—namely obeying orders, fetching water, and doing homework. But here was the really odd thing: during these performances, the adults signified their approval by tossing coins at the youngsters. Mostly the coins skittled across the floor, but because many were lobbed from quite far back in the assembly, the trajectories were often such that the missiles struck the children about the head and shoulders. This hail of metal did not dim the young actors' enthusiasm, as the performers were free to collect the coins at the end of their skits. But I found myself flinching on their behalf every time a piece of currency arced across the nave, and in my mind I could hear my mother saying, "It's all fun and games until someone loses an eye."

More singing and drumming ensued, punctuated by a crack of thunder and the dull hammer of rain on the metal roof. The lights blinked and went out, and the rain pelted down harder. It did not stop, nor did the choir. When I left after two hours, it was still raining, and they were still singing.

**Jan, who had no kids of her own,** became a surrogate mother, big sister, and teacher to the children who shared our courtyard. On most mornings she would have her coffee (which we hoarded from our shopping trips to Accra) out on the top step to our flat, surrounded by several kids before they left for school. She would read to them, or share songs on her iPod, or sing camp songs. I suspect these meetings exposed the youngsters to far more English vocabulary than they got in school, and in return Jan learned about the singular dynamics of Ghanaian family life.

"As the children and I sat on the step," she wrote on her blog (from a speech she gave back in her hometown of Wenatchee, Washington), "they would periodically call down to greet an adult, usually with the one syllable 'Ma' or 'Da,' then wave wildly when the adult looked up to see them with the *obruni*. Before long, I realized that the same child might yell down 'Ma' at two or three different women at different times."

She went on to describe the family of two of "my kids," as she called them, six-year-old Precious and her thirteen-year-old sister, Pamela, whose father and older brother were living and working in London:

> Pamela and Precious live in the compound behind us with their mother and grandmother, their mother's brother and his wife and two children under five, and their father's younger brother, who is also called their "Small Father." They also call their mother's brother Father, and his wife Mother. So, in the house they have two mothers and two fathers, only one of whom is their biological parent. Strange as it may seem to you and me, in a culture where the average income is less than two dollars per day, where people may have to travel to find work,

and where there is no daycare, this is the way families
work.

Today we would instantly recognize this dynamic as evidence of the over-
used cliché "It takes a village to raise a child." But even clichés are based
on fact, and community child-rearing in Africa has been noted by outsiders stretching back centuries. This custom is so imprinted in the African
psyche that it has made the transition to urban life—where children today
arguably face more external dangers than in remote villages. Our little
courtyard functioned as a village within a city of one hundred thousand.
Younger kids, who loved to follow us around and tug at our clothes, knew
better than to leave the safety of the courtyard; when we crossed the
street they dutifully stayed on their side, waving good-bye to us, even
though no adult was present to "herd" them. They understood the boundaries of their community. Even little Patrick, a three-year-old whose nose
disgorged an apparently limitless charge of snot (most of which ended up
on my leg), knew enough to stay on his side of the street.

On the Republic Day holiday of the First of July, Jan and I decided to
treat Precious, Pamela, and Pamela's best friend Savannah to a picnic at
Boti Falls in Krobo territory. Despite being just half an hour's drive from
Koforidua, this significant natural attraction, famous throughout the
country, might as well have been the Isle of Capri. Only one of the girls
had ever been there, and all were fairly breathless with excitement. Yet as
soon as we pulled away from the street in front of Burro, little Precious
grew notably frightened. She was with her teenage sister and two *obruni*
adults she knew well, but leaving the courtyard without an adult family
member filled her with anxiety. Fortunately, she soon got over her fear
and had a great day, although she seemed pretty happy to get home that
evening.

Strong family and social ties are a matter of survival in poor cultures.
But modern society assumes our children will do more than merely sur-
vive in the Darwinian sense and actually thrive—still a tall order in
Ghana. "Despite all the adults around," Jan continued on her blog, "there

is very little adult interaction on day-to-day development—little help with homework, no extracurricular activities to speak of, no organized sports or music, and few youth organizations or clubs."

This became clear to me the first time I saw grade-schoolers in the courtyard playing with the shards of a broken mirror—veritable crown jewels for kids who traded bottle caps with numismatic fervor. With no sports leagues and no money to buy balls or other legitimate toys, parents didn't exactly fret about jagged glass playthings; in fact, these same children were supplied with old-fashioned double-edged razor blades to sharpen their school pencils.

Determined to improve the kids' play area, Jan concocted a plan to build covers for the disgusting open sewer that ran through the courtyard. One Saturday, the two of us drove out to the timber market, where hulking bare-chested men used handsaws to cut inch-thick, foot-wide planks of mahogany and other incredibly dense woods. (There was a table saw in one of the mill buildings, but electricity was too sporadic to be relied on.) We filled the back of the truck with cut lumber and headed home, where an army of kids waited with one hammer and a handful of nails to fashion the platforms. This project was greeted with enthusiasm by the adults in the neighboring buildings, who quickly saw the gains in space, safety, and overall quality of life afforded by concealing this defilement.

One could argue that life was nominally better for these city kids than their country cousins, who had no electricity and not even occasional plumbing. But the urban version of African poverty, with its grime, indifference, anonymity, open sewers, and shattered mirrors, felt particularly Dickensian, and encouraged the moniker "urchins" when describing these unlucky youths. "My neighborhood children are hungry not only for food," wrote Jan, "but for attention, education, and anything to call their own."

Jan regularly hauled back suitcases of stuff from the States, much of it donated by friends, for her Kof-town kids, everything from books to shoes and backpacks to pencil sharpeners that weren't made by Gillette. Tired of being called *obruni* ("That's not my name!"), she made sure the kids knew our names, to which they invariably added the prefix "Uncle" or

"Auntie." That made it easy to tell which kids didn't go to school and thus had virtually no English: they were the ones who shouted "Auntie Max" and "Uncle Jan."

Jan held school of her own after dinner most evenings. Several kids would come up to do homework and get a little extra practice in English, the lack of which would pretty much guarantee a life of penury in Ghana, despite the obvious cultural importance of their native tongues. They would spread their workbooks around the dining room table and use the Burro whiteboard as a blackboard. One night, as the younger kids played a round of Memory, a preschool game with cards and symbols, I helped an older girl named Elizabeth with her composition homework.

The assignment page of her workbook dealt with the subject of "Homes." First she had to write a sentence describing her home, based on one of several prompts: flat, bungalow, condominium, hut. "I live in a flat," she wrote carefully, which seemed debatable considering the concrete bunker with no indoor plumbing or cooking facilities that she called home. Then again, it wasn't exactly a hut, *bungalow* sounded far too charming, and it certainly wasn't a condo. The next section dealt with describing the rooms in the home, with prompts like living room, dining room, bedroom, kitchen, and terrace. Elizabeth's home had no kitchen, dining room, or terrace; even the concept of a living room seemed a stretch; Ghanaians live outside. "Why don't you write a sentence describing how many people sleep in your bedroom?" I suggested.

She held up her fingers and counted: "Sister . . . sister . . . sister . . . brother . . . grandma . . . me. Six." She wrote: "Six people sleep in my bedroom."

The last section was called "Near the Home," with a list that included market, park, MRT station, and "hawking centre." There were no parks (except for the cracked concrete expanse that hosted the Thursday bead market and various school and church pageants), and all of Koforidua was one giant hawking centre. On her own, Elizabeth came up with "bank," several of which stood nearby. She wrote "Our house is near the . . ." and then she slowly penned B and A. "What's next?" she asked. "R?"

I made the N sound.

"*N!* What's next?"

I made the *K* sound.

"*K?*"

"Yes," I said.

"I'm going to urinate." And with that, she set down her pencil and repaired to the relative luxury of our indoor facilities.

## 3. Mena

Mena was the old deaf lady who lived behind the courtyard and hand-washed our laundry when we got tired of doing it ourselves—meaning after about two weeks into January. I didn't know her real name; Mena is a contraction of the Twi words *me ene*, or "my mother," and is typically used as an honorific for any older woman—like we would call an old woman generically "Grandma," although Mena was in fact Precious and Pamela's real grandmother. She was bent over with arthritis and had just a few teeth, but taking in laundry was one of the only ways she had to earn money—not that she would have starved without our cash, as she was surrounded by supportive family, but every cedi counted. There was no set price; we gave her a bag of laundry, it came back clean and folded the next day, or the day after (delivered by one of the children in the courtyard, who expected a coin or a banana), and we paid what we wished, generally around ten cedis, which was a lot of money for an old lady in Koforidua. Whenever we returned from a stay in the United States, Mena knelt at our feet and made a prayer sign, in gratitude that her benefactors were back, dirty laundry soon to follow.

Communicating with Mena was always a challenge because she talked mainly with her hands—not formal sign language but her own invention of wild gesticulations, accompanied by guttural vocal sounds. She seemed to be a naturally animated person, so that even the most routine communications were delivered as if she were directing firemen to a burning orphanage. Quite how I'm unsure, but the children in the courtyard were able to comprehend her; mostly what they comprehended was Mena's generalized desire to beat the tar out of any child within arm's reach, so they kept their distance—especially Kwabena, the ten-year-old who did not go to school, spoke no English, and was the punching bag of every adult in the courtyard. Whenever Mena passed Kwabena, she would give him a slap just on general principle.

I couldn't understand much of Mena's sign language, but the basics were accessible enough. If she meant to say your laundry would be ready later that day, she would point to her wrist (not that she actually had a watch) and make several tight spirals with her finger—signifying hours. Laundry that would not be completed until the next day was indicated by a wrist point followed by a wide circle drawn in the sky—the passing of a day. Equally easy to understand was Mena's opinion of your payment, which was theoretically voluntary but in practice subject to her stern regard. When you picked up your finished laundry and paid her, she would register happiness with your donation by kneeling in supplicant pose and bowing her head. Displeasure at the amount (for reasons that were never clear, perhaps a stubborn stain that required more work) was met with a scowl followed by finger wagging and grunting vowels, ending with the universal hunger gesture of hand to mouth. In this way we managed a crude business rapport over several months and many bags of laundry.

## 4. A Bitch Named Future

Jan and I invited the families around the courtyard to dinner one Sunday. Somehow over the course of the weekend it transpired that Pamela and her best friend Savannah would teach Jan and me how to make fufu. From this grew the addition of peanut soup, and once you make a pot of peanut soup in Ghana, you are setting yourself up for a big event. So that's how it happened.

It began around three in the afternoon, when Jan and I took Savannah to the public market, quiet on Sunday but many stalls still open for business, with the shopping list she had written down. For the fufu we needed two simple ingredients: cassava and plantains, green and quite hard. Her list for the soup, spelled perfectly in English, read:

- Groundnuts [peanut butter, made by hand and sold in thin plastic baggies knotted at the top]
- Onions
- Tinned tomatoes [what we would call tomato paste]
- Ryco [a brand of bouillon cube]
- Pepper [meaning ground dried chili peppers of an incendiary variety]
- Chicken [bought hacked up and frozen from the cold store]

Back at the flat, Pamela joined us in the kitchen and we began to make the soup. First the girls peeled and chopped several onions, then tossed them into our enameled cast-iron pot along with the chicken pieces, the "tinned tomatoes" (maybe twice as large as an American can of tomato paste), and the bouillon cube. They added salt and copious handfuls of chili powder, covered the pot, and turned the heat on high.

Next we moved on to the fufu, which required peeling and cubing the cassava and plantains. This was being done outside in the courtyard, at the foot of our stairs; I was in the kitchen washing a few dishes when Jan came up and said, "Max, you've got to come down and see how they cut the cassava."

I went down and noticed that Jan had been peeling the cassava root as I would—with a twin-bladed vegetable peeler. She had not made much progress. The girls, on the other hand, were almost through the whole basket of roots. Wielding massive long kitchen knives—almost machetes—in one hand and grasping a cassava root in the other, they deftly whacked the plant lengthwise, splitting the skin like bark off a log, then effortlessly tore the whole clean. A couple more whacks—again, holding both knife and plant in bare hands—and the roots were reduced to large chunks suitable for pounding. The plantains, of course, were simple to peel.

Into a pot of water went the washed plantain and cassava chunks, and onto the stove. "Uncle Max, please, we need a rubber for on top," said Savannah. It took a minute for me to figure out they meant a plastic shopping bag which, laid over the boiling water and under the lid, helped to seal the steam.

By this time the chicken had steamed sufficiently in the other pot to add the liquid. Savannah and Pamela tore open the baggies of peanut butter and squeezed them into a large plastic bowl to which they had added water (from the tap, not completely safe; we generally cooked with purified water). Using their hands, they stirred the mixture and added more water until it reached the consistency of gravy, then poured it into the pot. We threw in a few snails for good measure, and let it all simmer. Although I did not have a cigar or a crime novel, around this point in the proceedings I truly felt like Felix Naggar over his Nairobi stove.

An hour later, the cassava and plantain chunks were cooked and ready for pounding. Back in the courtyard, the girls set up a station, assembling a bowl of water and another of the vegetable chunks. In the center of this operation was a carved hardwood mortar the size of a small stool, worn smooth from years of pounding, with a flat center and a wide lip. Joyce, who is Savannah's aunt but also functions as her mother, sat on a bench and began to toss handfuls of plantain chunks into the mortar. Savannah stood above her, wielding the eight-foot-long pestle—nothing more than a straight tree trunk, roughly four inches in diameter. On the bottom of the pestle, the wood fibers had been pounded out into the shape of a mushroom cap, so that the surface greeting the vegetables was wide and smooth. As Savannah pounded in a steady rhythm, Joyce deftly added chunks of cassava and plantain along with a sprinkle of water; as the mixture solidified into a paste, she would then quickly flip and turn the whole mass, sort of like kneading bread, constantly repositioning the mound under the crushing pestle while slipping her hand away at the last split second.

This became hard to watch, because it was obvious that if Joyce and Savannah got their rhythm off, Joyce's hand would be instantly mangled under the pile-driving action of the pestle. When I had been told earlier in the day that I would get a chance to pound fufu, I hadn't realized that a woman's hand would be at the mercy of my skill. "Just keep the same rhythm," said Savannah when she handed me the pestle. "Let Joyce worry about her hand."

Easier said than done. Try as I might to focus on my rhythm, I couldn't stop worrying about Joyce's hand—which of course caused me to lose my rhythm, which of course was the worst possible thing from Joyce's standpoint.

The pounding proceeded without incident, however, and soon dinner was served. We had invited about twenty guests, and double that showed up—quite a party. Someone handed Mena a glass of wine with the warning, "Drink it slowly." She sniffed it, took a sip, and sagely pronounced, "Beer!" It was also the only word of English I'd ever heard her pronounce.

The snails went quickly as they are a Ghanaian delicacy, on par with lobster in America, and were fished out of the stew by fast-moving children. For dessert Jan had made an apple crisp (South African apples, quite expensive, were generally available in the market) that the children thought strange; they much preferred the strawberry ice cream we had sent Savannah out for.

As bowls and plates were cleared, scraps of bones got tossed outside to the courtyard's resident cur, a bitch named Future. This benign mongrel seemed generally better fed than the average slab-sided African pariah dog, perhaps because her agreeability encouraged human sympathy. Future's charms were evidently not lost on the local canine studs, as she appeared to be constantly suckling new broods. Sometimes late at night I would wake to the terrible clamor of a dogfight somewhere out on the street; there are few alarms more piercing than the sadistic skirmish of a feral turf war, and I often wondered if Future was part of the fray, and if the next morning there would be, so to speak, no Future. But there she always was.

In the summer of 2010, Jan told me that Future had disappeared. Apparently there was a new shop in town that sold dog meat, according to Mary, who was Precious and Pamela's mother, and dogs were disappearing left and right. They planned to get another dog.

## 5. Another Day, Another Doxy

Personal health required constant vigilance, given all the ways one could get sick, possibly very sick, in Ghana. Many of the serious diseases raging in the country, including cerebrospinal meningitis and polio, could be prevented with vaccines, and like all sensible Westerners (and most elite Africans) I had a full round of shots and boosters before traveling. But other afflictions were not so easily prevented. Cholera and dysentery—different bacterial infections of the intestine which begin with the foulest bodily eliminations imaginable and progress, if untreated, to death—coursed through the water of Ghana and lived on feces and food. Many of the insect-borne ailments had no vaccination, such as trypanosomiasis ("sleeping sickness"), the fatal disease carried by the tsetse fly. Fortunately, tsetse flies are rare in southern Ghana, and even the ones in the north of the country are now said to be the noncarrying variety. Not so mosquitoes, which carry the parasites causing malaria and the viruses of yellow and dengue fever.

Malaria was the biggest concern because there is no vaccine, only a series of prophylactic drugs that may or may not prevent infection. Although most strains of malaria are not fatal in otherwise healthy adults, at least one is—and even the nonfatal versions might make you wish you were dead as you lie in bed, wracked with fever and night sweats. Meanwhile, the drugs all have various side effects. Lariam, the standard brand name for Mefloquine, is a synthetic analog of quinine developed by the U.S. Department of Defense in the 1970s.* Among its side effects are vivid, hallucinogenic-like dreams or nightmares, depending on your point of view.

Malarone, the brand name for a cocktail of atovaquone and proguanil, is considerably more benign except for one major side effect: severe strain on the wallet. A daily dose costs more than three dollars when ordered online from Canada, and more than twice that at a U.S. pharmacy. Since most American health insurance policies won't pay for malaria prevention

---

* Quinine, an alkaloid derived from the bark of the South American cinchona tree, has been used for centuries as a somewhat effective treatment for malaria.

at all, and virtually none will pay for more than thirty days of prophylaxis, a Malarone course adds up quickly over a long stay.

Finally there's doxycycline, a tetracycline-type antibiotic that can cause stomach upset and, for some people, extreme sensitivity to sunlight—a notable side effect in a tropical clime. And you need to take it for a month after returning. On the other hand, doxy is dirt cheap and may provide the side benefit of inoculating against at least some bacterial bad guys.*

Sorting through all these options was only the beginning. Once you decided on your malaria drug of choice there was a daily debate over how to avoid side effects: Should I take it before bed and risk nightmares or sleeplessness? Or should I wait until morning and chance nausea? With dairy, or without? Before a meal, or after? These decisions sapped huge amounts of mental bandwidth. Meanwhile, we all carried stashes of cipro-floxacin, the powerful antibiotic used to treat dysentery, and arguments raged about the proper timing of a cipro course. Whit's Seattle doctor told him not to panic at the first sign of diarrhea, which was most likely garden variety and not a serious infection; why risk building immunity to the antibiotic over nothing? My doctor in Maine, on the other hand, said, in effect, bullshit—if you get the runs in Africa, start the cipro, pronto. Since my doctor had actually worked for several years in Uganda, I tended to believe him. At any rate, we spent more time discussing our medications than a roomful of nursing home residents.

Of course there is a fine line between vigilance and paranoia, and awareness of the range of ailments tended to breed, if nothing else, a virulent strain of hypochondria. Every sneeze and cough raised the specter of tuberculosis. A muscle ache brought on worries of yellow fever. That skin rash could be nothing—or it could be *a three-foot-long parasitic worm festering inside my thigh!* One day I noticed, for the first time in my life, coarse hairs growing from the rim of my left ear. They were so stiff you could have scrubbed a pot with them, and there were none on my right ear. I panicked: What evil African flagellate causes boar bristles to grow from

---

* Whit finally did get malaria, resulting in feverlike symptoms for several days. Treatment was a drug made from wormwood that has been proven to cure the disease.

your left ear? I found nothing in the literature, but treatment seemed to involve careful application of a razor.

Africans themselves are no better; they pop more pills than the French, a habit facilitated by the easy procurement of powerful drugs from any pharmacist, without a prescription. Every time a Burro employee got a cold, he or she would race down to the chemist for a round of antibiotics. "It won't help," said Jan over and over again. "Colds are viruses; antibiotics won't do anything." She was preaching to a brick wall. Charlie and his family took deworming medication every three months, which actually seemed like a good idea—"especially if you eat a lot of fresh food," said Charlie.

I finally did get genuinely sick in October. For some karmic reason that I cannot fathom, I am one of those chosen to experience regular episodes of kidney stones. Roughly every three years I am blessed with this exquisite form of torture, so I know the onset symptoms, and the treatment, only too well.

"Do you want to go to the hospital?" Whit asked as I lay groaning on my bed during the first, relatively easy round of spasms.

"No," I said through gasps, imagining myself curled up in the fetal position on a wooden bench in some vast Conradian waiting room. "All they do at home is give me morphine, then send me home with Oxycodone. I bet you can get that shit at the pharmacy here."

"Morphine?"

"No, Oxycodone. It's a prescription synthetic opiate, but I bet you can walk in and get it here."

"I'll do my best."

He returned half an hour later with a blister pack of Oxycodone tablets. "Wow, that was easy," I said.

"The pharmacist definitely gave me the once-over," said Whit. "He wanted to know what it was for, and it probably didn't hurt that I'm an *obruni*."

"Yes, because *obrunis* are never drug addicts. How much do I owe you?"

"Two cedis."

"Jesus. This shit sells for like eighty bucks a pill on the street back home. It's a wonder this whole country isn't junked up."

"Well, like I said, I don't think they hand it out like candy."

"Thanks." I don't remember much of the next two days. I floated off into opium dreams and stopped thinking about kidney stones or malaria pills or boar bristles on my ears or anything else that keeps mere mortals awake at night.

## 6. The Black Star

One night in the fall, Whit and I dragged Charlie and Afi to a musical performance at the National Theatre of Ghana. According to the full-page color ad in the *Daily Graphic, The Black Star* was a musical tribute to Kwame Nkrumah, Ghana's venerated first president and, as leader of the first post-colonial state in sub-Saharan Africa, the father of African independence. It was the centennial of his birth, and celebrations were planned around the country. Over the years, Nkrumah's flame has burned both bright and dim for Africans. In the early 1960s, Ghana under Nkrumah became the center of a new back-to-Africa movement. Many black Americans, including Maya Angelou and W.E.B. DuBois, packed up and moved there. (DuBois became a Ghanaian citizen and died in Accra in 1963 at age ninety-five, the day before Martin Luther King's "I Have a Dream" speech. He and his wife, the writer and activist Shirley DuBois, are buried at Accra's Osu Castle, but you can't visit their graves; the heavily guarded castle is the home of the president and closed to the public.) Martin Luther King, Louis Armstrong, and Malcolm X came to pay homage to the new leader.

But Nkrumah's vision of a united Africa never came to pass. At home, his centralized, socialist economic reforms failed miserably, although he did improve the country's infrastructure and educational system. Nkrumah himself was an ascetic, gnomelike man with a broad forehead and receding hairline that gave him the look of a black Mao Tse-tung—an unfortunate physical comparison in light of his increasingly oppressive policies. Facing dissent, he jailed opponents without trials, banned political parties, and clamped down on the press. Although he never sank to the sadistic

brutality of so many later African leaders (and was apparently uninterested in personal enrichment), he was well on his way to dictator-for-life
status when, while visiting Hanoi in 1966, he was deposed in a CIA-
engineered coup, despite his avowed nonalignment. ("We face neither
East nor West; we face forward," he famously said.) Until his death in
1972 he lived in exile, a symbol of Africa's lost opportunity. In Ghana he
was essentially written out of the history.* By the late 1970s, however,
Nkrumah's legacy was getting a polish—perhaps because he seemed like
Churchill compared to the despots who succeeded him across the continent. Today he is lionized all over Africa as one of the great statesmen of
the post-colonial era, a galvanizing if imperfect visionary.

As it turned out, the advertisement for The Black Star was somewhat
misleading. Far from being a musical celebration of Nkrumah, the performance was in fact a revival of a 1970s satire of the rise and fall of a fic-
tional Nkrumah-like leader, set in a make-believe African country. The
play was written by the Nigerian-born, Chicago-based dramatist and painter
Uwa Hunwick (whose husband, John Hunwick, is a distinguished British
scholar of Islamic Africa at Northwestern University) and first performed
by the same Ghanaian acting company that was putting on this new
version.

Surely one strikingly different aspect of the revival was its production
in the ungainly National Theatre, an upside-down concrete soufflé built
by the Chinese and opened in 1993. This ambitious folly of a building was
commissioned under the Rawlings regime—one of those all-too-common
African public works projects that are meant to demonstrate Big Ideas,
but without nearly enough thought given to practicalities.

Indeed, as the anemic turnout that evening demonstrated, Accra night-
life, once a sprawling incandescent quilt of clubs, theaters, galleries, and

---

* In January, Harper, Whit, and I visited the Gramophone Records Museum and Research Centre in Cape Coast—basically an archive of some fifty thousand Ghanaian
highlife recordings, mostly on old 78-rpm discs. The museum's director, Kwame
Sarpong, showed us a record from the sixties that celebrated Nkrumah; scratched
across its surface in yellow paint were the letters NTBB—Not To Be Broadcast.

intellectual dinner parties, from Osu to Asylum Down, was long past its bedtime, so to speak—a victim of austerity programs and the very real concern, under a variety of oppressive military leaders, not to flaunt wealth or social status. Oblivious to these dreary modern realities, the government ordered up a cultural palace so over-the-top that its operating expenses alone virtually guaranteed vacancy.

Inside, the theater was conceived in a style that might be called African Outerspace Modern: a vast, raked orchestra below two soaring, cantilevered mezzanines, apparently made of whipped meringue. The ceiling was almost high enough for indoor baseball, although David Ortiz would have to swing hard to hit the mezzanine rows from the stage. The designers of this cavernous pile did not seem to understand that balconies are supposed to allow for greater intimacy at higher elevations; starting the mezzanine rows at the very back of the orchestra, as opposed to stacking them over the stage, serves no functional purpose. On either side, private VIP boxes hovered like alien UFO pods, their tenants concealed behind tinted (and perhaps bulletproof) glass.

I am certain that the air-conditioning contractor could have bought an island nation with the proceeds from ducting this equatorial Caracalla. Not that any tenants, which currently include the National Symphony Orchestra, could actually afford to cool the place. On the night we attended, mosquitoes buzzed around the stage lights, and the theater was about as comfortable as a rain forest, which come to think of it is what much of Ghana is. But at that point in my African sojourn, air-conditioning had become like grated black truffles—a luxury you might be lucky enough to experience every now and then in life, but hardly anything you expected on a daily basis.

We arrived right on time for the seven-thirty performance, bought our general-admission tickets (twenty cedis each, about the cost of a movie), and strolled into a nearly empty auditorium. I counted forty-one people in a theater that I estimated could seat two thousand. Then I remembered we were in Ghana, where nothing starts on time. "The people are still coming," said Charlie reassuringly. "The show will not start until at least eight, maybe half-eight." And sure enough, by the time the curtain rose just after the hour, a couple of hundred more people had wandered in. Still, the auditorium was perhaps 80 percent empty.

The houselights didn't dim until well into the first musical number, which is when the ushers finally decided to pass out programs. And the stage lights didn't come up until after that, so the performers had to work in the dark for about ten minutes. I don't think this was organized for dramatic effect; Ghana is just like that. It's the same casual approach that guarantees no two diners at a restaurant table will receive their meal at the same time. In every restaurant in Ghana, you get the sense that you are the first customer the establishment has ever served and they are inventing the whole table-service thing on the spot. I suspect stage production is not too different.

Lighting glitches aside, the production began auspiciously enough, with an expressionistic dance of writhing bodies on the floor that aptly suggested the birth of African independence. The offstage orchestra was minimal—an electric keyboard, drums (both Western and African), guitar, and horn—but reasonably accomplished. (It would be a sad night indeed when you couldn't muster some talented musicians in Ghana.) And the story itself had all the elements of good tragedy: a visionary leader who starts to believe his own hagiography, overreaches, alienates his people, and finally flees in disgrace. Along the way, he imprisons his brilliant and passionate treasury minister for speaking truth to power, unaware that the young man is his son. The son dies, and the nation is again enslaved—this time under a succession of native despots and generals.

Several of the musical numbers were memorable, others less so; I had hoped for less Broadway schmaltz and more African rhythm. The cast was all over the map; a few standout performers could easily have held their own on the New York stage, but others were more at the level of community theater. The most disappointing aspect of the evening was the stage production. The set design consisted of a few white columns meant to evoke palace architecture and a small map of Africa tacked to the rear wall. Costumes were equally uninspired—a true mystery considering the elaborate and beautiful handmade outfits I had seen in Jonas's remote church. Three hanging microphones could barely pick up the actors; in such a vast auditorium I had to strain to hear, and we were in the sixth row. I told Whit that the whole production had the feel of a high school musical, but he said his kids' high school had put on better musicals than this.

The two-and-a-half-hour play was performed without an intermission— another curiosity, given the existence of a beer stand in the lobby. Wouldn't a troupe so obviously cash-strapped try to maximize revenue by pushing refreshments during an intermission? It was the sort of no-brainer West- ern business decision that just doesn't come with the culture here. By the end of the night I felt sad that this was as good as professional theater in Ghana gets. I wanted the country to do better—just a better-funded pro- duction of *The Black Star* would be a good start. When you think about it, a lively urban cultural scene in one of Africa's most democratic and pros- perous countries would seem achievable. But in row six of the National Theatre on a Saturday night in September 2009, it felt about as likely as Nkrumah's pipe dream of a united, prosperous Africa.

A final tragedy: to make room for the construction of the National The- atre, authorities razed the intimate and legendary Ghana Drama Studio, which had been founded in 1960 by the Ghanaian playwright Efua Suther- land. (A replica has been built on the campus of the University of Ghana, just outside Accra.) Over the years, under Sutherland's guidance, the Drama Studio housed the Drama Studio Players; a full-time traveling company called Kusum Agromba; the Workers' Brigade Drama Group; and a workshop for children's literature writers. Those would have been the days.

## 7. Satanic Lizards

Ghana's freewheeling press is often described as "lively," an unusual choice of word considering the country's editorial fixation on death and depravity. Newsstands here carry dozens of local tabloids, many of which would not seem out of place in an American supermarket checkout lane. SATANIC LIZARD STALKS PASTOR POLITICIAN! was one of my favorite summer headlines. Even the more reality-based publications are nakedly partisan,

with blistering allegations that one political party or another has un-
leashed violence and disorder on an otherwise pastoral land. They make
Fox News seem—well, fair and balanced. Then there is the gore factor:
spectacular car accidents and unspeakable crimes get major play, an obvious attempt to drive sales at the newsstand and in traffic jams, where
street hawkers hustle the latest headlines to bored drivers. Despite the
content, as a journalist I often found myself wishing the U.S. print media
were as thriving as Ghana's.

In early September, the press had a field day when Ghana Police arrested a sixty-five-year-old American man after he allegedly videotaped
eight children, some as young as three, performing fellatio on him. Authorities believed the man, Patrick K. La Bash, was a major international
child porn producer. On a website business directory, La Bash was listed
as a Ghana-based business consultant with a PhD in English literature, as
well as an author, acting teacher, motion picture producer (well, *yes*), and
former Marine. The day after his arrest, the *Daily Guide* devoted most of
its front page to the banner KIDS SUCK WHITE PENIS FOR FOOD, MOVIES.
Above the headline were four graphic close-up photos pulled from the
seized videos; other than black bars over the eyes of the children, nothing
was left to the imagination. This charming cover was prominently dis-
played at newsstands all over the country. In America, of course, printing
such images (to say nothing of displaying them in public) would constitute
a crime in itself; there is no acceptable editorial context for reproducing
child pornography. But this is Ghana, where journalistic standards, like so
many aspects of the culture, are baffling. To its credit the Ghana Journalists Association later condemned the *Daily Guide*'s coverage: "The GJA is
deeply saddened that three weeks after winning the Best Layout and Design Award at the 14th GJA Awards, the paper has tarnished its reputation
with this unprofessional presentation."

At any rate, police said La Bash lured the children into his home with
the promise of "toffees" and DVDs, an allegation that shocked me by its
familiarity. For Ghanaian children, simple pleasures like a piece of candy,
or watching a Disney movie, are rare luxuries. The children in our courtyard literally jump in excitement when we give them a banana; a serving of

ice cream might as well be Christmas. One Saturday afternoon, Jan and I set up a "screening" of *Finding Nemo* on my laptop (we had no TV), and our dining room was packed with eager kids. It became sadly easy for me to imagine a predator luring Ghanaian kids.

The wheels of justice can spin rapidly in Ghana. Just one month after his arrest, La Bash was sentenced to twenty-five years' hard labor—in effect the rest of his life. One imagines the catalog of fiction does not contain a living hell as grim as a Ghanaian prison labor camp, or an occupant more deserving of its charms.

In fact, the whole culture of child rearing in Ghana makes it easy for sexual predators to operate. Children are taught to respect and obey adults, no matter who they are. It is not uncommon to see people on the street blithely order a strange child to run an errand. Indeed Kevin would often do this, drafting some passing "small boy" (as the invocation invariably begins) to run off in search of this person or that thing in the course of Burro business. The fact that the child didn't know Kevin from King Faisal hardly mattered: in Ghana, if a grown-up tells you to do something, you must do it. This rule extends to sanctioned forms of abuse like hitting children, which is also tolerated from strangers.

That year, an eight-year-old schoolgirl was caned to death by her teacher. The girl's father told a newspaper, "The child was caned in the head, the back and the spinal cord so the brain was injured and blood from the brain ran down through the throat and to the chest, that is the cause of her death." Ghanaian authorities arrested the teacher—pointing out that only "head teachers" are allowed to cane students.

The day after the American pedophile was arrested, I witnessed Joyce, the aunt of Savannah with whom we had made fufu, slap Kwabena across the face hard enough to send him sprawling. She is not related to him. Kwabena, who has a rebellious streak unusual for Ghanaian children, hit her back; he is learning to solve problems with his fists.

It is possible to condemn African domestic abuse and still appreciate African family values, just as Ghanaians might appreciate American democratic institutions but not the Central Intelligence Agency that toppled their first leader. It is possible to see Mena, who stoops over soapy buckets of laundry in deafness and old age but is surrounded by caring family, as having a better life than my own mother, who does nothing all day in a nursing home. It is possible, I decided, to appreciate Kwame Nkrumah as a brilliant catalyst for African independence despite his political failings. It is even possible, as Nkrumah said, to face neither East nor West, but forward.

eleven

# SKIN IN THE GAME

**FALL 2009:** The team

Rose warming up the crowd with her standard Burro spiel.

## 1. Stop Means Stop

The offices of the local bank, a leading microfinance organization in Ghana, were on the top floor of a modern five-story complex in downtown Koforidua. There was, of course, no working elevator, and the stairs were outside. With the temperature in the nineties and humidity near the dew point, Whit and I were soaked and gasping as we reached the entrance to the bank. Outside the door, a wall was covered with illustrated posters—cartoon characters and slogans that are supposed to motivate or inspire you, like you'd see in the break room of a factory. One poster showed a farmer in ragged, patchwork pants standing with his goat. Next to him, a man in a necktie was holding out a bag of bank notes. The farmer was turning away from the money. The poster said: "Do not take a loan if you do not need one." We pushed open the door and recoiled from the icy blast of air-conditioning as if hit by a fire hose.

Walking over from the Burro office, Whit had explained that the bank made loans to local farmers, merchants, and other small businessmen—anywhere from a few hundred to a thousand cedis—for seed, fertilizer, equipment, inventory, and other capital costs. He had an appointment with the branch manager to discuss several ideas, including financing for agents to build Burro franchises, financing for customers to spread their battery costs over a year, and partnering with the bank to identify potential agents in villages.

"He will see you now," said a woman behind a beat-up desk, motioning to a side door.

We opened the door and found the manager asleep at his desk. Hearing us enter, he bolted upright and began pretend-typing at his laptop. "Come in, please," he said, straightening his tie. We sat down and Whit explained Burro, then delivered his pitch for partnering with the bank. "It's a very good idea," said the manager. "Please come back on Monday and discuss this with my field representatives." The meeting was over.

"In other words," said Whit as we tramped back down the stairs, "stop bothering me with something that might resemble work. Actually he seemed pretty responsive. We couldn't really have asked for more out of a cold call—especially if the field rep meeting comes off."

The bank manager was an archetypal white-collar worker in Ghana. Although most Ghanaians—from farmers to market ladies to entrepreneurs like Charlie—work incredibly hard, for some citizens a college degree is seen as a ticket to a job with benefits and no accountability in an air-conditioned office. I make this observation without condemnation. As the Tunisian-French writer Albert Memmi put it in his influential 1957 book *The Colonizer and the Colonized*, "One can wonder, if their output is mediocre, whether malnutrition, low wages, a closed future, a ridiculous conception of a role in society, does not make the colonized uninterested in his work." In the aftermath of Memmi's book, the African has thrown off the yoke of the colonizer. But as the last half century of African history has sadly demonstrated, independence has not wiped the slate clean. It will take time for Africans to find their place in the modern work world.

Meanwhile, Whit needed to find Ghanaian college graduates with an enterprising spirit. He had learned when publishing a help wanted ad that he could eliminate most of the idle opportunists by stating that the office had no air-conditioning. The résumés that flooded his inbox showed alarming job mobility: people tended to change jobs every six months. "I think a few years ago Barclays must have offered some sales position to anyone in Ghana who could speak English and wear a tie—or a short skirt," said Whit. "It's like they hired everyone, and paid them literally no salary; it must have been all commission. So of course they all quit, and now every résumé in the country says former sales rep at Barclays."

Interviews could be surreal. "I went over to Polytech and asked a professor about hiring some electrical engineering grads," Whit told me. "I said I'm not looking for rocket scientists, just someone with some technical aptitude who can help keep the batteries charged and recognize bad ones. You wouldn't believe some of the people he sent over. The first guy was this big dude; he comes in and we explain the battery offer. To make sure he understands it, I ask him to pretend he's pitching the batteries to Rose. So the first thing he asks her is, 'Where are you from?' You know, people here can be sensitive about their ethnic background in different contexts, so she was a little taken aback. She says, 'I live in Koforidua.' He says, 'But where are you *from*?' She says, 'Well, I grew up in Accra.' He keeps pressing: 'But what language do you speak?'

"She finally says, 'I'm Fante. Why does it matter?' He says he wants to know what language to do it in. She says, 'Just use Twi.'

"So he starts out and devolves into this harangue about the program, how it will never work because people can't afford the batteries, on and on. So I say, 'You know, you raise some good points, and these are things we are all discussing on an ongoing basis as a team, but right now, when you're trying to sell Rose the batteries, this is not the place for that.'

"Then I ask him if he knows how a multimeter works. He says yes, so I hand him the meter and a radio and I say, 'How would you measure the power this radio consumes?' He takes the device, and Max, it was like voodoo. He's just passing his hands over it, and playing with the knobs and crossing the wires; he obviously doesn't know the first thing about it and doesn't seem to realize that I do. He thinks he's fooling me with magic or something. It was fucking laughable. I mean, why didn't he just say, 'I don't know how to use one but I'm a fast learner and I'm sure you can teach me quickly.'"

Even when Whit found job candidates who were honest and enthusiastic about the company and its mission, training required huge reserves of patience, with daily lessons that emphasized the basics. For example, the notion that emails benefit from subject lines describing their content came as a revelation to much of his staff. And all three of his employees needed to learn how to drive. After taking formal classes (paid for by Whit) and getting learner's permits, Kevin, Rose, and Adam required hours of practice behind the wheel; it fell to Whit and Jan to fill in the skills.

One day, on a harrowing trip to Accra, Rose (in three separate incidents) hit a Barclays Bank, ran a red light, and brushed back a traffic policelady. "Well, she was in my way!" said Rose in self-defense about the last infraction.

"It doesn't matter," said Whit calmly. "You still can't hit her."

Rose might have hit another pedestrian had Whit not reached for the emergency brake. "Rose, when I say stop, stop," he said. "Stop means stop. Right away."

"Am I doing that bad?" Rose asked.

"You're doing fine," said Whit. "You only hit one person and one building in two hours; that's one incident per hour, so I'll try to keep your missions under an hour."

"Oh, you are so bad!" she said.

"Just watch your clutch. It stays all the way in or all the way out, not in between."

## 2. Thinking for Yourself

"So when are you going to interview me?"

Small of frame and often quiet, Rose could easily be mistaken for a shy person; in fact she was confident and poised. She spoke with an inflective tone that turned every sentence into a challenge, which could seem jauntily flirtatious, in a romantic-comedy kind of way, or playfully mischievous—a fickle streak that was also reflected in her personal appearance. While she usually wore her hair braided into fine cornrows, sometimes she coiffed it into a straight perm, so one never knew what to expect. And contrary to the conservatively dressed women we encountered in the villages, Rose mostly wore blue jeans so improbably tight that I wondered if machinery were required to don them. She was smart, and not unpleasant company on a drive, so long as she was in the passenger seat. It was fall and we were traveling, the two of us, to set up a gong-gong in a Krobo village an hour northeast of Koforidua.

"What do you want me to ask you?" I replied.

"You should ask me about school."

"Okay, shoot. Tell me about school." I already knew that Rose was a 2009 graduate of Accra's Ashesi University College, a private four-year business and computer science school, with a strong liberal arts core, that emphasized entrepreneurship and ethics. Ashesi was founded in 2002 by Patrick Awuah, a Ghanaian graduate of Swarthmore and Berkeley's Hass

School of Business (and like Whit, a former Microsoft manager, although the two did not know each other then). *Ashesi* means "beginning" in Twi, and Awuah's goal was to begin by training students as good citizens and critical thinkers, reasoning that success in business would naturally follow. And if his school could also train the next generation of political leaders, so much the better.

"The whole idea of liberal arts, thinking for yourself, analyzing, not cheating on exams—it's very un-Ghanaian," said Rose. She went on to describe a depressingly cynical system of higher education, in which credit is contingent on bribing or sleeping your way into favor with key professors. Perhaps she was exaggerating; perhaps academic corruption is more the exception than the rule in Ghana, I don't know. But based on Whit and Jan's experience sorting through stunningly inept job applications from Ghanaian college graduates, I was giving Rose the benefit of the doubt. Then, in 2010, a sex-for-grades scandal erupted at Kwame Nkrumah University of Science and Technology (KNUST), the country's second-largest college. Apparently Rose was not exaggerating.

"How did you end up at Ashesi?" I asked her.

"I didn't want to go to a big school like Legon," she said, using the shorthand location name of the University of Ghana, one of seven public universities in the country. Legon was founded in 1948 as an affiliate of the University of London and now has forty-two thousand students.* "And I didn't like the national system where your major is determined by your test scores, regardless of your interests."

Ashesi, which currently has about four hundred students, appealed for its promise of individual attention. "Unfortunately it is very expensive," Rose said. Tuition ran more than three thousand dollars a year, a fortune by Ghanaian standards. Rose's family is not poor but hardly affluent—the Ghanaian version of middle class, such as it exists, which is to say *lower* middle class. Her father, Francis, works for an NGO that supports youth groups; he travels often to London and to southern and eastern Africa.

---

* Maya Angelou worked there as an administrator in the renowned School of Music and Drama from 1963 to 1966. She also performed in school plays.

Her mother, Becky, is a caterer, preparing Ghanaian specialties for weddings, funerals, and other social events. The family (Rose has a younger sister, Gracelove, who is studying accounting and fashion design) lives in Osu, the central business and shopping district of Accra, where Rose grew up in a modest two-room home behind a block wall on a narrow one-way street. A childhood in Osu is the equivalent of an American kid's growing up in midtown Manhattan. In much the same way as New York kids seem to know everything (or at least think they do), Ghanaians from the streets of Osu carry themselves with assurance.

Rose was actually born in Winneba, the large fishing town on the central coast and the easternmost stronghold of the Fante ethnic group. In colonial times the Fante maintained close relationships, in every sense of the word, with the Brits. Fante tend to be lighter-skinned than other Ghanaians, and they often have British surnames (as in Rose Dodd). President Mills is Fante.*

Rose managed to get about three quarters of her first-year tuition covered by financial aid, but she still needed to come up with eight hundred dollars, which she earned by working in a real estate office owned by a family friend. "The second year was the hardest," said Rose. "I did not have the tuition by the start of the semester, and the rule was if you did not have your tuition you could not get textbooks. So I had to study all year in the library. I still got all A's, and I told the school, 'I deserve a scholarship because I got A's even with no textbooks.'" The school agreed, and in 2007 Rose became the first recipient of an annual twelve-hundred-and-fifty-dollar scholarship in honor of a beloved professor named Princess Awoonor-Williams, a development economist and head of the business department who had received her own doctorate from Howard University.

"Turn here," said Rose. We bounced up a dirt track that climbed steeply, and when it turned into a path, we left the Tata and walked the last few hundred yards to the high village of Djamam. Along the path, delicate

---

* The Fante people speak an Akan tongue similar to Twi and getting more so in today's mobile society. At this point the two languages share many words.

Chinese lantern flowers, drying in the sun, hung from rangy bushes over our heads—Ghana's version of fall foliage. Wild begonias, pink and blue, crowded along the shoulders of the path like seedling racks at a nursery. Behind us, the land dropped off and the sky opened to a cyclorama of Lake Volta, its water stretching to the horizon and pulsing like a mirage in the heat. For a minute I imagined a distant human ancestor standing in this spot and enjoying the same view, although he would have seen a wide, branching river and not the man-made lake. Thanks to a unique geology that created rich fossil beds, eastern Africa's Great Rift Valley has become ground zero in the study of human evolution, but man may have also taken his first steps here in western Africa.

"So what are your plans for the future?" I asked Rose as we tramped along.

She laughed. "I have so many ideas. My problem is I get bored. I want to clean up the beaches of Accra, but not as a charity. You see these groups come in and do a big cleanup, but a year later it's covered in filth again. I want to do it in a way that keeps them clean forever. So people have to see clean beaches as a benefit."

"You mean tourism?"

"Yes, that could be part of it."

Indeed, with its miles of sandy coastline, formidable slave castles, animal reserves, friendly citizens, and English language, Ghana has the natural and cultural resources to support a first-class tourist industry. The potential is there, but the problem always boils down to infrastructure. The country needs better roads, safer transport, Western-style hotels and restaurants, cultural attractions that are well maintained, and yes—beaches that aren't vast public toilets. Rose talked about starting a targeted tour bus service that takes visitors directly from the airport in Accra to the slave castles and the national game park up north; currently there is no easy way to link those sites, and existing public transport, while dirt cheap, is unreliable, unsafe, and downright shocking to Western sensibilities. She also envisions organizing cultural homestays in small villages, and renovating the few tired old beach resorts that do exist.

"Do you think you'll get bored with Burro?" I ask.

"Not now, because it's a challenge; every day is different. If it really becomes successful, then I might want to try something else."

"Spoken like a true entrepreneur."

She laughed again. "I like working for Whit."

Left unspoken was the alternative, which for a young woman in Ghana often means working for lecherous creeps. Ask just about any Ghanaian working woman and you will hear stories of bosses who simply assume sex is part of the job description. Indeed, help wanted ads in Ghana often call out young ages and female gender as a requirement; some go so far as to call for "attractive" candidates. Like some cheesy porn movie, engaging in sex can even be part of the "interview" process, but it doesn't stop there. In late 2010, a story broke about a junior banking rep who came out with some colleagues (all anonymously) to state that the bank set impossible sales targets and that they were expected to sleep with potential major clients to secure their deposits.

The harassment often starts with flirtatious talk and moves on to work dinners, out-of-town travel to conferences (Ghanaian enterprises seem to spend much of their time conferencing, which if nothing else keeps the hotel business humming), late-night work in the room, and so on, with dreary predictability.

A related issue is the secret world of some Western aid workers and businessmen who, under the pretense of being in Africa to help poor people, are more pointedly interested in helping themselves to African women. While not as awful as the criminal pedophiles like the American "businessman" whose arrest I described in the previous chapter, these more garden-variety creeps still rate pretty high up on the icky scale. Whit and I would occasionally run into these malingerers—middle-aged white men living semipermanently in lower-class hotels around Accra, where they run businesses of questionable efficacy and spend their evenings around large dinner tables conducting their own version of social entre-preneurship with much younger locals. I'm thinking this subject doesn't come up at international conferences on developing-world business oppor-tunities, but based on our observations, the phenomenon is quite real.

The chief of Djamam had traveled, so we greeted an elder who was shaving rattan fronds into strips with a sharp knife, preparing to weave baskets. Rose explained the plan for the gong-gong, speaking in Twi and some Krobo she had been learning, then concluded in English: "So you understand it? There is a one-cedi deposit with each battery. Do you think people will still buy them?"

"I am telling you, they will come," said the elder. "Do not fear."

We walked back to the truck, past huts plastered with faded campaign posters emblazoned with a rooster—the symbol of the Convention People's Party (CPP), founded by Nkrumah himself in 1949 but now a perennial third-place finisher in national elections.* "These people all vote," said Rose wearily. I think she was tired from all the walking in the hot sun. "If I were them, I would not vote."

"Why not?" I asked.

"Because it doesn't matter. Nothing ever changes for them."

## 3. An Akan Proverb

On Wednesday mornings we had a staff meeting, which lasted about an hour and was run by Jan, following a printed agenda put together by Rose. Jan passed out sheets of colored graphs and bar charts, culled from the Fodder database, that illustrated battery rentals and business growth. "We're at one thousand sixty-four batteries with a hundred and fifty-seven clients on the new program," Jan reported one day in August. "Twenty percent are on grid." Gaining new customers on the electrical grid was significant because it suggested the business could work in cities as well as remote villages.

"That's great, Jan," said Whit. "I'm wondering, what's the best way to get at revenue per battery? It feels like something we should report. Any idea how that's running right now?"

"It ain't pretty," replied Jan. "July revenue was thirty-one pesewa per battery."

"Ouch," said Whit. "It's hard to see how that sustains our business,

---

* Nkrumah's daughter Samia was elected a member of parliament for the CPP in 2008.

long-term." At one point he had come up with a figure of fifty pesewa per battery per month as a bottom line. Calculating that the Koforidua branch could support at least three hundred agents if the routes were designed well, and figuring an average of one hundred batteries per agent, a fifty-pesewa average would yield revenue of fifteen thousand cedis per month—a real business, in other words.

"Well, remember, we're giving away lots of free coupon books to chiefs, queen mothers, and youth leaders in the new villages," Jan countered. "So we're doing a lot of promotions right now, and that's skewing the number."

"Can we just run a trailing thirty-day so we don't have to wait until the end of every month for an update?" asked Whit. "That will give us a meaningful number we can constantly track."

"What does that mean?" asked Kevin.

Whit and Jan together explained the concept of a trailing thirty-day average, and I could see a flash of insight in Kevin's eyes; he got it right away, but apparently no one in his previous business career had ever bothered to explain it.

"Speaking of promotions, we need to send another all-agent text message," said Jan.* "We're running a four-coupon bonus promotion till the end of September and giving agents an extra cedi for every client they convert from the old program."

"I can do that," said Whit. "Is the agent contact info in Fodder up-to-date?"

"As far as we know," said Jan. "Okay, let's move on to our monthly goals. We have twelve days remaining toward our goal of twenty new agents in August. So far we've added eleven. How's that going?"

Kevin and Rose detailed their plans for adding several new agents by Friday.

---

* Whit and Jan initially saw texting as a great way to communicate with agents, since virtually all of them had cell phones. But it turned out that the messages were relatively expensive (the price added up when you had a hundred or so recipients). And many agents, especially those living in villages with poor or no cell coverage, kept their phones turned off until they needed to make a call from a better signal area. Also, while Burro agents had to be functionally literate, few had ever used text messaging and most didn't even know how to access messages on their phones.

"How many of the first agents have converted their clients to the new program?" asked Whit.

"There are still many more to go," said Kevin. "Only two of twenty-six have been converted so far. Jonas and Yirenchi."

"What's our goal for total conversion—end of September?" said Whit.

"Right," said Rose.

"So we need to stay focused on that while also training new agents."

"And we need to make sure the new agents are signing new clients," said Jan. "I think client growth should be our main goal in October, and we'll need to come up with some new promotion. Now I'd like to spend a few minutes talking about the coupon inventory. Those coupon books are like money, and they need to be under lock and key. I created a database for managing the inventory, but Adam, you'll need to oversee it."

Adam, the twenty-eight-year-old accountant, was generally quiet but could be made to laugh easily. Tall, rangy, and handsome, he lived with his brother (a student at the local polytech, where Whit had searched in vain for job candidates) and wore immaculately pressed shirts and slacks. After graduating from Accra's Institute for Chartered Accountants, he worked as the finance officer for Youth Empowerment Synergy Ghana (YES Ghana), a local NGO. Adam was from Volta Region, stronghold of the Ewe, where he grew up in a village under sacred Mount Adaklu, an imposing butte that marks the spot to which the Ewe first migrated (from lands farther east) some five centuries ago. Although steeped in traditional African customs (his father, as mentioned earlier, was a chief), Adam was also devoutly Christian. Sometimes I would notice Post-it notes on his computer with biblical aphorisms he had jotted down for the day. He never touched alcohol and was apparently an excellent singer in his church choir, although I never heard him intone. We did, however, have several conversations about music after he became aware of the rhythm-and-blues collection on my iPod, and it was clear to me that he had an ear for all sorts of music. Sometimes on village trips we would hear some indigenous music (live or on the radio), and he would explain to me its exact tribal provenance and even the style of dancing one was expected to perform to the beat. I came to think of Adam as the sensitive-artist

employee, which is possibly not the best recommendation for an accountant. Indeed, Whit worried that Adam was occasionally in over his head
(and was quite frank to him about it), but as we all did, he liked Adam and
felt certain he was honest, if not always sharply focused. Part of the problem was that we *obrunis* had a hard time understanding Adam's English,
which was grammatically correct but heavily accented. This disconnect
appeared specific to the Ewe—I also had to listen carefully to understand
Charlie's technically perfect English—and was, perhaps not surprisingly,
reciprocal. While Whit and I had little trouble trotting out a handful
of basic Twi phrases, our attempts at Ewe were generally met with polite
laughter. We simply could not pronounce the words comprehensibly, let
alone properly.

"It seems my work day is getting bigger," said Adam in response to Jan's
request.

"That's good!" said Whit. Adam laughed self-consciously.

"Well, I was going to suggest that route managers handle their own
Fodder input, which would take some pressure off Adam," said Jan.

"Oh, but we get back so late!" Kevin protested. "That could be a problem."

"I don't think it will take that much time under the new system," said
Jan, "but let's think about it. Maybe you guys can come up with a solution
and present it to us. Let's move on. Where do we stand on the replacement
battery sleeves?" She was referring to the green plastic Burro labels that fit
over the battery; Whit was concerned that the beat-up labels on older batteries were contributing to the perception by some customers that the
batteries were not good. "Does China have the file yet?" meaning the digital artwork.

"Ready to go," said Whit. "The sleeves should be no problem. They're
being air-freighted so it won't take long."

"How do we put them on the batteries?" asked Kevin.

"Heat shrink," said Whit. "You just use a hair dryer. I asked them when
I was there if they would be cut to length and they said yes."*

"What about more D adapters?" asked Kevin. "We are almost out."

---

* This did not happen, and the sleeves had to be trimmed by hand in Burro's office.

"They're on the way," said Whit.

"I hope they are better than the last ones. I've been seeing some in the villages that are already corroded on the contact point. Customers are complaining." Kevin was keenly attuned to customer complaints, or at least ostensibly; sometimes it seemed like his reports from the field, generally downbeat, were more projections of his own issues than anything the customers actually noticed. When Whit and I talked to customers, they seemed mostly buoyant about the batteries—but then we were *obrunis*, so praise in our direction had to be devalued by the sycophancy factor, like a currency exchange. "The new ones should be better," said Whit. "Three-Sixty* tested them in an environmental chamber—blasting them with high humidity and water that's supposed to simulate two or three years of use. I can't say they looked pretty after that—I can show you the photos they emailed me—but they still worked fine."

"Speaking of water damage, I do have a housekeeping issue on the agenda," said Jan. In fact there it was, "Housekeeping," on the agenda. "Men, can you please put the seat up when you tinkle and down when you're done? The rest of us would really appreciate it."

"Nice segue, Jan," I said.

"Thank you. Anybody have anything else? Okay, this meeting is over."

The weekly meetings, which focused on problem solving and follow-up on tasks, encouraged initiative and personal responsibility—qualities not always emphasized in Ghanaian work culture. But Whit wanted—in fact needed, if he were to spend much time at all back home with his family— Rose, Kevin, and Adam to take even more "ownership" of the business. They needed some skin in the game. So he designed a bonus plan, which he unveiled at the August 26 meeting.

"I'm open to feedback on this," he began, "but here's what I'm thinking

---

* An American-run, Hong Kong–based company that helps Western companies source and manage manufacturing partners in China. Burro's start-up operation was an insignificantly small—if not actually bothersome—client for Three-Sixty, but Whit had a strong relationship with the company from his game manufacturing days, so they were basically doing him a favor while placing a long-odds bet this crazy Cranium guy might really crack the nut on expanding developing-country markets for a range of manufactured items.

so far. I don't want to set impossible goals; this year we'll be hard-pressed to just break even, and I want you guys to be motivated. So this is based on some realistic goals that will help make the company a success. These bonuses aren't pocket change. We're not talking bags of rice here. We're talking real money. Each of you has a chance to get a thousand-cedi bonus, paid in January, based on Burro results through December. That would be the maximum per person."

A thousand cedis was considerably more than a month's pay for each of them.

"Now, don't get your hopes up; frankly there is little chance you will get all that money. It's incremental, and we're asking all of you to do a lot of crossover work and build as a team to grow the company. So here's how we see it."

Jan went to the whiteboard and started diagramming as Whit continued.

"Two hundred cedis of your bonus will be based on your own personal goals and objectives."

"You mean like our job description?" asked Rose.

"No. That's different than goals. Adam and I are already working on very specific objectives for him, with completion dates, and Jan and I will get similar detailed goals for you guys. If, in the fair and reasonable decision of management, you have met your objectives, you will get this two hundred cedis.

"Another two hundred cedis will be tied to the other two people meeting *their* goals. Because we are a team. So Kevin, you have an interest in Rose and Adam meeting their goals, and Rose, you want Kevin and Adam to meet their goals. You guys have to work together.

"Then two hundred cedis is tied to meeting cost targets, keeping our costs down. These will be based on things you can control, not salaries or rent, but things you guys can control in the day-to-day way you run the business, like buying supplies and maintaining the cars. I'll work with Adam and Jan to define what reasonable costs are. This will be a sliding scale, it's not all or nothing. So if you hit the cost-control target completely, you get the full two hundred cedis, but you may get one third, or whatever, depending on our business costs. I need you guys to pay attention to spending, okay?"

Nobody said anything. I was thinking this could possibly lead to short-cuts, possibly even dangerous ones when it came to car maintenance, but I kept my mouth shut. Jan probably had a formula for that.

"Finally, the last four hundred cedis will be tied to revenue. We'll work with Adam to define some specific revenue targets and how to report on them daily—probably some evolution of the thirty-day trailing number. Maybe the bonus will be tied to revenue per battery as well as overall revenue, I don't know."

Silence.

"Well?" said Whit. "Like I said, we're open to feedback."

Nothing.

Whit was turning red. He grabbed a marker and jumped to the white-board, crossing a giant X through the whole schematic Jan had just written. "Or we can say forget it. I'll just *keep* the three thousand cedis! Because I'm not hearing anything from you."

Jan stepped in. "We need you guys to tell us what you think. This bonus plan represents about fifteen percent of your annual income. That's considered quite an attractive bonus in the U.S., but we don't know about in Ghana. Is that normal? Better than usual? Less than usual? We need you to tell us. Does this interest you at all?"

"I'm not looking for pats on the back," Whit added. "I'm looking for constructive feedback."

"If we get this bonus, you will have so many pats your back will be aching," said Kevin.

Everybody laughed. "That sounds like an Akan proverb," said Whit.

"It's good," said Kevin. "We're not saying the bonus is not good. But it will remain to be seen if we can make these goals and numbers."

"Well yes, that's the whole point," said Whit.

"Have you taken into account that our clients have very little money?" said Kevin.

"No!" said Whit emphatically. "What I mean by that is, these will be numbers that we have to hit or we're out of business. So it doesn't have anything to do with our clients' spending power. We need to have a hundred agents with a hundred batteries each to start making a profit—and that's with you guys, a staff of three. The bottom line is, we've gotta hit these numbers by the end of the year or we're done. We pack it up. We've got to show to investors—and I include myself as the guy who has already invested a quarter of a million dollars into this business—that we can start up a regional branch that makes money in a year."

"And the fact is," said Jan, "Whit has done a lot of research into what our clients are spending on batteries, and they spend a lot—several cedis a month."

"The whole country spends fifty million dollars, eighty million cedis, on batteries every year," said Whit. "We have an offer that beats the competition hands down. Frankly I think that anyplace we are in business we should be grabbing one hundred percent of the market share. All of it."

Jaws hit the table. Whit paused and looked around.

"Okay, let's be generous and say we only get twenty-five percent, nationwide. That's still a *fifteen-million-dollar business* in Ghana. A business that makes money and helps low-income families live better lives! We are doing something very different here, and you guys are leading it!"

At that point I thought Whit might strip down to tights and a cape, and leap off the veranda to save Koforidua.

Finally Rose spoke. "For me, I don't take satisfaction from a bonus; I take it from not being bored on my job. But it's good that we have it."

"That's fair enough, and a good point," said Whit. "I think we should all feel proud and satisfied in our jobs. This is a country with thirty percent annual interest rates. Most businesses here have only one model: buy cheap, sell dear, move inventory quickly. It's the only way they can profit with those interest rates. But we are building a completely different model. The goal this year is to prove we can do it in one place. The goal next year is replicability."

## 4. Cronies

The bonus plan required cooperation, and getting everyone on the Burro team to cooperate could be complicated by ethnic differences. All three employees were from different regions and tribes, with different customs and languages. Ghanaians pride themselves on tolerance and rarely express ethnic prejudices openly. But the truth is, they *think* about them all the time, and when pressed they will gladly share:

"The Ewe, they are very suspicious," said Kevin one day as we were driving the battery route. "They won't buy anything until they are sure it is good. The Krobos, if they see their uncle or brother buying it, they will buy it. The Ashanti? Oh, they will buy it if it is good, but only because they make up their own mind."

Kevin, of course, was Ashanti.

"Now the Ga," he concluded, "they all have the big mouth."

After Whit hired Kevin as his first Ghanaian employee, Charlie lobbied strongly for the hiring of Adam, an Ewe, for the accounting position. Fortunately for Whit, an equally qualified Ashanti candidate was not available for six weeks, allowing him to avoid the issue. But he and Jan had several discussions about whether it was right to consider ethnicity in hiring. Did it make sense to spread the jobs out equitably among ethnic groups? Or was it wrong and racist to even care? The issue was never settled, but Whit felt satisfied that his Ghanaian staff, accidentally or not, reflected a broad pool of ethnic groups.

Politics, as in national politics, could make for office tension as well. One day, again in the car with Whit and Kevin, I wondered out loud if there were any real ideological differences between the country's two main parties. Whit answered no, but Kevin disagreed. "The NPP is more business-friendly," he said. "They favor less taxes."

"Well, that was certainly their campaign manifesto," countered Whit, "but as a practical matter I don't discern any substantive difference between the parties. It's all about patronage, and not just in Ghana. I mean, hiring your cronies is how you stay in power. Breaking that cycle is a huge challenge. Somebody has to have the courage to step up to the plate and say it ends with us, but nobody has done that. I mean, Kufuor's government gave *thirty percent* raises to state employees three weeks before leaving office."

Indeed, there is virtually no accountability for government spending in Ghana. A 2004 report by the World Bank and the International Monetary Fund found huge discrepancies between budgeted and actual expenditures. For example, from 2000 to 2003, the Ministry of Education spent 39 percent less money than budgeted on actual services, while spending 45 percent *more* on salaries. The situation in the Ministry of Health was even worse, with services receiving 67 percent less than budgeted, and salaries going overbudget by 76 percent. As Tony Killick of the Overseas Development Institute wrote in a recent paper on Ghana: "There is evidence of large leakage in allocated funds between their release from the centre and their arrival at the point of service delivery."

Kevin laughed nervously at Whit's mention of Kufuor's vote-buying "raises."

"You think that's funny?" challenged Whit. "I don't. Because it's your money, and really, money that isn't there. Money that could be paving these messed-up roads." He swerved to dodge a pothole, paused, and took a long breath. "I think it's scandalous." Conversation dropped off.

## 5. Unknown

I walked to the immigration office in Koforidua's ministries complex to pick up my passport, which I had to submit (along with twenty cedis) for a visa extension. It's a queasy feeling to surrender your passport in a foreign country—"Come back in a week," the stern-faced immigration lady told me—and especially troubling when you come back in a week and she says, "Come back in one more week." But finally the day arrived. "Have a seat," the same unsmiling lady said, motioning to a plastic patio chair. I thanked her and bowed, although her invitation troubled me. I had assumed I would simply grab my passport and hit the road, but apparently not. I crossed the tattered linoleum floor and sat down. The small, dusty room was crowded with six beat-up desks, at which sat six women, nearly identical in their starched green uniforms with gold epaulettes and shoulder braids. There was not a scrap of paperwork on any desk, and no work apparently in urgent need of attention.* Instead, all six women sat with their eyes glued to a TV in the corner, which was playing a Nigerian movie. The woman whose desk was closest to the TV presided over a sizable library of DVDs, suggesting that film appreciation was, in fact, the real work at hand.

It was midday and meltingly hot—sweat poured from my brow even though I sat utterly motionless—yet the overhead fan was not turning, was perhaps broken. One of the women took my "Document Retention Receipt" and left the office; now I had no passport and no proof of ever handing it over to this zombie bureau, but I tried to remain calm, if not cool.

I focused on the movie, a typical Nigerian potboiler. Most revolve around deceitful businessmen, crooked politicians, beautiful women in danger, and one misunderstood but honest man out to save the country, who invariably dies, usually slowly and after prolonged torture at the hands of corrupt cops, orchestrated by an evil shaman. This particular film was not breaking any new ground. Minutes passed, scenes changed. A couple was asphyxiated by carbon monoxide in a Mercedes-Benz. The immigration ladies were arguing about whether the dead woman was pregnant and by whom.

Finally my passport arrived. But instead of handing it over, the lady sat down at her desk and withdrew a large dog-eared ledger book that appeared to predate the Ashanti-Fante War of 1806. She opened my passport, turned to the ledger book, and started writing. And writing. And writing.

The movie plot thickened. There was a motorcycle crash, a man ended up in the hospital. His wife came to see him. "You shouldn't do this to yourself," she said to him. Still the passport lady wrote.

---

* Computers were nonexistent; most government offices, at least in the provinces, conducted business on paper.

The movie ended. The credits rolled. I noticed that the character of "Deacon" was played by "Unknown," which I found curious. I guess by the time they finished making the movie, they had forgotten all about that guy who played the deacon. Maybe he will turn up one day and identify himself. Maybe, like me, he was a man without any identity documents. Still the lady kept jotting in her passport ledger book. The woman with the DVD collection popped in a new movie. During this entire time, no one else in the office took any action that I would classify as work; in fact, never on my several visits to Immigration did I see any worklike action undertaken at all, other than that pertaining to my own visa. Finally the lady closed her ledger book and handed over my coveted passport. "Check it, please," she said, "to make sure the extension is correct."

## 6. Your Woman Has Spoken for You

"Can I see your driver's license and fire extinguisher, please?"

Fire extinguisher? Rose and I were driving out to Fantem, a postcard African village of thatched-roof huts on Lake Volta, where a fisherman had promised us some fresh tilapia and duck eggs. The police roadblock was in the usual market-day location just outside Koforidua, and I was used to slowing down and waving as the police eyed our registration and insurance stickers on the windshield. But today's demand for a fire extinguisher was new—or rather a new variation on the too-familiar police shakedown. It begins with a citation for some obscure infraction. You will have to go to the police station, or to a judge in a distant town. All of this will take time. For a small consideration the matter can be settled right now.

As the young officer wrote me up, I told him, "I was not aware I needed a fire extinguisher," imagining that in the unlikely event my car were to immolate, I would leap out and run before it exploded. But the law was hardly about safety or logic. Perhaps some importer of fire extinguishers was on friendly terms with the government; a crackdown on missing extinguishers (who knew?) would drive business. The policeman who pulled me over was threatening to withhold my international driver's license until a court date. I was already without a passport, at that time still in the bureaucratic labyrinth of a visa extension. My license was my last proof of identification.

I called Whit while Rose talked to the cop in Twi. "Sit tight," said Whit. "We're on our way."

Rose and the cop kept on talking amiably; he was clearly curious about our business. Soon Rose was holding up a battery and launching into the spiel, which I could almost recite in Twi at that point. Soon they were laughing about something. Then the cop turned to me.

"Your woman has spoken for you," he announced in English. It was meant as an insult: a man who needs a woman to get out of trouble is not a real man. And by calling Rose "my woman," he was, I think, implying that I was one of those lecherous Westerners who come to Africa for all the wrong reasons. But it was all sticks and stones. He could have called me a child molester as long as he gave me back my international driver's license.

"I will tear up this ticket," said the officer, "but you must pay for the paper."

Ah, the paper! I was ready to hand him a ten-cedi note and be done with it, but Rose stepped in and negotiated the payment down to five cedis (about $3.50). He handed back my license, and we were off to get fish and eggs. I called Whit: "We're in the clear. See you this afternoon. Get a fucking fire extinguisher."

# twelve

# PAINT IT GREEN

**LATE 2009:** The brand

Burro's office and two thirds of the company's fleet.
The Kia Pride was undoubtedly in the shop.

## 1. Branding Fatigue

In mid-September of 2009 we got the Tata "branded," in the current business lingo—that is, painted Burro green with the Burro logo and slogans affixed to it in black self-adhesive vinyl (known in the trade as SAV). Branding, or "impact advertising," is pretty much what marketing is all about in Ghana; the country's low literacy rate and dozens of languages make it a challenge to convey information about your product. TV commercials have limited reach, since relatively few people own sets (although radio is popular). When you consider that Ghanaians spend virtually all of their waking hours outdoors (their tiny huts and houses, meant for sleeping, are cramped and stuffy by day), it's not surprising that outdoor advertising is the primary marketing space.

Commercial signage is everywhere; on the low end are hand-painted shop signs created by relatively skilled artisans, with studios on seemingly every block. These colorful kitsch masterpieces are designed for illiterate customers and illustrated with representations of the wares for sale—shoes, fish—or bizarre interpretations of the services rendered, such as severed hands and feet to announce a manicurist's shop. Many, perhaps most, small businesses in Ghana are named after seemingly irrelevant inspirational passages, such as the God Will Do Welding and Body Shop, Not I But Christ Fashion, Thank You Jesus Spare Parts, It Is Jesus Catering ("This is delicious, what is it?" "It is Jesus.") and my favorite: the unfortunately named Never Say Die Until the Bones Are Rotting Fish Store. In his recent book *The Masque of Africa*, V. S. Naipaul succinctly described the proliferation of African Christian signage "as though religion here was like a business that met a desperate consumer need at all levels."

In recent years, however, the Man from Galilee has faced stiff competition in naming rights from President Obama, a hero in Ghana and indeed most of sub-Saharan Africa. Now you can stay at the Obama Hotel in Accra while snacking on Obama Biscuits, a locally made sugar cookie that even appropriated the famous poster art by Shepard Fairey.

But the charming hand-painted business signs are merely the bottom warp in a tapestry of outdoor advertising dominated by big multinational impact campaigns. When Vodafone, the British mobile phone giant (45 percent owned by Verizon), bought Ghana's state telephone company in early 2009, they literally painted the country red. Along roads from east to west and from the Atlantic to the Sahel, entire villages of adobe huts were brushed, seemingly overnight, in bright Vodafone red, punctuated by the company's white apostrophe logo. Streetlights were draped in Vodafone banners, bridges transformed in red; even major landmarks, like Accra's Nkrumah Circle, were co-opted by Vodafone flags and signs.

It's not terribly hard to get your brand plastered across Ghana. Until recently, rural Ghanaians who lived along main roads were happy to let companies turn their huts into giant advertisements at no charge; the association with an "important" brand connoted status and was considered desirable—plus you got your house painted for free. "At first people were ridiculed for letting the companies paint their houses," said Kevin, who used to work in promotions for Guinness, "but then it became fashionable."

But as often happens with outdoor advertising, the branding of Ghana has devolved into an arms race. Today you can drive through villages that have been transformed into kaleidoscopic brand wars—every other home is either Vodafone red or the yellow of MTN, a mobile phone competitor and the largest carrier in Ghana; across the street are whole-house ads for Pómo tomato sauce (red and green) and Snappy peanut snacks (red, blue, and yellow). On the next block, Coke and Guinness duke it out in the beverage wars. (Besides its beer, Guinness owns the Malta soft drink brand.) Kevin told me that Ghanaians have started to show signs of branding fatigue and are no longer willing to offer up their homes as free billboards. Payments are increasingly common, especially in prime locations. And of course, companies pay towns and cities for the right to brand public spaces. These companies understand the importance of brand identity in Africa. Whit argued that brands matter even more to low-income consumers, precisely because they cannot afford to take chances on unknown products.

Yet despite the relentless branding of commodities like phone services and taste-alike beverages, the African retail segment is otherwise surprisingly under-branded; most consumer products, from housewares to appliances to clothing, are essentially generic and undifferentiated. Nobody, it seemed, was as focused as Whit on building a brand that would earn the trust and loyalty of low-income African consumers in products that are essential to them.

With revenue of some two hundred cedis a month, Whit was a long way from branding the countryside—not that he didn't have dreams of seeing entire Ghanaian villages painted in Burro green. For now he'd have to settle for company T-shirts, shop posters, and branding the two vehicles, starting with the Tata.

Through Rose we had established a relationship with a company in Accra that specialized in orchestrating brand campaigns; basically they took care of the details involved in ordering clothing, signage, car branding, and any other impact promotions you needed. If you wanted to face-paint Ghanaian market women in the color of your brand, they could probably arrange it.

Or at least, say they could. It didn't take long for us to figure out that what the company promoted best was itself. The outfit was run by a physically imposing man I'll call Dave, a member of the Ga ethnic group of greater Accra. Perhaps because they are primarily an urban people, the Ga have a reputation among Ghanaians as being aggressive and in-your-face. They are the New Yorkers of Ghana. They talk fast. With his thick-rimmed glasses and shaved head, Dave certainly fit the physical bill of a Big Man not to be messed with; I have no doubt his intimidating image was carefully cultivated—branded, you could say. In fact, as testimonial to the importance of protecting your brand, Rose had stumbled upon Dave's company by accident, its name confusingly similar to a far larger, better established, widely known competitor she thought she'd found when first meeting him.

At our first meeting in Burro's Koforidua office, Dave could hardly sit still in his chair, so eager was he to share his brilliant ideas for taking Burro to the top. Whit wanted T-shirts; Dave talked about vests with lots of pockets for the batteries. Jan wanted to know what a public-address system for the truck would cost; Dave was already talking about composing a Burro jingle and hiring actors for radio ads. He was going ninety miles an hour, but he didn't really understand the business yet. It was, in short, all talk, and not a lot of details at that.

Nevertheless, Jan managed to pin him down on a T-shirt order, and within a few days he had provided some paint samples (on twelve-inch-square metal plates) for branding the cars.

Burro's green color was somewhat hard to reproduce, a concern known to Whit when originally adopting it. The Burro brand identity was developed under the direction of Michael Connell, Cranium's former creative director, by the Los Angeles design firm Creable. To make a green that would really pop in print, the designers chose a Pantone spot color and specified two "hits" of the ink on a super bright white stock. If done properly, it looked great, popping vividly—almost neon. But it proved difficult to duplicate in Africa, where printers did not necessarily have the ability to match Pantone colors or to provide the correct coated paper stock. Even harder were clothing dyes and automobile paint tones because (at least in Africa) they were not as standardized as printer ink.

So it took a few weeks, but finally Dave managed to source T-shirt dye and car paint that Whit felt were close enough to move forward. We drove down to Accra on a Saturday to pick up the truck and the T-shirts, pulling in front of Dave's office, in a neighborhood with the exquisitely colonial name of Asylum Down, right on time at two o'clock. The truck was nowhere in sight along the narrow street.

"Where is our truck?" Rose asked the receptionist, an attractive and slightly cross-eyed woman in her thirties. She sat behind a large desk in a cramped and cluttered foyer of the building. On one wall was a glass case displaying shirts branded with the colors and logos of perhaps a dozen multinational companies.

"It is still being washed," she said. "Please wait."

"But we called two hours ago and it was being washed," said Rose. "That is quite a washing."

"Please, wait," she said again. "I will prepare the bill."

She left and returned a few minutes later with an invoice. Rose looked at the bill and said, "This isn't right. The shirts were supposed to cost five and a half cedis each, and you have billed us six cedis."

The receptionist extended her hand and took the bill, then perused it. "Dave will be here soon," she said.

"Can I look?" said Whit. He took the bill and turned to the second page. "Whoa! Six hundred twenty-eight cedis for the sound system?" He was referring to the charge for buying and installing the amp, microphone, and rooftop speakers. "On our pro forma, which I have here, Dave said that would cost a hundred and eighty cedis. I know he did call and say that he couldn't get that system and the one he found would cost more. But I figured, like, ten or fifteen percent more. This is three hundred and fifty percent more! I'm sorry, but that's unacceptable. I would expect a phone call for that much more."

"That is what it cost," said the woman blandly.

"I don't doubt it," said Whit. "But it's not even close to what I agreed to pay. So maybe I'll say just take the whole system out. I mean, I will talk to Dave when he gets here, but that's just outrageous."

Dave walked in, handshakes were made. Still no truck. "It's on the way," he said. "It looks fantastic."

"We can't wait to see it," said Whit. "But Dave, I am concerned about the invoice." He pointed to the audio system charges, comparing them to the estimate. "I'll be honest with you, Dave. I don't understand why you didn't call me about this. I don't like surprises in my business, and this is a very big surprise."

Before Dave could respond, a worker came through the door, jangling the Tata keys. "It's here," said Dave. "Let's go."

We walked out to the street and beheld the Tata, which was now a very bright green. It was, indeed, very cool. We walked around it, inspecting the paint job. We hadn't been sure quite what to expect in terms of quality—we had joked earlier that we hoped they wouldn't paint the tires green—so the professional workmanship came as a pleasant surprise. Although Whit noticed a couple of small drips around the windshield-wiper base, it was overall a very clean job. Even the doorjambs were properly painted. The vinyl logo applications were all done to spec. On top of the roof, mounted to the rollbar, were two large gray cone speakers. Inside the cab, a public-address amp with a tape deck was mounted on the console; connected to it was a microphone. Whit couldn't resist. He climbed in, turned on the ignition, switched on the amp, and grabbed the mike. *"Better battery, half the price!"* It was loud. We jumped, at first from the surprise, then with delight. This could be all sorts of fun.

"Man, we can really scare kids in the villages now," said Whit. "Nice job, Dave," he added.

Back inside, Dave offered to take fifteen percent off the price of the audio equipment. Whit grudgingly accepted but pointed out he still didn't understand what he was paying for. The invoice itemized two amps—an Ahuja "complete public address" for four hundred thirty-two cedis and another, with no brand listed, for one hundred forty-eight cedis; we could only see one amp, and it was not made by Ahuja. Where was the other amp, and what did it do? Dave didn't know, he admitted. The technicians installed everything. "Can I see the owner's manuals for this stuff?" asked Whit.

"I will get them for you," said Dave. "They are not here." Whit rolled his eyes. I went out to the truck to see if I could locate all the equipment. I looked under the seats, under the hood, under the dash. I saw only one amp, but I also noticed that the truck's original radio was missing; there was a hole in the dashboard where it belonged.

"Whit, the radio's gone," I said, back inside.

"Huh?"

"As in, not there."

"Oh, we have it," said Dave. "We took it out so it would not be stolen." A few minutes later an employee emerged from the back room with the radio, wires dangling. I went out to monitor the installation. The guy couldn't get the antenna cable hooked up—for some reason it was now too short. I went back in and found Rose and Dave in a heated discussion about the T-shirt invoice. "I am not paying this," she said. "The agreement was for five and a half cedis each, not six. I will pay the original price and no more."

Dave seemed like the type who was not used to women standing up to him; I thought I detected steam coming out of his ears. He hovered over Rose and jabbed his finger at her. "You are Ghanaian!" he bellowed. "Surely you understand the problem of inflation in this country!"

Up to now Whit had been listening, letting Rose take charge—which she was doing very well. But I could tell he was getting angry that Dave would try to bully her (not that it was working). "Inflation?" said Whit incredulously. "Ten percent a week? Sorry Dave, but you are insulting our intelligence. The price was five and a half last week when we paid you a deposit. If it was going to be higher, you should have told us then."

Outnumbered, Dave backed off. The technician came in and announced he could not connect the radio antenna without adding an extra length of cable. Whit rolled his eyes again. "It's definitely not good to cut and splice coax," he said, "but it sounds like we have no choice." Whit shot me a look that said "What next?"

We had arrived in the Kia, with plans to leave it behind for its own paint job. But at this point, Whit wasn't sure he still wanted to do any business with Dave. The guy had also been playing us along on getting posters printed; every week it was "next week" when his printers would get the right ink, and as with the car branding, price seemed to be arbitrary. Meanwhile, Burro was developing a network of agents who owned shops in key market towns and along main roads. Unlike "freelance" agents, who could walk around and introduce the battery to their neighbors, shopkeepers couldn't leave their stores and sell door to door. They needed signage to announce the product. Without what Whit called "promotional air cover" to drive sales, he was worried that busy shopkeepers would lose their enthusiasm for Burro—a deadly setback for a start-up.

So the need for posters was immediate, and Dave was punting. Fortunately we had found a reputable printer on our own—thanks to a brochure in a hotel, of all places. He was a charming and very professional Lebanese immigrant named Stephane Fawal, with many years' experience as a printer both in Ghana and France. While Dave hemmed and hawed about getting ink (and revised his price daily), Stephane was ready to roll; in fact we had met with him earlier that day to talk about options.

The next day, Sunday afternoon, Whit and I decided to take the truck out for a test run on one of the battery routes. We headed west out of town on a dirt road to Ampedwae. You could say our first test was more anthropological than technical. There is a part of the male brain, fully developed by the fifth grade and requiring no further academic discipline or apprenticeship, that recognizes categorically the intrinsic hilarity of amplified bodily noises. Mel Brooks paid homage to this branch of connoisseurship when he declared that as long as he was making movies, farts would be heard. In that spirit, Whit and I quickly performed a rigorous field test of belching into the microphone before moving on to more technical trials. I plugged in my iPod and cranked up some best hits from E. T. Mensah, the father of postwar Ghanaian highlife music who synthesized American big-band jazz with African rhythms. That turned some heads along the road: it's not exactly the sort of music you heard every day in Ghana in 2009, especially blasting from a bright green truck with two *obrunis* in it. We waved at farmers and market ladies and children along the road, and they all stared and laughed at the spectacle. *"White folk actin' stranger every day!"* Whit said like a 1930s Hollywood plantation mammy. We switched the soundtrack to Bob Marley, which is to say the soundtrack of life in Ghana, and watched children break into frenzied dance moves as we passed. They dropped their loads of water jugs and plantains and chased us like we were an ice cream truck.

*"Better battery, half the price!"* Whit recited into the microphone. *"Get more power for less! Burro batteries! Get them from Benjamin the chemist in Supresso!"* We drove on, finally reaching a village, called Asampanyie, that Burro had not yet opened up. As we scaled a rise into the village center, our speakers met their match: a circle of drummers under a mango tree were beating out a steady rhythm as dozens of people in dark robes and dresses shook their hips. It was a funeral, which in Ghana generally turns into a big party with lots of alcohol—the African version of an Irish wake. We pulled over and were instantly swarmed by tipsy mourners. Whit gave a spiel on the batteries and signed up a few new customers, who would be served by an agent in nearby Mangoase. I pictured them waking up sober on Monday morning and wondering where the hell they got these new green batteries.

Our fun with the sound system was short-lived. After just a few days of Ghana's punishing roads, the cheesy die-cast U-brackets meant to hold the heavy speakers onto the truck's roof bar had twisted and snapped. Whit called Dave, who said it sounded like we would need heavier brackets, as if the road conditions in Ghana were some surprise to him. Back we drove to Accra, back to Dave's office, where two of his workers brought out a pair of new brackets. I could see they were indeed much heavier, but they were also obviously homemade, with amateur welds that looked weak. The black paint was still wet.

"I think these will break," I said to Whit. He agreed.

"No good," he told the workers.

They went back inside and brought out a pair of new factory brackets in packages, better and stronger than the original ones. But although these brackets were made by the same company that made the speakers, Whit and I could see that they didn't quite fit. To attach them involved removing from the back of the speaker a gasketed metal ring that protected the magnet and all the circuitry from rain; the new bracket didn't work with the old gasket ring, and there was no seal. "These will leak," said Whit, pointing at the fit.

At this point the two guys ignored us and started assembling the brackets to the speakers. "What will keep the water out?" asked Whit, pressing on. One of the men started yelling at Whit in Ga, a language we understood even less than Twi. "I'm sorry, I don't speak Ga," said Whit.

The man scowled. "Do you speak any Ghanaian languages?"

"Yes," said Whit. "English."

"They will not leak," he said firmly.

"Okay," said Whit, holding up the water sachet he was drinking. "Let's pour water on them and see." The man ignored Whit, who took out his cell phone and called Dave. "Tell your men to take it all out. The whole system."

The worker's cell phone rang. He spoke briefly to Dave in Ga, then hung up. "I have been a technician for ten years," he said to us, seething. "I know what I am doing." It took over an hour to remove the sound system, because the technician didn't have a Phillips head screwdriver and had to use a penknife.

## 2. The Mad Men of Asylum Down

Our next meeting was just around the corner, at the Asylum Down office of MMRS Ogilvy, the Ghana branch of the global advertising firm. We had an appointment to meet with the business development director, a woman named Josephine Komeh, to discuss possible ways the company could help shape the Burro brand. Whit knew his business was (at least for now) insignificant to an agency that handled the Ghana accounts for giants like Nestlé and Unilever, but he also felt it would be good to make the introduction. So when Rose set up the meeting with a friend who worked there, Whit was happy to follow through.

We filed into a large conference room and shivered from the air-conditioning. There was a flat-screen projection system and a glass trophy case filled with Gold Gong-Gong trophies—shaped like cowbells—which I gathered were Ghanaian advertising awards like the American Clios. Whit unpacked his laptop and was connecting to the projector when a young man came in. "I'm very sorry," he began, "but there seems to be a misunderstanding. Josephine is in another meeting and cannot make it, but I will be happy to listen to your presentation." He seemed pretty low-level, and his English was only fair.

"Umm, okay," said Whit, tentatively. "How much time do you have?"

"Five minutes."

"Oh, then forget it," he said, closing his laptop. "We can't explain our company in five minutes. Thank you for your time."

"One moment please," the man said, leaving. A few minutes later he returned. "Can we do it next Monday?" he asked.

"No, I'm sorry," said Whit. "We are based in Koforidua and we are very busy up there. It's hard to find time to come down to Accra."

"One moment." He left again. This time he came back with the big shots: Josephine Komeh herself, plus the agency's creative director, Kweku Popku. After pleasantries, apologies, and business cards had been exchanged, everyone sat down and Whit launched into his presentation.

"I'll be honest with you," he began, "I don't think we'll be able to afford you. But I'd like to introduce you to the company so you are aware of us, and as we grow, hopefully we might be able to work together. At Burro we believe passionately in the power of the brand we are building, and we know how serious your agency is about brand development." He described his career and his previous time in Africa, then turned to the slide show. After a few introductory images came a slide titled "Burro Vision." Next to a photo of Whit, Kevin, and Hayford riding triple on Hayford's bicycle were four bullet points:

- Profitably deliver affordable goods and services that empower very low-income consumers to do more with their lives
- Leverage direct sales channel across multiple categories
- Collaboratively craft a world-class company
- Build a new kind of brand for the developing world

Whit explained the points, then clicked to the next slide, titled "The Burro Brand":

### "Burro"
- Memorable and short
- Easy to spell and pronounce

### The Donkey
- Cost-effective productivity enhancement
- Trustworthy, hardworking companion
- Tangible thing, simple, real presence

### "Do More"
- Aspirational promise—Burro does more
- Proactive call to action—you should too

The next slide laid out the financial opportunity:

- Consumers are currently spending $2 to $6 per month on throw-away batteries
- Additional energy demand can be met with batteries
  - $2 to $4 per month on kerosene for lighting
  - $2 to $4 per month on cell phone charging
- Substitute Burro battery service for these existing expenditures
- Put the economics of rechargeables within reach of low-income households
- Burro is better—and half the price
- $50 million market opportunity for batteries in Ghana alone

There were twelve slides in all. At the end, Whit said, "Our most immediate need from you is a multilingual audio pitch to create an initial exposure to the Burro brand and to drive sales of Burro's initial offerings. We need a signature sound, a music track, a drive-by pitch, and a stationary pitch for our vehicles, and we need all the creative and production. Are there any questions?"

"I am very impressed," said Kweku. "I like the two-in-one pitch with the adapter, which makes your product very versatile. What I would still want to know is, what is the *character* of the brand in terms of tone of voice? Before we could do the music, we would need to know more about that. Clearly the voice must be Ghanaian, but what kind of Ghanaian? How old? The music could range from traditional highlife, which is rather dated and conservative, to contemporary hiplife. Do you see what I mean?"

"Absolutely," said Whit, "and that's an excellent question. Right now I would say our sweet spot for customers is in the thirty- to forty-year-old range, but I know that's still a big demographic, and we have many younger and older clients. So we need to think about that."

"Another thing I would add," said Kweku, "is that every Ghanaian has aspirations to be better than what he is. Even the person in the gutter today dreams of doing better. So I would not focus too much on the poor as a concept."

"I hear you," said Whit. "This is really very helpful."

It was getting late and Whit was exhausted—too many meetings, too many late nights in the battery room, too many decisions, and too much fucking heat. Rose was staying with her parents in Accra that night; I took the driver's seat for the haul back to Kof-town. The lights of Accra were twinkling on as I pivoted the truck around the hairpin turns up the Akwapim Ridge and around the promontory of Kitase, where the presidential weekend retreat called the Peduase Lodge hovered in fog over the capital. The lodge, a sprawling modernist slab with its own theater, zoo, poultry farm, and cricket oval, was built by Nkrumah in 1959 as a place to house, entertain, and impress foreign dignitaries visiting the newly independent nation. Unlike Accra's Osu Castle, the president's primary residence and the seat of government, this new building would have no colonial references, no imperialist baggage, no slave history. It was sleek and modern—a new, updated look for the new "brand" of Africa.

At least that was the idea. To me it looked like an oversized Rat Pack playhouse—too ungainly and vulgar even for Sammy and Dino, but maybe perfect for, say, Jackie Gleason. Still, over the years it had gained a certain notoriety. In 1967 the lodge hosted the mediation talks between rival Nigerian factions that resulted in the ill-fated Aburi Accord. (Biafra seceded anyway, plunging Nigeria into civil war and mass starvation.) But by 2002, Peduase, like many of the slave castles, was abandoned and in ruins—terrazzo floors cracking, roofs leaking, giant termites feasting on the custom cabinetry, and curtains "reduced to rags," according to a firsthand report in the *Daily Graphic*: "There is nothing to write home about the pantry and the once magnificent fountain."

Peduase Lodge was renovated under President Kufuor and is now in use again. Unfortunately, the motorway out of town that provides the only access to Peduase—the same road to the university in Legon and on to Koforidua—is in a semipermanent state of rebuilding, and traffic crawls over dirt and around detours night and day. When President Obama and his family came in July 2009 (his first state visit to a sub-Saharan nation), they stayed at the airport Holiday Inn.

Whit was snoring by the time we passed Rita Marley's gated recording studio, just up the road from Peduase Lodge, and I drove the last, dangerous hour in tense silence, straining to focus on gutters and goats along the twisting pitch-black road. It was nine o'clock when we rolled through the gate of Koforidua's Mac-Dic Royal Plaza Hotel for a relatively expensive but welcoming dinner of grilled octopus and tough steak.

"I think Ogilvy will want twenty thousand cedis to do something for us," Whit said, pouring a glass of wine. "But I'll give them five thousand."

"And how will you convince them to take that?"

"I just won't do it. I'm ready to walk away. But they want to do it. It's good for their company, good for employee morale, good for their image, good for recruiting. They'll do it."

## 3. It's a Battery

Even if Whit wasn't ready to paint Ghana green, he was dying to paint Burro headquarters green. It was a largely symbolic gesture, since Burro did relatively little walk-up business, but Whit's lease was up for renegotiation, and in Ghana the landlord typically pays to paint the exterior, so the timing was right. We had seen a green tint on a building in the town of Aburi that looked just about right; I took a picture of the Burro truck in front of the green building, and you couldn't tell the difference. I walked around to the courtyard and asked the owner what the paint was. "Green Apple," he said, showing me the can with the brand. Back in Koforidua, I found it in a paint store.

Jan arranged with a local crew to do the painting, but the landlord felt their price was too high and strongly suggested they consult his cousin Seth, also a painter by trade, for a "competitive" quote. Seth came over and met with Jan. "Do you have equipment?" she asked.

"Yes, I have all the equipment," he said.

He got the job, but when he showed up to paint the façade of a building half the length of a city block, he had just one small putty knife, a couple of ratty paintbrushes, and a roller caked in dried paint. He had no drop cloths, no large scrapers, no masking tape, no cleaning supplies. He had no ladder.

"I will rent the ladder from the fire department," he told Jan, for two cedis per day, and off he went to secure what was apparently the only ladder in town; fortunately the city's cinder-block buildings rarely catch fire, but it does happen, given the haphazard electrical wiring that appears to be standard in Ghana. The few fires I had noticed over the course of a year all smelled electrical and blotted the sky with foul black smoke.

Meanwhile, Seth's assistant showed up and introduced himself as a pastor.

"A pastor?" said Jan.

"Actually I'm a prophet," he replied. Jan raised her eyebrows. "A minor prophet," he clarified.

"We were hoping for a painter."

He ignored her and went to work, perhaps already deep in revelation.

As the job progressed, it became clear that neither painter had received much divine inspiration with the brush. Both were slopping paint all over the veranda floor. Jan came out and noticed Seth was painting the spaces inside the decorative cinder-block balustrade, which were caked with years of urban grime.

"You can't paint the dirt," she told him. "You have to scrub off the dirt with a brush and water."

"I don't have any water," he replied. Jan brought him a bucket and a brush.

"If I wash it, I will have to wait for it to dry, and that will slow me down," he said.

"I don't care," said Jan. "The paint won't stick to the dirt." And she took his scraper and showed him how the paint he had applied slid right off.

"Oh, I get you," he said. But the next time she came out, he was still painting over the dirt.

By the end of the weekend they thought they were done and returned the ladder, but when Jan came back from Accra on Monday she noticed lots of missed spots and mistakes. Seth went back to the fire department to reclaim the ladder, but it was in high demand and someone else had rented it. Eventually the work got done; the total cost was seven hundred and three cedis, including paint. To no one's surprise, the new green-and-black building attracted a wave of walk-in business. More important, it established the brand in downtown Koforidua. One day Precious pointed at the façade and said, "Auntie Jan, it's a battery!"

thirteen

# MOTOR CITY

**LATE 2009:** The demographics

Makeshift sound trucks like this cruised past the office daily, blasting Ghanaian rap music as young men (almost never women) danced in the flatbed.

## 1. In Camelot

"**This sucks.**" Whit was talking as usual and driving, or rather braking, in a typical Accra traffic jam. In 1971 Nadine Gordimer described Accra's "vast chatter and surge of the streets, the sense not of people on their way through the streets but of life being lived there." I'm not sure if she was writing about the traffic per se, but as far as I was concerned I had already lived nine lives on the streets of Accra and was now entering the gates of hell. It was late morning and the sun was pounding like a railroad sledge on the roof of our defenseless Kia, which had no air-conditioning and was fast approaching the temperature required to fire porcelain. Outside, a river of street hawkers flowed around the stalled cars. In an effort to stave off ennui and Whit's endless prattle, I took out my notebook and started recording the merchandise as it moved past our car. This was my list:

Steering wheel covers, baby dolls (Caucasian) in strollers, Jesus wall clocks, chocolate bars, Ghana flags, yams (whole, extra large), full-length mirrors, reading glasses (assorted powers), sunglasses (fastened to a large sheet of plywood), belts, blue jeans, Sylvester Stallone DVDs, English dictionary, shoes, sandals, socks, button shirts, oversized foam alphabet blocks, plantain chips, Obama DVDs, neckties, cuff links (Ghana flag design), Michael Jackson DVDs, shorts, boxers, briefs, briefcases, ginger snaps, bracelets (brass), Sprite, Coke, toothpicks, newspapers (headline: "YOU'RE A BEAST," JUDGE TELLS RAPIST), cashews, single book (*Everywoman: A Gynecological Guide for Life*), soccer balls, car-washing chamois (Shell Oil logo), toilet paper (Chinese brand), child's spinning top (demonstrated by salesman on dashboard of car, through open window, uninvited), air fresheners (Liverpool Football Club logo), plastic coat hangers, plastic clothespins, onions, toenail clippers, power adapter plugs, carved wooden masks, Swiss Army knives, screwdrivers, Tummy Trimmer girdle (as seen on TV), Ping-Pong paddles with ball, watches, puppies (two, cute), Salif Keita CDs, crucifix (framed), caps, pillows, limes, tiger nuts, boiled peanuts, windshield wipers (assorted), doughnut holes, end tables, Super Glue, hair brushes.

I gave up at that point, partly because of heat exhaustion and partly because if you accidentally allowed your eyes to cast more than the merest peripheral glance at any particular ware, its seller would take you for a potential customer and hound you like an auctioneer until traffic moved again, which was to say a long time. And while some of the items had a clear marketing logic in the inferno of an Accra traffic jam—cold beverages, a snack—and others, like key chains or pocketknives, could be understood as impulse purchases, most seemed like a stretch. Who buys reading glasses in traffic? Or bedroom furniture?

"Look, nightstands! Just like I've been wanting, and the price is right!"

"Sorry I'm late, traffic was nuts and I bought a really cute puppy."*

Still other items reflected the desperation of poverty. Who but the hungriest would spend all day in shadeless ninety-degree heat, breathing car exhaust, in the hope that somewhere in that river of traffic was a driver looking for an outdated gynecological textbook? There is an optimism to indigence that is both admirable and sad.

"I'm sorry, were you saying something, Whit?"

"I was saying how pointless this traffic jam is."

"I meant, were you saying something insightful?"

"What I mean is, even without doing some kind of sophisticated computer tracking system, they could just get the existing traffic cops who are sitting around doing jack to really do their jobs. Put them at every corner, and teach them how to direct traffic, which right now almost none of them seem to know how to do." He slammed on the brakes to avoid rear-ending the *tro-tro* that was crawling three feet in front of us, spewing black smoke.

If solutions to Accra's traffic nightmare seem painfully evident to a

---

* Whit has reflected that Ghana's primitive retail environment and nightmarish infrastructure has expanded the definition of an impulse purchase. In other words— yes, you do buy that nightstand or that puppy on the side of the road because it's so much easier than even contemplating "shopping" for one in some later all-day episode.

Westerner, the causes of individual tie-ups can be pointedly African. One morning a busy quarter of the city was brought to its knees after a man trying to harvest honey from a beehive high in an acacia tree decided to simply burn the tree down. It crashed onto the main Ring Road and blocked traffic for hours. "The tree was said to have fallen at dawn," a newspaper reported, "however as of 10 am, the road had not been cleared, and there was no sign of the Ghana Highway Authority or the Parks and Gardens whose responsibility it is to evacuate the road. Some of the commuters who could not endure the searing morning heat . . . were continuing the rest of their journeys on foot."

Walking started to sound like a good idea. We were running late, as usual, this time for a meeting in Osu. Whit had an appointment at a Nigerian-based company called Camelot that specialized in security printing—gift certificates, lottery tickets, the sort of things you wouldn't want copied or counterfeited, like Burro's battery exchange coupons.

Camelot's facility, off a busy main road along Accra's tattered urban beachfront, certainly seemed imposing. A large mechanized gate swung open and we entered, under the stern gaze of a guard, past signs warning NO MOBILE PHONES OR CAMERAS and ALL CARS WILL BE SEARCHED. Our dull and dented Kia limped rather pathetically past a fleet of shiny, tinted-glass SUVs belonging to other customers who, at least in my imagination, possessed an acute need for security printing and security everything else.

The offices were mercifully air-conditioned, and we were ushered into a small room and greeted by a pleasant enough representative named Bernard, who got right down to business. "These are some samples of what we can do for you," he said. "I regret that you cannot take any of these with you, as they are actual jobs we are doing for clients, but you are free to examine them here."

The first sample, some sort of grocery-store contest certificate, was printed on a simple watermarked paper called CVS1, used mainly for checks. "This is our design but we import it, it's not made in Ghana," Bernard stressed. I hadn't thought about it before, but his comment made me realize that paper provenance was important; if employees are going to be pilfering watermarked paper, you want the paper plant far away from where you do business.

Next came examples of various ways to imprint security systems on the paper. The first was called thermochromic: a small reddish dot appears to the eye, but when you apply slight heat—like from your finger—it magically disappears. "People don't realize it," said Bernard, "so when they copy it, the red dot doesn't work on the copies. We can shape the thermochrome to match your logo." That would mean a donkey head that disappeared when you rubbed it. Might be fun for kids, I thought, but as usual I kept my mouth shut.

Next came a special gold seal, called a foil print. Then he showed us a silver hologram, then a serial number that bled through to the other side of the paper and was hard to copy. Another option was ultraviolet printing, which requires a special UV light to see. Similarly, some inks can only be seen after rubbing with a reactor pen, or what we used to call a Dick Tracy decoder pen. Then there was microtexting, which involves printing lots of minuscule lines of text as background; every seventeenth or so line says something slightly different, which crooks are unlikely to notice when copying.

Finally there was a simple but fascinating process in which a company logo is "sculpted" in a different color using lines similar to a topographic map, creating a 3D illusion. When copied, the logo doesn't "pop" in the same way as the original.

If it had been up to me, I would have ordered everything—a watermarked, invisible-ink, thermochromic gold-foil donkey hologram that says *hee-haw!* when hit with an ultraviolet strobe light. But it wasn't my money.

"It's all pretty amazing," said Whit, reading my mind. "But I'll be honest with you, Bernard, I suspect a lot of this stuff is out of our price range right now." (This was becoming Whit's standard refrain with vendors.) "I do like the idea of watermarked paper and possibly that sculpted logo, which I don't imagine is too expensive, right?"

"That's right, compared to the hologram and some of these other things," said Bernard.

"And the more coupons we can get on a standard page, the cheaper each coupon will be, right?"

"That's right."

"Can you print a full page of coupons perforated to this size?" Whit took a postage stamp–sized Burro coupon out of his pocket and handed it to Bernard.

"Not that small," he said. "We use a roll press and can only perforate to a minimum of three inches square."

"Really?" said Whit, surprised. That would effectively make each coupon cost about twice as much. "In China I've seen this done with a hand machine where they can set the perfs as small as you want. The guy just puts each page in the cutting machine and presses it down."

"We don't have such a machine," said Bernard flatly.

"I hear you," said Whit. "But it's actually not that complicated. The ones I saw in China were just made on the spot."

Changing the subject, Bernard said he would consult with the company's designers and put together an affordable proposal. We left amiably and agreed to stay in touch. No one searched our car.

## 2. We're Not in Shanghai

Our next errand was replacing the Kia's four worn tires, which meant another tedious slog through traffic, to Accra's tire district—a multiblock stretch of shops along a busy artery. As one who has owned and maintained cars in New York City, I was fascinated to find a country that had downgraded tire buying to an even lower circle of hell than I thought possible. In Accra, all of the tire shops were on one side of the street, and all of the installation shops were on the other side. So after haggling for your tires on the first side, you needed to negotiate your car through six lanes of traffic to the other side for installation. As the road was bumper-to-bumper and divided by a median that eliminated all opportunities for U-turns, the drive across the street meant another half hour in traffic, circling the block. Meanwhile, an army of youths, all of them expecting a tip, were waiting to carry your new tires across the street for you. Whatever.

Accra's tire business was run, if the verb's meaning can be stretched, largely by the Kwahu, an Akan ethnic group from the Kwahu Plateau and the Afram Plains, north of Koforidua. *Kwahu* means "slave died," and according to Akan mythology, the slave of a wandering tribe died on the plateau, fulfilling a prophecy and marking the place for the tribe to settle. It remains a strange and exotic corner of Ghana, pastoral and wide open like the American West, also home to the nomadic and sharp-featured herdsmen called the Fulani, whose women blacken their lips with henna. Whit and I ventured up the Kwahu Plateau one Saturday, encountering a group of Fulani and their emaciated livestock as we coaxed the Tata over a hillock of boulders. They spoke not a word of English (their language is called Pular) and seemed as surprised to see us as we them; the men wore tall conical straw hats that looked more Asian than African, and the women wore turbans and colorful beaded necklaces; all had long, hand-embroidered robes.

The Fulani and the Kwahu are constantly at odds—in part it's the age-old conflict between herdsmen and farmers—and life on their remote highland is undoubtedly arduous. Still, it is difficult to imagine the Kwahu people descending from this mythic escarpment to adopt a life of haggling over steel-belted radials in Accra. The motivation, of course, is obvious: money, and the quest for a better standard of living. The Kwahu have a reputation for being excellent businesspeople—hardworking and innovative. Some of Ghana's wealthier citizens are Kwahu, and many return to the plateau to build incongruously outlandish trophy homes with their Accra-earned wealth. "Every Ghanaian has aspirations to be better than what he is," the Ogilvy man had told us. You can't really argue with that, especially if you haven't personally embraced the life of a highland hut dweller over indoor plumbing and electricity.

Having bought our new rubber and made the schlep across the street to the installer's shop, Whit and I settled down—way down—into a flaccid sofa that leaned drunkenly, springs akimbo, alongside an outdoor shop floor of exquisite commotion. A platoon of grease-encrusted workers rolled tires back and forth, shouting in Twi, fighting over hand jacks, and sliding under cars that were pitched up on stands and listing like deck chairs on the *Lusitania*. More cars waiting their turn had been backed obliviously into the traffic lanes, so it was hard to tell which cars were being worked on and which were merely unfortunate enough to be stuck in traffic behind them. There was a lot of honking. It was a spectacle, choreographed in that particularly African sense of order that bears a distinct resemblance to chaos.

"That whole thing about the perforation cuts was interesting," said Whit. He was still thinking about the meeting at Camelot.

"What do you mean?"

"I mean the guy saying they couldn't do it to my specs. The die-cutting machine I've seen in China must cost like three hundred dollars. The guy sets it up by hand; the dies are just pieces of metal with razor-sharp edges built on sheets of plywood. He sets it up any way you want and off he goes. There's no bullshit answer like 'the machine can't do it.' So yeah, you need a few guys to do some welding, so what? Workers in China are totally coachable. You tell a Chinese worker it's not okay to have the label come below the edge of the adapter and you will never see it again. It will bring dishonor to his family."

"How much do factory workers make in China?"

"About a dollar an hour; here maybe half that."

Whit stared out at the gridlocked traffic. "The lost productivity in this country is just staggering. In Shanghai they've got this mag-lev bullet train that goes like two hundred and fifty miles an hour and whisks you from the airport to downtown in about fifteen minutes, for less than ten dollars. It's almost as far as from here to Koforidua, which takes us almost three hours."

"We're not in Shanghai," I said, trying as always to bring insights to my brother's business plan. "Besides, here we get so much quality time in the car together."

"Shut up."

I think he said something else, but it was lost in a sudden chorus of shouting and even more honking than the default din. Although it seemed contrary to the laws of physics, somehow the traffic was parting. Into this void drove a loaded and impeccably detailed Range Rover, which creaked to a royal halt in front of the main tire bay. Out stepped a pair of shiv-pointed patent leather loafers, followed by a beige linen abacost of generous yardage.* Here was a Big Man of the Very Big variety, and his shaved pate was wrapped in thick black glasses. He barked something in Twi, and workers scurried. Moments later, four underlings returned, each hefting a massive tire and a chrome wheel with more facets than the Hope diamond. The Big Man grunted his approval and checked his gold watch impatiently. The "old" tires on his SUV still looked new—as new as the vehicle itself—but off they came.

Some things in Africa, such as labor and okra, are reliably cheap, but high-performance SUV tires and titanium alloy wheels are not among them. One of the shop guys told us the Big Man's new tires cost nine hundred cedis each, the rims five hundred—a total rolling package of about four thousand *dollars*, or more than my brother's entire car was worth.

"Your aid dollars at work," Whit whispered my way.

"Looks like he works for the government," I said, "but who knows."

"That's what I mean."

## 3. Control Yourself

When Africans aspire to a better life, they generally aspire to the urban life. There are exceptions, like my farmer friend Jonas who aspires to be a bigger and better farmer, but the massive and ongoing urbanization of the continent tells the larger tale. Across Africa, people come to the city because the city offers hope whereas the village will never change, as Rose

---

* Abacost: from the French *à bas le costume* or "down with the suit," referring to Western-style business suits that were rejected during the African independence movement as patronizingly colonial, especially by venal dictators like Zaire's Mobutu. Oddly enough, the abacost is in fact a suit, but a distinctly African version with short sleeves and large external pockets. Ghana's President Mills wears them almost exclusively.

said. Electricity is not "coming soon" to a village near you, despite what the politicians promise. And even if it were to come, who can afford the hookup?

Of course, the chances of becoming a Big Man (or a Big Woman) in the big city are virtually nil, but that's not the point. Most urban migrants are happy if they can secure a small but steady income, possibly enough to support family back home in the village. It is understood in Ghana that when a "city cousin" comes back to the village for a visit, he will bring gifts—food, alcohol, a new Chinese radio, or just money. For many Ghanaians, including the ones who stay behind, city life connotes the good life.

But as with politicians everywhere who promise more than they can possibly deliver, there is not nearly enough good life in the big city to go around. As a result, the default condition in cities across Africa has become chaos and misery—vast, wheezing slums, crimes of breathtaking human indifference, coma-inducing traffic delays, and a whole new playbook of deadly contagions. Still they come.

While Burro's initial business plan was targeted at the millions of Ghanaians who still live in the villages, there was a battery business to be built in cities too. A lot of Whit's customers lived on the grid, in Koforidua and smaller electrified towns around it, but still used flashlights, such as when walking around at night (streetlights are virtually nonexistent in Ghanaian cities). Other urban battery uses presented themselves on the ground; nobody could have modeled them in a business plan from America. Like the wedding photographers.

Actually they photographed all sorts of social events, some of them quite specific to Ghanaian culture, like the party-all-day funerals and the so-called "outdooring" ceremonies, another big party that is sort of like a baptism for newborns. Documenting these milestones was a lucrative second income for Ghanaians who could make the investment in some basic digital camera equipment and had weekends free. Since even most urban Ghanaians do not own cameras, the market was robust. Dozens of photographers plied their trade in Koforidua alone. It didn't take long for them to figure out how many more flashes they could get from Burro's NiMH batteries than from the crappy competition, and they literally beat a path to our door.

Which is how I met Celestine Galley, a Ghanaian woman of singular charm. She rang the bell one day and came in clutching a handful of batteries. She was middle-aged, a large, gap-toothed woman with a big mop of curly permed hair, a cavernous voice, and a motorcycle. A nurse in the outpatient department at the local hospital, Celestine worked as a photographer on weekends; she had zipped over on lunch break from the hospital, on her bike in her starched white uniform, to exchange batteries. "They are the best for my camera," she said. "Four batteries give me one hundred pictures. You people are so good to me!"

"Well, we appreciate your business," said Whit. "Tell your friends."

We chatted while Celestine waited for her new batteries. "How are things at the hospital?" I asked.

"Oh, it's very bad," she said, waving an arm in disgust. "We have so much sickness. The young girls, they pull up their dress and then you fuck and you get AIDS." She illustrated her point with the universal finger-in-the-hole gesture. Here it should be noted that even Ghanaian men rarely drop F-bombs; for women the word is considered unspeakable. As for the obscene hand gesture—no matter how long I thought about it, I couldn't recall a time in my life when I saw any woman making that, and I worked in rowdy bars for years.

Somehow I felt Celestine's biker-chick conversational style required a suitably salty repast, but all I could come up with was "No worries for me, I'm happily married."

"Well, pray to God you control yourself," she said with evident suspicion.

Celestine lived a short walk from Burro, in the ground-floor flat of a tidy apartment block, across the street from a popular watering hole called the Bula Spot. One day after work I called her up and arranged to come and visit. Her Yamaha 250, quite a beefy bike by Ghanaian standards, was parked in the courtyard. "You are welcome!" she said, motioning me inside. Remembering her frat-house vocabulary in the Burro office, I half expected to see empty schnapps bottles all over the floor and velvet paintings of dogs playing poker. But it was nothing like that. Her apartment was certainly crammed with stuff—cookware, stacks of plastic storage bins, fake floral arrangements, and shelves overflowing with enough Christian curios to open a votive shrine. But even with all the bric-a-brac, the place felt roomy under high ceilings. She had two bedrooms; a living room; a small kitchen with a sink, a four-burner cooktop, and a fridge; and a bathroom with toilet and shower. The floors were terrazzo. It was, all things considered, a very comfortable home—bigger than the apartment in Brooklyn where Sarah and I lived for ten years.

We sat in the living room, where a small TV with grainy reception was playing an American soap opera. Celestine told me she was fifty-four years old and had been a nurse for thirty years. She was Ewe, from a village in Volta Region. She ended up in Koforidua because that's where the job was. Her parents had long ago made the urban migration to Accra. Although never married, Celestine had two boys—a seventeen-year-old who attended boarding school in Begoro, about an hour north, and a thirty-five-year-old who was getting his master's in finance at Towson University in Maryland. "He wants to stay in the U.S.," she said. "If he gets a green card, I will go to visit him."

Meanwhile, just about every weekend for the last fifteen years, Celestine would hop on her motorcycle with her two digital cameras and travel to weddings, funerals, "any event," she said. The five-by-eight prints she had made at a local lab cost her fifty pesewa each, and she sold them to her clients for twice that. She could also get larger prints laminated onto decorative panels for fifteen cedis, and her living room was cluttered with stacks of samples. But the profit margin was smaller on those, she said, as customers only seemed willing to pay about twenty cedis.

Celestine said she planned to retire from nursing in six years, at age sixty, at which point she would receive a small pension. "I have been saving," she said. "I plan to open my own photo studio."

"I have no doubt you will succeed," I replied.

"I am always fighting," she said, jabbing her fists like a boxer. "Struggle, struggle. You can't rely on anybody, only God. As soon as you rely on another human being, that's trouble for you. That's my life. No boyfriend, no husband, they are very bad. God doesn't like that. It's a bad habit. It's not godly." I wondered about the no-account men who had passed through her life, breeding fatherless children and misandry, but I didn't ask. "I praise God and thank Him every day for what I have," she said. Then she took my picture.

## 4. Money Pit

If you want to get a sense of how the urban elite in Ghana shop, you go to the Accra Mall. The mall looks pretty much like malls in America. It's clean and air-conditioned with lots of free parking, a well-designed multiplex, and a large anchor tenant on each end—Shoprite, a South African grocery chain, and Game, a South African version of Target. In between are trendy clothing and accessories boutiques that look vaguely familiar until you realize they are mostly South African knockoffs of popular Western chains. There's a Pottery Barn lookalike called La Maison, for example. Walking through the Accra Mall is sort of like being in a parallel shopping universe, or a *Star Trek* episode about a planet where everything is sort of like home, but tweaked in some weird way. There is even an "iShop," which sells Apple products but is not a real Apple store.

I'm not much of a mall rat even in America, and when I spend lots of time in a country where daily shopping is done in chaotic public markets and along trash-strewn boulevards lined with shacks and lean-tos, I tend to forget all about things like Pottery Barn and Cinnabon. I just never wake up in Koforidua thinking, "Damn, I wish I could go browse wrought-iron candlestick holders." (Actually, come to think of it, you can get some pretty cool hand-forged iron stuff in the Koforidua public market.) I get used to not having that stuff around, and then I forget about it, which makes seeing it all the more shocking.

All of which is to say that while entering the Accra Mall would fail to dazzle back home, in Ghana it's like walking through the main gate of the Emerald City.

With gemlike prices, I might add. Stuff in that mall is just mind-bogglingly expensive—far more than in the United States for the same merchandise. I don't know if it's the lack of competition, the inability of Africans to buy mail order on the Web, stiff import taxes, or all of the above, but if you want the good life in Ghana, you will pay dearly. Even the food in the grocery store is out of reach of most Ghanaians, but there too the merchandise is obviously geared to an elite crowd looking for prime steaks, Parmesan cheese, and vintage wines. Naturally, the crowd at the mall is relatively upscale, and you see plenty of *obrunis* from the diplomatic corps and the NGOs. Still, not everyone is as high-toned as you might expect. Whit maintains that the guards shoo away people who look "too bush"—radically indigent farmers with tattered clothing and matted hair. But there are plenty of very poor urbanites with a clean pair of jeans who stroll through the mall window shopping—aspiring to be modern consumers, as it were. I often found myself silently rooting for these apprentice materialists: "C'mon, you can get that blender if you work hard and save! Think of the mango smoothies!" Maybe someday, when you have electricity.

From the mall parking lot you can get on Ghana's only expressway, which runs from there to the port of Tema. It was built under Nkrumah and was supposed to go all the way to Kumasi, the inland capital of Ashanti Region and Ghana's second city. But Nkrumah was deposed before it could be finished. Under former President Kufuor, the government awarded a contract to a Chinese company to install streetlights along the busy tollway. The lights were substandard, made of cheap fiberglass and aluminum, and many have twisted and broken in the wind. Now they dangle limply over the roadway. "They were never hooked up anyway," said Charlie.

We were driving, Charlie and I, on a weekend trip to Volta Region. Charlie generously offered to be my tour guide in what is one of Ghana's most rugged and beautiful areas, so I picked him up on a Saturday morning at his house in a suburb of Accra called Adenta. His neighborhood was laid out in a loose grid of dusty and unnamed dirt roads, each block enclosing several sprawling one-story homes whose tile roofs were barely visible behind high walls. It reminded me of Phoenix, or possibly Phoenix when they completely run out of money for road maintenance. Although you couldn't see much from the street, most of the homes appeared to be comfortable but not ostentatious. Some, however, aspired to considerably more grandeur; bougainvillea and bird-of-paradise cascaded over ornate gates scanned by remote cameras. Some had walls bunted with razor wire, or a row of electrified strands, or with menacing shards of glass cemented into the crown, reflecting the determination of the African elite to hold on to that which they have gained, and their lack of faith in the rule of law. In Western societies, the middle class functions as a buffer between the haves and the have-nots, providing a path for advancement without resort to guns and machetes. In Africa, the buffer is a wall.

Charlie's property had a wall, a gate, and barking dogs but was otherwise undefended—partly because he wasn't rich enough or elite enough to require further emplacements, and partly because the whole concept of residential fortification struck him as overkill, despite his readiness to believe Ghanaians capable of almost any contravention. "What are they so afraid of?" he asked me once.

His youngest son, ten-year-old Kosi, met me at the gate and led me inside. Charlie and Afi have five children—one older daughter, two sons who are away at boarding school, another daughter in junior high school, and Kosi—and their home is suitably capacious yet clearly built for function, not frills. Charlie designed and built it about fifteen years ago, and he claims his newer homes are much nicer. Still, it's pretty nice—breezy and casual in layout, with hand-carved hardwood doors, four bedrooms (all with attached bathrooms), and a large, open living and dining area. It would be a perfectly nice home in America (it even had an attached garage), but some features, or lack of them, would seem strange in, say, Denver. Despite the amazing amount of good food that comes out of Afi's kitchen, the cooking area is small; one reason is that Afi and her daughters still do much of their cooking on an outdoor brazier, village-style. There is no dishwasher, which would strike any African as superfluous when you have five children. And there is no washing machine or dryer—again, not counting the children, who do all the family laundry by hand. The children also sweep and mop the terrazzo floors throughout the house every day. To do all these chores they must first haul water, because Charlie's well isn't working. It seems a neighbor drilled a well that tapped into

Charlie's aquifer, draining his own supply. During my visit, Charlie was in the process of getting a new well drilled, but these things take time in Ghana.

As a contractor Charlie mostly works in the field, but he also maintains a comfortable home office with well-stocked bookshelves, a late-model computer with Internet service, and a CD player. Charlie loves American soul music, especially Motown, and books about American history. On his desk was a copy of Bill Clinton's autobiography. I picked it up. "Have you read it?" he asked me.

I confessed I had not.

"It's good," he said. "I liked him. He was very respected in Africa."

One of Charlie's daughters had made us omelets, but for Charlie the repast was fatally compromised by the absence of his fresh daily bread, which had not been delivered that morning. Saying he would eat some bananas on the road, he left me to my breakfast and went to load his bag into the truck. Soon we were on the road, the smog and traffic of Accra disappearing behind us. After a couple of hours we crossed a steel arch span over the Volta River south of the Akosambo Dam and headed north and east. Overhead, high-tension power lines hummed. Charlie said that for years after the dam was built in the early 1960s, Volta Region was still being powered by creaking British generators left over from colonial times. "All the power from the dam was sold to Togo and Ivory Coast, to line the pockets of the politicians in Accra," he said. That changed in the 1980s under the military rule of Rawlings, who is Ewe.

Along the road, under shade trees, we passed displays of wooden djembes and peg drums for sale. "This is the land of the Peki," said Charlie. "They are an Ewe tribe known for their drums, and for starting wars." I wondered if the two were related, but Charlie wasn't sure. He told me that an incident in a tribal war against this group is how his family got its name. "My great-grandfather was fighting the Peki," he said, "and a bullet was deflected off his machete in a scabbard at his side. It would have killed him. Our name means 'metal trap' or 'money trap.'"

"'Money trap'?" I said.

"Well, metal and money were typically the same thing."

"Of course. So you could say your family is a money trap."

"Possibly even a money pit," he said, alluding to his several homes and kids in private schools.

We drove on, the landscape providing Charlie with a running commentary on the catalog of his entrepreneurial ventures. Here was a cattle ranch; Charlie had tried that once. There was a teak plantation; Charlie knew all about that. "The teak forests in Volta are the best in the country because the rain pattern is ideal," Charlie said. "You get lots of rain, but interspersed with dry periods, which makes the grain very tight," and he balled up his large fist to demonstrate. "In other parts of the country where it is too wet, the grain is not so tight. The Volta teak is as good as Burmese teak and can even be sold as such if it is shipped through Asia."

It seemed obvious to me that Charlie had made the right decision when he gave up his studies in medicine. Not that his career has followed a linear path—he's been a serial entrepreneur, with plenty of ups and downs—but the consistent thread has been a willingness to try just about anything new, from mechanized salt farming to building a better cement block. His business career actually started in college, at Kwame Nkrumah University of Science and Technology, where he wrote his master's thesis on a technique he developed to inoculate a local plant with palm wine to create a substitute for hops (which don't grow in Ghana) and thus brew a genuinely local beer. "I decided I didn't want to go into the business of making people intoxicated," he said. (Charlie enjoys an occasional beer or cognac, but he swears allegiance mostly to coffee.) And so he moved on to the next idea, and the next, in the process employing a lot of his countrymen, which he still does on his construction crews.

Although he grew up in Accra, like most Ewe Charlie maintains strong ties to Volta Region. He and Afi have a house in Keta, a windswept barrier island of fishermen and salt farmers hard by the Togo border, and relatives throughout the region. On a trip that spanned several hundred miles over two long days (I did all the driving), Charlie knew the location of every single speed bump and police checkpoint, most of which he complained about. The speed bumps that really got him going were the homemade ones built out of mud and stone by local communities. "They are much too high, they ruin cars," he said. I wasn't sure how speed bumps could be any worse for cars than the sinkholes all over the roads in Ghana. As for the police—well, how much time do you have?

"It used to be hard to become a policeman here," Charlie said after a cop at one barricade glared at us with more than the usual suspicion. "They had to pass exams and physicals; now it's just who you know. Many of them today don't even speak English. Sometimes when I get pulled over, I pretend I don't speak the local language, only English. They get confused and just let me go!" He laughed solidly at the thought.

No, Charlie wasn't too intimidated by the police, despite their stern roadside queries and loaded Kalashnikovs. One time he scolded a cop soliciting a bribe from Whit. "This man comes over here to try and make a business, to provide jobs for Ghanaians, and you give him trouble!" he said to the officer. "How do you expect this country to grow?"

As we advanced north, the landscape narrowed to a twenty-mile sliver of land between the giant lake on the west and the mountains along the Togo border due east. We stopped for a lunch of street food—goat meat kebobs, bananas and coconut shards—in Kpando, a chaotic market town on the lake. Along the breezy shore, fishermen in dugout canoes raised sails sewn of flour sacks and scudded out over the waves with their long nets. There was supposed to be a ferry from Kpando to Donkorkrom, ten miles across the lake, but lately it had not been running. We continued north to the city of Hohoe, where Charlie had an uncle he wanted to visit. His uncle, an herbal healer, or medicine man, of royal ancestry, lived in a dark stuccoed hut off a courtyard in the center of town. He was at least in his seventies and quite small, especially standing next to Charlie, who had to stoop as we entered the small home. We sat in plastic chairs and shared water from a cup. The pair spoke in Ewe for about twenty minutes. Charlie apologized to me for the perceived rudeness, explaining that his uncle's English was poor. I didn't mind; after a long drive, the singsong rhythm of their conversation was soothing in a musical way. Soon we got up to leave, and Charlie gave his uncle fifteen cedis. Back in the car, he said the old man complained that the country was going to hell and the younger generation had forgotten the traditional ways. Old people are pretty much the same everywhere.

Charlie told me that despite his uncle's humble trappings, the man was sitting on a gold mine—literally. Apparently he possessed a box stuffed full of ancestral gold jewelry that his family had collected over centuries of royal service in Ewe villages around Volta Region. Rather than sell the stash, which would clearly have artistic value well beyond its metallic worth, he made money by renting out the finery to chiefs for their festive gatherings called *durbars*—sort of like Harry Winston loaning gems to starlets on Oscar night. Not all Ghanaians are as poor as they look, Charlie reminded me, and his uncle was certainly proof. And yet it was still expected that Charlie, the big-city nephew, would slip him some bills during a brief visit.

Getting out of Hohoe proved a significant order, as every road was blocked by several long funeral processions, a fact of life in Ghana on a Saturday afternoon. We sat in traffic and watched columns of marching mourners in black and red robes file past the car. It was a curious custom, the Ghanaian funeral party. In a country where, to put it mildly, discretionary income was at a premium, people spent copious sums on these extravagant send-offs—catering meals and alcohol for hundreds of people, hiring bands and sound systems, to say nothing of the elaborate hand-made coffins and cemetery memorials. Guests too must pony up—traveling from far away and paying tailors to make custom robes out of fabric chosen by the next of kin. In her book *The Imported Ghanaian*, Alva K. Sumprim writes of a boy whose parents spent more on his funeral than they were willing to spend on the drugs and medical treatment that might have saved his life. It is commonly said in Ghana that you never know how many friends you have until you die.

"It never used to be this way," said Charlie, munching on a banana as we waited. "The whole funeral thing really started in 1979 with the crackdowns related to the military coups. The curfews shut down the nightclubs in Accra, and it became dangerous to act wealthy or even middle class. If you had money, you didn't want to show it. So no one had parties

or went out. Instead, the funerals became the parties. Now it's crazy."
Eventually the crowds thinned and we escaped Hohoe, bearing east toward the mountains along the Togo border, where jagged faces of exposed
rock creased the horizon.

Togo, population around seven million, is in many ways very different
from its larger western neighbor. The sliver-sized country has been ruled
by the same autocratic family (father and now son) for more than forty
years, and the economy has stagnated along with most pretense of representative government, despite recent controversial elections. By comparison Ghana is the land of opportunity, and many Togolese have migrated
west. Some thrive in the food service industry: a former German and then
French colony, Togo has a francophone culture that extends to its cuisine.
Togolese chefs, schooled in the sauces of Escoffier, find steady work in
Ghanaian hotels and the homes of the elite.

Lomé, the capital city, rises on the coast just east of Charlie's home in
Keta and only a hundred miles or so from Accra. It used to be a wild place,
said Charlie, with hedonistic nightclubs and candlelit French restaurants.
"The Togolese, they really knew how to have fun," he said. "We would go
over there just for dinner and dancing. Now it's all gone to hell." Poverty
and desperation have spiked a dangerous crime wave in Lomé, with mug-
gings and carjackings common. According to the U.S. State Department,
the beaches and public markets are unsafe even by day.

"The last time I went to Lomé, I threw up," said Charlie.

"Literally?"

"Literally."

But along the Togo-Volta border—a line drawn in Europe in the nineteenth century—the differences between the two countries become insignificant. The people on both sides are simply Ewe. Although we passed
several official border crossings (all closed on Sunday), dozens of dirt tracks
wandered into the bush, back and forth across the border. At places, our
main road actually veered into Togo. "We are in Togo now," said Charlie as
we cruised along.

"Are you sure?"

"Believe me."

I pulled over next to a woman carrying a sack of charcoal on her head. *"Bonjour, madame."*

*"Bonjour, monsieur."* She smiled broadly and waved, balancing the sack on her head.

*"S'il vous plaît, est-ce qu'on est proche au Togo?"*

*"Ici Togo,"* and she pointed at her feet.

"I told you," said Charlie, laughing as we drove off.

"My first African dictatorship," I said. "I think I'm supposed to have a visa."

"Don't worry, we're back in Ghana again."

Charlie needed to go to Keta to pay the electric and water bill on his house there. "You can't send checks?" I asked.

"They won't take checks from a bank in Accra."

"Really?" I was surprised because while credit cards are rarely accepted in Ghana (and often subject to fraud), checks are pretty standard; Whit paid his employees with checks, and he wrote checks for business supplies at several Accra merchants. "What is your bank?" I asked.

"Barclays."

"They won't take a Barclays check for your utility bills?"

"Not in Keta from an Accra branch," he said. Apparently there was no reliable financial infrastructure to verify interbank checks, at least not on the level of personal accounts. Like the traffic jams, the information jams ate up huge productivity bandwidth, forcing businesspeople like Charlie to drive hours to pay simple bills.

"It's a lot of work, owning houses here," I said. Charlie had another place up on the Akwapim Ridge, near the president's Peduase Lodge.

"You know, in Ghana, houses are like retirement accounts," he replied. "If you have money, it's where you put it. Saving in a bank is risky because the cedi is so unstable. I used to keep money in a London bank, but that's also risky, because you have currency fluctuations. Real estate is much safer."

"It's real."

"Exactly. As long as you are careful what you buy, it will always be there."

"What do you mean, careful?"

"Private land sales are not always honored," he said. "You can buy land and before you know it, someone else is building a house there. Then you must litigate. It's a big mess."

"So what do you do?"

"It's best to buy land from the government. Also if you are smart, you will start building right away."

"So that's why I see so many half-built houses in the middle of nowhere."

"They are asserting their claim. You put up something, whatever you can afford."

In many ways Ghana seems like a modern capitalist society, but dig a little beneath the surface and you find all sorts of weird idiosyncrasies, like the lack of basic, reliable title laws. Indeed the whole concept of private property, a relatively recent idea even in the West, is still highly ambiguous in Ghana and many other African countries, where the ancient notion of the commons is often still respected. Much like the European nobility of the Middle Ages, chiefs in Ghana are typically stewards of common land in their communities, with the power to decide how it is used, and by whom. (Chiefs are not, however, part of the government; in fact they are barred from participating in politics.) Friction occurs where the modern world of private land intersects with the traditional world of common land. It's not unusual for a Ghanaian to purchase property and find out later that another family claims use rights, based on long-held chieftaincy grants. The nebulous world of land use is another reminder that Africa can be a dangerous place for the uninitiated to do business.

Around a corner, at another checkpoint, a cop waved us over with his rifle. I groaned and rolled down my window. "Please, I would like a ride to my barracks," he said, motioning down the road.

"A ride?" said Charlie. "Where is your car?" He was being a wise guy: Ghanaian police almost never have cars.

"I have no car," said the cop, who looked to be maybe twenty and probably didn't know how to drive.

"Are you smart or stupid?" asked Charlie.

"Please?"

"We only let smart people in this car."

"Oh, I am smart," said the young man, straightening visibly.

"Okay," said Charlie. "You may get in, but we will see how smart you are. If not, you will walk."

The young man climbed in the back. He was a new recruit, he told us, from a tribe in the far north of Ghana; he did not speak Ewe and knew no one in this region. He and Charlie spoke briefly in Twi, but after a few miles we reached his barracks and let him out.

"Don't you think you were pressing your luck?" I asked Charlie.

"I just like to make jokes," he said. "If you just wear a frown all day, what's the point?" I thought about the sad face I'd be wearing in a Ghanaian hoosegow, then realized there probably wouldn't be any mirrors.

"Good thing for us he seemed like a nice young man," I said.

"Maybe even smart," said Charlie.

Over dinner at our hotel in Ho (the large regional capital, not to be confused with smaller Hohoe), Charlie and I talked about Burro. "Do you think Whit will go for nonprofit status and try to get donations?" he asked.

"I don't think so," I replied. "He's pretty committed to making this business stand on its own."

"It's taking so long," said Charlie. "I admire Whit for sticking with it, but I hope he doesn't lose his money."

As for his own exposure, Charlie had no cash in the company; his deal was an equity stake in return for six months' work getting the business off the ground—basically providing his local expertise and advice. That time frame had long since passed, and Charlie was pretty busy with his own construction business, but he remained actively involved in Burro. Whenever Whit needed a contact in Accra, or someone to speed a shipment through customs, or advice on how to deal with a personnel matter, Charlie was the man. Still, Whit and I sensed he was getting impatient. With scarce access to capital and sky-high interest rates, the concept of nurturing a start-up for several years was understandably foreign to Ghanaian entrepreneurs like Charlie.

Our primary tourist destination for the weekend was Wli Falls, at two hundred sixty feet the highest waterfall in Ghana. Arriving at the turnoff for the Agumatsa Wildlife Sanctuary, we parked and walked a few yards, until the mighty cascade, still perhaps half a mile distant, came into view. Vultures circled high above where the water exploded from a deep fissure in the side of a red rock wall and tumbled down a sheer face lined with moss.

"Now, that is really something, isn't it?" said Charlie.

"Indeed," I said.

We both stood and stared for a good long minute. Finally Charlie said, "It looks like a woman urinating."

"You know I hadn't considered that," I replied, "but now that you mention it, I can see your point." For better or worse, it was now all I could think of.

Accessing the dramatic lower pool of the falls entailed a forty-minute walk along a jungle trail that crossed the Agumatsa River in ten places, over rustic wooden bridges. In typical Ghanaian style you had to hire a local guide, for no reason other than to spend some money. As it turned out, however, our guide proved handy when, ten minutes into our walk, the heavens opened with a monsoon downpour. Samuel (that was his name) quickly located a large banana tree and proceeded to bite off the stems of two giant leaves to use as makeshift umbrellas. The leaves did nothing; the rain still soaked us. But it was funny to walk along holding banana leaves over our heads.

The rain had stopped by the time we reached the giant pool at the base of the falls. It was an awesome sight: mist thrown off by the thundering cascade vaporized in a massive cloud, bending rainbows over the spray and drenching the treetops. On the rock cliffs surrounding the falls, thousands, maybe tens of thousands, of giant fruit bats dangled like effigies over the abyss, waiting for their twilight wakeup call.

All of this nature would have been quite enough to write home about, but there was more. This being a weekend, a gang of youths had hiked in with a generator and enough sound equipment to address the North Korean Workers' Party. In fairness you needed a lot of wattage to compete against the roar of that waterfall, so the wall of speakers did not seem excessive in context, once you got past the very weird idea of a public-address system blasting Ghanaian rap music at the base of the country's most spectacular natural attraction. Honestly, I don't know how the bats managed to sleep. But it all made perfect sense to the busloads of city kids in the water, splashing, yelling, and dancing.

The compulsion to improve the great outdoors with gasoline-powered amplification is not exclusively African. But as practiced in Ghana, it is almost certainly rooted in drumming traditions combined with the simple fact, which cannot be stated too many times, that here all life happens outdoors. Westerners tread reverently in the woods, but Ghanaians crash in with as many comforts as they can call home—slashing at snakes, waking up fruit bats, and rudely interrupting the great cascade, Mother Nature going about her business.

fourteen

# HOW TO MAKE MONEY

**SPRING 2010:** The expansion

*"Blessed is the servant who loves his brother as much when he is sick and useless as when he is well and can be of service to him."*

—St. Francis of Assisi

Trade show queen? Burro intern Tara Hair in the back of the Tata, preparing for a gong-gong.

## 1. Sorry

**T**wo nurses in white and one white brother leaned over my face, prone at the end of a narrow hospital gurney. *"Sorry,"* said the head nurse, an imposing woman of the type in Ghana who typically addresses a white man as *"you, white man!"* although on this particular day I can't be sure if she actually said that. I do recall her chanting "sorry" like a mantra.

And I vaguely recall other hospital employees around my legs and arms—comforting me with their touch, I thought at first, until I tried to bend my knee and could not resist the pressure of African arms, and then understood, through my haze of apprehension, that I was being pinned down in preparation for a "procedure" that did not involve anesthesia.

*"Sorry."*

I had spent most of 2009 in Ghana, returning home in late fall. Shortly after Harper's high school graduation in May 2010, I traveled back to Ghana. It felt good to be back—almost like home at that point—but contentment was short-lived. After enjoying all the comfort, privilege, and respect (however unearned) that accrue to a Westerner in the developing world, the day came when the Ghanaians stopped looking up to me as a fortunate *obruni* and instead stared down pathetically at the heap of my existence on a gurney. I hesitate to report how I got there, in the interest of sparing the reader not so much discomfort as disappointment. For although the Gothic catalog of pox, pestilence, and horror waiting to befall the traveler to sub-Saharan Africa is long and well documented—from malaria and ebola to AIDS and dengue fever, from car crashes to heatstroke, and from mammals (lions, mercenaries) to microbes—none of these plagues led me to Koforidua's Eastern Regional Hospital. On the contrary, I must report that my day of infirmary was the result of a freak accident while sitting at a desk. It could have happened in Manhattan, or the Seventh Arrondissement, or downtown Dallas, but it happened in Burro's Koforidua office on Hospital Road. Fortunately, as the street name suggests and as I have mentioned before, the hospital I never wanted to visit was nearby. Equally fortunate, on that morning the Burro office was swarming with roughly a dozen employees, interns and volunteers, all of them anxious to help me. Burro had come a long way by May of 2010.

Whit's company was still small and not yet making a profit, but it was no longer operating in a vacuum. Earlier in the year, my brother had met with product designers at Ideo in San Francisco; traveled to Utah to consult battery experts at a company called Power Stream; organized a Burro internship program with the Marriott School of Management at Brigham Young University; and partnered with Greenlight Planet, maker of an innovative solar lantern for the developing world, to produce a nonsolar (battery-operated) version for Burro. Word was getting out, and Whit was being asked to address organizations as diverse as the engineering department of Brown University and the Program for Appropriate Technology in Health (PATH), a Seattle-based nonprofit working in more than seventy countries to break cycles of poverty and disease.

Yet just as interest in Burro grew, it became hard for Whit to commit to American speaking engagements, since business in Ghana was consuming more of his time. Four BYU interns were arriving in May, as well as an accounting consultant from Seattle and her twenty-two-year-old son, a QuickBooks savant, both of whom had volunteered to help Whit get his books in order in return for a free place to stay, a few tourist insights, and the occasional use of a vehicle (they had bought their own plane tickets). I had arrived in the middle of the month, and Jan would return in June. Whit was running out of room at the combination Burro office and residence; he needed a home of his own. Still not ready to buy property, he engaged a local real estate agent to secure a decent rental.

In Ghana one finds not so much a home as a project to take over. Virtually no house available to rent is actually finished, at least not in the Western sense. With no mortgage market to speak of, people build homes (and for that matter commercial buildings) in stages, as they acquire the money.* And a key way to get the money is by finding a tenant, who is

---

* As virtually all buildings in Ghana are made of reinforced concrete—wood is used only for doors and window trim—unfinished structures can sit exposed to the weather for years with little or no harm.

generally expected to pay at least two years' rent in advance. The landlord then takes that cash and invests in the house, adding amenities and moving the project further down the line. In other words, tenancy is used to add incremental value to the property, not to generate income. In this way Whit secured a commodious but unfinished four-bedroom home on a rutted dirt road outside town, behind the Capital View Hotel where we often ate dinner.

Whit's African version of the starter château, while unremarkable by the exuberantly vulgar standards of many upper-class Ghanaian homes, would strike most Americans as the fortress of a rapacious drug lord. A one-story contemporary complex finished in pebble-textured stucco, the house was defined largely by a series of arched porticos and a roof cornice ornamented (in contrasting tones of crushed pebble) with repetitions of the traditional Akan pictograph for *Gye Nyame* ("Except for God"). Not that you could see much of the house from what I hesitate to even dignify with the term *road*. Like most detached African homes above the level of village huts, Whit's estate cowered behind an imposing concrete wall, albeit without razor wire.

Inside the house, large rooms with terrazzo floors radiated from a wide central hallway designed to facilitate cooling breezes; there were three toilets, a large concrete shower stall, and, in the master bathroom, an actual soaking tub, which apparently sealed the deal for Whit.

But it was hardly habitable. As with his renovations to the Burro office, Whit had to add external storage tanks to compensate for the sporadic public water supply, as well as a hot water heater, kitchen appliances, and cabinets. There was also a complete interior and exterior paint job to oversee and substantial upgrades to the wiring. This is the sort of work that in Ghana can take months to organize and execute, as the Ghanaian's commitment to heart-stopping highway velocity does not translate to the building trades. Months, however, were precisely what Whit did not have. Specifically, he had a few weeks. As luck would have it, an incentive to alacrity materialized in the desperation of the landlady, a woman named Nancy.

Whit and Nancy had agreed on a two-year lease of one hundred fifty cedis a month, all of it payable in advance. In return, Nancy would invest the bulk rent payment in the home—paying for electrical wiring and water hookup, among other basic necessities. But after a couple of weeks, Nancy contacted Whit and said the money was gone. "Please," she said, "I beg you, I need more money to finish the work."

"So I agreed to give her more money," Whit said, "but I made a deal with her. I said, 'I will pay for one more year, but I need to move in next week, and this is what needs to get done before then.' We made a list. We divided up the work into inside and outside jobs, basically defined the scope of the work. I said, 'This all needs to get done by next week; every week that it's not done, I get one month extra free rent.' She was three weeks late, so now I have three years and three months on my lease. And I got an explicit agreement that I can sublet."

Getting the jobs done was not the same as getting them done well, however. An electrician was engaged to install lights and ceiling fans, the latter of which were mounted so that the metal blades rotated about two inches below bare lightbulbs hanging from wires, which created two problems. The first was that at night the spinning fan blades created a stroboscopic effect as they whirled under the lightbulbs, lending the effect of a silent movie to our motions. This was amusing for about five minutes and then generally annoying, possibly even seizure-inducing. The second problem was that occasionally a gust of wind from the jalousie windows would cause a fan to wobble slightly—just enough for the blades to strike the compact fluorescent bulb (the only kind widely available in Ghana) hanging above it with explosive force that would send razors of glass and poisonous dust raining down on floors, beds, and occupants. As I said, these fans and bulbs were installed by a professional Ghanaian electrician, which perhaps adds context to the hurdles Whit faced in training his own employees.

On that front, the first casualty was Kevin. Whit had fired him in the spring over a handful of issues, including absences with company vehicles and a reluctance to work as part of a team, that eroded confidence. "He seemed shocked," said Whit, "but he took it like a man." I knew I would miss Kevin, who had taught me so much about his country, but his sacking was a reminder that Whit was building a real business, not a charity. "It was like a giant exhale when he left," said Whit. "Morale improved overnight. I started driving his route; you know how he used to drag himself back at seven o'clock looking like he'd been hit by a car? I'm finished every day at like four. I have no idea what the fuck he was doing out there."

In his place was Nkansah, the young Krobo medical salesman who had taken Jan and me to the "secret farmers" a year earlier and who seemed intent on conquering the world. Also new in the office was a full-time route driver, James (not his real name), who had approached Whit at the local car wash about a job for his twenty-two-year-old daughter. After hiring his daughter as an office administrator and battery technician—she was a fast learner and had the charming but unsettling habit of curtseying to "superiors"—Whit hired James himself. Then there were the Americans, who could be divided into two groups: the Mormons and the bean counters.

The Mormons, of course, were the four interns from BYU's Marriott School of Business. Jennia Parkin and Tara Hair shared what was usually Jan's bedroom (she was back in Oregon), and Justin King and Andrew Stewart were sleeping in my former bedroom. When they weren't out in the field doing research, they huddled over MacBook Pros and worked diligently on spreadsheets and reports on Burro's business and marketing plans. Housekeeping apparently ran a distant third on their priority list. Had I been asked in advance if I believed Mormons to be culturally disposed toward residential cleanliness, I would have certainly guessed in the affirmative; they sure *seem* clean. Yet based on the general indication provided by this cohort, I would have been wrong. I had never seen the Burro quarters in such disarray. Trash was piled everywhere, dirty dishes languished on every surface, and the refrigerator was a science experiment. Then again, they were college students.

One in their group, however, could not be held accountable for the hazardous wastes inside the fridge. Jennia, blond and cherubic-faced, was disarmingly frank about her food phobias, which might reasonably complicate a one-month sojourn in Ghana. "What are you eating here?" I asked.

"I brought all my own food from home," she replied.

"For a month?"

"Yeah. MREs."

"You brought military meals ready to eat?"

"Well, similar. Check it out."

She led me into her bedroom and opened the wardrobe. On the shelves normally reserved for spare sheets and towels were dozens of Hormel Compleat meals. "Three hundred calories each and shelf-stable," she said with pride. "The real MREs are a thousand calories."

"So you brought, like, a suitcase of these over from Utah?"

"Two," she said. "I also brought fruit leather, trail mix, Clif Bars."

"And you haven't eaten any local food at all?"

"I bought some peanut butter," she said.

"Oh my God, you ate the *peanut butter*?"

"Why?" she asked, putting a hand to her mouth.

"Just kidding," I said. "Anything else?"

"I tried a piece of grilled corn."

I didn't have the heart to tell her that my father-in-law once contracted dysentery from a piece of street-grilled corn in Yugoslavia. That was actually one of the few foods in Ghana that I avoided. "Well," I said, "*bon app!*"

The bean counters were the mother-and-son team of Debi Nordstrom and David Martin. Debi was a Seattle business consultant whom Whit had met through Cranium's former CFO. David had just graduated—literally, a few days earlier—from the University of North Carolina at Chapel Hill. An economics major, David told me he had been balancing his own checkbook since he was six years old, and after watching him power-slam data into QuickBooks, I believed him. They arrived in Accra the night that I flew in, ready to whip Burro's books into shape and explore Ghana. Burro was putting them up at Rose's modest but charmingly appointed home, a few miles out of town.

Most of these people were in the office on the morning of my accident. The night before, I had noticed that the antenna of my cell phone was loose, the plastic threads at the base having been stripped. So when we got to the office that morning I scrounged around the storage room for a tube of Super Glue and sat down to fix it. The glue was old and the tip was clogged shut. I took out my pocketknife and dug around the tip while squeezing the tube and pointing it down at the desk, over a slip of paper. To see better, I had taken off my glasses. I was trying to squeeze the tube lightly, but Super Glue tubes are made of fairly rigid plastic and you have to apply a good amount of pressure to get any movement at all. Suddenly the blockage cleared—but instead of squirting down at the desk, in the direction I was pointing the tube, it cleared at an odd angle, sending a fountain of Super Glue straight up and directly into my right eye, bathing my cornea in glue. Naturally, I blinked. Except as soon as I blinked, that was it; my eyelid was sealed shut.

"*Fuck!*" I think I said that several times, loudly, more out of fear than pain. It actually didn't hurt at all. There was no sting from the glue; in that sense it may as well have been water in my eye. But of course it wasn't water, and my eye was glued shut—permanently, as far as I knew. I would have been terrified if this had happened across the street from the Mayo Clinic, but here I was in a small town in Africa, in a state of complete panic. Whit and the others rushed to help me, but nobody really knew what to do. I remember being led to the shower and my eye going under a stream of hot water, which did absolutely nothing. I remember staggering out to the couch on the veranda, lying down moaning, and Debi bathing my eye with a warm towel. I remember asking Whit to check on my medevac insurance. "I want a *fucking* Lear jet to Germany!" I commanded him, obviously under delusions of self-potency.

Justin came out; he'd been on the Internet, on the Super Glue website. "It says there are no known cases of permanent injury from Super Glue in the eye," he said. "After about four days it will degrade and your eye should open."

"*Fuck*," I replied. A word that had generally been a significant if selective element of my vocabulary was now representing its length and breadth.

"He looks pale," someone said.

"Maybe he's going into shock."

Whit hovered over me. "Maxy, we should take you to see someone. We can drive you to Accra, where there are good private clinics, or try the hospital here; they do have an eye clinic, and it's supposed to be pretty good." I found out later that Rose had called the best eye clinic in Accra, then insisted on speaking directly to the doctor, who recommended the clinic at the Koforidua hospital. "What do you want to do?"

Driving through Accra traffic was excruciating even in good health. "*Fuck,*" I said. "Let's go down the street."

I remember staggering up several flights of outdoor stairs at the hospital, shielding my one good eye from the glaring sun, holding hands with Whit and Adam, trying to imagine what the rest of my life would be like with just one eye. There was a huge waiting room, wooden benches packed with patients, babies crying, a grainy TV blaring from within its iron security cage, fans barely moving. I don't know if it was the nature of my wound or the color of my skin, but I didn't have to wait. They took me right in, asked me some questions, gave me an official Ghana health card, and stretched me out on the gurney.

The health-care system in Ghana does not involve a lot of patient hand-holding. Doctors don't call you into their diploma-lined office, swivel in a big chair, and sagely lay out the scenario and discuss your options; they just roll up their sleeves and go to work. So I was not consulted before the staff pinned me down and the large nurse started to rip open my eyelid with tweezers. "*Sorry.*"

"Not as sorry as I am!" I spit out, feeling like my eyeball was being skinned alive. Apparently my caregivers hadn't consulted the Super Glue website.

"We must cut off the eyelashes first," she said after a few minutes of futile tugging. "They are glued together." Out came the scissors, then more agonizing torture with the tweezers. "Men are not supposed to cry," said the nurse.

"I'm not crying, I'm screaming!" Still, every excruciating yank on my eyelid revealed a slightly larger sliver of formless daylight, so I held out hope that her brutal ministrations weren't leaving me permanently blind in one eye. After several more interminable minutes of persecution, she pronounced my eyelid fully opened. All I could see was a blurry kaleido-scope of moving shapes. "Now we must remove the glue from your eye," she said. "Sorry."

"Holy shit," said Whit, who sounded like he was leaning over my face. More tugging and scraping followed; this time it felt like my eyeball was being pulled out of its socket. "Okay," she said.

And suddenly I could see again. There was the nurse. In her tweezers was a chunk of dried Super Glue the thickness of an orange peel and the diameter of a nickel.

Next stop was the eye doctor himself, down the hall. Reassuringly, his office had all the familiar equipment, and his exam appeared thorough. "Your cornea has many sores," he said, which I think was the Ghanaian way of saying scratches.

"You can thank Nurse Ratched for that," I wanted to say.

"I will give you some drops to take away the worst pain for a little while, but your eye will be uncomfortable for a few days." As a semiprofes-sional kidney stone patient, I knew that "uncomfortable" was medical doublespeak for agony. Here I was expecting the whole hospital experi-ence in Ghana to be completely unfamiliar, possibly satanic, but it was basically the same as ours, with the same vocabulary. I wanted to ask the doctor if he played golf and subscribed to travel magazines, then thought better of it. "The biggest danger is infection," he continued. "I will give you a prescription for antibiotic drops. Use them three times a day. Come back next Tuesday and we will see how you are doing." We thanked the doctor and went downstairs to fill the prescription and pay the bill. The total, including eyedrops, came to sixty-six cedis—about forty-six dollars.

I was doing much better by the next morning, and better again the next day. My use of the F-word had returned to its traditional frequency. Within a week I felt my eye was back to normal, albeit without eyelashes and still a bit bloodshot. I ran into the big nurse on the street, and she treated me like a son. "Oh, how *are* you?" she said with a wide smile, clutching my hand with both of hers. "Your eye looks so much better!" I thanked her for helping me, and I meant it. I decided that while I would still want that Lear jet to Germany for a seriously traumatic injury (medical supplies in

Ghana are limited and blood transfusions still carry the risk of HIV con-
tamination), the country's government-run medical system wasn't nearly
as scary as I had imagined. Nurses and doctors were just as caring and
professional as their Western counterparts, perhaps more so. For the rest
of my time in Ghana, I considered myself a proud, card-carrying member
of the Ghana Health Service.

## 2. Akosia

"Whit, breakfast is ready," I said. "And there's a woman peeing in your
backyard."

"That would be Akosia," he said from his bedroom, sprawled out over
the sheets with his laptop, crunching numbers. I brought in his morning
mango smoothie, as usual. Some men might be humiliated to find themselves, at age fifty-three, serving breakfast in bed to their younger brother
every day, but I didn't mind. Our morning ritual of mango smoothies gave
us a chance to talk before the insanity of the office, where at any given
moment a half dozen people vied for Whit's attention.

I pulled up a chair next to Whit's bed and took a swig of my own
smoothie. "Akosia?"

"She lives in the blockhouse in the courtyard. The landlady said I
could evict her if I wanted, but I won't. She has a little boy and another
kid on the way. I mean, she's got a sweet deal—no rent and free electricity, but no plumbing."

"So I see."

"I pay her to do my laundry."

"What happened to Mena?"

"She still does Jan's laundry, but now that I'm out here, it's just easier."

"Does she have a husband?"

"Victor. He travels a lot. I think he's a bit of a rogue. I feel bad for her;
she seems well educated and speaks very good English, but I don't think
she lives on much except what I give her for laundry and what she can grow
in the backyard."

"Are those her roosters?" The property appeared to come with five cocks who started crowing outside our windows at the break of three A.M. every morning.

"No, but thanks for reminding me. I need to ask her about them."

At this point her boy was stooped outside our kitchen window, emptying his bowels onto the concrete patio. His mother watched with a worried frown as he cried. "Oh man, that doesn't look good," I said. "The kid's got serious runs." Diarrhea caused by unclean drinking water is a major cause of child fatality in Ghana.

Whit got up and went to the back door. "Good morning, Akosia," he said.

"Good morning, Whit," she said. We walked outside; Whit introduced us and she smiled.

"Your boy, he is sick," said Whit.

"Yes," she replied. "Please, can you loan me some money so I can take him to the clinic?"

"Where is your husband?" Whit asked.

She frowned. "He has traveled."

"He left you no money?"

"No."

"When will he return?"

"Please, I do not know."

"When is your baby due?"

"I do not know."

"Have you been to a clinic since you got pregnant?"

"No."

Whit dug into his pocket. "Here is ten cedis—an advance against laundry. I want you to get checked for your baby as well, okay?"

"Yes, please," she said. "Thank you. Bless you."

"Oh, Akosia. Do you know who owns the roosters?"

"Agbe," she said, pointing over the wall of the backyard. Agbe was a nearly toothless hunter who trekked about the encroaching suburban sprawl with a cocked and loaded shotgun, on constant alert for ferrets, small antelope, and other game he could annihilate and sell.

"If you see Agbe, can you please tell him he should take his roosters away? They make too much noise."

"Yes, please," she said.

"Good luck with that," I said to Whit as we went back inside.


## 3. Nkansah

Herding roosters might be a fool's errand, but back at the office Whit and his team had made a lot of progress since my last visit in late 2009. The counterfeiting issue was solved with new battery coupons printed by Camelot, the security printer we had visited last fall, with a watermark and an engraved Burro donkey logo. Six thousand new, high-capacity batteries had arrived—each one holding 2500 mAh, versus 2300 mAh on the old ones. "And we've gotten much better at certification," said Whit on the bumpy drive into town, referring to the process of determining whether a freshly charged battery was strong enough to be sent back into the field. Being able to cull bad batteries was essential to maintaining customer loyalty.

"We're doing one hundred percent testing of batteries before they go out, which has completely changed the game," said Whit. "We had hundreds, maybe thousands, of batteries that were somehow damaged in circulation, and we weren't weeding them out. We still occasionally get a complaint, but it's nothing like before. Shit, we were losing so many customers. We had agents quitting, saying they couldn't put their name on this. That whole problem has been eliminated. And we've learned we can't test batteries right out of the charger. Several experts told us that's nuts; you'll get a false reading. You have to wait at least an hour, preferably eight to twenty-four. We're also re-skinning the old batteries with new labels, which has helped with perception. We engrave them, so we know which ones are old and we can track them. I also got a hundred Sanyo NiMHs, widely considered the best in the world; they cost three times as much as ours. We re-skinned and engraved those, and we'll track them through the system as well, to see how they compare.* So we're learning a lot, and it's all adding up. I can't say there are no problems; you're bound to have issues with all this growth, but we're getting much better at our business."

Another big driver of growth was the battery-powered phone chargers I had brought over in my luggage—nothing more than a plastic case holding four AA batteries with a pigtail wire that could be spliced to a mobile phone's charge plug. The cheap carbon-zinc AA batteries sold all over Ghana (Sun Watt brand) weren't powerful enough to charge phones, making Burro just about the only game in town for that application. The chargers, selling for three cedis, were a hit in nonelectrified villages, but they weren't perfect; they didn't work with every phone (some phones had circuitry that shut down the current, mistakenly thinking it was an overload), and cutting and splicing the wires to the phone's AC charger was a pain. Whit was working with a Chinese company to bring in more sophisticated Burro-branded phone chargers that could be coupled with a diode to get around the circuitry issues, as well as a selection of charging tip adapters so customers wouldn't have to splice wires.

Also contributing to fast growth was a new Burro credit policy—interest-free short-term loans to villagers so they could afford the one-cedi battery deposit or the phone charger. As Whit designed the plan, anyone in a village who was deemed creditworthy by a committee of the chief and elders could borrow the deposit money from Burro, so long as they paid it back within a month. It was plainly modeled after the microfinance innovations of Muhammed Yunus, whose Grameen Bank relies on peer pressure to guarantee loans. As Whit explained it, "We make it clear to the chief that if somebody doesn't pay us back, the whole village loses credit, and then we start calling back batteries. So you have to let the chief advise you on who's creditworthy or it's not fair. You can't have the chief saying later, 'Oh, you gave credit to Larry? I would never loan money to Larry. He borrowed my saw last year and never returned it.' There has to be some accountability." (Burro later refined the policy to make the

---

* Some of them held up quite well, others seemed to fail prematurely.

agent responsible for the credit of his clients, which significantly improved repayment rates.)

Then there was Nkansah. "I have no idea what Nkansah is telling people in these gong-gongs," said Whit, since they were generally conducted in Krobo, "but he moves like three hundred batteries at each one. Maybe he's telling them the batteries will make their penis large or their kids smarter, I don't know. And he does this clever thing at the end where he says, 'I need three volunteers who can read and write to help me sign up customers.' So he's pre-screening new agents in the village."

Nkansah, twenty-five, had a broad smile and the easy manner of a natural salesman. He was comfortable with himself, and when he spoke he drew you in with mannered gestures and broad sweeps of his long fingers. There was something actorly about him, but it didn't seem put on or exaggerated. He grew up near a busy market town about twenty kilometers north of Koforidua. His father was an English teacher; his mother owned a small shop—nothing more than a shack selling dry goods, hard-boiled eggs, and a few groceries. Every day after school, Nkansah's mother gave him money to buy bread at the market in town for the shop. He quickly learned how to leverage his mother's cash: by buying directly from the bakery at a discount (instead of from the resellers in the market), he could sell the bread at a profit in town, then turn around and buy more bread for his mother—getting home in time to do his homework, with spare change in his pocket. "I have always known how to make money," he told me. "I sold bread until secondary school, but then I stopped because the other kids would laugh at me."

After graduating from high school, Nkansah moved to Accra and found a job as a receptionist at a restaurant. "There was a Big Man who always came in, a regular," said Nkansah. "One night he put a note in the suggestion box. Nobody ever read the notes except me. I read them all. In his note he said he didn't like it when his tilapia soup took too long, and he complained that no one ever brought him hot water and lemon to wash his hands after a meal. So the next time he came in, I served him myself. I went to the kitchen and made sure his soup was ready in two minutes. I brought him his hot water and lemon. That night he put another note in the box. It said, 'Tell whoever served me to call me.' And there was a number. I called and he offered me a job as his houseboy. He lived in a big house with his wife, and I did everything—folding laundry, cooking, cleaning. But then Kufuor became president and the man was appointed ambassador to Liberia, so they had to move there."

Nkansah wants desperately to go to college, preferably in America. "I shall go to Brigham Young University," he told me confidently. Clearly he had been spending a lot of time with the Mormon interns.

"Really?" I said.

"Yes. I know I can go there because I don't smoke, I don't take alcohol, and I can stay away from women."

"So you are familiar with the school's honor code?"

"Oh yes, I have been on the website. I am hoping to impress your brother so that he will help me get in."

"Well, I'm sure Whit would be happy to help you get in to any school."

To save money, Nkansah was living with his parents in the distant town of Somanya. (His family had moved when his father took a job as headmaster of a Presbyterian school.) The arrangement made Whit and Jan uncomfortable because Nkansah was commuting an hour each way in unreliable *tro-tros* and was often late. Typically Whit advanced new employees rent money, payable directly to the landlord, so they could get situated in Koforidua. (Most came from Accra.) But Nkansah convinced Whit to loan him money directly—fifteen hundred cedis, the equivalent of almost four months' pay—so he could buy a motorcycle and continue living with his parents. On a motorcycle, he reasoned, he could zip into Kof-town fast. And by living at home he could save more money for college. Whit agreed, but after several weeks the motorcycle had still not materialized. Nkansah said it was being repaired in Accra, but when asked to produce a bill of sale, he stalled.

Despite this distracting sideshow, Nkansah continued to rack up phenomenal sales. Nobody could work a crowd like him. He understood that the best salesmen don't simply talk about their products; they ask questions designed to make their prospects aware of their own wants and needs.

"How many people here would like to save money on batteries?" he often began.

*I know I would!*

"If you could save money on batteries, when would be a good time to start?"

*Umm, now?*

I tagged along on one of Nkansah's gong-gongs in a village called Aframase. Only about fifty people showed up because someone had died and many villagers had left for the funeral; the chief said he had tried calling Nkansah, but the village had poor mobile coverage and he couldn't get through. So the show went on, and Nkansah had them in the palm of his hand. Knowing that customers who handle the merchandise are far more likely to buy it, Nkansah made sure everyone got to hold a battery and adapter. He called for villagers to bring up their flashlights and radios, then removed their rusty Tiger Heads—handling them with dramatic disdain—and replaced them with the bright green cells. You didn't need to speak Krobo to know he was regaling the villagers with how bright, and how loud, the Burro batteries were. At one point he said something that made the whole audience roll with laughter.

I turned to James, our driver, who was also working the crowd as Nkansah's assistant. "What did he say?"

"He was explaining the credit policy," said James. "He told them, 'We will come back next Friday to collect the payment. If you cannot pay then, we will come back the next Friday. If you still cannot pay, we will paint our truck black and it will say POLICE on the side.'"

Nkansah was a model salesman for the agents and other employees, but other basic job skills were lacking, especially when it came to managing his territory. One morning Whit called him into the office. "Nkansah, what do we need to do to get to the point where you are filling out receipts in a way that can be entered by Adam into the books? Because we've been through this before, and Adam has trained you, but there are still issues."

"I can explain," said Nkansah.

"Well, it isn't about explaining it to me, it's about doing it."

"It will be done."

"Remember it's not just about bookkeeping," said Whit. "This information will help you grow your business. For example, we're really trying to get the resellers to focus on exchanges over the last two weeks, because that's something they can really impact.* One week is too short—maybe they've traveled, maybe someone is sick—but two weeks is a good measure. You see what I mean?"

"I do," said Nkansah.

"So let's look at Daniel Larweh." He was one of Nkansah's resellers in Adenya. "He went from two hundred and seventy-four exchanges to a hundred and fifty. So his numbers are down forty-five percent. That's troubling because he is one of our biggest resellers. Why is he down so far? Are his clients sick, or angry with him? This is something to watch."

"I understand," said Nkansah.

"You should also be paying close attention to phone chargers," Whit continued. "Chargers I believe are one of the biggest things driving exchanges and thus revenue, so someone with low exchanges, it could mean they have not sold many chargers. That's why we are tracking charger sales. So if a reseller has one hundred clients and sold one hundred chargers, the number in this column is one hundred percent. If he has one hundred clients and has sold fifty chargers, what would the number be?"

"Fifty percent."

"Right."

## 4. Whit Is My Angel

I went out one day with James on his route, a broad loop up to the Akwapim Ridge and back down through the junction town of Nkurakan. James, a youthful forty-two, navigated this treacherous mountain circuit with one hand on the wheel and the other on the horn all the way, in approximately half the time it would have taken me. It may be possible that

---

* Agents were now being called *resellers* because it more accurately reflected their independent status as required by Ghanaian tax and labor law.

he clocked more miles in the oncoming-traffic lane than his own, but I had my eyes closed for much of the trip. Unlike Whit's other employees, at least James was an *experienced* crazy driver.

In fact he had spent eight years as a delivery driver for Guinness. He and his wife and five children (including Burro's new office administrator) had been living in Guinness company housing—a one-room apartment—when he met Whit at the local car wash.* "Guinness was very tough," said James. "They would never loan me money for my children's school fees. Burro pays more, and I can borrow for school fees. When I resigned from Guinness to work for Whit, they offered me more money, but I said it was too late." With his increase in salary he was able to move his family into a more spacious two-room house in Koforidua.

"Whit is my angel," he said. "I pray for Whit to have everlasting life."

His gratitude extends to Whit also hiring his daughter, who had been staying with an uncle in Accra, attending college, but things didn't work out and she came home. "She will return to university, maybe next year," said James. He drove on. "I wanted to go to university," he continued, "but my father died and I had to go to work."

"He died young?"

"Poisoned by a friend."

"Some friend."

"He was working in Lagos, and he had a car. His friend wanted the car. One night they went out drinking; the next day my father got very sick, and he died. His friend disappeared with the car."

## 5. Adventures in Bookkeeping

I took Debi and her son David to the bead market one afternoon. Since arriving several days earlier, they had been holed up in the office, poring

---

* Ghanaians keep their cars surgically clean, a Sisyphean obsession considering the country's sloppy roads. I view it as an extension of the Big Man conceit; very few people own cars or even drive company cars, and those who do take great pride in their good fortune.

over QuickBooks reports and bank statements on their laptops. David
worked nonstop all day with earphones firmly implanted, listening to
sports podcasts; Debi just worked. They needed a break. Besides, I wanted
to learn why Debi, at age fifty, would pay her own way to Ghana to help
Whit straighten out his books. I got the impression she had a pretty nice
life in Seattle; she was talking about buying a boat, and the boat she had
in mind (I happened to know) was not exactly a dinghy. Okay, she was a
divorced empty-nester, but that could describe lots of middle-aged women
who satisfy their wanderlust by going to yoga retreats in Costa Rica; how
many set off to the world's poorest countries and volunteer their professional services for a month?

"I just get bored," said Debi as we walked over to the market grounds.
"I like adventure. I mean, lots of people say they'd like to do stuff like this,
but they never do."

Sorting through Burro's books didn't seem all that adventurous—I was
glad when Debi and David took some time off to see the country—but there
were plenty of issues for them to resolve. For a modest start-up, Whit's business was complicated from an accounting standpoint because it involved
rental inventory (which depreciated), security deposits (which could not
be counted as regular income), and coupons that functioned a lot like gift
certificates but cost different amounts depending on how many you bought.
"You definitely can't count coupons as revenue until they're exchanged,"
Debi told Whit over a poolside lunch, also attended by David, one Sunday
at a new hotel in Aburi.

"The problem is, some of them will never get used," said Whit. "They
get lost, or whatever. So at some point I need to move unexchanged coupons into the revenue column. And to do that, we need to get a weighted
average value of coupons, which means tracking how many are bought at
each price point." Whit was no accounting savant, but he knew enough to
understand the issues.

"Right," said Debi. "I'm starting to look at depreciations and values this
week—what can be counted as what. So far we've just been getting up to
speed on Adam."

David looked up from his menu. "It's scary."

"Adam doesn't know how to balance the checking account," said Debi, "and he's never balanced the cash account. He just plugs the accounts every month to make everything reconcile."

"Great," said Whit.

## 6. Stays Strong

Thirteen of us gathered in the Burro conference room one morning to hear two of the BYU interns, Jennia and Tara, deliver their final presentation after three weeks of field research. The pair's assignment had been to come up with recommendations in two areas: marketing and human resources—that is, hiring, training, and retaining good resellers. "To compile our data we interviewed eighteen agents in the field," said Tara, "nine high performers and nine low performers. That was the qualitative research. We also interviewed forty clients, mainly to look at brand perception. That was a relatively small quantitative study, but we feel it was valid, as you'll see." The pair had put together a PowerPoint show that we all loaded onto our laptops and followed along with.

"We wanted to get a handle on why some agents are exchanging hundreds of batteries every month and others are only exchanging ten," said Tara. "The idea is that Burro can apply those best practices to hiring and training. One interesting thing we found was that both high-performing agents and low-performing agents face similar issues in their villages—people have little money, people are farming and busy, it's a lot of walking, and so on. That tells us the discrepancies between high and low sellers are not based on market forces; it's about the sales abilities of the individual. When asked why people don't buy Burro batteries, low sellers often cited strangely negative social pressure: 'They think I'm selling to make money for myself' was one response. Another was 'They are jealous because I'm making money from it.'

"On the other end, we found that high sellers had several things in common. They typically go house to house instead of waiting for customers to come to them. People who sell other things seem to do better with

Burro. My guess is they love business and have sales skill. And the top sellers have an understanding that Burro is a *service*, not just a product. They're selling energy."

"I'm wondering," said Whit, "since there is not a rich range of potential resellers to choose from, what hiring practices are we doing that you think are good, and what do you think we could be doing better?"

"Well, your policy of meeting with chiefs about potential agents seems to be working well," Tara said. "Perhaps the interview process could be more codified: pick five candidates with the chief, then interview them with a point system for possible answers. So the answer 'I plan to make customers come to me' would be worth zero points. Then select a candidate based on that process."

"One problem I see," said Rose, "is that the chief could pick five people and they could all be his sons. We use them for two months and it's a waste of time; then we just have to find someone else."

"The chief is often too simple," agreed Nkansah.

"Still," said Rose, "at the end of the day the chief has to know the reseller and respect him. But he doesn't necessarily have to pick the person."

"However they end up being chosen," said Tara, "I think Burro should promote the perception that this job is important and the person has been selected for their skill. They need to be made to feel serious about it."

She moved on to the issue of agent training—arguably even more important than the initial hire, since even natural-born salespeople would be unfamiliar with Burro's business model. The challenge, she noted diplomatically, "is training people who have very different cultural values. We recommend Burro move to a hierarchical system of divisions within each branch, where top sellers become division leaders who can reach out to other sellers and help them reach their sales goals. The division leaders in turn would be trained by a specialized training staff—trainers who can train the trainers, basically."

"It's possible these division leaders could also be exchanging batteries for their agents," said Rose. "We tried getting Dorothy in Bomase to do that for Seth and Victor; it didn't really work, but then again we weren't offering her any incentive."

"I like the idea of having someone at the village level with training expertise," said Whit. "Tara, you had mentioned a company in Accra with some experience at this."

"Health Keepers," she said. "They've had a number of BYU interns, and they work around here."

"I'd love to learn more about their operation."

Debi spoke up: "I think you have to be able to have these division leads if you're going to grow as fast as Whit wants. Rose and Nkansah can't do it all. It can be really hard to give up control and delegate, but you have to be able to do that, and find people who can do that."

"You're right, Debi," said Whit. "I mean, right now we have about ninety resellers in the pilot branch. To pay a return on investment with net profitability, I figure requires about three hundred and seventy-five resellers per branch. Now, can I see Rose and Nkansah training that many resellers with one or two other people? Yeah, possibly. As effectively or as rapidly as with this division lead structure? Probably not. And I'd like to see us get to the point where we can spool up a new branch in six months, versus eighteen."

"Rose, you mentioned incentives," said Tara. "I'd like to go back to that idea. One challenge we identified is that resellers make very little in commission—currently one pesewa per exchange. That is less incentive than other comparable sales jobs and it could be more competitive."

"Well, actually they're making more like two or three pesewa per exchange when you factor in coupon sales," said Whit. "And keep in mind that other sales opportunities around here require a buy-in: you need working capital to buy inventory, which is often perishable, so there is risk. With Burro there is no buy-in. Having said that, it would be interesting to explore more ways to incentivize and reward high performers. We especially need to rethink the mix in compensation for registering a new battery versus exchanging a battery for an existing client. We've favored the former at the expense of incenting exchanges, and we need to flip that."

Next came Jennia's presentation. "Our objective in the marketing research was to better understand Burro customers and why they consistently use Burro over other brands," she said, "then to apply what we learned to a marketing and brand-awareness plan. The most consistent positive comment about Burro we heard was that the battery 'doesn't rot in machines.' Virtually everyone knew someone whose device had been ruined by a leaking Tiger Head."

"I'm not surprised," said Whit. "Isidor Buchmann, the battery expert, told me that *all* carbon-zinc batteries will leak if you run them all the way down, which is what people do here. It's the nature of the chemistry. It's not a matter of *if*, it's a question of *when*."

"So Burro can definitely own the phrase *Doesn't Leak*," Jennia continued. "Another negative feature of Tiger Head was the child-safety issue. Several customers told us they had seen children putting discarded batteries into their mouths. One subject told us how a child she knows had sucked on a battery and was taken to the hospital. Because Burro batteries are not thrown away, and possibly also because they don't leak, Burro is perceived as safer for children.

"But Tiger Head also has many positive perceptions," she went on. "The first is huge familiarity; people seem to trust the brand, despite the leaks. And many customers perceive them as lasting longer or being more powerful than Burro."

"And as we know from our tests," said Whit, "Tiger Head is slightly more powerful at first, and it does last longer, albeit at very low output levels."

"Because of that," said Jennia, "we think Burro can't really own the phrase *More Power*, because it isn't always more powerful, depending on the device. It's also a bit vague: does it mean *Lasts Longer* or is it *Brighter-slash-Louder?*

"In addition, the phrase *Do More* did not elicit any response. In all of our interviews, the idea of *doing more* never came up. It made me wonder if that is a Ghanaian value, at least expressed in that way.

"However, we did identify a phrase that we believe Burro can own: *Stays Strong*. People liked the fact that Burro batteries are not constantly getting weaker and weaker like Tiger Heads."

"I love *Stays Strong*," said Whit.* "As far as *Do More* goes, it's important to keep in mind that we are delivering productivity enhancements. Every Burro product has to either enhance income earning potential, or substitute for something else they already spend money on. So we need to get people excited about doing more. It may not be a pithy tagline to sell batteries, but in terms of overall brand positioning, I don't see us backing away from that. However, we do need to figure out how to make money from the battery offering. The throwaway battery market in Ghana alone is fifty million dollars. And beyond that is the low-hanging fruit of devices like lanterns and phone chargers that showcase our batteries. Near term, that's where we're headed."

A few days later, I sat in on a meeting Whit called with Andrew to discuss his own project, which involved some follow-up on ideas raised by Tara and Jennia. Andrew said he wanted to pick four villages and see if he could raise the reseller exchange rate with Nkansah.

"I'm for this," said Whit, "but I'd go bigger. Let's identify one or two zones we want to test in. Then you can work with Rose and Nkansah and try to speed those interventions with multiple resellers. That would have a multiplier effect, and it will help us test this idea of zoning and the division manager organization."

"So you mean we should be training zone managers?"

"Yes, picking people who have at least five resellers under them, making sure they're selling effectively, identifying new territory effectively. Rose is already working on that, and you could jump in. So you guys train the trainer. Then you've really made an impact."

The next day they met again, with Rose. After reading a lengthy written plan that Andrew had drawn up, Whit said, "You've gotta keep it real simple. Remember there's not a big tradition of reading here; it's all about oral interaction. There are cognitive studies showing that humans can

---

* Subsequent fieldwork by Rose suggested that *Stays Strong* was as potentially ambiguous as *More Power*. She convinced Whit that a better slogan was *Brighter/ Louder*, which also helped justify the battery's shorter duration.

process like five plus-or-minus two concepts at a time. I think we should err on the lower side. Keep these training materials to chunks of three or four things with at most three or four layers under them. It's gotta be really crisp, something they can completely memorize in one setting. Distill it into brief, bulleted stuff—three things you need to do this job; under each of those, three or four things you need to do for each point; under those, three or four things you need to do to achieve those goals. It's gotta be that simple."

## 7. A Weird Nexus

Meanwhile, Justin was organizing a business plan that would help Whit present Burro to potential investors. He was a bit older than the other interns—he had a wife and baby daughter back in Utah—and came with real-world experience executing business valuations. He met with Whit one afternoon to talk about the plan. "What's the exit strategy for an investor?" Justin asked. "Would they take dividends? How much of the company would they get for a million dollars?" He was asking the right questions.

"Well," said Whit, "I've got a quarter million of my own in this company, so I've got some skin in the game; I wouldn't give up control of the company. But I'm also comfortable putting more of my own money in if revenue continues to grow. My financial guys would say I'm out of my mind, but if things look good I'm willing to roll some pretty big dice. As for exit strategies, I know dividends are less attractive to investors than going public, or a strategic acquisition. Maybe I have people invest in starting a branch, and they get convertible three-year notes."

"If Burro were acquired, do you have any companies in mind?" Justin wondered.

Whit shrugged. "I could see P&G, Unilever—some monster consumer goods company. Or I could see a major Chinese manufacturer being a strategic investor, but they're so shitty at brands. For me, I'd want someone who understands the value of the brand."

Justin asked how Burro would use venture capital.

"Well, first, we'd beef up our training and marketing materials, deepen the team more quickly, show that we can spool on growth more rapidly, and of course move towards a first trial of replicability with a second branch," said Whit. "We'd also invest against medium-term technology to better support growth—especially a low-budget IT solution that integrates all our current operational needs more robustly than the Fodder program Jan and I hacked together in Access. We probably need a more industrial-strength charging capability as we scale up. It might also make sense to invest in a proprietary battery design that could get costs per cycle way down, provide better performance for clients, and protect much better against fraudulent charging. More product development definitely makes sense. People want better entertainment and information solutions, better communication solutions, more versatile lighting solutions, maybe even battery-operated tools. Expanding the line of efficient, battery-powered appliances makes sense so long as we stay focused on things true to the brand—creating new income capabilities or displacing existing expenditure. We need to demonstrate that we're building assets far more valuable than a battery store. Hell, who knows, maybe I'd even pay myself a salary."

Justin asked if Whit would be interested in smaller stakeholders who are as passionate about the company mission as making a buck.

"I've definitely thought about it," said Whit. "We're operating in a weird nexus of social enterprise and creative capitalism where the reality is, even if you're just barely sustainable, you could probably get people to underwrite and subsidize and help roll out additional branches. I'm not terribly interested in that, but I wouldn't rule out keeping the baby alive that way. It would mean getting donor support of some sort to play the role of a central corporate structure that manages the whole thing and rolls out new branches. So the branches stand alone and are sustainable, but there's not enough fat in the system to make it scalable. You'd have somebody who's driving the opening of new branches and who is advising and training new branch teams; they would need donor assistance at their level, but they'd be creating viable and sustainable small businesses on the local level that deliver energy and increased efficiency to poor communities. I personally would see that as a failure, but many people involved in social capitalism are aiming for exactly that. In other words, you could design a template that puts donor money to work on a rollout that could be a screaming economic success, or barely sustainable.

"So yeah, I could see angel donors where you say, look, for fifty or a hundred thousand you can provide power to these rural villages. We'll manage the whole rollout and operation for you, we'll keep you posted on agents and clients, and you're gonna feel real good about it while earning some modest return on your investment. I mean, I think it's pretty impressive what we're doing here. We've got close to a hundred semiliterate agents out there, selling batteries to hundreds of customers, advising them, counseling them, getting information on them, building a business model that has never been tried before in this country or continent. And people are saving money on batteries and doing more for their money."

Outside, as if on cue, a cheer erupted across Koforidua and floated up over the streets and into our windows like smoke from the charcoal braziers of the snack sellers. But they weren't cheering Burro; the Ghana Black Stars soccer team had just scored a goal in a lead-up match to the World Cup.

Whit continued. "I think right now we've got a pitch that a lot of donors or socially minded investors would love. But we're driving instead to demonstrate truly attractive unit economics—you know, like a branch spinning off fifty or seventy-five thousand dollars a year in after-tax profits. That would be huge. Then it's like the McDonald's model. But you can't franchise something that loses money; you'll just lose money faster. So we have to demonstrate that running a branch is a good business. Then maybe, if we go for outside money, you can sell branches to investors for a hundred or two hundred thousand dollars once you prove that within a year or two you can get them spinning off substantial nets. That's going to be attractive to a lot more people, real investors. Like me."

## 8. They Like the Sound

Burro also had a Ghanaian intern—another recent graduate of Ashesi University, named Priscilla Osman, who had been a classmate of Rose's. Priscilla—quiet, very dark, with a wide face and high cheekbones—was from Bole, a town in the country's dry and sparsely populated northwest. She was a member of the Gonja tribe, of whom there are about a quarter million people. Their language (also called Gonja) is a subset of the Guang linguistic group; many people in her remote region don't even speak Twi, let alone English, but Priscilla was fluent in both. She told me she learned English by listening to the Ghana News radio broadcasts as a child. "Many Gonja do not speak English, but they listen to the news anyway," she said, "because they like the sound."

Rose and Priscilla were teamed up writing scripts for a Burro pitch that could be played over the loudspeakers on the truck—the pitch Whit was hoping to have created by MMRS Ogilvy in Accra. Despite many email follow-ups, Whit had been unable to get any commitment from the global agency, and he couldn't wait any longer. Burro was a do-it-yourself operation, and Whit was not exactly a marketing neophyte; he and Richard Tait hadn't waited for permission from any multinational corporations to start Cranium, and he wasn't going to wait now. Besides, Adam's brother knew a small recording studio in New Tafo, a town about an hour north of Koforidua, that said it could handle the physical production. The cost would be only a few hundred cedis; it was worth a try.

The plan was to create two pitches—a short, thirty-second teaser that could be played from a moving vehicle, and a more detailed one-and-a-half-minute pitch for stationary events like gong-gongs. "Make them like testimonials," Whit told Rose and Priscilla, "so we hear other voices, not just the narrator."

After lunch, Whit asked me to help review the drafts that Rose and Priscilla had put together. Since the actual recordings would be done in Twi, Ewe, and Krobo—the three languages commonly spoken around

Koforidua—the English-language versions were really just for the benefit of Whit and me, a common base to work from.

I read the first draft. The opening line was: *Attention all battery users, Burro batteries have broken barriers and status quo!* To my ear that sounded a tad wooden, but I had to remember that the advertising culture in Ghana, while pervasive, was untainted by the jaded irony that characterizes current Western salesmanship. In Ghana there were no TV commercials with wise-guy babies pitching brokerages, no cavemen selling car insurance. Billboards and TV commercials—we did occasionally watch TV in restaurants—generally featured smiling, happy people embracing the object of their desire—a naïve enthusiasm that, for me, evoked a lost world of postwar optimism. "You are too *known*," Africans would often say to us—a polite Ghanaian way of calling us uptight honkies—and when it came to advertising, they were dead right.

So I read on: *Thanks to Burro, no longer will we pay more for expensive, leaky and fast-failing batteries.*

"Doesn't that imply that now we will pay *less* for expensive, leaky, and fast-failing batteries?" I asked.

"I see what you mean," said Priscilla. She changed it to read: *Thanks to Burro, no longer will we buy expensive, leaky, and fast-failing batteries.*

We read on, and Whit weighed in: "This is really close and very strong, but I would just jump right into *the Burro battery is better*, somehow. I don't know the word in Twi, but Priscilla, I would just encourage you to take the first two sentences and make the point very explicit and as crisply and quickly as possible. You mention how other batteries *expose your children and the environment to danger*, but I wonder if for the short version we should just focus on the no-leak guarantee. So I guess where I'm headed is, what's our overall positioning and what are the three things behind it? I just want to hammer those three points as quickly as possible. So the overall message is *it's a better battery*. Then the three things are the no-leak guarantee, stays strong, and more value for less money. I don't know the tightest and most impactful way to get at *more affordable* in Twi—you guys need to tell me—but that's the kicker. So it's a better battery, no-leak guarantee, stays strong, and—*you're not gonna believe this*—but it costs less."

"Should I add something about how you get the batteries?" Priscilla asked.

"Good question," said Whit. "I don't think in the short pitch. This is definitely a case where less is more. I wouldn't even mention the coupons. But certainly in the longer one."

To make sure we could better understand what the actual African scripts were saying, Whit asked Rose and Priscilla to translate the final revisions into Twi and then "reverse translate" them back into English from Twi. It was sort of like a game of telegraph, but it worked. After a few more revisions, here was the final script:

MAN'S VOICE: Attention all battery users, there is a new battery in town called Burro! Burro batteries do not leak, stay strong, and the best part is that they cost less.

WOMAN'S VOICE: Thanks to Burro, I will no longer buy leaky batteries that do not stay strong and cost more!

MAN'S VOICE: Try Burro too, and you will testify to it. Burro! Do More!

As artificial as the dialog sounded to us, we had to remember that a lot was getting lost, or garbled, in the translation from an African tongue that has no etymological correlation to Western words and phrases. And Rose and Priscilla were not professional translators. So it was natural that the English version of their script (which no one would ever hear) sounded a bit like something from Google Translate. Rose promised that the Twi version sounded completely natural, and there was no reason to doubt her. Nkansah translated both the short and long pitch into Krobo (from Twi), and Adam handled the Ewe versions. Priscilla and Rose drove up to the studio in New Tafo to start work on the rough cuts. The next day, Whit, Priscilla, and I went up to watch some of the voice-overs be recorded.

Quayem Productions was located in a nondescript stuccoed hut no larger than a standard garden shed. We pulled into the dirt yard under an oil palm tree and were greeted by the owner, an easygoing young man whose name, Stocky, adequately described his athletic build. Sitting around a wooden table outside the studio were several other young men, all of them appearing to be weight lifters, who would be performing the voice-overs in the various languages. For now they were handfeeding small chunks of dried fish to a ravenous kitten no wider than one of their wrists. Stocky explained that he and his colleagues had a rap act called DNA. "It's short for Drugs 'n' Alcohol," he explained matter-of-factly, although I couldn't picture any of those guys taking drugs, except maybe steroids.

The studio itself had barely enough room for a battered wooden desk covered with computer equipment, a small electronic keyboard, and a couple of plastic chairs. The walls were draped in woven sisal fabric to deaden the sound of car horns outside. A bare compact fluorescent lightbulb hung above. In one corner was a phone booth–sized recording chamber with a stool and a microphone. Stocky sat down at his desk as several of us squeezed into the room. Then the light blinked out: power failure. We moaned and filed back outside. Whit called the office and reached one of the interns. Power was out in Koforidua too. This could be a while.

We sat around the picnic table and watched Jah, a tall member of DNA who would perform the male Twi voice-over, feed the kitten more dried fish while we talked. Stocky, it turned out, was an ambitious young man. Besides his Accra-based band and his recording studio in New Tafo (where he grew up and still had family), he was also studying supply chain management at Koforidua Polytech, where he had met Adam's brother, a fellow student. Before deciding to pursue college, Stocky had spent three years in Guangzhou, China, exporting clothing and footwear for the Ghanaian market. It was not an experience he held fondly. "The Chinese are racist," he said. "They spit on the sidewalk when a black man walks by."

"Are you serious?" I asked.

"I am serious. Especially African blacks. They always thought I was American because I'm big, so they didn't hate me as much."

Which is not to say they showered him with respect. "One Chinese man couldn't believe it when I bought my own plane ticket," Stocky recalled. "He wondered how I could afford it. They think we are slaves."

Stocky had also worked in Egypt and Dubai. Besides a passport filled with entry stamps and visas, he possessed an encyclopedic knowledge of the Ghanaian import business, which operated by its own strange logic. "The things I have seen you couldn't believe," he said. "People bring in used American cars and smash the bonnet to pay less duty," he said. "Then they fix it here."

Jah screamed and shook his hand, which was dripping blood. The kitten had taken a chunk out of his index finger.

Stocky glared at the cat. "Biting the hand that feeds you!" It looked up and purred.

"He didn't mean to," said Jah. "He thought my finger was food."

So does the lion, I thought. Never much of a pet lover even back home, it was easy for me to avoid the village dogs and cats in Ghana. But Whit was always petting and holding these frail creatures, despite my nagging warnings.

The light flickered on and we tramped back into the studio. The Krobo voice guy (I never got his name) had to leave soon, so he went first into the booth with a script. As he started reciting his lines, Stocky directed from the computer terminal: "Shout!"

The guy started again, louder.

"Shout!"

Again, louder.

"Shout! Excitement!"

This went on for about twenty minutes, running through all the lines over and over. Stocky clearly got it, and knew how to drive his actors to perform. At one point all the guys started laughing at a joke we didn't understand. "What's so funny?" Whit asked.

The question made Stocky laugh even harder. "There is a word in Krobo, twɛ, which means 'patience,' or 'have patience.' But in Twi it sounds like the word for 'vagina.' In this context it would mean 'Burro is the only vagina.'"

"Well I don't think we can make that claim," said Whit. "Seriously, is it okay?"

"It's okay," said Stocky.

"It won't offend people?"

"No, it's a different language," he said. "It's understood." And he laughed again.

Out went the power, again. After an hour of sitting around, we decided to leave; Priscilla needed to catch a bus to Accra. Stocky and his crew promised to work through the night once the power came on.

Sure enough, he called Whit the next morning and told us to come up.

The cat was still eating. Jah had a bandage on his finger. We sat down in the studio and Stocky ran the audio files. Whit had brainstormed an idea for a signature Burro sound: two *clicks*, like a finger snap—the sound made when clicking a Burro battery into the D-sized adapter. The short pitch began with the *click-click* sound, which Stocky had enhanced, followed by the voice-over: "Hey!"

The rest, of course, was in Twi, or Ewe, or Krobo, over an instrumental music track of generic, bright-sounding Ghanaian pop music. The only English was at the very end: "Burro! Do More!" *Click-click*. And then it started all over again, in a constant loop.

Whit listened carefully, grinning. "Can you give it another, you know, split second to come down before the *click-click*?"

"Okay. So, *Do More . . . click-click*," said Stocky.

"Yeah. It's like the *click-click* is coming a little bit into the *Do More*, you know? So just a little cleaner break on the *Do More*. It's awesome though, man, it's great."

Stocky adjusted the levels and beat measures, then replayed it.

Whit paused. "Play it one more time. It's weird, it's almost like there's a little reverb on the *Do More*."

"There is."

"Yeah, and it sounds like the *click-click* is hitting the echo. Which might be okay."

More adjustments followed.

"Yeah!" said Whit. "That's good, huh?"

Jah came in. He was shivering with a fever. "I am going to the clinic," he said, as a taxi pulled up outside. I wondered about that cat bite yesterday. Stocky's girlfriend from Accra had come up, and she offered to take Jah to the clinic. We kept working.

"Who did the woman's voice?" asked Whit, assuming it might have been Stocky's friend.

"That's me," said Stocky.

"That's you?"

"I pitched it," he said—electronically manipulating the pitch to turn his own deep voice into a woman's.

"I would never be able to tell," said Whit. Stocky smiled.

The last job was rendering all the recordings through a program that would "brighten" the playback by subtly shifting up all the frequencies. "It will give it a 'wall of sound,'" explained Stocky. Almost fifty years after Phil Spector invented the concept in an analog New York City recording studio with a legion of African-American girl groups from the Bronx, a young African man was using a computer program to duplicate the effect in a mud-walled village hut in Ghana.

When it came time to pay, Stocky asked for two hundred and twenty cedis. "That's not enough," said Whit. He gave him three hundred cedis and a brief Business 101 lecture about pricing strategy and the value of services.

Driving home, Whit said, "That was amazing. I paid like two hundred and thirty dollars to make two commercials in three languages over three days."

## 9. Pork Show

We threw a party at Whit's house one Friday night. Actually we put on a pork show, as we called it, having bought a shoulder of pork from a guy along the side of the road, next to a hand-painted sign announcing PORK SHOW. This odd nomenclature was typical in Ghana, where the words *sale* and *show* can be interchangeable. Pork can be hard to find in Ghana, so in that sense any pork retail experience is something of a show. But our local pork merchant's presentation fell somewhat short of spectacle. It was, in fact, nothing more than a large aluminum bowl filled with fly-covered chunks of pig, shaded with a banana leaf. Nevertheless it made a fine barbecue.

Everyone from Burro except Adam showed up; he begged off, claiming an engagement in Accra, although I suspected the evangelical voice in his head was dissuaded by the all-day preparations, which included strategic planning by Rose, Debi, and David on the variety and quantity of liquor to be offered. Still, that didn't seem to put off the BYU interns, who turned out to be pretty good dancers. Considering that my brother's sprawling home had approximately five pieces of furniture including both beds, there was plenty of room for dancing.

My clearest memory of the pork show was Rose dancing with a drinking glass perfectly balanced on her head, which may be the Ghanaian equivalent of wearing a lampshade. My second clearest memory was of Nkansah and James complimenting me on my barbecue, a new taste experience for them—until I told them it was pork. "Oh," said Nkansah, setting down his fork politely. "We are Krobo; we do not eat pork."

Late in the evening, while watching Rose and James dance in the dining room to a very loud techno-funk beat, I looked out past them and saw Akosia, the pregnant woman who lived in the hut in the backyard. She was outside, her elbows on the cement-block balustrade around the porch, watching the party through the open jalousie window.

"Akosia!" I said, waving to her.

But as soon as we made eye contact, she disappeared into the night like Cinderella.

## 10. Loafers in the Temple

The local Mormon meeting house was a few blocks from the Burro office. On a Sunday in late May, Justin, Andrew, and I were the only white people in the large congregation. We sat in straight-backed chairs. All the men wore white shirts and dark ties, except me, who never brought a tie or even a sport coat on any of my trips to Africa. I had put on a clean shirt and pressed slacks, but my sincerest nod to sartorial formality was a pair of pointed white leather African loafers I had bought a few days earlier. Although I meant well, in hindsight they were a poor choice for the service. I'm not sure why I bought them, other than thinking they looked cool. But as I sat in church clutching the Book of Mormon, I remembered that when I was a kid spending summers in Detroit we used to call similar footwear "pimp shoes." So I was wearing pimp shoes in the Mormon church on a Sunday morning. Perhaps worse in the eyes of God, I was *thinking about pimps* in the Mormon church on a Sunday morning. If only it had been like Jonas's church, where you had to take off your shoes at the door.

But it was nothing like that. There was no dancing, no drumming, no music at all except for one hymn sung a capella by the children in honor of their mothers. (It was Ghana's Mother's Day.) The service was in English. In his sermon, which constituted pretty much the whole event, the leader talked about the importance of learning English. "I have heard the Mormon service in Twi," he said, "but it was not good for me."

## 11. Ointments and Balms and Medicated Soaps

"Maxy, wake up."

"Piss off." I was already awake, a condition I had been trying to reverse since three A.M., when the roosters started crowing directly outside my open bedroom windows.

"C'mon. We gotta go," said Whit.

"Go where?"

"Accra."

"Fuck." Another day of traffic in Accra, another conference room. Whit had an appointment with the people who ran Health Keepers, the agent-model NGO that Tara, the BYU intern, had mentioned in her presentation. It was one of those companies operating in that "weird nexus" (to use

Whit's phrase) of charity and for-profit. And it had a network of agents, some around Koforidua, selling useful products that did not directly compete with Burro but certainly complemented Burro's brand. All in all, it made sense to get to know them. I crawled out of bed like it was a foxhole and grabbed a shirt.

A combination of bad directions and an obscure location made us late for our meeting at Health Keepers. When we finally arrived, executive director Daniel Mensah greeted us warmly. A large man with thick glasses, he seemed genuinely eager to hear about Burro. We sat around a conference table and were joined by Sandra Manu, who was in charge of training agents for Health Keepers. Whit presented his updated PowerPoint show, which reflected the latest Burro figures of fifteen hundred clients served by eighty or ninety active agents in about two hundred locations. When he mentioned the challenge of finding good agents, Sandra nodded knowingly.

"We are learning that good agents make a huge difference," said Whit. "Currently our average exchange rate is twenty to twenty-five days," referring to the time it takes a client to use up a battery and exchange it for a fresh one. "We think it should be fourteen, and agents who are good at servicing clients typically achieve this."

Whit finished, and Daniel narrated his own PowerPoint show. "We are an NGO but we believe in sustainability," he began. "We distribute at a profit and plow the money back into the business. And our agents are profitable at their level. So we use private-sector business approaches."

The company was founded in 2006 by a California nonprofit called Freedom from Hunger. Over the years, fifteen BYU business-school interns had come over to help design marketing plans and improve productivity. "But none came this year," said Daniel. "It seems Burro took them all," he added, laughing. Meanwhile, Freedom from Hunger decided to focus its efforts on the humanitarian crisis in Darfur, so Health Keepers lost its U.S. funding. "But they generously let us keep this office space and all the local assets," said Daniel, "so we reorganized into a local group. Just last week we received a grant from USAID to distribute condoms and birth control pills."

Health Keepers' products included many items Westerners would buy at a drugstore: diarrhea medicine, reading glasses, wound care, feminine hygiene products, toothpaste, anti-lice and anti-dandruff shampoo, moisturizers, and laundry soap. Other goods were more specific to the developing world, like insecticide-treated mosquito nets and water treatment tablets. The company also provided services like mosquito net re-treatment (the pesticide eventually wears off), optical screening, blood pressure testing, first aid, and national health plan subscription sign-ups.

Unlike Burro's consignment model, Health Keepers agents needed to buy their products in advance. So an agent might buy a six-pack of razors for eighty pesewa, then sell them for one cedi, a little less than the going rate in shops.

Daniel said the company was at first reluctant to advance credit to agents, but they found that a cash-only policy discouraged agents from trying new items. "So now we offer a four-month product loan of one hundred cedis' worth of stuff," he said. "They must pay back twelve and a half cedis every two weeks, interest-free. Even with that, sometimes it is hard to get the money," he added. "We have had to send the police to make the point." His comment made me realize that Nkansah's police-car gag in the gong-gong was a joke with a serious undertone.

Whit asked if the company had experienced any push-back from local pharmacies and chemist shops, which were often located in smaller towns, if not remote villages, and sold many of the same products. "Well, there are things they have which we cannot sell," he said, "such as antibiotic ointments and ibuprofen."

I found it odd that, in a country where scheduled narcotics can be obtained by asking the pharmacist politely, ibuprofen is strictly regulated. Only pharmacists and chemists (the difference is in level of training) can dispense it—the former in up to four-hundred-milligram doses, the latter limited to two-hundred-milligram pills.

"Sandra, I'm wondering how you find new agents," said Whit.

"Often we find them through existing agents," she said. "They make a small commission if they sign up a new agent."

"And what about training?" Whit asked.

"We do training at our cluster meetings," she said, explaining that clusters are groups of agents from several towns. They meet every two weeks to exchange money and get new products. "Training involves some role playing, drama, and discussion. It can be a challenge. Our best agents are typically older, at least in their thirties, because the young people have too high expectations." She said the most profitable products, like antibiotic soaps, hand lotions, and feminine sanitary products, require a degree of salesmanship that is not always second nature.

"We would love to see how your training works," said Whit. "I understand you have agents in Nkurakan."

"Five or six," said Sandra.

"And Mamfe?"

"Around twenty."

"Nkurakan, Mamfe, that's our sweet spot," said Whit. "I'd love to see if we can encourage mutual sales in those towns. Also, we're happy to try supplying your products to our people in other areas."

"Clearly there are areas for collaboration," Daniel said.

We left with Sandra agreeing to invite Burro to the next cluster meeting in Mamfe.

On the drive home we talked about ibuprofen. "Last week when Rose had a fever, I tried to find her some," said Whit. "I went to the chemist and they had never heard of it. Finally I found some at a pharmacy; they call it *profen*. It was from India and it was candy-coated, in bubble packs. It was very cheap, like three cedis for maybe sixty pills. But it's so hard to get. People in villages can just never get it unless they take a taxi or *tro-tro* into town. I'd like to partner with a pharmacy chain like Interpharma to sell Burro-branded ibuprofen up here. I'd say, 'Look, you're selling it, so it's a pharmacy making the legal sale, but we'll provide marketing and delivery.' I mean, these poor farmers—they're getting all these fucking ointments and balms and medicated soaps for backache, and they can't get ibuprofen. I wish we could go into a village and say, 'If your back hurts take two of these.'

"But the truth is I don't have time to pursue all this stuff right now," he went on. "First we've gotta get these resellers more productive. English is such a challenge. Guys like Jonas and George, in their forties, their English is good but not as good as Hayford's, who's sixty-four. There has been more emphasis in the schools on local languages, but most everyone will agree that the education system has declined; there's definitely a decreasing curve of English fluency with the younger agents. Edward Mintah, this agent in Beware, great guy, hard worker, excellent salesman, twenty years old—tough to communicate with him in English."

It was now long after sunset, and the narrow road with its unforgiving shoulder of an open concrete drain was getting hard to see. People in dark robes walked along the edge of the blacktop, their ghostly forms nearly invisible until close range; goats the color of coal darted back and forth. Sometimes oncoming drivers would dim their lights, sometime they wouldn't; either way, with no streetlights or reflective road stripes, the beams of opposing traffic blotted out all reference to the highway long enough to swerve into any number of pedestrians and livestock. Just outside Koforidua, in the village of Okurase, the bobbing lens of a flashlight signaled a police roadblock. "Please open your boot," said the officer. The trunk was full of groceries from Accra; he made us take them all out. One kilometer up the road, another cop at another roadblock inspected the groceries again. I thought Whit might lose it, but he kept cool.

We pulled into Whit's garage and noticed the car was leaking oil. Inside the house, a fan had hit another lightbulb and showered Whit's bed with glass.

I woke up at two o'clock, not to the usual noise of roosters but to the unmistakable clamor of what police delicately call a "domestic disturbance." It was coming from Akosia's blockhouse in the courtyard. I had lived in New York apartments long enough to recognize the difference between an argument and actual abuse, and this sounded more like the former, so I left it alone.

At five-thirty the next morning Akosia, at this point looking very pregnant, knocked on the back door. "Please," she said to Whit, "will you talk to my husband?"

Victor had returned from his "travels" in the middle of the night—with a woman from Accra. Naturally, Akosia had protested the unwelcome guest; they argued. "Please tell him to go away."

"I will talk to him," said Whit.

"Thank you." She looked down at the ground. "Please," she said, "I need to go back to the hospital. Can you give me some money?"

"I will give you money this time because I want you to go to the hospital for your baby," he said, digging into his pocket for a ten-cedi note. "But I am traveling to America next week, and I can't take care of you. You need to find a way to get by." It was the only time in Africa that I saw Whit break his own rule about handing out money to people who weren't obviously handicapped. Outside, Victor was slinking out the gate with his girlfriend, who wore tight jeans and a big hairdo. Whit watched and shook his head: "What an asshole."

# fifteen

# CHARGING

**FALL 2010:** The upsell

*"If you want to save souls, try China."*

—Sammy Glick in Budd Schulberg's
*What Makes Sammy Run?*

The competition: A generator was one way villagers could
charge their cell phones; another was sending them out by
taxi to grid locations. Either way cost a lot more than
using a battery-powered Burro phone charger.

## 1. Try China

**T**here is a place in the world for the corkscrew that breaks after one use, the faucet that leaks out of the box, the gas oven that blows out when you shut the door, the refrigerator that won't stay closed, the garlic press that bends into a pretzel, and the tongs that lacerate your hand like scissors. That place is the African kitchen. I illustrate my point with these common household appliances because of my intimate familiarity with them, but you could as easily find examples in office supplies or mechanic's tools or consumer electronics. Any product that is too shoddy or unsafe for the West ends up getting sold in Africa, alongside the cast-off Goodwill clothing and the refurbished four-track cassette decks.

The main engine today is China, scouring Africa for natural resources with which to power its manufacturing colossus, and repatriating the continent's raw materials in the form of shiny junk for which there is no warranty, no return, and no exchange. Against this tsunami of stamped tin and thin plastic paddled my brother, trying to bring well-made but affordable products to rural Ghanaians. "They deserve better," he would say, and he meant it—but by the summer of 2010 it had become clear that his business was unlikely to thrive on batteries alone.

Indeed, with battery quality issues seemingly under control, a nagging question remained: why were so many people in Burro's villages still using Tiger Heads? It seemed that even the best Burro resellers had a hard time keeping customers coming back for more exchanges. Since the first battery use was essentially free—you could return the dead battery and get your deposit back, having paid nothing—ongoing exchanges were crucial to the business; otherwise it was just a free-trial giveaway. But instead of exchanging old for new every week or so, many customers were giving up, returning their dead batteries, and collecting their deposit.

Presumably those customers were going back to buying Tiger Heads, as the only other option was living in darkness after six o'clock every night. Whit knew his batteries were better than Tiger Heads and cost less money; the Burro team was working to ensure that every battery sent out had been properly charged and tested for strength. What was not to like? It took months of work on the ground for Whit to fully understand that the problem lay in the nature of the local battery-powered devices, and in the peculiarly subjective nature of human vision.

Whit knew from all his testing that Burro's NiMH batteries provided bright light for about thirty more hours than the cheap carbon-zinc Tiger Heads. The problem was that the Tiger Heads continued to provide at least *some* light for several more days, whereas the Burro battery quickly died at the end of its useful life. In the modern world of smart, high-tech devices and ready power supplies, the Burro power curve would be preferable; you'd get a lot of steady power, followed by a steep drop-off that signaled it was time to recharge. But rural Ghana was not the modern world. Whit's customers didn't have smart devices, much less electricity to recharge their batteries. Instead, virtually all of Burro's clients used "dumb" flashlights sold (also by Tiger Head) for two or three cedis—lights that by their very simplicity were ideally suited for the long, slow voltage trickle of Tiger Head batteries. "They're killing us with these cheap LED flashlights," said Whit. "They have no serious circuitry, so instead of keeping power constant as the battery voltage falls, they actually draw less current—a lot less. It would be like if you were climbing a mountain and the more tired you got, the more weights people along the trail would remove from your pack. You could keep going forever. So as Tiger Heads die, their voltage just tracks lower and lower in a straight line. And those cheap flashlights respond to the lower voltage by demanding less and less power."

"So what's wrong with that?" I asked.

"Well, the light gets dimmer and dimmer. Think of brightness as being the weights in that backpack. The more you take out the easier it is to climb, but the less light you have. Laws of physics apply here."

Indeed, Whit's tests demonstrated that the light provided by a dying Tiger Head was barely visible, perhaps on the level of a dim night-light. But here was the problem: the human eye does not readily perceive differences in light intensity; it simply adjusts and gets on with things. Only when compared head-to-head with a more powerful light do we say, "Aha! Big difference!" As far as the average Ghanaian villager who owns only one flashlight was concerned, that faint glow was still light. Explaining to her, "Well yes, but, you see, it's not really very much light, and Burro gives you much better light for a lot longer, at least at first," presented a qualitative marketing challenge, to say the least.

In short, Whit was trying to sell "brighter" to people who really wanted "long-lasting." And while he couldn't change the physics of the NiMH battery curve, he felt there had to be some way to work around their disadvantage in cheap devices. After all, the batteries were inherently better.

Then one night in the battery room, it hit him.

"Hey Max, check this out," he said. "I'm thinking you could run one of these flashlights on just one Burro battery." He had fashioned a sort of faux battery with a roofing nail and a ball of tinfoil, which he was jamming into a flashlight canister.

"One battery in a two-battery flashlight?" I asked. "Wouldn't that be incredibly dim?"

"Well yeah, it would be running at 1.2 volts instead of 2.4. But it would still be brighter than people are used to on their rundown Tiger Heads. In fact, I'm thinking the power required to operate at that lower voltage would be so low that . . ." He paused.

"That what?"

"I'm almost afraid to say this. But I'm thinking the flashlight might actually run *longer* on one battery than on two."

"That's crazy."

"Maybe so, but I think I'm right. It would be incredibly cheap, much cheaper than two Tiger Heads. It would make Burro the cheapest way to get fresh light *today*, and as we've seen, with most of our customers it's all about current expenditure."

We stared at each other and smiled. It was like the moment in *The Producers* when accountant Leo Bloom realizes they can make more money creating a Broadway flop than a hit. But while Bialystock and Bloom never imagined their flop would become a hit, Whit realized from the beginning that his battery saver would be a crowd pleaser.

"This is huge," said Whit. "Shit, though. It means bringing in a device that diminishes the need for my product; that's a little scary, but we're losing these people anyway."

"And couldn't people just use the eliminator with a Tiger Head?" I asked. "Then you're back in the same hole."

"Well, you could design it with an insert on the top that wouldn't work with Tiger Heads," he said, "although people could probably game it with a piece of tinfoil. But a single Tiger Head in one of these flashlights would get really dim really fast, and it'd be especially prone to leaking. I'm pretty confident that most users would pick Burro in a head-to-head running this way."

Whit shoved a single battery into the flashlight with the makeshift tinfoil "battery eliminator" as he quickly dubbed it (later christened the battery *saver*) and turned it on. "I need to test this."

**The other way around** the cheap flashlight issue was to sell better lights and other smart devices optimized for Burro's NiMH batteries. One example was the jerry-rigged battery-powered phone charger that Whit was already selling for three cedis, but he wanted a Burro-branded phone charger, ideally with a built-in flashlight, that wouldn't force customers to cut and splice wires from their wall charger.

Through Three-Sixty, his China-based sourcing partner from his Cranium days, Whit had located a low-cost consumer electronics manufacturer in Guangzhou that was ready to work with him. During a visit to their plant in the summer of 2009, Whit was shown a standard catalog of flashlights, most of which were too expensive or included useless frills like flashing disco lights. He told them he wanted a simple but elegant four-battery phone charger that incorporated an LED light, including a red light for preserving night vision while hunting. He was also interested in selling a Burro-branded headlamp, but it would have to cost a lot less than the forty-dollar versions Americans buy from L.L. Bean, and even less than the twenty-dollar versions sold at Walmart. Whit laid down a few thousand dollars to commission hand samples—prototypes that must be approved before actual production begins—for the combination phone charger and flashlight and the headlamp. It went downhill from there.

Whit had specified that the phone charger include circuitry to shut itself off when the power from the batteries dropped below 3.6 volts. That was crucial to prevent damaging Burro's expensive NiMH batteries, which lose capacity if they are run down too low. Bernice, the manufacturer's English-speaking sales rep, confirmed by email that the company could make the unit as described for a wholesale price of $1.32 "FOB China," which means free-on-board China—the cost before shipping and customs. After factoring in those additional expenses, each unit would probably cost Whit about two dollars, or three Ghana cedis. He figured he could sell it for five cedis, which represented a modest but acceptable gross profit margin. (Net profit would of course be much less after factoring in the cost of his operations.)

Everything was falling into place. But when the hand samples for the charger and the headlamp arrived in Ghana in October 2009, it was clear that a lot had been lost in translation. Whit detailed the problems in a follow-up email to Bernice:

PHONE CHARGER:

The battery compartment requires a screwdriver to open. This is not acceptable. Our clients do not have access to screwdrivers. The compartment must snap closed securely and cannot require a screw for closure.

The battery contacts do not work well yet. I had to use a piece of tinfoil to get the negative contacts on the lid to contact the battery terminals. Please be certain you are testing with high-capacity, NiMH AA cells that are custom labeled as these tend to have slightly different dimensions, smaller electrode contacts, and larger diameters. Such batteries fit a bit too snugly into the unit currently and do not make electrical contact. This is a major concern.

The lights should stay on when the button is pressed and turn off when the button is pressed a second time. Our clients will be using the lights for extended periods. It is not acceptable to have to hold down the button to keep the light illuminated.

The green is not our Burro green. Please confirm that you will able to hit PMS 802 C 2X in the final plastic.

HEADLAMP:

The switch on our sample unit is defective. It is nearly impossible to turn the unit off once it is on. It takes many attempts before the mechanism finally clicks in correctly and turns off the unit. This is very troubling since I don't know how we could count on the quality of production units if the one sample is so flawed.

The clicking angle adjustment seems quite prone to breaking. I'm concerned that the plastic part that provides the ratchet might easily snap after repeated use. I'd like to know more about your testing on this and any return issues or complaints you might have had. At a minimum, we would need to have spare parts of the piece with the ratchet so that we could field service any that might break in the service of Burro clients.

Whit concluded by pointing out that the phone charger did not cut off below 3.6 volts, as specified, and did not seem to work with many phones, including his own.

"We can't reach this," Bernice responded in an email, referring to the 3.6-volt cutoff requirement. "It needs professional IC* which is used for rechargeable Lithium battery. The extra charge is USD 1.5-2/PCS."

---

* "IC" in this context means *integrated circuit*. Whit had no idea what she meant by "professional IC."

That would more than double the cost of the unit, evaporating Whit's profit.

She went on, "We have sold this item to Europe and USA 5 years ago. Why Africa has more strict standard?"

As for the headlamp, she wrote: "The price deserves the present quality. We can't match low price products with higher quality products. . . . I think it's suitable for African market also."

In other words, Bernice was proposing to send my brother the same old junk that Africa always gets. Whit was insulted, and furious that she had been wasting his time. He wrote back:

Wow! I'll be honest with you. Your responses to my email providing feedback on the samples were extraordinarily disturbing. Note that on 24 August I specified precisely the functional requirements to control maximum output voltage, to cut off current flow at 3.6 volts, and to ensure current could not flow back into the batteries. Based on this exchange, I agreed to proceed with the design and arranged to wire transfer the design, tooling, and sample fees early in the following week. Now, weeks into the process and thousands of dollars later, I learn that to achieve what was specified from the beginning and agreed upon will require additional circuitry that would more than double the unit price I had been quoted. Frankly, your comments about Africa add insult to this injury. My business is all about introducing more appropriate products into this market, Bernice. While I welcome your product insights, please do not presume to dismiss critical market requirements we have garnered on the ground here while building a new kind of brand and business. Your suggestion that cheap is the right answer for our market is, frankly, insulting—especially after having agreed to deliver the functionality we need at a price we had agreed upon.

Perhaps most disturbing to me was your comment about the headlamp, "The price deserves the present quality. We can't match low price products with higher quality products." Bernice,

perhaps I wasn't clear. The headlamp does not work. The switch
is broken.

More generally, let me reply specifically to your comment and
question about the charger, "We have sold this item to Europe and
USA 5 years ago. Why Africa has more strict standard?" Call me
crazy, Bernice, but if I buy a phone charger, I expect it to charge my
phone. Your sample does not charge my phone, it fails to charge
other phones we tested on the first day, and its present circuit
limitations will hasten the destruction of our valuable battery
inventory. Why should Africans care more than Americans or
Europeans that something they buy actually does what they bought it
for? That answer is simple, Bernice. Because they have so much less.

I think we are done here.


**Whit was done with trying** to extract Burro-worthy product from this
particular factory, but he viewed the whole snafu as a delay, not a defeat. As
long as he was going back to the drawing board, he decided to keep it simple
and make the phone charger a stand-alone product with no light—basically
a square plastic battery holder similar to the generic ones I had schlepped
over in the spring of 2010, only Burro-branded and with a removable adapter
tip to match any kind of phone connection. That would be easy to source
through Three-Sixty. As for a lantern, he was brainstorming bigger ideas—
and he already had a new design and manufacturing partner in mind: a
young American engineer living in China who shared Whit's passion for
bringing quality products to the world's lowest income families.


## 2. The Green Book

I came home from Ghana in June of 2010 and spent my first summer with
my family in Maine in two years. As soon as the leaves started falling in

October, I was back on a plane to Accra. Whit had arrived the night before, from a two-week Italian vacation with Shelly. My own absences from home were difficult for Sarah, but they paled in comparison to Whit's: he was spending most of his time in Ghana, with only brief visits home. The long separations were straining his marriage. The original plan was for Shelly to join Whit in Ghana after a year or so, once both kids were away at college; maybe they would rent Charlie's house in Peduase, about halfway between Accra and Koforidua. But then she got her big job at the Gates Foundation, and that became impossible. Shelly was totally self-sufficient, adept at running their Seattle household and holding down a demanding job that could find her flying to India for two days. But with both their kids out of the nest, Shelly, like Whit, was living in an empty house—one even bigger than Whit's African bachelor pad. "It's pretty stressful all around," said Whit as we drove off from the airport and into the boil of Accra. "I mean, we had a great time in Italy. We still really love each other, enjoy each other's company, share the same values. We talk on the phone every few days, and I try to stay engaged in her life and with the kids. But it's hard."

Whit's vacation was compromised by a tenacious intestinal disorder that was eventually diagnosed as giardia, a type of flagellate, pervasive in Ghana, spread through fecal-contaminated drinking water. Antibiotics can kill the flagellates themselves but not the reproductive cysts, so it can take several courses to wipe out subsequent generations. As a result, despite a vigorous round of antibiotics before Whit left for Italy, the little bastards were still hanging on when he came back. The situation wasn't helped by an almost comically grim layover in Libya on Afriqiyah Airways, which was, until the Arab revolutions of early 2011 and the NATO-imposed no-fly zone over Tripoli, Muammar el-Qaddafi's showcase commercial airline.

Afriqiyah didn't fly to the Western Hemisphere, but its colorful Airbus jets (one of which crashed in May 2010, killing 103 people) crisscrossed Africa, Europe, and the Middle East. The late-model planes were reported to be exceedingly comfortable, with ample legroom and leather seats— green, to match the Libyan flag—even if there was no alcohol served. But

Afriqiyah's real draw was its rock-bottom fares. Perhaps realizing few Westerners would make it a first choice, the airline had managed to lure travelers with fares roughly half that of its competitors. Always anxious to save
money that could be better spent on his self-financed business adventure,
Whit decided to give Afriqiyah a go, connecting through Tripoli to Rome.
It was, to put it mildly, a learning experience.

. What he learned is that the hub is the rub. To hear Whit describe it,
Tripoli International Airport is a nexus of such uncompromising sadism as
to warrant revisions to *The 120 Days of Sodom*. Upon debarking into
Tripoli's transit "lounge" (dominated by a monumental portrait of Qaddafi)
after an overnight flight across the Sahara, Whit and the other passengers
were frog-marched through a reception line of redundant document and
baggage checks performed by shouting, mustachioed security operatives
resembling those weasely bad guys in spy movies who are always lurking
around foreign airports, just before James Bond gets klonked over the
head and shoved into a waiting Deux Chevaux. Copious signage, with lots
of bold passages and exclamation points, covered the walls, but only in
Arabic. Having survived the pat-downs and random confiscations (Libyan
authorities took all eight of Whit's Burro batteries, plus a plastic D adapter,
on the grounds of "travel security"), the weary nomads at last encountered
an oasis: a pleasant little café bar, around which perhaps a dozen or so urban Bedouins sipped aromatic espressos and enjoyed fresh local pastries.
Alas, this "Traveler's Café & Restaurant" did not accept credit cards or any
foreign currency, despite the fact that by definition all travelers in the
transit lounge were changing planes to and from other foreign countries
and thus were highly unlikely to possess even a single Libyan dinar. There
was, needless to say, no currency exchange office in the transit lounge; a
decrepit looking ATM was out of order.

Well, coffee and breakfast would have to wait until Rome. But given
Whit's condition, what definitely couldn't wait was the restroom. Here the
term *restroom* must be stretched even beyond its usual euphemistic sense,
although the British moniker *water closet* turned out to be pointedly apt.
In this cruel dungeon, above a floor covered with an inch of gray fluid
vaguely resembling clam liquor, the culture gap widened into a chasm. As

in many Islamic countries, Libyan toilets are set up to accommodate the religious hygienic rules known as *Qadaa al-Haajah*. These rules, established by Muhammad himself, require "purification" with water after defecating. In modern Islamic toilets, the ritualistic ablution is accomplished with a flexible rubber or metal hose having a manually controlled spigot and an ergonomic tip. While the rules do not prohibit the additional use of toilet paper (Muhammad recommended using smooth stones), in practice many Muslims just rely on water. Nevertheless, in a public restroom in an airport transit lounge frequented by non-Muslims, one might expect to find a roll of tissue in the stall. But a country that requires all visitors to have an Arabic translation of their passport is not about to compromise on the weighty issue of Islamic ass wiping. There was not a scrap of paper to be found. Everyone, regardless of religion or background, was required to spray down with the hose. (Fellow passengers confirmed to Whit that the ladies' room was no different.)

Intending to be better prepared for Tripoli Airport on his return flight, Whit secured toilet paper in Italy and scoured the country for Libyan dinars but could find none at any exchange bureau. Miraculously, on his return the sad little Libyan ATM was working, which allowed him to buy coffee and, in the souvenir shop, a new English translation of Qaddafi's 1975 *Green Book*, in which the dictator shares his wisdom on the tyranny of representative democracy and Western capitalism. It's a slim tome. Perhaps it was meant to be used as toilet paper.

### 3. Have You Ever Worked with Money?

Whit's Koforidua estate was much quieter in the fall. The courtyard was empty, the door to the hut shuttered and locked. "Where's Akosia?" I asked.

"Gone. Victor threw her out."

"What?"

Apparently Whit had followed through on his promise to Akosia, telling her husband he could no longer bring other women to the house. Victor retaliated by throwing Akosia into the street—pregnant, along with their young son. She disappeared, presumably to her mother's place up on the Akwapim Ridge. When Whit found out, he evicted Victor. Now the place lay empty.

Nkansah had also disappeared. Over the summer things came to a head about his use of Burro's fifteen-hundred-cedi loan, which was supposed to cover an apartment lease but which Nkansah said he had used to buy a motorcycle so he could continue to live with his parents out of town and commute to Koforidua. After Whit and Rose pressed Nkansah repeatedly to come up with the bike, he admitted he had used the money to invest in a taxicab, which another man was driving for him. (A man whom Burro had hired to drive Nkansah until he got his license; Nkansah stole the driver too.) It was just another of his many business ventures. Enraged that Nkansah had essentially gamed Burro's generosity and then lied about it, Whit put him on leave and ordered him to return the money, even if it meant selling the taxi. But Nkansah simply vanished after sending Whit a string of barely comprehensible text messages lamenting what he perceived to be unfairly harsh treatment—never accepting any responsibility in the matter, calling Rose "Juda," and assiduously avoiding any discussion of a repayment plan.

The whole experience left everyone dispirited, in part because Nkansah had shown so much promise. On the other hand, as Whit pointed out, his sales skills were not matched by even the remotest flair for management or any capacity for details. It was probably just as well.

At any rate, in Whit's absence, Jan and Rose had hired an even more promising manager—a twenty-three-year-old Ashesi grad named Nii Tettey. While he lacked the protean carnival-barker sales skills of Nkansah, Nii was considerably more polished. A member of the Ga tribe of Accra, he had grown up in an elite family. His father, who died when Nii was seven, was a Ghanaian diplomat and former undersecretary of the United Nations; his mother was a retired accountant. Nii was born in Italy and attended Achimota, the renowned secondary school in Accra mentioned earlier (as the alma mater of Whit's partner Charlie) that has groomed African business and political leaders (including Zimbabwe's despotic Robert Mugabe) since the colonial era.

Perhaps reflecting his privileged background, Nii favored an archaic

manner of speaking that seemed professorial even by Ghana's formal standards of English. Instead of "yes" he would often say "exactly." Offer him
any small favor—a cookie, a sachet of water—and he invariably replied,
"That would be nice." One day in a village we encountered an unusual
curly-haired dog of the type more likely to be seen on the Faubourg Saint-
Honoré, and Nii remarked that lately he had been observing a profusion of
"randomly exotic dogs in villages." Rose teased him about his baroque syntax,
but he was self-assured and paid no mind. "I should like to write a book,"
he told me. "A book about cultural and social changes in Ghana."

I told him I felt he was in a good position to do so. We had just left the
Burro office, Nii and I, driving out of town toward the northwest, scouting
off-grid villages for new Burro agents. This was uncharted territory, so to
speak—places and people as yet unaware of Burro and its offerings. Nii
was a good and experienced driver—the first employee besides James, the
route driver, whom Whit and Jan did not have to train in this skill—but
like most Ghanaians he grew a lead foot behind the wheel. This com-
punction for haste had very nearly proven tragic two weeks earlier, when
Nii and the newest intern, a nineteen-year-old college sophomore from
the Bay Area named Alec Scott, rolled the Kia onto its side after losing
control when a wheel broke off the axle. This was the same car in which
Whit and I had burned up a wheel bearing more than a year before, but
this latest malfunction was considerably more serious.

The accident happened on a weekend; they were headed down the
coast to Busua Beach, an idyllic tourist spot popular with adventurous
surfers. Somewhere along the way, the car began swaying ominously, but
they pressed on—the pair had what pilots call "get-there-itis." They did
not get there. When the wheel fell off, the car pitched, rolled, and landed
on the passenger side, skidding along the roadway. Photos taken later by
Rose showed the entire right side creased and crumpled from stem to stern,
the windshield smashed. Nii was driving; had he not been wearing his
seat belt (a Burro rule), he would have landed on top of Alec, who was riding shotgun. Luckily, both ended up only briefly in the hospital, with minor injuries. (It would take several weeks to fix the Kia.) "For the rest of
my life I will always wear this seat belt," Nii said to me as he drove.

When Whit, still in Italy, heard about the accident, he was aghast. Alec's parents were old friends; they had worked together decades ago in Niger. "Imagine if something had happened to Alec," said Whit, shaking his head. "I mean, yeah, it wouldn't have been my fault—both of those guys should have known better and stopped before the fucking wheel fell off— but still. I would feel totally responsible." The accident caused Whit to rethink letting employees or interns borrow cars for personal trips. Besides the risk of injury, Burro was growing fast and simply couldn't afford to lose vehicles.

A lot of that growth was in the new territory that Nii was opening up. He and Alec had been using Google Earth satellite imagery and local topographical maps to zero in on population centers, which were not always visible from the road; thousands of people might be living down a narrow trail, out of sight. Although the Google maps were useless in much of Burro's territory due to out-of-date and low-resolution satellite imagery, it so happened that relatively new and more detailed imagery had been added to Google Earth for this particular test area. The topographical maps were thirty years old and unreliable for population data (some villages had sprawled and grown over three decades, others had withered), but they typically contained a more comprehensive set of place names, sometimes for even the remotest settlements, as well as elevation contours. By cross-referencing Google Earth and the local topo maps, Nii and Alec were able to discern in advance the latitude and longitude of locations with greater potential. Those coordinates could then be entered into a handheld GPS for field location. They had begun to articulate what was becoming an increasingly sophisticated and efficient way for Burro to identify potential sales areas.*

So armed, Nii and I were striking out to find new customers—or more

---

* Alec and Nii eventually obtained national census data from the Ghana Statistical Service that listed the year 2000 population of every village in the country. Along with the phone book–sized volumes (organized, less than optimally, in a single alphabetic listing for the whole nation) came a rough disc version that Whit was able to import into Microsoft Access and integrate into Fodder. While the data contained no geographic coordinates, Burro could now narrow down potential sales areas within districts and sort by population—a "game changer," as Whit called it.

accurately, new agents (make that *resellers*) who could serve customers in new villages. Building on the fieldwork done by the BYU interns last spring, Burro had refined and codified the process of reseller selection, and I wanted to see how that was working. Now reseller candidates were nominated in an open-forum village meeting (often with special input by village elders), then interviewed and scored by a Burro manager—Nii or Rose, whoever was running the new territory in question. The "winner" was then announced with fanfare, a process that not only helped ensure the best reseller but also reinforced the idea that the job was important.

Nii dodged potholes at high speed along a theoretically paved main road on which I had never traveled, not that the landscape offered any novelty; stretches of plantain groves, teak plots, half-built concrete churches, and roadside vendors with their gallon jugs of crimson palm oil under raffia pergolas could have been just about anywhere in Eastern Region. As usual, three-phase electrical lines ran on high poles along the road—in fact they appeared to be getting upgraded, as large wooden spools of bright chrome wire had been dropped every few miles—but no power went back into the villages.

Nii turned onto a muddy tire track that ran alongside a teak farm and drove about fifty yards until the road turned into a footpath. The map data had suggested there was a substantial village down this path, a place called Nkrankrom Dadasu.

We got out of the truck and looked around. A shirtless man was hacking at the trunk of a teak tree with a machete, work that I imagined to be exceedingly difficult in the midday heat; I have fashioned teak accessories on my boat and respect it as a wood with the approximate density of alabaster. He stopped and greeted us, sweat glinting off his bare chest. Nii and the man spoke in halting Twi, which was not Nii's first language or, I gathered, the stranger's. "He says he will take us to the village," said Nii. Ghana was like that. Everywhere you went, someone in the middle of some important exertion would cheerfully drop everything and help you. Then again, any excuse to stop chopping down a teak tree in ninety-degree heat might be welcome.

It had rained buckets the day before, and at some point the trail actually went underwater. Villagers had fashioned makeshift bridges with logs, but the logs themselves were now floating, so there was no way to cross without getting wet. I had on Crocs, which were fine except for being dangerously slippery, but Nii was wearing leather street shoes and socks. It may have been the last time he sported formal footwear on a recon mission. After about half a mile we reached the village and met the chief, a small man about my own age. Nii introduced us and the chief gathered several of his elders.

We sat under a tangerine tree, the tiny fruit still green, as Nii explained Burro to the assembled dignitaries. It turned out that the villagers were Ewe, from Togo. Nii spoke no Ewe; my French was rudimentary but serviceable, although not as good as Nii's Twi, which was better than their Twi or English. Between this Babel of languages we managed a crude but effective communication. Our cold call was warming up.

Nii explained the battery program and passed around some samples. "You must always keep using them," he said. "They are like a footballer who must always stay excited to perform well."

The elders were duly impressed.

"We are very community centered," Nii continued. "We like to talk to people, find out what they need, and so we talk to our agents. If they tell us they need this thing in their neighborhood, we look for the best way to bring it at the best price. And we found out that a problem was charging your phones. For a place like this where there is no electricity, you have to take your phone far away to charge it."

The elders nodded. The chief explained that villagers pay fifty pesewa to send out their phones for charging, plus forty pesewa in taxi fare each way, for a total of 1.30 cedis.

Nii continued: "So we said, 'What can we do to solve this problem?' And so let me show you the Burro phone charger." He pulled the small green device out of a plastic bin.

"This is what it looks like. It uses four of our batteries that I showed you." He opened the charger to reveal the batteries.

"I'll show you how it works," he said, pulling his own phone from a pocket.

"Everybody gets their phone pin," he said. "Everyone gets one free when you buy it. And so you put it like this"—he inserted a phone pin into the female receptacle on the charger wire—"and then you put it inside your phone, and you have your phone charging."

He held up his phone so the chief and elders could see the blinking battery symbol on the screen. "Look at it, you can see it charge."

They gathered around, amazed. "Charging!" confirmed one man.

"Charging!" agreed another. They said the word in English but pronounced it almost like Chinese: *CHAH-jing!*

"It's as simple as this," said Nii. "Now you can always have your phone with you; you don't need to send it away, wasting time and money to charge it."

"How much for this?" asked another man.

Nii replied that the four batteries cost a total of eighty pesewa and are good for at least two phone charges but often as many as four, depending on the phone. "So you would be paying twenty to forty pesewa to charge your phone," he said. "That is on average a cedi less than what you currently pay. You must also pay five cedis for the charger, which is yours to keep. So after just five charges, the money you have saved will pay for the charger itself."

The men indicated they understood, and they did not seem fazed by the upfront cost of the charger.

"But the main reason we have come is to talk to the chief," said Nii, "so I can schedule a day that we will come to select a reseller. A reseller, also called an agent, is someone we need to see every week to give them more batteries and give them the things they would like to sell. So that is why we came."

The men conferred in Ewe, then spoke to us and agreed on a date the following week. "How many people are in this village?" Nii asked.

"Oh, we have many," said a man.

"How many?"

"Here we have thirty or thirty-five."

Nii's face fell. That was not enough to justify an agent. "Okay, so I want to know how many in all the surrounding villages."

The men consulted again in Ewe. There was much shouting and gesticulation. "Perhaps a thousand," said the spokesman.

"Excellent," said Nii. That was about what he had expected based on the map data. We shook hands all around, said good-bye, and trudged off down the slippery trail.

On the appointed day we returned to select a reseller, this time wearing farm boots. But it had not rained in several days, and the trail was dry. We met again under the tangerine tree, now with a larger crowd of villagers that included four men selected by the elders as reseller candidates. Nii ran through the basic Burro spiel, pointing out what he called the three most important points about the batteries: stays strong, no leak, and costs less. Then we broke off for the job interviews, moving to a bench under a cocoa tree, next to an elaborate double still that bubbled under a thatched roof.

The interview process had been codified into a series of questions designed to evaluate a candidate's competence in seven critical areas:

- Literacy and Numeracy
- Honesty
- Reliability and Motivation
- Trainability
- Sales Experience
- Ability to Commit Time to Burro
- Personality and Character
- Service-oriented

Each criterion was followed by several sample questions and a "scoring aid" to facilitate analysis of the answers. So a question under *Service-oriented* was "How would you deal with clients that came to you saying their batteries do not work in their flashlight?" The scoring aid noted, "Saying something like 'I would tell the client to hold on while I report to the company,' at this stage is a good enough answer to earn them a high score. Saying something like 'I will collect it from them and tell them to stop spoiling my business' or 'I would tell them that they are lying' would give a very low score on this."

Under each criterion, candidates were scored on a seven-point scale, from negative three to positive three. At first I thought the whole thing was a bit artificial, but then I remembered that if the business were to expand across the country, route managers would have widely different backgrounds and education levels, and they all couldn't be trained personally by Whit or Jan. It was important to have a clear set of guidelines. In this case simplicity was a virtue.

The first candidate sat down and Nii handed him the written portion of the interview. The paper had two questions:

1. If a client buys 2 chargers costing 5 cedis each, and registers 4 batteries, how much does the client pay you?
2. How much is 52,000 old cedis in the new Ghana cedi?

"Please write your name," said Nii, "and your location and your phone number." Nii watched as the man struggled to compose his name. "Now please read the two questions aloud and then write your answers." He read the questions slowly, laboring over each word. His brow creased like origami as he tried to process the math, but it was no use.

"Have you ever worked with money before?" Nii asked.

"Yes."

"What was the job?"

The man thought for a minute. "In Nigeria."

"Doing what?"

"I organized a football club on Sundays."

"How did that involve money?"

He scratched his head. "I don't know."

"Can you remember the three most important points about the batteries?"

There was an awkward silence. Finally Nii reminded him: "Stays strong, no leak, costs less."

"Okay," the man said, but he seemed unable to repeat them.

"What would you say your village needs?"

The man considered the question carefully for a long minute and said, "Water."

"Okay, thank you," said Nii. "Can you please tell the next candidate to come?"

The second guy was more assured and obviously better educated, although his English was almost nonexistent. He told us in French that he traveled to Togo every year, which probably disqualified him.

"When does it work for you to meet us?" Nii asked.

"Anytime."

"But not anytime; you said you had a farm and you also travel to Togo."

"My wife can also come."

After the interview he walked over to the still and changed one of the drip containers, which was close to overflowing with the clear, potent brew.

The third candidate, a man named Francis Ataglo, was better yet—well groomed in a polo shirt and poised, with a fluent command of English. He had no trouble doing the math and seemed to understand the concept of Burro. It transpired that he was either a preacher or some sort of lay leader in his church, a sign of respect in the community.

The fourth interview went well enough, but the best candidate was clearly Francis. We reconvened the villagers and Nii announced the new agent, leading everyone in applause. Then Nii spent an hour and a half training Francis and setting him up with an initial inventory of batteries and phone chargers. In a week Nii would return and hold a formal sales gong-gong to help Francis develop his new customer base. I was glad to see that the fourth candidate sat in on the training session, apparently out of simple curiosity; he would make a good alternate agent if things didn't work out with Francis.

"That went very well," said Nii as we drove away. "Sometimes it comes down to picking the lesser of two evils, but in this place I think we got a very good agent. He fits the image of a reseller. Plus he is already an evangelist, so the people trust him to send them to heaven." I detected a note of irony in his voice. Of all Whit's employees Nii seemed the most likely atheist, not that many Ghanaians would dare identify themselves as such, and I didn't ask.

It had been a little more than two years since Whit first arrived in Koforidua with a new Tata, looking for a place to live that could double as a business. Now he had three vehicles, five full-time Ghanaian employees (two of them college graduates), with more on the way, nearly a hundred part-time agents and a revolving group of American and Ghanaian interns. He had invented a brand that was trusted and respected by thousands of Ghanaians, mostly by respecting them.

He had not expanded nearly as fast as originally planned; indeed he hadn't expanded at all beyond the first Koforidua test branch, although the branch itself was growing rapidly and poised to demonstrate replicability. But he had done it all with his own money—more than a quarter million dollars at this juncture, not counting his own opportunity cost—which meant that when the time came to scale rapidly through outside investors he'd be well positioned to retain control of his brand.

Burro had reached a turning point of sorts, at least in my mind. The new protocols for finding villages and hiring agents felt more mature, less seat-of-the-pants, than a year ago when we just drove around looking for crowds. The new phone chargers were spiking revenue; trailing four-week sales had more than quadrupled in the last month and would soon top twenty-five hundred cedis. And that was mostly just income from the chargers themselves; the tail of the battery exchange revenue was beginning to lengthen dramatically once new customers started charging their phones regularly. "It's obviously not enough," said Whit, "but it's going in the right direction." The company was applying months of hard-learned lessons at a quickening pace and seemed to be within striking distance of real success.

This was all good news, and I was happy for Whit, but I also felt myself pining for the primal chaos of the early start-up days. I missed the adventure of the random hunt for new villages, the improvised and ever-changing battery spiel in God knows how many languages, the palm-wine toasts with one-eyed chiefs, the villagers who gave us duck eggs and mushrooms, the game of wits against the coupon counterfeiters. I had met men who ate cats. I had seen dead cows and live sheep in the trunks of taxicabs. Now what was I doing? Now I was tailing a hotshot African college boy who punched coordinates into a GPS. I missed being an explorer. And yet—just when I was starting to think there was not much more for me to see, we pulled into the village of Owuratwum.

Electric lines stepped down from the main poles that ran past the little brown-and-beige outpost of huts, so we knew at least some citizens of Owuratwum had power. But a teenage boy returning from school told us that only a few homes right along the road were wired; most of the village, he said, confirming our analysis of Google Earth imagery, was back in the bush where the lines didn't run. "Where does the chief live?" asked Nii.

"I will take you," said the boy. We parked and got out.

Along the road, huge sisal bags filled with cocoa beans were stacked several feet high, waiting for transportation by taxi or *tro-tro* to the central depot—on their way to becoming Belgian truffles, oozing exotic liqueurs and sold in boxes with red velvet ribbons on Valentine's Day. Ghana is second only to neighboring Ivory Coast in global cocoa production, growing about 14 percent of the world's crop. It was cocoa harvest time, and prices were high this year; the farmers were flush.

We headed down a footpath, which dropped into a low, swampy area thick with cocoa trees. The broad leaves blocked out the sun, and the gnarled trunks looked like spineless space aliens in some 1950s sci-fi movie. Moss dripping water like mucus dangled from branches. It was dark and creepy, and I half expected flying monkeys to hatch from the strange, elongated cocoa pods. Instead, mosquitoes and tiny gnats swarmed. Soon we reached a residential compound—a U-shaped complex of rectangular stucco huts, fronted by wide porches under the shade of metal roofs. In the central clearing were three large, flat bamboo racks, each waist-high and the size of a large Persian rug, covered with dark cocoa beans drying in the sun. The thumb-sized beans had already been fermented under wet banana leaves, and they exuded a strange smell, like chocolate vinegar, that was pungent but not unpleasant.

*"Master!"*

I turned, and from the corner of my eye caught a fleeting glimpse of a satyr rushing toward us from across the clearing. It was, in fact, a small old man, arms flailing like a pinwheel and bent over from what must have been years of physical labor. His long white beard hung down in front of him like a turkey's snood.

"Oh master! Oh master!" he cried. I looked behind me to see whom he might be addressing, and before I could spin back around the old man had wrapped his arms around my legs in a bear trap. "Master, you have come!" he said, looking up and smiling. His teeth had rotted in a peculiar way that left his lower incisors stepped like an Aztec pyramid. "Master, you are welcome!"

This was, to put it mildly, disconcerting. Having lived and worked for many years in Hollywood, I can report from personal observation that there are men who thrive on such obsequiousness. As for me, all I could do was stand gape-jawed and try to retain my balance as this groveling lickspittle hugged my kneecaps and genuflected in the dirt. Finally he arose and screamed orders in a strange tongue at a younger man, who scurried to find a plastic chair and a tin cup of rainwater for me, the inexplicably honored guest.

Up to this point Nii had been watching the whole affair bug-eyed. Now he spoke up. "I don't know what this is all about," he whispered to me. "I can't understand his language." The younger man spoke to Nii in Twi. "Okay," said Nii to me again. "That man is the chief. This is his son. They speak Larteh, a language specific to this area."

"Great," I said, "because I was just thinking we didn't have enough languages around here."

"He says his father thought you were someone else."

"Livingstone?"

"No. It seems his daughter works for an *obruni* in Accra, a man who keeps promising to come and visit. So he thought you were his daughter's boss."

"Would that be a typical way to greet your daughter's *obruni* boss?" I asked Nii.

"I should think not."

"I am very sorry," said the chief sheepishly, in his best English.

"It's okay," I said, smiling weakly. He was, after all, the chief. The whole experience reminded me of those Tarzan movies where the natives fawn over the very important bwana, just before tossing him into the cook pot.

## 4. Strict Standards

The package arrived from DHL with a distant, handwritten return address:

> Greenlight Planet Inc.
> Bldg 3, Rm 3A, Conrad Garden
> Binhe Rd & Caitian Rd, Futian Shenzhen
> China 518026

"It's here," said Whit, and people in the Burro office dropped their work and gathered around the conference table. We knew exactly what it was: the final engineering prototype ("FEP" in the lingo of product development) of the new Burro lantern, the African village version of the "killer app"—in this case, Whit hoped, the appliance that would lead Burro into profit and sustainability. "This is the final consumer packaging," said Whit, pretending to admire the makeshift cardboard shipping container, crudely bound in clear tape.

"Just open it already," I said.

Whit carefully cut into the package. It was Christmas in November.

**Shenzhen is a sprawling** manufacturing and financial hub narrowly separated from Hong Kong by the slate waters of the Sham Chun and Sha Tau Kok rivers. It's where you go if you're looking to buy lighting devices, among thousands of other electronic products. In the summer of 2009 Whit had traveled there on a weeklong tour of manufacturers. After several days politely nodding at pulsating disco flashlights and other useless and poorly made devices, he began to realize that nothing "off the shelf" was going to work in the tough conditions of a Ghanaian village. He'd have to create his own products. But he needed a partner.

Whit couldn't remember exactly when he first heard about Greenlight Planet, the for-profit company founded in 2008 with the idea to design efficient lighting products for the world's poor. "I was just searching around, looking for alternatives, and Greenlight Planet popped," he said. "And then I met Patrick."

T. Patrick Walsh was the young American engineer living in Shenzhen who cofounded Greenlight Planet right out of college. As a sophomore at the University of Illinois at Urbana-Champaign (the same school where Jan studied engineering), Patrick had joined the campus chapter of Engineers Without Borders, a group that connects student engineers in the United States with communities in the developing world. Patrick, trim and dark-haired, with eyebrows like coal smudges, worked on a project designing affordable electrification for a village in northern India, a country that still has four hundred million people living off the grid. "It was really stunning to me as a city kid to go and live in this village for two months," he said in a speech at his alma mater in late 2008. "On the first night when I got there I walked into a dark room and I went to turn on a light switch"— here he waved his arm, groping for an invisible switch—"and I went 'Holy cow! I'm not gonna have light—not only tonight, but for the next couple months.'"

The villagers had a diesel-powered generator to pump water and process spices, a chief source of income. But they couldn't afford the fuel needed to light the whole village. They did, however, have a surrounding forest thick with trees that produced an oil-bearing seed. Patrick and his fellow students designed a system for extracting the oil from the seeds; then they modified the diesel engine to burn the vegetable oil. "It's a workable system," Patrick said. "It produces two or three dollars' worth of fuel for half a day's work, so it's doubling or tripling income plus lighting the village. After a year, the people had wired about half the village and put lightbulbs in sixty homes."

It was an elegant local solution, but much to his disappointment, Patrick came to realize it wasn't scalable. The project had been funded with a twenty-thousand-dollar charitable donation, but there was no money to duplicate it in the other fifty thousand nonelectrified villages in the state, much less the whole country. "We've got four hundred million people with no light, and they're not gonna get it through charity alone," he recalled thinking. "We've got to have a way for these villagers to afford light themselves. It can't be donated, it can't be pushed down from the top, it's got to be demanded from the bottom. And what we looked at was how can we develop an individually affordable solution—something that the private sector could have a motivation to sell, and something they could actually scale."

Thus was born Greenlight Planet and the company's flagship product, the Sun King solar-powered lantern. The product was a flying saucer–shaped pod of tough polycarbonate plastic encasing an array of LED bulbs and a lithium-ion battery that was charged by a plug-in postcard-sized solar panel. A hand strap allowed the light to be palmed in one hand or tied to the forehead with a bandanna. A heavy-duty steel stand transformed the light into a table lamp or (if hung from a nail or clothesline) an overhead fixture. On its lowest setting the device provided as much light as a kerosene lamp, without the expense and danger of fuel. On its highest setting (which burned through a full solar charge in a few hours) it provided twice the light of kerosene. The unit was virtually indestructible—Patrick liked to demonstrate by dropping it onto a hard floor—and watertight. It won a Mondialogo Engineering Award, a student competition sponsored by UNESCO and Daimler.

Whit loved the Sun King's rugged construction and clever functionality, but the solar design didn't fit into his immediate business plan: if your primary business is renting low-cost grid-charged batteries to off-grid villagers, you ought to be able to provide them with compatible battery-powered devices, not a much more expensive solar device. (The Sun King solar lantern retails in India for eight hundred rupees, almost nineteen dollars.) But it was obvious to Whit that Greenlight Planet shared his commitment to selling quality, productivity-enhancing products to the world's poor.

"I talked to Patrick on the phone at first," said Whit, "then I went to meet him in China, and I was blown away. He was my kind of product guy, so passionate about developing amazing products. He took me through the whole efficiency chain of lighting devices, from photons emitted from the sun hitting the ground to photons reflecting off a kid's school book at night, and the whole chain of conversion that has to happen for that to work efficiently."

Patrick was also intrigued by Whit's ideas, but he was cautious. "He told me it was kind of interesting but that he was very focused on solar," said Whit. "He wasn't saying everything has to be solar, and I got the impression that if something could be useful in his product line, he'd think about it.

"So I started spec-ing this thing a little bit. What I originally wanted to do was something that would be forward-compatible with some kind of proprietary battery format—a form factor that would work with legacy double-A's but also with an integrated LFP battery.* As I was sending Patrick drawings and ideas, he was playing along at first, but finally he threw up his arms and said, 'This thing is getting too hard, it's distracting me from what I should be doing.' That's when he backed out. So I was like, fuck, what do I do now? I decided to recalibrate and say okay, we'll tackle the lithium-iron forward-compatible device later on. I went to Patrick and asked him what we could do now. He said he could modify the existing Sun King to work with our current batteries. I said great.

"What I didn't realize," Whit continued, "was that he was talking about more than just changing the Sun King to take batteries. At the same time he had also been thinking about moving away from an array of conventional LEDs to a power LED, and he had found a good source for them.†

---

* Jargon decoder: LFP, for lithium iron (ferrous) phosphate, is an emerging-technology chargeable battery that is much more stable (i.e., noncombustible) than standard lithium-ion batteries, with a longer life cycle. Whit was talking about designing a device that could eventually use such a battery as they became more cost-effective, while also working with his current NiMH double-A's.

† Power LEDs, also known as high-power LEDs or HPLEDs, are driven by high currents and are extremely bright. They are also expensive, in part because they require special heat-dissipation elements.

So the Burro light in a way became a test for what he wanted to be doing with power LEDs."

The Burro light would also differ in other ways. "Patrick's original Sun King had three brightness settings," said Whit. "I wanted four. He was resistant to that, and he knows that stuff so well, but I was pretty adamant. So with strong input from me we came up with four power settings, each with some element critical to our market positioning. We wanted one setting that matched the perceived output of a kerosene hurricane lamp, so people could do the same shit they do with kerosene but at a huge cost savings. Lots of people talk about beating kerosene, but we truly deliver it in this mode—eighty percent cost savings, cleaner, safer, more convenient light. It's huge for anyone with access to the Burro battery service.

"We wanted a second mode that blew kerosene out of the water—you know, any observer would say that's brighter than kerosene, but still at a thirty percent lower cost than kerosene.

"Then we were both in agreement that we wanted something really bright. Exactly how bright was the question. I said, 'How high can this thing go?' Patrick was like, 'The human eye isn't linear, I wouldn't recommend pushing it all the way; buy yourself a little more battery life and go dimmer, people won't notice it all that much.' I said, 'You know what? Go for it. What's the maximum current?' He said, 'Three hundred and fifty milli-amps.' He was saying we should go for like three hundred or two eighty. So we did the math on it, and for any of these currents, even assuming typical degradation of our batteries, we'd get maybe only five or six hours of life. I was like, 'Dude, that's an evening. Let's go all the way. Give 'em the brightest fucking light in the village! They'll get it—they'll know it's gonna use more power. Plus they'll still get another five or so hours in the lower modes after the batteries run low on juice.' I talked him into it."

"So that's three settings," I said. "You've got kerosene equivalent for a fraction of kerosene's operating cost, better than kerosene for still less money than kerosene, and bright as physically possible for five hours. What's the fourth setting?"

"Well, I told Patrick how we're facing this competitive threat from

Tiger Head on the insanely long tail they deliver in those stupid flashlights. So I asked him how low we could go and still get some useful
light—like an ambient night-light or something like that."

"What did he say?"

"He said, 'Try it yourself. Buy an LED and just drive it.' He explained
how to dial in the input voltage and use different resistors to play with different ranges of current. I was home in Seattle then, so I went to Radio
Shack and bought an LED and some resistors. I'm doing all this and looking at the output, blocking out the windows, turning out the lights, and I
email him and say, 'Okay, I can go as low as six milli-amps and still get
useful light.' He says, '*Really?*' I say, 'Yeah, I mean I guess there's maybe a
photon or two there. But I'm looking at these Tiger Head flashlights after
a hundred hours of use with Tiger Head batteries, and *that's what they
look like!* It's a really low bar. It's like a candle. You're not going out hunting
with this light, but there is a glow there, and I've learned that villagers like
a night-light.'

"Patrick said if we went that low we'd have to factor in the circuit,
because the circuit itself would draw as much current as the LED at
that point. I actually wanted to go lower. I did a lot of tests, and you
could argue that a Tiger Head flashlight with a pair of Tiger Head batteries was maybe usable as a night-light for two hundred or two hundred
and fifty hours. So I wanted to beat that, to hit *three* hundred hours. But
we couldn't really go below six milli-amps, which would give us two
hundred-plus hours once we factored in the draw of the circuit, so that
was it."

Whit and Patrick settled on an initial order of three thousand lights
and worked together to dial down costs as low as possible. As the project
advanced and estimates of manufacturing, shipping, tax, and other import
costs firmed up, it became clear that Burro could not hit Whit's ideal retail price of ten cedis (about seven dollars) while maintaining adequate
margins. Even using sea freight, which was dramatically cheaper than air,
wouldn't cut it. It would have to sell for fifteen cedis, roughly ten dollars.
But Whit felt the market could bear the price, given the huge cost savings
over kerosene.

A hand sample of the light was manufactured and sent to Ghana in September. Whit responded with a detailed email to Patrick, who continued the conversation in a series of answers to Whit's questions:

From: T. Patrick Walsh
Sent: 9/18/2010 10:03:23 AM
To: Whit Alexander
Subject: Re: Fwd: DHL sample

**WA: Couple early thoughts/questions, Patrick: We are seeing flicker really only when first entering any given power mode. Is this the extent of the issue, or is it impacting in ways we aren't yet noticing?**

PW: That's the extent of the issue.

**WA: Battery lid does not seem excessively tight in sample. Was it fixed by hand in the sample?**

PW: Yes.

**WA: Battery lid is able to be closed in four different orientations, three of which prevent switch from functioning. Not a showstopper, and I wouldn't want to delay initial order to address this, but should we consider "keying" the lid somehow and/or marking correct orientation?**

PW: Already being done. If you look on the back side of the cover there is a stopper that is supposed to prevent the cover from being inserted in the wrong direction. This was designed poorly so it doesn't work, we have already started altering the tooling to fix it.

**WA: Is there added schedule risk if we wanted to go slightly cooler on the light color? Not sure we want this yet, and not sure if it's**

all or nothing. Some early feedback that the color combined with the frosting is creating an impression that we're an "old-fashioned" incandescent. It may be the kind of thing where usage preference is different than purchase preference. Is slightly cooler possible, or is a major shift the only option? Would there be any supply or functionality risk from making such a change so late in the game?

PW: Interesting. We could try to go with some middle-ground between what you have and the Sun King—maybe 4500K–5000K. There will always be a range of colors in each batch of LEDs, so these are ballpark figures. Let me know if that's what you want to do based on feedback there. There is always some supply risk with LED chips, sometimes you just can't get exactly the bins you want. But even if we can't get the exact target bin we can always get something close, and the lead times have become very reasonable nowadays.

WA: Will wire stand be identical to Sun King in shape? The new lamp is slightly wider. Old stand seems to function fine with new lamp, but it does change the "bearing" angle a bit. If the stand was changing, I'd consider trying to make the wall-mounting screw/nail affordance more pronounced.

PW: The regular Sun King and the AA version are actually the same outer dimensions, so we should keep the exact same stand at least for now, as producing this part in low volume is not trivial.

WA: The new lamp is, no surprise, pretty darn heavy when loaded up with three cells. I'd like to reduce the prospects of lamps crashing to the floor if practical. On that topic, how do you think we'll perform in drop tests when loaded with cells? I managed a small such test by accident already, and nothing bad happened, although the battery lid did pop off.

PW: This is what we have seen: battery cover pops off if the lamp is dropped on the top side. The mechanism is pretty clear—the batteries hit the cover and push it out. I have done a few drop tests with batteries loaded and even spiked it into the ground touchdown-style and ended up with a blown-off cover but no permanent damage outside of a nick or two. We could try to add more of an undercut to the bosses that hold on the battery cover, but that may be a bad idea as if they are too undercut and the batteries really want out, they could break the bosses right off instead of simply pushing the cover off without damaging it and letting the energy dissipate. Let me know what you think.

**WA: What's been your experience with warranty, Patrick? We'd like to offer one year, but we'd want some backing from you guys.**

PW: In India we offer a 1-year warranty against manufacturing defects. We also offer the same to international customers even for the original Sun King. The question is how to implement this in practice. If you have defects that lead to returns we will replace the units for sure, we just need to make sure they are actually defective and not abused. Standard warranty against defects in material/ workmanship only, obviously.

**WA: What caveats do you have to make and how do you know if someone dropped his lamp into a pond? Should we consider any field servicing? Should we order any spare parts? On branding, the seam between the battery lid and the back is so smooth, we actually might be able to pad print over the two when assembled. This would give us some good real estate upper and lower right for logos. It could also provide that visual hint on correct battery lid orientation.**

PW: I don't see why not!

**WA: We're still playing with our baby all weekend and are likely to have further insights or questions, but this should get us going. We want to order on Monday, so let's resolve anything we need to do to get you guys unblocked and into manufacturing ASAP.**

PW: OK, we should be ready to quote and take your order by Sept. 25th. If we can do so by then we will get this on a plane certainly by the end of October.

**WA: Thanks again, Patrick.**

PW: My pleasure!

**I'm old enough to remember** the TV repairman (ours was named, perfectly, Ray) making house calls, a concept even more anachronistic than doctors knocking on your door (I remember that too) since at least doctors still exist. In Ghana, however, TV and radio repair shops are everywhere—wooden shacks with mountains of electronic carcasses overflowing onto the street and where men labor six days a week over circuit boards with tweezers and soldering irons.* Nothing in Africa gets thrown away, because there is no money to buy new, so Africans have learned how to repair just about anything. Ghana's manufacturing sector may be sadly underdeveloped, but its knowledge base on how stuff works, based on the country's vibrant repair business, is profound.

The console television that Ray the Repairman serviced in our living room was made in America. It seems reasonable to observe a correlation, and perhaps causality, between a society's ability to fix things and its ability to make things. Could it be mere coincidence that our throwaway cul-

---

* Ghanaian cell phone shops also repair phones on site, usually the same day and for a few dollars. I try to imagine the tattooed Gen Y'ers who staff cell phone stores in the U.S identifying and replacing a faulty microchip on a printed circuit board, but I give up.

ture parallels the demise of our manufacturing sector? After all, people who don't know how to make things will soon lose the skill to repair those things. Of course it could be argued that even poor Americans are too affluent to bother with repairs. Whatever the reason, we now have a consumer society almost completely divorced from production. Everybody knows where our widgets come from—China—but almost no one knows, or seems to care, how they get made. We fetishize the latest gadgets and venerate the entrepreneurs who run the companies who make them, but the self-evident miracle of creation itself, the process of designing and engineering and molding and assembling all our gear, takes place off camera. Whatever happens before the UPS truck delivers the new gadget to our door is like the era B.C. (Before Consumerism), a dark time when molten plastic roiled upon the Earth and our merchandise was formless and void. It's as if the subject itself makes us uncomfortable, reminding us of the loss of our esoteric knowledge of the assembly line. Modern manufacturing is indeed complex, but the basic process can be readily grasped.

It begins, like most modern things, with a computer—in this case a program used by the designer to generate a detailed three-dimensional model of the product. This computer drawing then goes to a tooling engineer, who is charged with designing the best way to make the "tool," which is factory lingo for the mold—a two-piece apparatus held together in a powerful vise and into which molten plastic is injected. The tooling engineer must figure out where on the mold to inject the plastic and how the mold will come apart after the plastic cools. Some shapes (like a sphere composed of two halves) are simple to tool. But if the product has a complicated surface with lips and returns, the tool could require elaborate moving parts called slides and pulls, which shape the plastic within the mold. That kind of tooling gets expensive; a good tooling engineer will always be looking for the most cost-effective solution, which may involve molding several parts for later assembly. Once the tooling engineer has designed the tool (or tools), a final 3D computer drawing of the part is created. That design is then electronically transferred to a milling machine, where a high-speed cutting wheel similar to a router bit automatically carves a full-sized model of the part out of a piece of solid copper.

This copper model, called an electrode, is then placed under heavy pressure against a block of steel and charged with massive electrical power at high voltage. The surging power and high pressure (tempered by a special cooling liquid) causes the copper electrode to physically cut a "negative" version of the shape into the steel, which becomes the actual mold. The finished steel mold is then fitted to a machine that injects it with heated liquid plastic that has been tinted with dye pellets to a specified color.

Elsewhere in the factory, workers (and robots) put together the product's internal subassemblies—the circuit boards, LED boards, and other components that will go into the finished piece. Once the molded plastic pieces and the subassemblies are finished, the product goes to final assembly, where workers (in China mostly women) in white gloves and hairnets sit along a line, fishing the various parts out of plastic tubs.

But before thousands of identical widgets start rolling off the assembly line, the factory has to turn out just one very important widget—the final engineering prototype to be approved by the customer.

**Whit slowly cut away the** packing material on the DHL package from Shenzhen. "Here it is," he said, "the final engineering prototype of the Burro light. There's the Burro logo and the Greenlight Planet logo. *Do More* is, I guess, kind of legible. The color looks nice; they really pumped up the green. The battery lid doesn't close as well as I'd like already; it's not flush. Supposedly it's keyed so it will only fit one way. Aha! It is keyed. I wish it would fit more flush. Let's get some batteries and try it, shall we?"

Alec, the intern, grabbed three fresh Burro batteries. "Here goes," said Whit, and he pressed the switch. The white plastic dome glowed with a dim but observable light, even in the daylight of the office. "That's what we're calling *Super-Saver*," he said. "More than two hundred hours of light for about forty cents operating cost."

He hit the switch again. "This is *Saver*—comparable to kerosene at one fifth the cost."

Again. "*Bright*—much better than kerosene, still more than twenty-five percent cheaper."

And again. "*Super-Bright*—more expensive than kerosene but the brightest light in the village. It'll really light up your room." He turned the light toward his eyes and squinted. "Wow, that's bright!"

So was my brother's face. I remembered what Beatrice, the Chinese rep from Whit's first potential partner, had said in defense of her crappy headlamp: "Why Africa has more strict standard?" Finally Whit had a light that met his strict standards for Africa. "I'm thinking we could put kerosene out of business," he said.

## 5. Sacrifice

"Don't even think about it."

"Think about what?" I asked, glaring at my brother. We were at the fetish market in Accra, where voodoo priests buy curatives and offerings like frankincense, dried herbs, monkey heads, and crocodile skins. It was probably my last trip to Ghana and I wanted to check this legendary place off my to-do list. Tucked into the bowels of the timber market outside the vast slum of Agbobloshie (known locally as Sodom and Gomorrah), the fetish market was definitely not on the tourist maps, and I ended up paying a guy a few cedis just to lead us there.

We probably could have followed our noses; the place reeked of rancid flesh and pungent, unidentifiable spices. Sellers glared at us from behind baskets filled with decomposing dog heads, their lips frozen in gnashing snarls. Desiccated, coiled lizards were stacked artfully on tables next to crude wrought-iron daggers. Whole python skins, rolled up like sleeping bags and tied with raffia, shared table space with black, shrunken monkey heads and empty tortoise shells. Hanging from a stall like coats at Macy's were dozens of whole animal skins—antelopes, crocodiles, and several large wild cats, the latter priced at three hundred cedis each (about two hundred dollars) but negotiable. That's a lot of money in Ghana, which probably explains the cat knockoffs on the same rack—antelope hides on which feline spots had been obviously painted. The real cat furs were stunning and sad, luxuriously soft and improbably tame. "I said don't even think about it," Whit repeated as I brushed a feline pelt.

"What do you take me for, anyway?"

"I take you for someone who if he thought he could get away with it would smuggle a leopard skin home, or at least a leopard-skin hat."

"Give me a break. These animals are endangered. I'd go to jail. And Sarah would divorce me. Is it legal to bring back a python skin?"

"It's illegal to bring a python skin into my car."

"What a wenis. But just as well. Hey, check out these voodoo dolls. This one's painted white; it looks like you."

"Seen enough? This place creeps me out."

Voodoo wasn't the only bad medicine bothering Whit. His giardia was still hanging on, and the doctor at the clinic in Koforidua had prescribed the nuclear option: a broad-spectrum antibiotic called chloramphenicol. While I was driving to Accra, Whit swallowed his pill and googled chloramphenicol on his smart phone. He read aloud: "'Due to resistance and safety concerns, chloramphenicol is no longer a first-line agent for any'— repeat, *any*—'indication in developed nations. In low-income countries, chloramphenicol is still widely used because it is inexpensive and widely available.'"

"In other words," I said, "it's being dumped on the poor, like all the other shitty products over here."

"Listen to this," said Whit. "'The most serious adverse effect is aplastic anemia, a bone marrow toxicity that is generally fatal.'"

"Are you kidding?"

He read on: "'There is no treatment and there is no way of predicting who may or may not get this side effect. The effect usually occurs weeks or months after chloramphenicol treatment has been stopped, and there may be a genetic predisposition. The highest risk is with oral chloramphenicol, affecting one in twenty-four thousand.'"

"One in *twenty-four thousand* that you could die? Holy shit, those are pretty bad odds. I mean, it's better than Russian roulette, but still. I don't think I'd lay money on a bet that had a one in twenty-four-thousand chance of killing me."

"No shit."

"Listen, man, if you die, I'll be there for you."

"Fuck off."

"You know that shop in town that makes the cocoa-pod coffins? I bet we could get them to do a Burro battery coffin. We should probably order it now."

"Just watch the road."

As far as I was concerned our primary destination was the fetish market, but Whit kept insisting the trip was actually about picking up a hand sample of his new battery saver, which had just cleared customs. For about fifteen hundred dollars Whit had hired an industrial designer in Madison, Wisconsin, to work up the model, then worked with his partner Three-Sixty in Guangzhou to source a Chinese manufacturer. The design was simple: a hollow plastic shell the shape and size of a D battery with two poles and internal wiring that could replace one of the Burro batteries in a two-battery flashlight. The first sample, which had arrived in the early fall, fit a little too tightly; it was a little too long, and Jan observed that it needed a beveled edge around the "positive" end, which would make it easier to fit in next to the real battery in some devices. So we were down in Accra picking up this second version. But as soon as Whit stuck it in a typical radio (he had brought one with him), he realized the new version had a new problem: the beveled rim made it nearly impossible to grab the thing with a finger and pull it out. It needed some kind of "affordance"—a plastic nib or ridge that the finger could grasp. Before we even got to the fetish market he had emailed his designer in Wisconsin with the new request.

As Saturday trips to Accra go, it was a fairly productive day. Traffic wasn't bad, Whit got one step closer to a usable battery saver, I crossed what was, in my mind, a major Ghanaian attraction off my travel list, and we shared a charming lunch of wood-fired pizza (the kind of Western food you can only get in Accra) with Rose, her sister Gracelove, and their friend Sarah, all of whom graciously pretended to be amused and entertained by the doddering old graybeards who were picking up the check. After dropping off that trio at the sprawling and crowded Makola market (their own fetish hunt ran to shoes, handbags, and fabric), gassing up, and stopping at the Shop-rite for precious cargo like Parmesan cheese and olive oil, we drove home in the dark with considerably less cash but a trunk full of Italian groceries, a Chinese battery saver, one dried lizard, and a rusty sacrificial dagger.

## 6. Stop Talking and Let Us Pay

Revisions to the battery saver were trivial compared to the ongoing discussions with Patrick about the lantern. After Whit conducted a thorough examination of the latest FEP sample, he sent Patrick an email detailing seven areas of concern before granting approval to place the initial order of three thousand units. Patrick responded to each concern, and Whit responded again. The conversation was cordial (the men respected each other as obsessive about quality) but with an undercurrent of urgency; Whit needed these lights soon. He had already been teasing the sample light in gong-gongs, and agents were getting impatient.

1) Final units will run well on alkaline or other primary cells with no damage to unit from higher voltage.

PW: I fixed this theoretically, but we will definitely test it thoroughly before shipping. I am waiting to get a handful of completed units to do more rigorous testing like you mention.

WA: Sounds good. If it doesn't work, please advise before considering changes. We might be able to accept this limitation in the first run so long as we know about it up front.

2) Final units will withstand a drop to a hard surface from eight feet high and not break, continuing to operate normally.

PW: I will do more drop testing to make sure they don't break in any permanent way, but depending on the angle it hits the ground the batteries are most likely going to come out. In my opinion this is really barely acceptable, but I don't have any quick way to fix it. I think if we enlarged those undercuts, we might wind up with broken bosses when the heavy batteries try to find their way out and can't. My suggestion would be to try enlarging the bosses after this production run, and hope for the best. If not, go back to the way it was or think of a better design. Including planning and testing and such this process will probably take 2 weeks or more, as it's not a straight-pull mold.

**WA: It is okay if the battery lid opens in this initial shipment. It is much more problematic if a drop from the ceiling breaks it permanently. If you are seeing this, let's talk. Otherwise, let's ship. I concur that we should find a more robust solution for the next shipment.**

3) Final units will withstand monsoon rains in all orientations while operating and continue to operate normally.

PW: I think the units as is are water resistant at best. I don't think we're going to get waterproofness without a gasket. We are already on sample mold 2 in attempting to put a gasket in there, but I'm worried it makes the cover too difficult to close. We're still playing with this and will update you—new samples are due on Monday. My *guess* is that with the waterproof switch, this thing will survive pretty well even if it gets water inside (for example while somebody has the cover off for battery replacement). We will also test this once we have enough units in hand.

**WA: We can't take a huge slip to dial in the gasket fit. If it works well in the Monday sample and is easy to integrate into production tooling, then great, otherwise, let's get the cover fitting as nicely**

as we can over the next day or two and set realistic, tested expectations that we can position as best as possible for our clients in this initial run. I concur that in the next run we want to dial-in water resistance to support operating while exposed to monsoon rains. We do not need submersion capabilities, but it's sure nice to have if the cost delta is close to nil.

4) Please confirm light will ship individually bagged in a reusable Ziploc bag.

PW: Clear zip lock bags—got it.

WA: Thanks!

5) Please attempt to get back cover fitting more flush with back of lamp. This sample has a perceptible edge where the cover rises above the back. I do not want to delay initial shipment for this, but want to express desire to improve this ASAP.

PW: I also noticed that the cover is sitting farther up than the first samples. I assume this is really hard to fix, but we will look into it. I also know that with the O-ring gasket I tried, it makes the cover sit slightly higher up and creates significant resistance when you try to turn it into the locked position. I've had a sample mold made up for a square gasket which should be ready by Monday and we will try this.

WA: Per above, let's evaluate on Monday if we have a viable and superior solution with an incremental day. If not, the fit is acceptable for the first run assuming it doesn't cause massive fail following even momentary exposure to moderate rains.

6) Would love to have our *Do More* pop more clearly. Let's not slip further for this, but would want to dial it in down the road if it's not

a quick fix now. We should also be TM [trademark] and not circle-r. [U.S. federally registered trademark].

PW: Got it—to save time let's make these tweaks after this run?

**WA: Concur. Ship as is. Fix on next run.**

7) Confirm increase in base circuit power consumption that has Super-Saver, lowest power mode drawing 8.5 to 9.0 mA.

PW: So this would be about right for 6 mA through the LEDs plus 2 mA through the MCU/opamp [the circuitry]. The first sample may have been running low—it's hard to dial in that lowest current mode very accurately. At 8.5 mA / 2000 mAh you're looking at 235 hours; is this sufficient or do we want to go to 6 mA total (4 mA LED) and 300 hours? I'd rather not tweak the code again but if you're set on 300 hours I understand.

**WA: Ship as is. Please don't touch the code at this stage. I think it is fine. I just wanted to alert you that it seemed to be running a bit higher than the previous sample. We've been specifying runtime against 1800 mAH cell as our realistic level post field degradation. This puts us at slightly below 200 hours, but we'll be fine. We'll just change our positioning on it to be more like, "run it all night, every night for less than 5 pesewa a day." The light is actually quite nice. Comps well to a candle. Can even read by it if in close proximity.**

Let's ship, ship, ship!

PW: Indeed!

**WA: Seriously, Patrick. I really need you guys burning on this 24/7 until we ship.**

Whit swallowed hard, reconciled himself to the tougher sell of a fifteen-cedi price, and wired Patrick a down payment on the first order. Burro's first collaboration with Greenlight Planet was officially greenlit.

It was early November; the finished lanterns wouldn't arrive until at least December and possibly January. Meanwhile, the new phone chargers were flying off the shelf, and as a result battery inventory was dwindling. Six thousand new batteries were on order, scheduled to be flown from Hong Kong to Accra on Air Emirates, via Dubai. That was in late October—just as al-Qaeda bombs were discovered in two packages originating from Yemen, one of them at a parcel facility in Dubai. Whit groaned at the news. He knew it would mean delays getting anything through Dubai, especially thousands of powerful batteries.

But there was little time to worry about bombs in Dubai. We had a gong-gong scheduled in a village called Akorabo, another new place west of town where Nii had trained a new agent. Like the reseller selection and training process, the protocol for an initial sales gong-gong had been re-fined and formalized. After the new agent had been trained and was ready to sell, Nii or Rose would consult with the chief and elders to schedule a sales gong-gong, at which one of them would present the Burro offering and products to the village and give the new agent a chance to sign up clients. In advance of the gong-gong, the agent was given a stack of promo-tional flyers bearing the date and time of the event. He distributed the flyers to villagers, who were encouraged to hold on to them by the promise of a raffle at the gong-gong: anyone with a flyer could enter the raffle and win a valuable prize—usually a green Burro T-shirt, which (to even Whit's surprise) was rapidly becoming a status symbol in the area around Ko-foridua. The gong-gong was also a chance to preview new products, like the battery saver and the lantern, and get a feel for customer demand.

On the drive out to Akorabo, Whit coached Nii on how to introduce the lantern sample. "Tell them it's a torchlight, it hangs on a wall, you can hold it on your head—it needs to be really short. The four settings are Super-Saver, Saver, Bright, and Super-Bright. If we actually name those modes, it will help explain what we're trying to do. So if you're spending five cedis a month on kerosene now, you're gonna spend one cedi with this. Keep it really crisp and on-message."

"Perfect," said Nii.

We rolled into Akorabo in the Tata, speakers blaring the recorded Burro pitch. The place was already humming with activity. It was market day in some larger nearby town, and residents were rushing to prepare for departure, gathering baskets and packing their wares with the usual African trifecta of yelling, laughter, and commotion. Taxis brimming with sacks of cocoa beans, looking about as mobile as overstuffed sofas, groaned into motion. Dozens of passengers squeezed into crowded *tro-tros* like rush-hour commuters. In the village square, cocoa beans dried on a giant section of a four-color billboard print—thick rubbery paper that had been spread out on the ground like a carpet. The print had logos for the National Football League and the ESPN television network; giant faces of thick-necked American football players grinned out from under the fermenting beans. I tried to imagine how a section of an American football billboard had found its way to this distant off-grid village in Ghana. Did someone roll it up and stuff it into a Goodwill box outside a shopping mall in St. Louis? Did a church group haul it over in checked luggage, and why? Or was it counted as a charitable tax deduction by some corporation? Maybe it was part of the "5 percent of profits donated to charity" that some companies boast about. Every scenario I could think of begged the question, What *were* they thinking? Clearly no one in Akorabo had paid good money for it; when Ghanaians take the time and effort to build their own cocoa drying racks, they elevate them off the ground for maximum airflow and to keep goats and chickens away. This makeshift version, lying in the dirt, was far from ideal, but as a handout it would suffice.

We gathered in the shade of a tree. Nearby, a gasoline generator was set up under a corrugated metal-roofed gazebo, next to a sign that said CHARGE YOUR PHONE HERE. This was the competition. Children wandered up, many of them wearing school uniforms embroidered with badges identifying the Akorabo Islamic Primary School and the Akorabo Islamic Kindergarten. A man explained that the town had a *zongo*, the Ghanaian

term for an Islamic section, as well as many Christian residents. The new
agent, I forget his name, was Muslim. He had gone off to round up more
villagers as Whit, Nii, and I took seats on a wooden bench.

Villagers started to arrive and sit down. Soon there were forty or fifty
people, men and women, waiting for the gong-gong to begin. I looked out
at the crowd and noticed that lots of people were clutching cedi notes in
their hands. "Whit," I said out of the side of my mouth, "I don't know
much about sales, but I'm gonna take a wild guess and say these people
are ready to buy."

"Do you think?"

Finally the gong-gong rang out and the show began. Nii ran through
his standard demonstration of the phone charger ("*CHAH-jing!*" several
people said), then pulled out the lantern sample. "Coming soon, this is our
new torchlight," he began. "It has four settings . . ."

But before he could go any further, a man in the crowd stood up. He
was wearing a University of Georgia Bulldogs cap and a golf shirt from the
Palms Casino Resort in Las Vegas. *"White man!"* he said to Whit, gesturing with a handful of crumpled bank notes. "Tell him to stop talking and
let us pay! We need to get to market!"

"No more talking!" said another man. "We want to pay."

Another stood up, then another, and another, as if we had just asked
which one was Spartacus. And so began a buying frenzy not seen since
the Dutch tulip bubble of 1637. One aspect of British culture that Ghanaians appear to have wholly rejected is the polite queue, so we were not
totally surprised at the swarm that quickly engulfed us. And yet, as we
stared at the jostling crowd and the outstretched arms holding cell phones
to be tested (most but not all phones worked with the Burro phone charger)
and money to be collected, we realized that this was something new for
Burro. "Nii, you sign up the clients while I test their phones," said Whit hur-
riedly.

"I'll make change," I said, grabbing the cash box. Within minutes we
had fallen into a rhythm like short order cooks:

"He's got four batteries. Make that four and a charger, with a Motorola
plug."

"Adapters, adapters, I need adapters here."

"Change for a twenty on this woman, she bought four and a charger."

"Give this guy a micro-USB. No, that's a mini, he needs a micro, a micro."

"Sir, where is your slip? You need to register first."

"It's a Nokia, old Nokia. No can do."

"Try the blue diode."

"She's back for more batteries. Nii, change her slip to eight batteries. What's your name, ma'am?"

"I'm dyin' here, boys, my kingdom for an adapter."

This went on for nearly two hours. People would buy chargers and batteries, then leave and come back with more money, more phones to be tested, more orders for chargers and batteries. It didn't even stop when a customer came running up holding his new phone charger, which was plugged into his phone and spewing black smoke, the wires melting in his hand.

"Unplug the phone!" said Whit, grabbing the charger and pulling out the hot batteries. "I'm very sorry. It must have some kind of short. Let's get you a new one. But you can see how powerful our batteries are! Don't worry, if your phone is damaged we will replace it."

The man smiled. Whit looked relieved. "Note to self," he added to Nii and me, "add a fuse to the next shipment."

We finally ran out of chargers and D adapters, and nearly sold out all the batteries we had brought. Nii raffled off two T-shirts amid great applause, and after rounds of thank-yous and good-byes we drove off. Nii had another gong-gong scheduled that afternoon, but first we had to race home and restock.

"Well, that went well," said Whit in the truck, with purposeful understatement. "Good job, Nii." The pair started planning for the afternoon gong-gong, but I wasn't paying attention. I was in the backseat, counting up the cash box. We had taken in two hundred and eighty cedis, a record. I wish Harper could have seen it.

*Stop talking and let us pay!*

As far as I was concerned, those six words pretty much said it all. Because while you could measure business success with any number of more sophisticated metrics (and Whit eventually would), you could get at the essence of success in that one sentence. You couldn't get there with a handout. People will always accept handouts, because free is everyone's favorite price. Ghanaians will dry their cocoa beans on the NFL billboard not because it is ideal, but because it is free. But when they tell you to shut up and throw money at you—that's a pretty sure sign you're on the right track.

*Stop talking and let us pay!*

It had been nearly three years since Bill Gates banged the gong-gong for creative capitalism, spurring a global discussion on helping the poor through profits that was still raging from classrooms to corner offices. In one corner of one country in the crucible of the developing world, it seemed to me that the time for talk was over.

# EPILOGUE

Satisfied customer: Emmanuel is a sixty-five-year-old
farmer who uses Burro batteries to power his radio,
always set to his favorite news channel.

**B**urro continued to grow, and to face new challenges. Two hundred of the final lanterns, with rubber gaskets around the battery compartment, arrived by DHL in December. Whit sent out a tweet on December 10: "Just confirmed in Accra hotel sink, the Burro Light keeps burning Super-Bright, even under water! Don't try this at home kids, but yeah!" That initial shipment sold out in less than two weeks; twenty-eight hundred more arrived in January of 2011. Whit was also hiring more full-time Ghanaians.

The Kia got smashed again, twice. Nii was teaching James's daughter how to drive—part of Rose's ongoing initiatives to get everyone cross-trained and capable in every job—and she lost control and hit a brick wall. "A guy in Koforidua said he could fix it for forty cedis," Whit told me over the phone, "but when I picked it up after the repairs, the whole engine was shaking. Turns out the crash actually sheared off the front engine mounts, which he hadn't bothered to check."

Then, on Christmas Eve—shortly after the car had been fixed properly in Accra—James smashed it even more, somehow creasing both sides while driving on a remote stretch of dirt road. Nobody fully bought into his explanations about why he was out driving the company car on Christmas Eve; his cash box was also missing fifty cedis that day. James had a wonderful spirit and worked hard, but he had issues. It didn't seem like a happy ending was in store, and I felt bad for him. Meanwhile, I decided that if I ever returned to Ghana I would not ride in that cursed car.

Nothing came easy. It seemed like every day Whit had to push back against the standard way of doing things. One day he got a call from his new clearing agent, who was paid to get the batteries, lamps, and other products through customs in Accra. He'd come recommended by a neighbor of Whit's, who happened to be an official with the federal Customs, Excise and Preventive Service (CEPS). The agent's first task was clearing the shipment of six thousand new batteries, which finally arrived in December. "The day they arrived he called me," said Whit, "and he said, 'Here's the deal. I can get them out today for five hundred cedis.'

"I said, 'You mean on top of everything else?' Because the duty and the VAT were supposed to be about two thousand cedis.

"He said, 'No, that's the total. Five hundred.'

"I said, 'Do I get proper clearance docs?'

"He said, 'No, it's a favor.'

"A *favor!*" Whit repeated to me. "And he said if I don't do it, the customs officer is saying the batteries have the wrong code and will be subject to twenty percent duty instead of ten percent, which is what they should be as rechargeables."

"Some favor."

"Yeah, he was making it pretty clear that the expedited way to get stuff through is to pay off somebody."

"What did you do?"

"Well, as soon as you start doing that, they've got you in their pocket. They know you'll pay the bribes, and you're compromised. So I said to him, 'You know, I really appreciate the favor but it's very important for my business to make sure everything is properly cleared.' He said then I'd have to come down and talk to the officer because he's insisting on twenty percent duty. I'm like *fuck*. I *know* those batteries should only cost ten percent duty. I can't make this business work on twenty percent.

"So I drive down and meet the head of CEPS at the DHL terminal. He was a smart guy who had obviously done his homework. He was telling me dry cells are subject to twenty percent duty and that only secondary-cell accumulators pay ten percent. He said he was even gonna forward this to the collections department and have them re-collect for all my previous batteries. So I'm really pushing back. I told him these *are* secondary-cell accumulators because they're rechargeable. But he was saying no, secondary-cell accumulators are wet-cell car batteries. I said, 'Sir, I'm in the battery business, and I can assure you that the definition of *secondary cell* is "rechargeable."'

"He said, 'Where did you get that information?'

"I said, 'Sir, I can look on any of about fifty thousand websites.'

"He said, 'Show me.'

"So I went on my smart phone, and I'm googling right there. And to his credit, he was pretty cool. He's looking at the ingredients, the chemical composition. I just sat there quietly for about fifteen minutes and let him come to his own conclusion. I knew I had to give him enough room to save face. Finally he backed down.

"Then just as I was leaving he said, 'What about lithium cell phone batteries? Should they be classified as secondary?'

"I said, 'Well sir, I won't tell the importers, but *yes*.' When I came back to pick up the lanterns, I gave him one. We're good friends now."

Burro's march to profitability continues steadily if more slowly than Whit had hoped. Less than nine months after the introduction of the first Burro battery-powered devices in October 2010, total monthly revenue more than tripled, and battery exchange revenue doubled. Non-battery sales passed battery sales in monthly revenue in May 2011. Burro is sourcing more battery-powered devices for introduction in the coming months and years and is also conducting trials with health and agricultural products and services.

As I observed in late 2010, the company is getting more efficient at picking good agents; by mid-2011, it was adding twenty new resellers every month. Even with the currently limited catalog of products, many Burro resellers are already performing at levels that will drive the company beyond profitability and on to very attractive rates of investment return. Whit expects many more agents will hit those numbers with an expanded catalog and increased marketing.

Challenges remain. Poor-performing batteries continue to occasionally elude Burro's rapid-testing protocols, but the problems have diminished, and Whit is working to source more robust and efficient charging and test equipment.

Meanwhile, electrification of some original Burro villages is great news for Burro clients but has also highlighted the vulnerability of the flagship battery offering as Ghana marches forward. Whit believes the Burro brand potential is bigger than any single product, however. Trust in the brand is high, and Burro is capitalizing on that to encourrage clients to save with

Burrro on layaway for more substantial investments, such as water pumps and improved seeds.

Whit essentially lives in Ghana, with brief visits home during the summer and around the holidays. He meets his family for vacations in Europe (alas no more cheap flights through Libya), and both of his kids have been back and forth to visit him in Koforidua. Shelly occasionally stops by on her travels for the Gates Foundation. With Burro growing rapidly, Whit can't yet envision the day when he can spend less time coaxing a green truck through red mud, and more time in Seattle sipping lattes. Burro has taught all of us that while there is a business to be made serving the world's poor, it's not a get-rich-quick scheme. It's not for people who wither in the heat, worship Wi-Fi, and like their food cooked just so. It's not for me, in short—but I admire my crazy kid brother for making it his.

Burro has already inspired other entrepreneurs. Justin and Andrew, the BYU interns, returned to Ghana in January of 2011 to explore alternatives for launching their own initiative—a franchise business to help rural Ghanaians design, implement, and maintain sustainable fish farms. Their company, called Tilapiana, won two business plan competitions at BYU. They are currently seeking funding to implement the program.

Jonas, still one of Burro's top resellers, the Farmer of the Year in his district and my host for a memorable village stay, ran for district assembly but was narrowly defeated. I called him from Maine and said I thought that someday he would be president of Ghana. His extra income from Burro has allowed him to take more risks on his farm, such as growing rice. In February 2011, his sixteen-year-old son, who rode his bike down dirt roads to school every day, died of an undetermined illness.

Whit has not yet heard from Akosia.

Rose became a good driver. Burro's vehicles continue to take a beating; in early 2011, the Tata needed a new engine after just 85,000 kilometers. Whit bought a motorcycle and now gets from Koforidua to central Accra in half the former time of two and a half hours. If it rains, he gets very wet.

Kevin, Whit's first employee, whose wife and child had been killed in a *tro-tro* accident, married an Ashanti woman, and they are planning to start a new family. He is working for an event management company in Koforidua. Adam was let go after Jan and Debi Nordstrom hired Modupe Dzorka, a Nigerian-born woman with many more years' experience as an accountant. In 2011, Adam was hired as comptroller of an NGO in another West African country. James was fired shortly after the Christmas Eve accident; he now drives for another local company. His daughter still works for Burro. Nkansah is running a taxi business, among other enterprises, but has still made no effort to repay his debt to Burro. Rose, Modupe, and Nii are Burro's top Ghanaian managers and, with the rest of the team, are able to run Burro's pilot branch autonomously. Charlie is still Burro's business partner, and still runs a very busy contracting firm.

Patrick, the boy with the snotty nose in the courtyard, died. Nobody seemed to know how or why; neighbors told Jan that Patrick had complained of feeling cold and was taken to the hospital. He died in the car on the way. "I realize the only picture I have of him is a grainy, cropped-from-a-group photo a year and a half old," Jan wrote in her blog. "Is his existence already a memory as life in Ghana goes on?"


**My own memories,** much more than news reports of regime change in Ivory Coast or revolutions in North Africa, confirmed daily the existence of a continent that seemed increasingly far away as I settled back into life at home. I started missing my friends in Ghana, which I had expected, and then missing Africa itself, which I had not. And of course I missed my brother. Our time together there had been a sort of second act to a childhood abbreviated when our parents divorced and Whit moved west with our mother. Who could have predicted it would take place so much farther east than west?

Separation, of course, has been the story of Africa since slavery. On the plane home from Accra one time, I sat next to an older Ghanaian woman and her American grandson, five years old. She explained that the boy was going back to his mother in Las Vegas after a visit to Ghana. He was totally American; he did not speak Twi, and he had a portable DVD player on which he watched a movie about Ninja Turtles. At some point in the ten-hour flight to New York, the battery died in his DVD player. He pulled a cell phone out of his knapsack and started playing Pac-Man video games, but he couldn't get it to work right; I tried to help, but I couldn't figure it out either. Frustrated and bored, the boy fell into a tantrum—crying and paddling the seat with his legs. When his grandmother told him to stop, he hit her.

In Ghana, where children show unerring respect for elders, hitting your grandmother would be scandalous. But the woman seemed resigned to the fact that her flesh-and-blood grandson was no longer African.

And yet, oddly, I had come to feel more African myself—spending less time worrying about what might happen next (to me, to my kids, to health-care reform) and more time embracing the unknown, as Ghanaians have learned to do over generations. We filed off the plane and through immigration, collected our bags in a chaotic African-style tussle around the carousel before pushing through customs and into the harsh corridors of Kennedy, perhaps the most unwelcoming portal in the world. This national embarrassment, perpetually under improvement yet never improving, always shocks me by its arrogance and lazy indifference—as if its master planners have never been to another airport (like Ghana's excellent Kotoka), and don't care to bother. As I waded into the swift current of the terminal, the relaxed, warm tones of Twi from my fellow passengers—the voices that had held me for more than two years in Ghana—became diluted by the disciplined cadences of Eurasian tongues, the languages spoken by people with definite plans. The French, the German, the Italian, the Russian, the Japanese, even my own English—they all sounded oddly foreign to me, and as disorienting as Terminal Three. Soon the Ghanaians disappeared into the crowd, and then Africa was gone.

# ACKNOWLEDGMENTS

This book could not have been written, or even pondered, without the cooperation and support of my brother, Whit. He gave me complete and uncensored access to his business, even when I poked and prodded in all the corners. He never—well, almost never—asked to change passages that made him uncomfortable (and there were many), but he did read every word and suggest many corrections, clarifications, and elaborations.

My other steadfast reader, collaborator, and companion was Jan Watson. Like Whit, Jan read every word of the book and improved it immeasurably. Her perspective made me think about issues I had not considered, and kept me from veering off course more times than I care to count. In addition, Jan's entertaining blog about her own Ghanaian adventure (skitocoast.blogspot.com) provided much inspiration and filled in some narrative gaps.

Whit's wife, Shelly Sundberg, read early chapters and made many good suggestions reflecting her knowledge and love of Africa.

In Accra, Charlie and his wife Afi (I wish I could use their real names) were my bedrock. Besides opening up their home for me, both tolerated my endless questions about their country, providing rich background and helping me to understand the Ghanaian people. Their joy, energy, and kindness testify to the indomitable spirit of the African and fills me with optimism for their future. Charlie and Afi: for you I would even pound fufu.

At Burro, Rose Dodd was a constant companion, interpreter, and inspiration who understood that older brothers are wiser, funnier, and have much better iPod playlists than their embryonic siblings. Nii Tettey was a patient and thoughtful guide. Kevin, Adam, Nkansah, and James— pseudonyms all, yet genuine friends: there are not enough ways to express my thanks in all of your poetic languages, so I will only say *meda'ase*. To the children in the courtyard whose English is slightly better than my Twi: Auntie Max misses you. Thanks to Pamela and Savannah for teaching me how to make peanut soup.

In the villages, Jonas Avademe and Hayford Tetteh were gracious and generous hosts. Thank you for sharpening my machete and story. Their wives—Rebecca and Rose, respectively—worked over open fires, often in the dark, to feed me three squares a day. Their extended clans—parents, siblings, children, and grandchildren—entertained and inspired.

In Utah, Justin King was enormously helpful organizing hundreds of photographs from the four BYU interns and getting them up on the Web for me.

In New York, my agent Sally Wofford-Girand got this book from the beginning and worked overtime to bring it into focus. Elisabeth Dyssegaard, editor in chief at Hyperion, encouraged me at every turn, probably because she understood that her deft editing would somehow make it all work.

In Maine, Sarah, Harper, and William were always there, even though I wasn't.